Gunnar Myrdal and Black-White Relations

DAVID W. SOUTHERN

Gunnar Myrdal and Black-White Relations
The Use and Abuse of *An American Dilemma,* 1944–1969

Louisiana State University Press
Baton Rouge and London

Designer: Laura Roubique
Typeface: Times Roman
Typesetter: G & S Typesetters, Inc.
Printer: Thomson-Shore, Inc.
Binder: John H. Dekker & Sons

Chapters VI and VII herein appeared previously, in slightly different form, as "An American Dilemma: Gunnar Myrdal and the Civil Rights Cases, 1944–1954," in *Journal of the History of Sociology,* III (Spring, 1981) and "An American Dilemma Revisited: Myrdalism and White Southern Liberals," in *South Atlantic Quarterly,* LXXIII (Spring, 1976), respectively.
The author gratefully acknowledges Alfred A. Knopf, Inc., for granting permission to reprint "Dream Deferred," from *The Panther and the Lash: Poems of Our Times,* by Langston Hughes, copyright © 1967 by Arna Bontemps; and Harper and Row for granting permission to quote from *An American Dilemma,* by Gunnar Myrdal, copyright 1944, © 1962.

Published with the assistance of a grant from the National Endowment for the Humanities

10   9   8   7   6   5   4   3   2   1

LIBRARY OF CONGRESS CATALOGING-IN-PUBLICATION DATA

Southern, David W.
    Gunnar Myrdal and Black-white relations.

    Bibliography: p.
    Includes index.
    1. Myrdal, Gunnar, 1898–   —American dilemma.
2. Afro-Americans.   I. Title.
E185.6.M953S68   1987   305.8'96073   86-20040
ISBN 0-8071-1302-6

For my parents

Dream Deferred

What happens to a dream deferred?

Does it dry up
like a raisin in the sun?
Or fester like a sore—
And then run?
Does it stink like rotten meat?
Or crust and sugar over—
like a syrupy sweet?

Maybe it just sags
like a heavy load.

Or does it explode?

—Langston Hughes

Contents

Illustrations

Preface

In 1944 Gunnar Myrdal, a Swedish economist, published his massive study of black-white relations entitled *An American Dilemma*. A huge collaborative effort, sponsored and generously financed by the Carnegie Corporation, Myrdal's book became an instant classic. No mere book, it constituted a historic event. Robert S. Lynd, the noted coauthor of *Middletown,* called the Myrdal study "the most penetrating and important book on contemporary American civilization that has ever been written." [1]

Although Myrdal's book contained more than fifteen hundred pages filled with vast amounts of data and numerous hypotheses, one simple, pervasive theme eloquently unified the gigantic tome. Myrdal asserted that white Americans experienced a troubling dilemma because of the discrepancy between the hallowed "American Creed," whereby they think, talk, and act under the influence of egalitarian and Christian precepts, and the oppressive way they treated Afro-Americans. Myrdal predicted that this moral dilemma, heightened by the democratic rhetoric of World War II and certain other social trends, would soon force "fundamental changes in American race relations" and end America's greatest scandal. [2]

Over the years powerful claims have been made concerning the impact of Myrdal's book. In 1964 the black social scientist Samuel DuBois

1. Robert S. Lynd, Review of Gunnar Myrdal's *An American Dilemma,* in *Saturday Review,* April 22, 1944, p. 5.

2. Gunnar Myrdal, with the assistance of Richard Sterner and Arnold Rose, *An American Dilemma: The Negro Problem and Modern Democracy* (New York, 1944), xix, hereinafter cited as *AD.*

xiii

Cook calculated its impact as follows: "Its influence has extended far beyond the gentle academy to high public officials—including U.S. Senators, Presidents, Representatives, and justices of the Supreme Court." In the same year the editors of the *Saturday Review* asked twenty-seven esteemed men and women of letters the question, "What books published during the past four decades most significantly altered the direction of our society?" *An American Dilemma* received more votes than any other book except John Maynard Keynes' *The General Theory of Employment, Interest and Money*.[3] In the quarter century following the publication of Myrdal's book, the term "dilemma" served as a common metaphor for black-white relations in America. Indeed, perusers of the Myrdal study commonly rendered the title of the Swede's book as *The American Dilemma*.[4]

It is no doubt difficult for some, especially the young, to appreciate the extent of Myrdal's boldness and foresight in the early 1940s. His insights inspired many racial reformers at a time when Sumnerian, laissez-faire social science still exerted strong influence on the study of race relations and when old-fashioned, overt racism conspicuously scarred the social landscape. The post–civil rights era, moreover, has seen a considerable amount of Myrdal-bashing. After the civil rights movement fell on hard times, it became fashionable to sneer at Myrdal's optimistic formulations. When Senator Edward Kennedy attempted to wrest the Democratic nomination from President Jimmy Carter in 1980, Henry Fairlie of the *New Republic* expressed his contempt for the New Dealish, Myrdalian mind-set of the Massachusetts lawmaker. "One suspects," Fairlie warned of Kennedy's retreat to nostalgia, "that his staff has been raised on sociology readings from Myrdal."[5]

In a review of the twentieth-anniversary edition of the *Dilemma*, the historian Oscar Handlin opined that the occasion of the new edition afforded a good opportunity for "stocktaking" in regard to the impact of the famous study. The Harvard professor maintained that it was time to consider "the influences and assumptions that guided the authors, to trace the effects of the book on its audience and to assess its relevance to

3. Samuel DuBois Cook, Review of Arnold Rose's *The Negro in America*, in *Journal of Negro History*, XLIX (1964), 207; Rochelle Girson, "Mutations in the Body Politic," *Saturday Review*, August 29, 1964, pp. 74–76.

4. See, for example, Harris Wofford, *Of Kennedys and Kings: Making Sense of the Sixties* (New York, 1980), 465; and "The American Dilemma: 1967—An Interview with Gunnar Myrdal," *Center Magazine*, I (October–November, 1967), 32.

5. Henry Fairlie, "Camelot Lost," *New Republic*, May 31, 1980, p. 5.

the present status of Negroes in America."[6] Now that the dust of the turbulent 1960s has settled and the fortieth anniversary of the *Dilemma* has passed, it seems that the time for a systematic, detailed stocktaking of the Carnegie project is all the more propitious.[7]

An underlying premise of this book is that ideas have consequences, that they occasionally shake and move. Few will deny that such books as Thomas Paine's *Common Sense*, Harriet Beecher Stowe's *Uncle Tom's Cabin*, or Henry George's *Progress and Poverty* in some degree altered American history. Skeptics, of course, may ask how many people ever read Myrdal's bulky work? The reply is that a book's impact cannot be measured solely by its sales, although the *Dilemma* enjoyed a surprisingly good market. More important was the circulation of Myrdal's report among influential Americans. As an analyst of public opinion put it many years ago: "What one thousand professors, writers, bishops think, write, preach, is handed on by three hundred thousand teachers, journalists and ministers to 130,000,000 Americans, and forms the consciousness of the entire nation."[8]

Americans generally like to think that they are independent, hard-nosed pragmatists who have not been sullied by the ideas of some remote economist, sociologist, or baby doctor. This is an illusion, argues Robert A. Nisbet, a discerning historian of ideas and social change. "We may think we are responding directly to events," Nisbet proclaims, "but we aren't; we are responding to the events and changes as they are made real or assimilable to us by ideas already in our heads."[9] This book thus attempts to show how Myrdal's ideas got into people's heads and how they helped shape racial perceptions and events during a crucial period of black-white relations in America.

To be sure, the international reputation of Myrdal and his late wife, Alva, helped mold attitudes toward the *Dilemma*. For half a century the Myrdals, who adopted the United States as their second homeland, have dazzled the intellectual world with their books, lectures, conversations, zealous promotion of political causes, and charm. In 1946 a journalist

6. Oscar Handlin, Review of *AD, New York Times Book Review*, April 21, 1963, p. 5.

7. For an unpublished study, see Walter A. Jackson, "Gunnar Myrdal and American Racial Liberalism" (Ph.D. dissertation, Harvard University, 1983). Its use is restricted at this writing, and it has not been available to me.

8. For a similar study to mine, see Thomas F. Gossett, *Uncle Tom's Cabin and American Culture* (Dallas, 1985). William S. Schlamm quoted in Van Wyck Brooks, *Opinions of Oliver Allston* (New York, 1941), 209.

9. Robert A. Nisbet, *History of the Idea of Progress* (New York, 1980), 4.

branded them "the Young Webbs of Sweden." Since then, both have won Nobel Prizes.[10] Gunnar Myrdal's frequent visits to America and his close friendships with scores of notable people since the 1920s have stimulated an interest in his books and ideas in the United States.

The influence of books and ideas admittedly is hard to measure. It seems obvious, however, that changing views of race were one of the many factors that led to the rise of the black freedom movement after World War II. To paraphrase John Adams on the American Revolution, the civil rights revolution occurred in the hearts and minds of many well-placed Americans before the legal and political breakthroughs took place. Like the influential pamphlets before the American Revolution, Myrdal's book played a significant role in changing the thought patterns and feelings of a people. For twenty years the Swede's authority was such that liberals simply cited him and confidently moved on. If historians need to understand the rudiments of Keynesian economics to teach effectively the recent American past, then they surely need to know something of Myrdal, the Keynes of American race relations.

The reader should know that this book attempts no thorough sociological treatment of black culture, race relations theory, or social science methodology. I have dealt with such matters when they seemed necessary to make Myrdal, or more precisely, his behavioralist critics, comprehensible, or when I wanted to place the *Dilemma* on the continuum of social science thought. My inclination is toward old-fashioned, humanistic history, even if interdisciplinary in nature. My aim was to assess Myrdal's influence in a traditional way—ordinary evidence mundanely gathered and sifted through common-sense judgment—and to present the findings, as far as possible, in jargon-free language.

10. George Soloveytchik, "Europe's Not So Quiet Corner," *Survey Graphic,* XXXV (August, 1946), 287. Gunnar won the Nobel Prize for economics in 1974; Alva won the Nobel Peace Prize in 1982 for her antinuclear activism.

Acknowledgments

Many people have assisted me in the preparation of this book. I owe my deepest debt to J. Harvey Young of Emory University, who suggested the Myrdal study as a research project and directed my early work on the topic. Though always burdened with a crushing work load, Professor Young gave freely of his time to this project. For nearly two decades his encouragement, advice, and example have been invaluable to me.

Professors Robert F. Durden and David L. Smiley graciously agreed to read portions of the manuscript. Professors Idus A. Newby and Arvarh E. Strickland read the complete copy. All offered encouraging comments, and all have helped improve the book by exposing errors of fact and interpretation and by making cogent suggestions for revision. Trudie Calvert, copy editor for the Louisiana State University Press, improved the text in countless places. Her uncanny ability to detect my mechanical and stylistic lapses was at once humbling and reassuring. Any errors that remain, of course, are my sole responsibility.

In the course of my research, I directed a substantial amount of correspondence at a wide variety of people. With few exeptions, I received responses that were prompt, full, and useful. Officials in the administrations of John F. Kennedy and Lyndon B. Johnson and historians were especially responsive. Gunnar Myrdal took an interest in the study from the start and has helped me in many ways.

I sincerely thank the many library staffs across the country for their efficient and courteous service. I would particularly like to express my appreciation to the staffs of the manuscript divisions at the Library of Congress, the Truman Library, and the Southern Historical Collection at the University of North Carolina at Chapel Hill. Elizabeth B. Mason aided me far beyond the normal call of duty while serving as acting director of the Oral History Project at Columbia University. Sara Engelhardt of the Carnegie Corporation assisted me in acquiring the elusive foundation files pertaining to the Myrdal report, a source that was vital for writing the early chapters of this book. Not least, the entire staff of the Westminster College Library deserves loud applause for cheerfully looking after my every request. Liz Hauer and Barbara Ault relentlessly pursued important items through interlibrary loan. Lorna Mitchell was a whiz at running down obscure names and facts for me. Karolyn Dickson did a marvelous job of typing.

A generous fellowship from the National Endowment for the Humanities, which enabled me to take leave from teaching duties during the 1982–83 academic year, gave me much-needed time to research and write. Two summer grants from Westminster College helped defray some of the expenses incurred in preparing the manuscript.

Finally, my eternal gratitude goes to my wife, Marcy. Her patience and understanding during my long preoccupation with this academic exercise have been heroic. She sacrificed countless amenities, including a honeymoon.

I

A Fresh Mind
for an Old Problem

Gunnar Myrdal originally intended to bury what he called the "short story" of how his famous study came about in the voluminous appendixes of *An American Dilemma*. The Swedish scholar considered the full story of the Carnegie project an extremely "touchy" matter. "We don't want to wash our dirty linen in public," Myrdal explained, "and so the story should be very short." [1] Ultimately, he told the short, diplomatic version of the large collaborative effort in a carefully worded preface to the 1944 book. Frederick P. Keppel, the president of the Carnegie Corporation, added some interesting but guarded details about the evolution of the study in his foreword to Myrdal's book. For reasons of prudence and space, however, both Myrdal and Keppel omitted many of the most significant, and often the most interesting, aspects of the making of the *Dilemma*. This chapter and the next explore those aspects.

The period of gestation for the mammoth social science work spanned almost a decade. In late 1935, in the middle of the Great Depression, Newton D. Baker, a trustee of the Carnegie Corporation, suggested an in-depth study of Afro-Americans. In early 1944, in the waning stages of World War II, the first copies of the *Dilemma* appeared. In the years between, numerous events, forces, and personalities put their mark on the book in consequential and complex ways largely unknown to a generation of readers. Many recently available sources now allow a

---

1. Gunnar Myrdal to Charles Dollard, July 16, 1942, Negro Study—General Correspondence, roll 1 of 2 rolls of microfilm, Carnegie Corporation Files, New York, 1956. In this chapter all letters, memoranda, and records of interviews and conferences, unless otherwise stated, are from roll 1 of the microfilm.

more complete and accurate view of how Myrdal and his associates proceeded. These sources, the most important of which are the Carnegie Corporation files and the Carnegie Oral History Project, illuminate how the Swede's personality, biases, experience, and methodology affected the contents of his noted study. They provide an inside view that goes beyond the terse official version told by Myrdal and Keppel.[2] Familiarity with the extended and arduous process of the collaborative effort helps explain the strengths and weaknesses of the *Dilemma* and casts light on the many controversies that have long surrounded the book.

The race problem was not a new concern of the Carnegie Corporation. From its founding in 1911, the foundation had shown, as one analyst put it, a "benign but fluctuating interest in the Negro." Andrew Carnegie, who ran the foundation with an iron hand until his death in 1919, contributed the bulk of his wealth, some $135 million, for "the advancement and diffusion of knowledge and understanding" in the United States and the British dominions. The steel magnate knew and admired the conservative black leader Booker T. Washington. The philanthropist, therefore, tended to direct whatever funds were reserved for racial betterment to black colleges and universities in the South.[3]

But the postwar period called for new approaches to the race problem. During World War I thousands of blacks migrated to northern cities and fell victim to poverty, prejudice, and violence. The appearance of the "New Negro" in the 1920s added another dimension to the racial issue. The Carnegie Corporation needed new ideas and new data on which to base a program of racial betterment. Realizing this need, in 1935 Newton D. Baker, a trustee of the Carnegie Corporation, first suggested a comprehensive, foundation-sponsored study of the Negro. Black leaders have long expressed skepticism about Baker's role in the Myrdal study. W. E. B. Du Bois, for example, doubted that the son of a Confederate officer deserved any credit for such a good work. Du Bois suggested that Carnegie president Keppel, who attributed the original idea of the study to Baker, was only paying a sentimental tribute to his old War Department boss, who had died in 1937.[4]

2. Carnegie Corporation Oral History Project, Columbia University, New York, 1969, hereinafter referred to as COHP.

3. Waldemar Nielsen, *The Big Foundations* (New York, 1972), 35, 351; Statement of appropriations for Negroes, May 11, 1938, 2, Negro Study, roll 2.

4. W. E. B. Du Bois, Review of *AD*, *Phylon*, V (1944), 121. Keppel paid tribute to Baker in *AD*, vi.

Du Bois' understandable suspicion, however, kept the black leader from giving the southerner his due. Although Baker grew up in the border states of West Virginia and Maryland and got his law degree at Washington and Lee University, he matured into a full-fledged progressive in the early twentieth century. He first achieved national fame as the successor to the well-known reform mayor of Cleveland, Tom Johnson. Later he served as secretary of war under Woodrow Wilson. Baker's experience as mayor of a major industrial city, as secretary of war during World War I, and as a businessman in Cleveland during the 1920s and 1930s made him acutely aware of the worsening race problem. Although the southerner never became an advanced liberal on the race question, he came to understand some of the broader dimensions of the problem. As a businessman and civic leader in Cleveland, Baker learned that the race problem was deep and complex. At a board meeting of the Carnegie Corporation on October 24, 1935, the southern progressive challenged the foundation's longtime policy of automatically appropriating the bulk of its racial funds for Negro schools in the South. According to Baker, race was no longer just a southern problem. The corporation, he argued, needed to know more about racism in America before it could spend its money with confidence that it was doing the most for the black minority.[5]

The energetic and imaginative president of the Carnegie Corporation seized Baker's idea and, until his death in 1943, devotedly shepherded the Myrdal project and made it the corporation's highest priority. Born on Staten Island in 1875, Keppel rose to be dean of Columbia College in 1910. In 1917 he entered the War Department as an assistant to Secretary Baker. By 1923 he was president of the Carnegie Corporation, where he remained until he joined the wartime State Department in 1941. Even in Washington the New Yorker continued to guide the Myrdal study through to completion. By all accounts, Keppel was a vivacious, cultivated, and highly likable man who had a lust to try new things. The records reveal virtually no negative feelings by any of his contemporaries. John Russell, who worked for Keppel at the corporation for ten years, later described him as the man who "humanized" Columbia College, the War Department in World War I, and the administration of modern foundations. Emmett J. Scott, who became ac-

5. C. H. Cramer, *Newton D. Baker: A Biography* (Cleveland, 1961); Emmett J. Scott, *The American Negro in the World War* (New York, 1969), 454.

quainted with Keppel when he worked as a special black assistant to
Secretary Baker during the war, recalled that blacks could always count
on the former dean to be compassionate and fair. Like many others,
Myrdal, who came to know Keppel intimately, remembered him as a
man "full of fantasies" and "prepared to take risks," "a glorious man"
and "a great liberal." [6]

Keppel grasped in Baker's 1935 suggestion a chance to go beyond
simply handing out money annually to black educational institutions.
The thought of undertaking a potentially important and controversial
project excited Keppel. He once said in a commencement address that
the American people trusted science but did not pretend to understand
it. He complained that they simply ignored the humanities. But with social science, the administrator announced, the average person feels "a
vague sense of lurking danger in meddling with our folkways." [7] Such
danger only served to motivate Keppel's interest.

Thus in 1936 Keppel and his aides began an intensive search for a
social scientist of unquestioned talent and stature to direct a definitive
study of blacks in America. At first Keppel and his associates compiled
a long list of American and European scholars who might meet the desired qualifications. But before long Keppel decided that Americans,
both black and white, had too many prejudices to write an objective and
fresh study. The list of potential directors grew even shorter when he
narrowed it down to European scholars from countries without imperi-
alistic interests. Essentially, the search then focused on Scandinavia and
Switzerland. [8]

For several reasons, Myrdal's name began to receive Keppel's concentrated attention at that point. Born in 1898, the Swede was still relatively young and yet possessed a reputation in Europe as an inventive
and productive scholar and a man of great intellectual breadth. Much to
his favor, he spoke fluent English (along with several other languages)
and counted several friends among the American social science and
foundation establishments. In 1929–1930 he and his highly intelligent
and attractive wife, Alva, had spent a year in America at the expense of

6. John Russell, in *Appreciation of Frederick Paul Keppel by Some of His Friends*
(New York, 1951), 115; Emmett J. Scott, in *ibid.*, 25; Myrdal, COHP, 12–18; Nielsen, *Big
Foundations,* 38.

7. Frederick P. Keppel, *Philanthropy and Learning* (New York, 1936), 25–29.

8. Negro Study List: Personal Suggestions, July 15, 1937; Charles Dollard, COHP,
108–109, 150; *AD,* vi.

the Rockefellers as Laura Spelman Fellows. Back in Europe, the Myrdals retained a strong interest in America, reading newspapers and magazines and watching American films. In 1937 Myrdal accepted an invitation from Harvard University to deliver the prestigious Godkin Lectures in early 1938 and to receive an honorary degree.[9]

On August 12, 1937, Keppel informed Myrdal by mail that the Carnegie Corporation had chosen him to direct "a comprehensive study of the Negro in the United States, to be undertaken in a wholly objective and dispassionate way as a social phenomenon."[10] The letter alternately puzzled and amused the economist. He wondered why the Americans would choose a man who knew nothing about the race issue, a foreigner who had never visited the southern states and whose contacts with Negroes were limited to elevator operators, lowly hotel workers, and Red Caps in train stations. "These Americans," Myrdal chortled to Alva, "they are a funny lot."[11]

In their prefatory remarks in the *Dilemma* Keppel and Myrdal did not reveal that the economist turned down the corporation's initial offer. In a polite letter to Keppel, Myrdal explained that he had recently been appointed to a well-endowed chair of economics at the University of Stockholm and that he had just begun a term in the Swedish Parliament. He expressed regret that these and other obligations—his wife's career as a teacher and an author was a consideration—made it necessary to reject the flattering offer. Myrdal calculated that it would be impossible to get away for the two-year period that Keppel estimated the study would take.[12]

Within about a month, however, the Myrdals changed their minds. Several factors figured in their decision. For many years John Kenneth Galbraith, who first met Myrdal in 1937, spread a garbled explanation of why the Myrdals accepted the Carnegie offer. They had seen an American film about Yellowstone Park, Galbraith said, and it made them eager to visit the United States to see all the national parks. In 1967 Myrdal remembered only that he and Alva had seen some "pathetic thing about doctors who went out in the jungles." Alva told Galbraith in the 1970s that the allegedly "decisive film" they had seen

9. *AD*, vi–vii; Myrdal, COHP, 8, 10–11. The lectures were published as *Population and Democracy* (Cambridge, Mass., 1940).

10. Quoted in *AD*, ix.

11. Myrdal, COHP, 2.

12. Myrdal to Keppel, August 30, 1937.

was not about Yellowstone Park but about yellow fever. The Myrdals reasoned, the revised Galbraith story went, that if Americans could go into a foreign country and inoculate the people to protect them from deadly pathogens, two Swedish scholars might be able to do the same for the disease of American racism.[13]

Probably more important than the film was Beardsley Ruml's trip to Sweden. At Keppel's request, Ruml stopped by to have lunch with Myrdal and to urge him to change his mind about the Carnegie project. Ruml, a psychologist and former dean of the social sciences at the University of Chicago, headed the Laura Spelman Memorial Foundation when the Myrdals were recipients of fellowships from that Rockefeller-supported organization and had plunged the Rockefeller Foundation deeply into social science research in the 1920s. A captivating and inventive man—he conceived the idea of withholding taxes during World War II—he was described by Myrdal as "a very outspoken, freewheeling, risk-taking American." Ruml apparently impressed Myrdal, particularly when he assured the Swede that the Carnegie Corporation would back the race study to the hilt, financially and in every other way.[14]

Another reason why Myrdal may have reversed his earlier rejection of the Carnegie offer concerned Swedish politics. Throughout the crucial political years of the 1930s, the Myrdals devoted considerable time to reform activities and exerted a strong influence on the Social Democratic Labor party. Through various publications, jointly and separately, and through Gunnar's presence on highly important government commissions, the Myrdals helped mold a Swedish welfare state that became a model for many Western liberals. But in early 1938 the Social Democratic party decided on a "pause" in its reform efforts and turned its attention more toward foreign and military affairs. This change of priorities made Myrdal lose some of his enthusiasm for politics. According to a recent article by the historian Allan C. Carlson, the revised political emphasis of the Social Democrats in 1938 may have prompted Myrdal to decide to accept Keppel's offer to come to America.[15]

13. John Kenneth Galbraith, *A Life in Our Times: Memoirs* (Boston, 1981), 83; Myrdal, COHP, 2.

14. James T. Carey, *Sociology and Public Affairs: The Chicago School* (Beverly Hills, Calif., 1975), 187; Myrdal, COHP, 5; Myrdal to Keppel, October 7, 1937.

15. Allan C. Carlson, "The Myrdals, Pro-Natalism, and Swedish Social Democracy," *Continuity,* VI (Spring, 1983), 71, 80, 82–84, 87, 89, and *passim.*

In any case, the Myrdals changed their minds. Gunnar, however, still seemed to take the proposed American project rather lightly. "They make all sorts of studies in America," he recalled thinking; "I should make one." So on October 5, 1937, he wired Keppel: "Having Met Ruml Changed Mind To Proposal Directing Negro Study. If Your Offer Still Open Prepared Discussion. Letter Follows." Immediately, Keppel wired back: "Your Cable Delights Us. We Shall Hold Everything." [16]

Two days later Myrdal sent a long letter to Keppel discussing the New Yorker's earlier proposal. The Swede agreed with Keppel that his main qualification for directing the study lay in his lack of preconceptions and knowledge about the race problem. He conceded that he was inclined to be critical of those who presumed great biological and intellectual differences between the races, but neither did he postulate "perfect parity." Myrdal expressed skepticism about reaching practical conclusions on solving the race problem. The emphasis of the study, he counseled, should be strictly on gathering facts. [17] These comments, as will be shown below, seemed to go against the thrust of his previous writings. Perhaps Myrdal chose his remarks to persuade Keppel that he was that "wholly objective and dispassionate" man the New Yorker desired.

In a side trip from Harvard, where he delivered the Godkin Lectures in the spring of 1938, Myrdal sealed the bargain with the Carnegie trustees at a cocktail party in the New York Century Club. He agreed to return to America in late summer and begin his two-year stint as the general director of a study on the Negro as "a social phenomenon." [18]

When Charles Dollard, one of Keppel's assistants, went to the docks on September 10 to meet Myrdal, he was shocked to find nine people waiting for him: Myrdal and his wife, their three children, Richard Sterner (Myrdal's research assistant) and his wife, and two Swedish wet nurses—not to mention forty-two very large pieces of luggage. To speed up the departure process of this unwieldy mass, Myrdal remembered, someone bribed the customs officials. This would be only the first of many instances when the corporation would, as Myrdal put it, "stretch its long tentacles" to clear the path for the project. Eventually, the corporation's efforts achieved such feats as obtaining plush office accom-

16. Myrdal, COHP, 110–11; Myrdal to Keppel, October 5, 1937; Keppel to Myrdal, October 5, 1937.
17. Myrdal to Keppel, October 7, 1937.
18. *Ibid.;* Myrdal, COHP, 109.

modations in the best places, bribing the British and the Russians to get the Myrdals back and forth across two oceans during the war, and arranging for draft deferments for Myrdal's collaborators.[19]

Besides Keppel, no one was more indispensable to Myrdal than Dollard. Occasionally, other Carnegie employees such as Robert M. Lester and John Russell received assignments relating to the Myrdal project. But Dollard assumed the role of the detail man from day one and devoted himself to the study even after he left the foundation to become an army captain. At first primarily a glorified errand boy, Dollard grew steadily in influence because of his intelligence, energy, tact, and, above all, his sound judgment. Unlike Keppel, he had some knowledge about the social sciences. His brother John was a noted social psychologist at Yale. Dollard, in fact, became a valuable critic of Myrdal's work. Myrdal praised his Carnegie aide privately and publicly, calling him "a very efficient, wise and good man." His tact and judgment rescued the mercurial and often rash Swede from many embarrassing situations.[20]

Hardly had Dollard gotten Myrdal settled in New York City when Keppel sent the foreigner off on an extensive tour of the South. Myrdal protested that he should do some reading before he tackled the race problem, but Keppel asserted that all the literature on the subject was greatly biased. The American wanted the European to see the problem firsthand. So Myrdal, Richard Sterner, his Swedish companion, and Jackson Davis, a white southerner connected with the Rockefeller General Education Board, left on an extensive trip. For more than two months in the fall of 1938, they traveled throughout the South in a stylish Buick. They visited all parts of the region and met academics, journalists, clergymen, public officials, farmers, and factory workers, both black and white.[21]

The trip left a deep impression on Myrdal, and it led him to two major conclusions. First, the journey made him realize that the race problem was worse than he had imagined. He was overwhelmed by the intensity and depth of racial prejudice in the South. "I didn't realize," he reported to Keppel, "what a terrible problem you have put me into. I mean we are horrified." As Myrdal noted in his preface, he tried to back out of the project by suggesting that an official advisory committee—

19. Charles Dollard to Myrdal, October 4, 1938; Dollard, COHP, 75–77; Myrdal to Charles S. Johnson, June 23, 1941, roll 2.

20. Robert M. Lester, COHP, 699; Dollard, memorandum to Keppel, March 12, 1939; Myrdal, COHP, 21–22, 115–16; John Russell, COHP, 134; AD, xvii–xviii.

21. Myrdal, COHP, 24; AD, ix.

similar to a Swedish royal commission—be set up to study the racial situation. This body would consist of a northern white, a southern white, and a black. He suggested the names of Donald R. Young, Thomas J. Woofter, Jr., and Charles S. Johnson. Keppel brushed aside Myrdal's suggestion and reminded the Swede that he had hired him to "take full responsibility" for writing a report free from political pressure. The burden was all Myrdal's, Keppel declared. But the Carnegie president reassured Myrdal that all the resources that the corporation commanded would be at his disposal.[22]

The other important conclusion that Myrdal reached on the trip was that a racial dilemma existed in the white mind. White racism ran tragically deep in Dixie, Myrdal acknowledged, but southern whites also believed in the American creed. "The difference between words and deeds was to us blatant," Myrdal remembered. When he returned to New York to prepare plans for the study, the word "dilemma" echoed in his mind.[23]

Another thought that lingered in Myrdal's mind was that many American scholars and black leaders resented his selection as the director of the Carnegie study. He sensed this feeling in his conversations with scholars on his southern trip. Though supportive of Myrdal, his old friends at the Rockefeller Foundation nonetheless informed him about the skepticism over his appointment. Donald Young, an influential race relations scholar highly placed in the Social Science Research Council (SSRC), argued strongly against Myrdal's selection. First he spoke to Keppel at length and then he sent him a long letter debating the idea that a European would bring a fresh mind to bear on racial matters. Young maintained that Europeans, too, had their biases, though often slyly hidden. Not only was Myrdal ignorant about blacks, Young complained, but he knew little about modern behavioral science.[24]

Many black scholars and activists expressed similar misgivings about Myrdal's selection. They felt that a black scholar should direct the study on the Negro. In late 1939, for example, Walter White, the executive secretary of the National Association for the Advancement of Colored People (NAACP), informed Robert S. Abbott of the Chicago *Defender:* "I want to say quite frankly that when I first heard that Dr. Myrdal was being brought to the United States to make this study I

22. *AD*, xviii; Myrdal, COHP, 28–29, 31, 52; Lester, COHP, 306.
23. Letter from Myrdal to author, October 1, 1982; Donald R. Young, COHP, 55–56.
24. Myrdal, COHP, 6–7, 44; Young to Keppel, January 30, June 30, 1937; Young, COHP, 38, 40–41.

was somewhat skeptical of an outsider doing the sort of survey which would be most valuable." Some blacks even saw conspiracy in the Carnegie project. Roy Wilkins of the NAACP reported to Walter White that several blacks feared that the Carnegie Corporation had predetermined that the Myrdal report would condone "Negro development within a segregated world."[25]

When Myrdal heard from Walter White about the suspicion surrounding his study, he told the NAACP director that such skepticism among blacks was "understandable even if unfounded." He added that the suspicion in the "other camp" was even greater and probably "more founded." Myrdal assured White that he had a completely free hand in the study and no results had been foreordained. Myrdal remained undaunted by the suspicion. As he put it, "I'm rather hard-boiled." Yet the suspicion and resentment generated by his selection clearly affected his initial approach to the project. As will be illustrated below, Myrdal would direct a vigorous public relations campaign in an attempt to allay the skepticism in various camps that had been created by his appointment.[26]

To be sure, even if Myrdal's mind had not been tainted by previous knowledge about blacks, his theoretical outlook and his leftist political leanings predisposed him toward a certain approach to the American race problem. Although Myrdal quipped that suspicion of him should be stronger among conservatives than blacks, his political views seemed to provoke almost no adverse comments from the center or the right. No dissent came from the trustees of the Carnegie Corporation. E. L. Thorndike, a trustee, described Myrdal as an "incurable romantic," but he felt the Swede was a good choice for the job. Likewise, trustee Frederick Osborn liked Keppel's choice, though he knew Myrdal had leftist views. Donald Young, a Parkian sociologist whose major work on minorities referred to blacks as "a culturally retarded race," ostensibly objected to the Swedish economist on academic rather than political grounds. In 1937 few could have guessed that in the postwar period Myrdal would be hounded as a dangerous subversive. In the days of the Popular Front and before the rise of the House Un-American Activities

25. Walter White to Robert S. Abbott, December 21, 1939, "Myrdal Study," Box 20, Addenda, Group II, Series L, NAACP Papers, Library of Congress, Washington, D.C.; Roy Wilkins to White, March 28, 1940, "Carnegie Study—Myrdal," Box 164, Group II, Series A, *ibid.*

26. Myrdal to White, April 3, 1940, "Carnegie Study—Myrdal," Box 146, *ibid.*; Myrdal, COHP, 6, 44.

Committee, liberals such as Keppel paid little attention to the ideological orientation of scholars thought to be well qualified. In truth, most Americans knew little about Myrdal's political views because most of his writing had been in Swedish and German. The foremost idea that American scholars associated with Myrdal was his advocacy of birth control, the subject of his 1938 Harvard lecture. In Sweden people often referred to contraception as "Myrdalling." [27]

By the 1930s Myrdal was an advanced but decidedly anti-communist Social Democrat. As a young rebel economist and disciple of his older liberal countryman, Knut Wicksell, Myrdal assailed classical economists with relish. He derided their pretensions of objectivity and their belief in natural laws. Both Wicksell and Myrdal anticipated John Maynard Keynes. When John Kenneth Galbraith was in Stockholm in 1937, he called on Gustav Cassel, a well-known economist. The former professor, whom Myrdal had recently replaced at the University of Stockholm, said to Galbraith: "I expect you have been seeing all my Red students in Stockholm." The American economist surmised that Cassel had Myrdal foremost in his mind. [28]

In a 1930 book entitled *The Political Element in the Development of Economic Theory*, first published in Swedish, then in German, and finally in English in 1953, Myrdal excoriated the natural law fatalism of Adam Smith and the Benthamite utilitarianism of John Stuart Mill. He denigrated such ideas as the "harmony of interests" and the "pleasure principle" as no more than fuzzy metaphysics. The young economist concentrated on revealing how laissez-faire scholars hid their norms in concepts, making their biases, he fulminated, all the more elusive and insidious. [29] In a 1933 article in a German journal, Myrdal charged that American social scientists were especially guilty of hiding their conservative biases in an exaggerated empiricism. Calling for an end to such deception, Myrdal advised social scientists to make their work relevant to the *"explicit and concrete value premises"* of the people. [30]

27. Frederick Osborn, COHP, 1, 54–55, 80–81; record of interview, Keppel and E. L. Thorndike, May 29, 1939; Young, COHP, 41; Myrdal, COHP, 45–46; Guy B. Johnson, COHP 25; Donald R. Young, *American Minority Peoples: A Study in Racial and Cultural Conflict in the United States* (New York, 1932), 584, 593.

28. Galbraith, *Life in Our Times*, 82.

29. Gunnar Myrdal, *The Political Element in the Development of Economic Theory*, trans. Paul Streeten (Cambridge, Mass., 1955), vii, 192.

30. The article is reprinted as "Ends and Means in Political Economy," in Gunnar Myrdal, *Value in Social Theory: A Selection of Essays on Methodology by Gunnar Myrdal*, trans. and ed. Paul Streeten (New York, 1958), 228.

In his early years Myrdal was an intensely theoretical or, in his words, "technical" economist. He wanted not only to expose the fallacies of the classical economists but to make it possible to introduce value premises into research and still "draw political conclusions on a scientific basis." He eventually abandoned that idealistic quest, calling it "naive empiricism." But through habit perhaps, he continued to refer to his writings as "scientific" for the rest of his career.[31]

In the early 1930s objectivity to Myrdal meant determining the actual concrete values of groups in society. But how could one discern the values of a people? Such a discovery, Myrdal admitted, entailed an exercise in social psychology, a very imperfect tool. Unfortunately, Myrdal observed, people's values were vague, inconsistent, and forever changing. Additionally, these values might be less than benign or even downright evil, as the period between 1914 and 1945 illustrated all too well. Myrdal knew that Max Weber, one of his favorite theorists, had struggled with the problem of conflicts in people's values, but he felt that the eminent sociologist had failed to find an answer.[32]

Throughout his life Myrdal's writings showed a deep concern for the relations between values and methodology. By the time he came to America to work on the Carnegie project, however, he had fallen back on common sense and impressionism to gauge the salient values of various groups in society.[33] Though he never solved the theoretical problems involving values and objectivity, he presented a tedious analysis of value theory in the *Dilemma*. Most of it, mercifully stricken from the text by sensitive editors, appeared in the controversial Appendix 2. The Scandinavian frankly acknowledged that the *Dilemma* did not prove the validity of his value theory. In America the dominant values, enshrined in the American creed, loomed so explicitly and authoritatively that Myrdal had no trouble finding an instrumental norm. But he conceded that America was an anomaly, a "historical accident."[34]

Myrdal, however, never allowed his theoretical or methodological

---

31. Myrdal, COHP, 9; Myrdal, *Political Element*, vii; Myrdal, "The Case Against Romantic Ethnicity," *Center Magazine*, VII (July–August, 1974), 27.

32. Myrdal, *Political Element*, 203. For essays on the problem of objectivity, see Max Weber, *The Methodology of the Social Sciences*, ed. Edward A. Shils and Henry A. Finch (Glencoe, Ill., 1949), 92–93, 103–104, 107–108, 111.

33. Myrdal, *Value in Social Theory*, esp. 9, 238; Remarks by Myrdal at a luncheon in honor of Gunnar and Alva Myrdal, *American Economic Review*, LXII (1972), 456–62; Gunnar Myrdal, *Against the Stream: Critical Essays on Economics* (New York, 1973), vii and *passim*.

34. Myrdal, *Value in Social Theory*, 260–61.

problems to blunt his exuberant optimism. Despite his criticism of nine-teenth-century liberals and radicals, the Social Democrat had much in common with the pre-Marxist utopian socialists. It took a leap of faith to believe that valuations of contending groups in society could be accu-rately assessed and that competing values could be satisfied without at-tendant disorder or violence. But Myrdal had convinced himself that people wanted to be rational and just. They simply needed to know the truth. Despite the examples of the Soviet Union, Germany, and Italy, Myrdal felt that if the people's values were not constructive, the right-minded social scientist could change them. Social planning should pro-ceed, he maintained, as "if they [the people] knew all that is actually known by contemporary experts." Like Carl Becker, the American who wanted to make "Mr. Everyman" his own historian, the Swede would make the common man his own social scientist.[35]

In any case, Myrdal clearly put social engineering above the aca-demic quest for an objective social science. He geared most of his re-search and writing toward the construction of a welfare state. In the 1930s he and his wife profoundly influenced the evolution of the Social Democratic Labor party in Sweden. The Myrdals' 1934 book on the population crisis, *Kris i Befolkningsfragen,* became, in the words of a historian, "the normative blueprint for the creation of a post-bourgeois Social Democratic order." The book's themes of equality, moral materi-alism, the inherent radicalism of the social sciences, and the efficacy of social engineering provided Social Democrats in Sweden with a gal-vanizing world view. More than a thinker, Myrdal was an effective or-ator and politician who won a seat in the Swedish Senate. As a member of the Population Commission from 1935 to 1938, he dominated that important body through intellect and "sheer energy."[36] Myrdal authored half of the commission's sixteen reports, white papers replete with rec-ommendations that ultimately made up much of what became known as the "middle way" between liberalism and socialism. In 1971 Myrdal pinpointed the theme of his life's work: "And so I came to be working on the equality issue, first in Sweden, then . . . in the United States . . . and in the last couple of decades in the world, focusing on the great majority of poverty-stricken masses of people in the underdeveloped world."[37]

35. Paul Streeten, Introduction to *ibid.,* xli–xlv; Myrdal, *Political Element,* 202; Carl Becker, "Everyman His Own Historian," *American Historical Review,* XXXVII (1932), 234–35.
36. Carlson, "The Myrdals, Pro-Natalism, and Swedish Social Democracy," 71–94.
37. Remarks by Myrdal, *American Economic Review,* 458.

In short, Myrdal had strong ideological and methodological leanings when he arrived in America in 1938. Though he was an incisive critic of nineteenth-century determinists, his own ideas were not without internal conflicts. Despite his search for a "scientific" study of human society, his emphasis was always on practical research designed to further social democracy. Like Richard Ely, the progressive economist of the Wisconsin School in earlier times, Myrdal felt that economics constituted a "moral science." Myrdal's idea of what objective science was, however, struck many American scholars as peculiar.[38]

Whether economics was a moral science or not, the Swede did not mind some hard financial bargaining on his own behalf. When offering the job as head of the Carnegie project to Myrdal, Keppel explained that the corporation's policy was to make an employee "neither richer nor poorer." The Scandinavian frankly informed Keppel that his price would run high. After extended negotiations in the fall of 1937 and the spring of 1938, Myrdal managed to obtain an annual salary of $19,800 for two years. In depression dollars, this amount would be roughly equivalent to $152,000 in 1986 currency. Myrdal estimated that he would lose about $8,840 in income by coming to America. In this figure he counted his income as a professor, as a senator, as a member of several royal commissions, and as a board member of a bank. He added his wife's salary, the estimated loss on his new house, his anticipated wage increases, and several other incidentals. The total amount shocked even Myrdal. "In this country," he confessed, "we are, of course, living on a rather European upper class level with our own house, two servants, etc." To continue the Myrdals' customary living style in New York, the corporation added almost $11,000 for living expenses. The Swedish scholar also got the right to any royalties that might accrue from the study. In addition, he insisted on bringing his Swedish assistant, Richard Sterner, who was paid $7,680 a year or about $59,000 in 1986 money.[39]

Young, who was an experienced evaluator of grants for the SSRC and the various Rockefeller foundations, believed that Myrdal received more money than any social scientist had been paid up to that time. He also

---

38. For an engaging critique of Myrdal's theoretical views, see Ernest Nagel, "The Value-Oriented Bias of Social Inquiry," in May Brodbeck (ed.), *Readings in the Philosophy of the Social Sciences* (New York, 1968), 102–104, 112–13.

39. Myrdal to Keppel, November 12, 1937, May 5, 1938; memorandum on estimated budget, September 10, 1940; Keppel to Myrdal, October 27, 1937. The Consumer Price Index of the U.S. Department of Labor was used to compare the value of money. For 1938 the CPI was 42.2; in early 1986 it was 326.1.

felt that it caused "some resentment" among American scholars. Not
only the Swedes were well reimbursed. Most of the American staff members, collaborators, critics, and even secretaries also proved enormously
successful at becoming no poorer by working for Carnegie. Guy B.
Johnson, a sociologist from Chapel Hill, happily came to New York for
$7,500, and young Arnold Rose, a graduate student from the University
of Chicago, expressed pleasure at the thought of getting over $3,000.[40]
That was about a thousand dollars more than Rose would have made as
an instructor, a considerable difference when a Van Heusen shirt cost
$2.25 and a Botany suit went for $45. If Myrdal's compensation caused
resentment, it did not stop others from trying to climb aboard the Carnegie gravy train. For this and other unforeseen reasons, the budget
mounted. In 1938 the trustees appropriated $25,000 for the Myrdal
study and estimated that the total cost would be around $75,000. By the
summer of 1939, Myrdal had proposed a budget of $166,921.15 to go
through August, 1940, about half the cost of the completed project.[41]
One might have to go forward in time to modern Pentagon accounting to
find such cost (and time) overruns.

Aware of the coolness toward him in American social science circles,
Myrdal orchestrated an extensive public relations campaign to curry
favor with certain important groups and individuals. As his staff member and confidant Guy Johnson later put it: "If you hadn't involved all
these people and spent all this money and had a thousand names on the
list . . . [who] helped, the reception [of the book] might not have been
as enthusiastic."[42] In Myrdal's defense, his behavior was not directed
solely at buttering up academicians so they would look more favorably
upon his study. Because of his ignorance concerning the race problem,
he sought to tap the best-informed minds on the subject. Thus the foreigner set out across the country again and again, consulting the stars of
the social science world in such universities as Columbia, Howard,
Fisk, Northwestern, Chicago, and North Carolina. The size of the country and the academic community made the job difficult. Scholars in
America, an amazed Myrdal declared, were "like grasshoppers in
Egypt." In a manner reminiscent of Lyndon B. Johnson, the boisterous
Myrdal pounded people on the back, grabbed their hands, and pleaded
for their "collaboration," reportedly his favorite word. Described by

40. Young, COHP, 60; Johnson, COHP, 12; Samuel Stouffer to Myrdal, May 28,
1941.
41. Appropriations for Comprehensive Study of the Negro, January 20, 1938.
42. Guy Johnson, COHP, 61–62.

some as the "Myrdal treatment," this technique often proved so effective that several academicians mistakenly believed that they had been offered a lucrative job with the Carnegie Corporation. This misunderstanding caused some injured feelings and embarrassments.[43] Actually, Myrdal usually was only soliciting goodwill and free advice. He intended no research projects for such notables as Franz Boas, Robert E. Park, Ruth Benedict, Melville J. Herskovits, Howard W. Odum, W. E. B. Du Bois, and E. Franklin Frazier. Eventually, he hired some collaborators primarily to soothe bruised egos or to increase the chances for a positive reception of his study.[44]

Try as he might to spread goodwill, Myrdal's forceful personality often proved a liability to that end. Articulate, extroverted, and supremely confident, the Swedish economist liked to be surrounded by bright and witty people. But when he met competitive people of high caliber, conversations tended to turn into heated debates. Myrdal's limited use for some of the ideas of the Chicago School of Sociology, the Columbia School of Anthropology, and the Chapel Hill School frequently put him at odds with some of the major figures of the American social science establishment. For example, when Myrdal came into contact with the combative Louis Wirth of the University of Chicago, their discussions sometimes turned into intellectual dogfights. And when people rebuffed Myrdal, he could be vindictive. When Wirth refused to join his staff, Myrdal called him a "very queer person who did not keep the truth." Like Robert Park, Wirth had some views about blacks that grate on the ears of the modern egalitarian. For instance, he informed Myrdal, "The Negro does not fit into the modern machine age." And "There is a looseness in his life which explains many of the statistical differences [between whites and blacks]."[45] Actually, Wirth was one of the most advanced thinkers of the Chicago School, and his consultation and criticism proved valuable to Myrdal's work. Still, Wirth's views only demonstrated further the wisdom of Keppel's choice to go outside America for a director of the Carnegie study.

Melville Herskovits, an anthropologist and racial specialist, also pre-

43. Myrdal to Gunnar Lange, October 28, 1941; Guion Johnson, COHP, 8; record of interview, Myrdal, T. J. Woofter, Jr., and Will Alexander, February, 1939, roll 2; Index of Interviews, n.d.

44. Guy Johnson, COHP, 3, 29–33, 61–64.

45. Young, COHP, 55–56; Guy Johnson, COHP, 27, 40–41, 48–49; Myrdal to Dorothy Thomas, April 19, 1939; record of interview, Myrdal and Dollard, March 21, 1939; record of interview, Myrdal and Wirth, February 24, 1940.

sented problems for Myrdal. Although these two scholars did not get along well from the start, Myrdal knew it would not be prudent to ignore the Northwestern University professor. In the planning stages of the project, Myrdal made a trip to Evanston to see the distinguished follower of Boas. In their meeting Herskovits argued that a comprehensive study of blacks would take not two but five years, and he stressed that black culture should be the crux of the study. Myrdal despairingly regarded Herskovits as a man obsessed with "Africanisms," but he nonetheless intended to assign Herskovits a small research project, just to bring him into the affair. According to Guy Johnson, the Scandinavian thought he had assuaged the noted anthropologist, but two more conferences and a luncheon at the Waldorf brought the ambitious professor a major assignment and a generous honorarium. In short order the enterprising Herskovits produced an important book called *The Myth of the Negro Past*, the first monograph published in the Carnegie Series on the Negro.[46] This book later raised problems for Myrdal when he began to draft the chapters on black culture for the *Dilemma*.

Myrdal also paid special attention to Howard Odum, the most influential social scientist in the South. Born of yeoman stock on a small Georgia farm in 1884, Odum began his higher education at Emory College. As an undergraduate he despondently described himself as "awkward, ugly, ignorant, and poor." In 1906, however, his life took on new meaning when Professor Thomas Pearce Bailey, Jr., introduced him to the behavioral sciences at the University of Mississippi. Social science became a shield for Odum's shyness and insecurities as well as an outlet for his ambitions. After acquiring a Ph.D. in psychology at Clark University in 1909 and one in sociology at Columbia University in 1910, Odum spent a decade researching and teaching, mostly in his home state of Georgia. In 1920 he found a permanent home at the University of North Carolina at Chapel Hill. In the 1920s he built a sociology department from the ground up, started the School of Public Welfare, founded the *Journal of Social Forces*, established the independent Institute for Research in Social Science, and served as an assistant director of President Herbert Hoover's Committee on Social Trends. In 1930 he became the first southern president of the American Sociological Society, and in

---

46. Record of interviews, Myrdal and Dollard, February 27, 1939; and Myrdal and Herskovits, February 27, 1939, roll 2; Myrdal and Herskovits, October 14–15, 1939; Myrdal to Keppel, August 21, 1939; Guy Johnson, COHP, 33–38; Melville J. Herskovits, *The Myth of the Negro Past* (New York, 1941).

1937 he accepted the presidency of the Commission on Interracial Co-operation. These activities did not deter him from publishing numerous books and articles, the most important of which was *Southern Regions of the United States* in 1936. A massive sociological work, it delineated the concept of "regionalism," which has been associated with Odum ever since. When Myrdal came to Chapel Hill in 1938, Odum had gathered a flock of talented students and had made the university the center of liberal thought in the South.[47]

As two scholars interested in elevating the poor and the down-trodden, one might guess that Myrdal and Odum would get along well. But such was not the case. Between the younger Swede and the well-seasoned southerner there was a clash of personalities, ideas, and ambi-tions. According to Guy Johnson, an Odumite who helped entertain Myrdal in 1938, the chemistry between the two men was bad. Flashy and ebullient, the foreigner enjoyed quick repartee and lively interaction between individuals. Odum, however, was a plain "country boy," who was not quick of tongue or wit. Myrdal's freewheeling style struck the Georgian as artificial. Odum also burned because he felt that the Euro-pean did not take him seriously enough.[48]

The leader of the Chapel Hill group was right about Myrdal's percep-tion of him. Myrdal's collaborators had briefed him about Odum's scholarship. The southerner's dissertation, published in 1910 as *The So-cial and Mental Traits of the Negro*, reads, Daniel J. Singal concluded, "almost like a parody of the scientific racism of its time." Although Odum repudiated his earlier racist views, he still retained an ambiva-lence about blacks. Furthermore, he judged that segregation was immu-table in the South.[49]

Beyond the differences of personality and philosophy, Odum saw Myrdal as one more person trying to tread on his academic turf. The

47. Daniel J. Singal, *The War Within: From Victorian to Modernist Thought in the South, 1919–1945* (Chapel Hill, 1982), 115–52. See also George W. Stocking, Jr., *Race, Culture, and Evolution: Essays in the History of Anthropology* (New York, 1968), 126, 242–43, 254–55; Morton Sosna, *In Search of the Silent South: Southern Liberals and the Race Issue* (New York, 1977), 42–59; Michael O'Brien, *The Idea of the American South, 1920–1941* (Baltimore, 1979), 31–93; and Daniel T. Rodgers, "Regionalism and the Bur-dens of Progress," in J. Morgan Kousser and James M. McPherson (eds.), *Region, Race, and Reconstruction* (New York, 1982), 3–26.

48. Guy Johnson to the author, November 22, 1982.

49. Singal, *War Within*, 141; Stocking, *Race, Culture, and Evolution*, 125–26, 242, 254–55.

North Carolina professor was an empire builder. He had a cozy relationship with the various Rockefeller foundations, the Julius Rosenwald
Fund, and many other similar agencies. He viewed all southern projects
not under his control as competition for funds and recognition. He long
had plans for a grand southern council to carry out a major study of race
relations, which he hoped to accomplish "before outsiders do the job."
Even before Myrdal arrived, an irritated Odum wrote to a subordinate
at the Commission on Interracial Cooperation: "Between the Right
Honorable FD[R], the Southern Conference for Human Welfare, and
twenty other groups that are literally taking the lead to do what the
Council ought to do, I think I'll presently go heat-wave hay-wire!!!"[50]

When Myrdal returned to New York from the South, he told Charles
Dollard that the Chapel Hill School could be marked down as "politely
antagonistic." The Swede characterized Odum as a "very kind old fool"
who was struggling to modernize his ideas. Odum in turn praised the
European's energy but thought that the foreigner did not understand the
"distinctive character of the American race problem."[51] Predictably,
sparks would eventually fly between the old native and the immigrant
student of southern regions.

Despite his low opinion of Odum, Myrdal wanted to have as much of
the Chapel Hill establishment as possible on his side when he completed
his study. Myrdal thus hired several of Odum's students. He selected
Guy Johnson as a permanent staff member of the Carnegie project. He
also employed Arthur F. Raper, Thomas J. Woofter, Jr., and Guion G.
Johnson as research assistants. Guy Johnson, a young, urbane Texan,
had a manner that Myrdal liked. More advanced than Odum on the race
issue, he was considered the "Negro expert" at Chapel Hill. After re-
ceiving his master's degree—doing a thesis on the Ku Klux Klan—
under Robert Park in Chicago, he came to North Carolina in 1924 to
study under Odum. At Chapel Hill he steeped himself in the study of
black culture. In his most notable book, *Folk Culture on St. Helena Is-*

50. Howard W. Odum to Gerald W. Johnson, April 12, 1944, Box 26; Odum to Mark
Ethridge, October 10, 1938, Folder 446, Box 21; quotation in Odum to Emily Clay, August 15, 1938, Box 21, Howard W. Odum Papers, Southern Historical Collection, University of North Carolina, Chapel Hill.

51. Record of interview, Myrdal and Dollard, March 7, 1939; Myrdal, COHP, 53;
Odum to Jackson Davis, October 28, 1938, Box 21, Odum Papers. The recent works of
Singal, O'Brien, Sosna, and Rodgers cited in note 47 essentially mirror Myrdal's view of
Odum in the late 1930s.

land, South Carolina (1930), Johnson impressively argued against the Herskovits thesis about African cultural survivals among American blacks, a view Myrdal considered to be potentially useful.[52]

Not surprisingly, Myrdal vigorously courted black activists and intellectuals. He did so for three major reasons. First, Myrdal wanted to overcome black suspicion about his selection to direct the Carnegie study. Second, and related to the first, he knew that any racial reform program based on his study would need the support of Afro-Americans. Third, Myrdal wanted extensive contact with blacks to enhance his understanding of the "Negro problem." Although the European had no romantic feelings about blacks, he was a natural friend of the oppressed. One of his first acts as director was to order all personnel connected with the Carnegie project to capitalize the word "Negro." It had not yet become common for even the most liberal whites on the Myrdal team to do so.[53] Such symbolic action did not allay the suspicion among black spokesmen, but in time, Myrdal disspelled many of their doubts about his intentions. Indeed, in 1944 no group reacted more favorably to the *Dilemma* than blacks. After Myrdal traveled to Washington and explained the proposed study to Charles H. Thompson, the dean of Howard University, the black educator's reservations about the Swede faded rapidly. When the skeptical E. Franklin Frazier proofread the final manuscript of the Myrdal report, he confessed that his earlier misgivings had disappeared.[54]

Many black scholars became collaborators on the Carnegie project. Dean Thompson aided Myrdal in what amounted to a brain drain of Howard University. Myrdal put Ralph J. Bunche, a political scientist, and Doxey A. Wilkerson, a professor of education, on his staff. He assigned an important research topic to Sterling A. Brown, a professor of literature, and initially a lesser one in sociology to Frazier. These scholars, whom Myrdal jokingly referred to as his "Howard boys," employed many other Howard teachers and graduate students to assist them. Charles S. Johnson of Fisk University performed substantial sociological fieldwork for Myrdal and kept half a dozen of his students busy

52. Singal, *War Within,* 317–25; Guy Johnson, COHP, 8–9.

53. "Main Viewpoints and Emphasis of Study," February 8, 1940, 7. At first, even Myrdal, Keppel, and Dollard (or their secretaries) spelled "Negro" with a small "n"; see Myrdal to Keppel, November 12, 1937; record of interview, Dollard and Myrdal, May 10, 1939, roll 2.

54. Thompson to Myrdal, February 23, 1939; Frazier to Myrdal, June 24, 1942.

preparing a memorandum on the "patterns of segregation." Still not wholly satisfied, Keppel urged Myrdal to make greater use of Alain Locke, the Howard writer and historian of the "New Negro" of the 1920s, and of W. E. B. Du Bois, the longtime protest leader and sage of Atlanta University. Locke often acted as a consultant and critic, and Myrdal twice visited Du Bois to pay his respects and get his views on the study.[55]

These friendly overtures toward the black community did not prevent difficulties with his black collaborators. One reason was that there were divisions and hostilities within Afro-American ranks. Charles Johnson, a conservative Negro who probably had the most white contacts, got little respect from more radical scholars such as Bunche, Frazier, and Wilkerson.[56] Frazier, a product of the Chicago School, a devastating critic of the black middle class, and a man full of racial pride, like Du Bois, was somewhat of an enigma. Bunche and Wilkerson tended to deemphasize race prejudice and pursue a strict class-analysis approach to the minority issue. Characteristically, Bunche asked Myrdal if he could get Carnegie stationery printed by organized labor and have a union label appear on it.[57]

Whatever his ideology, Bunche turned out more useful work for Myrdal than anyone else. He completed four memoranda dealing with black politics, leadership, ideologies, and betterment organizations. One, called "The Political Status of the Negro," ran to 1,660 pages. (No wonder rumors persisted in the black community that Bunche wrote the *Dilemma*.) Although Myrdal rejected Bunche's leftist approach, he respected the Howard professor's work and liked him immensely. Bunche reciprocated the feelings. When Myrdal had to return to Sweden sud-

55. Myrdal to Thomas J. Woofter, Jr., May 1, 1939, roll 2; summary of conference, Myrdal and Keppel, March 12, 1939; Herbert Aptheker (ed.), *The Correspondence of W. E. B. Du Bois* (3 vols.; Amherst, Mass., 1973–78), II, 177, 190–91; Shirley Graham Du Bois, *His Day Is Marching On: A Memoir of W. E. B. Du Bois* (Philadelphia, 1971), 67, 69.

56. Butler A. Jones, "The Tradition of Sociology Teaching in Black Colleges: The Unheralded Professionals," in James E. Blackwell and Morris Janowitz (eds.), *Black Sociologists: Historical and Contemporary Perspectives* (Chicago, 1974), 136, 162–63, 173–74, 200.

57. G. Franklin Edwards, "E. Franklin Frazier," in *ibid.*, 87–93; John Bracey, August Meier, and Elliott Rudwick, "The Black Sociologists: The First Half Century," in Joyce A. Ladner (ed.), *The Death of White Sociology* (New York, 1973), 13–19; John K. Kirby, "Ralph J. Bunche and Black Radical Thought in the 1930's," *Phylon*, XXXV (1974), 131–33; Bunche to Myrdal, September 29, 1939, roll 2.

denly in 1940, Bunche confided to the economist that he considered him "one of the truly great characters I have met in my life."[58]

But Bunche also caused problems for Myrdal. The black political scientist helped create tension between Myrdal and the national offices of the NAACP and the National Urban League. In his research memoranda for Myrdal, Bunche attacked these moderate, legalistic agencies with barely disguised contempt. Myrdal based his early assessments of the two New York organizations on Bunche's research. When Myrdal sent initial drafts of his manuscript to Walter White of the NAACP and Eugene K. Jones of the Urban League, they took offense.[59] White and Jones had cooperated with Myrdal in every way possible. Trying to put their best foot forward, they opened up their files to the Swede. When White and Roy Wilkins, the editor of the *Crisis*, worried that their first meeting with Myrdal had not gone well, they requested another. As Wilkins prophetically surmised, "this survey probably will be the most important study of the Negro in twenty years." When Wilkins received Myrdal's manuscript reflecting Bunche's hostile perspective, the black editor sent Walter White a sixteen-page rebuttal to the charges. White passed them along to Myrdal. Wilkins made a spirited defense of his agency, emphasizing its new political militancy and mass-oriented programs. He rebuked Bunche as "an arm-chair radical" who did not understand the real world.[60] Myrdal admitted to White and Jones that he had deliberately provoked them so they would respond with a vigorous defense of their agencies. This was but another example of the "Myrdal treatment." Though he still remained somewhat critical of the NAACP and the Urban League, the Swedish scholar ultimately rejected the harsh judgments of Bunche. When White read Myrdal's final draft of the *Dilemma* in late 1942, he informed him that his organization had received a fair assessment.[61]

When the generosity of the Carnegie Corporation became known,

58. Myrdal to Keppel, March 8, 1939; Myrdal, COHP, 61; Bunche to Myrdal, May 1, 1940, roll 2. For rumors about Bunche's authorship, see Guion Johnson, COHP, 65, and for skepticism about Myrdal's authorship, see John Russell, COHP, 154. Some of Bunche's research was published as *The Political Status of the Negro in the Age of FDR*, ed. Dewey W. Grantham (Chicago, 1973), xv.

59. Myrdal to White, July 24, 1942, roll 2; Myrdal to Eugene K. Jones, July 24, 1942, roll 2.

60. Memorandum, Wilkins to White, October 21, 1939; White to Myrdal, October 24, 1939; Myrdal to Jones, February 13, 1940; Myrdal to Keppel, April 23, 1940; Wilkins to White, March 13, 1942, roll 2.

61. Myrdal to White, July 30, 1942, roll 2; White to Myrdal, August 26, 1942; Lester Granger (Urban League) to Myrdal, August 7, 1942; Myrdal to Granger, August 24, 1942.

some blacks followed Myrdal's precedent by asking a high price for their services. To make him "neither richer nor poorer," Bunche wanted compensation for his salary, his lecture fees, and his wife's salary, and he requested that the corporation pay his wife's tuition at a graduate school in New York City. After calculating the extra expense of living in New York according to his customary style in Washington, which included a large house and a live-in maid, Bunche asked for $9,500 a year—or about $73,000 in 1986 dollars. Even the corporation officials and Myrdal balked at this figure. The corporation offered him $7,500. When Bunche declined, Myrdal interpreted the black scholar's action as a "bluff." He suggested that Bunche stay in Washington, where his wife could continue her job and the expenses were lower. So Bunche, though regarded as a member of Myrdal's permanent staff, stayed in the capital city and worked for $5,000 a year. Rumors nevertheless persisted that black academics were demanding salaries of $10,000 or more.[62]

A black social scientist's observation that "some black people got a little mileage out of" the Carnegie project was undoubtedly true.[63] Unfortunately, some black collaborators contracted to do research for Myrdal even though they already had too many academic irons in the fire. Sterling A. Brown, a black poet from Howard University, accepted a lucrative stipend from the corporation but turned in only a fragment of his assigned project, and that came in two years late. While a Myrdal collaborator, Brown still taught at Howard, lectured regularly at New York University, worked for the Works Progress Administration (WPA) Writers' Project, and—because he had a Rosenwald Fellowship—spent much of his time finishing an anthology of black literature. The black sociologist Horace Cayton of Chicago, who also worked for the WPA and had a Rosenwald Fellowship, lobbied Myrdal constantly for a full-time job at $5,000. When Myrdal learned about Cayton's other duties and income, he offered the Chicago scholar a modest stipend for a small research project. He accepted. Some black academicians apparently had little respect for Myrdal or the project and decided to milk the foundation as much as possible.[64]

62. Bunche to Dollard, May 6, 1939; John Russell to Bunche, May 15, 1939; Bunche to Russell, May 23, 1939; Myrdal to Bunche, June 1, 1939, all on roll 2; record of interviews, Myrdal and Russell, May 12, 1939, Myrdal and Dollard, May 29, 1939; Guion Johnson, COHP, 20–21.
63. Gerald A. McWorter, "Deck the Ivory Racist Halls: The Case of Black Studies," in Armstead Robinson, Craig C. Foster, and Donald C. Ogilvie (eds.), *Black Studies in the University: A Symposium* (New Haven, 1969), 70.
64. Myrdal to Dollard, January 26, 1939; Brown to Stouffer, November 5, 1941, roll

Doxey Wilkerson, however, proved to be the greatest puzzle and disappointment to Myrdal, though money was not significantly involved. Joining Myrdal's staff in September, 1939, the Howard professor of education and several of his assistants embarked upon a broad study of black education. The Swedish economist had high respect for Wilkerson's intellect and liked him personally. But after months, then years, Wilkerson produced almost nothing. Bernhard J. Stern, the man Wilkerson contracted to do a study of adult Negro education, wrote a tract that all the critics found to pulsate with class revolution.[65] Wilkerson had strong Marxist leanings when Myrdal hired him. While on the Carnegie project he underwent a personal crisis, which he described as the "dissolution of the Wilkerson family." Guion Johnson, who had many opportunities to observe Wilkerson, characterized the black educator as "very hostile" and "emotionally disturbed."[66] In his memoirs Myrdal speculated that he might "have gone mad." Wilkerson's affiliation with the American Communist party apparently had something to do with his behavior. A writer in the *Crisis* claimed that Wilkerson joined the party in 1943. In any event, Wilkerson wrote a foreword to the vicious attack on the *Dilemma* by Herbert Aptheker in 1946. Aptheker was probably the leading Communist party intellectual in America.[67] The failure or tardiness of so many black collaborators to complete their work aroused the suspicion of Charles Dollard, who wondered "if we are not facing something in the nature of passive resistance" from black scholars.[68]

2; Horace Cayton to Myrdal, June 9, February 23, 1940, roll 2; Myrdal to Cayton, February 27, 1940; memorandum by Dollard, March 1, 1940; Myrdal to Cayton, March 7, 1940. According to the black historian John H. Bracey, Jr., who interviewed Cayton, the Chicago sociologist admitted to "hustling" Myrdal (remarks made to the author by Bracey at a session titled "Blacks and American Social Science" at the annual meeting of the Organization of American Historians, April 6, 1984, Los Angeles).

65. Louis Wirth to Samuel Stouffer, August 30, 1940; Richard Sterner to Stouffer, August 27, 1940; Newton Edwards to Stouffer, September 14, 1940; Alain Locke to Stouffer, September 30, 1940, all on roll 2.

66. Wilkerson to Myrdal, January 26, 1942, roll 2; Myrdal to Keppel, April 28, 1939; Myrdal, COHP, 93–95; Guion Johnson, COHP, 39; Young, COHP, 42.

67. Myrdal, COHP, 64–65, 95; Coral Sadter, Review of Arnold Rose's *What the Negro Wants*, in *Crisis*, LI (1944), 395; foreword to Herbert Aptheker, *The Negro People in America: A Critique of Gunnar Myrdal's "An American Dilemma"* (New York, 1946). For more on Wilkerson's relation to the Communist party, see William A. Nolan, *Communism Versus the Negro* (Chicago, 1951), 56–57, 65–66, 69; Wilson Record, *Race and Radicalism: The NAACP and the Communist Party in Conflict* (Ithaca, N.Y., 1964), 138, 174; and Mark Naison, *Communists in Harlem During the Depression* (Urbana, 1983), 299.

68. Dollard to Stouffer, November 17, 1941.

Despite such problems, Myrdal's confrontations with collaborators of both races did not stem primarily from money grubbing, incompetence, or passive resistance. Faced with trying to complete a comprehensive study of blacks in two years, Myrdal assigned impossibly difficult topics with impossibly short deadlines. The Swede presided over what David Riesman called "fire-house research." Myrdal demanded speedy rather than polished research memoranda. Seemingly oblivious to the volume of material one had to master to produce some of these, Myrdal exclaimed: "Just dash them off, I'll cannibalize them." [69]

Those around Myrdal characterized him as a hard taskmaster. "You've assigned me . . . an impossible task," the saucy Guion Johnson told Myrdal. "I cannot possibly write a history of racial ideologies . . . between September [1939] and the 1st of March [1940]." Unmoved, the Swedish director resorted to his oft-used flattery. "You do what you can," Myrdal replied to Johnson. "I know that a person of your genius can do it." Habitually on the telephone, Myrdal hounded his collaborators to finish their work on time. "We must just have this thing," he would prod in his quaint English. In jest he referred to the driven assistants, both black and white, as the "niggers on the project." [70] Sometimes it seemed more than a jest. When one associate fell behind on her project, Myrdal threatened to ruin her academically unless she delivered her work promptly. When a collaborator missed a deadline because of a seriously ill son, the Scandinavian exclaimed that the project came first. [71]

Some of those close to Myrdal recognized that he often consciously employed rudeness as a tactic, hoping to evoke an uninhibited response from a person or group. He had used this tactic with the NAACP and the Urban League. The Swede's favorite reaction to the confidently spoken truth of another person was, "But, hell, now." He delighted in exercising the Myrdal treatment on white southerners. His sharp and provocative questions hurled their way often caused consternation and embarrassment—and sometimes fear—among his traveling companions. With the aid of Jackson Davis, who traveled with Myrdal through the South, Robert M. Lester of the Carnegie Corporation summarized the 1938 trip in a memorandum. Lester worried about what he heard and

69. David Riesman, COHP, 64; Young, COHP, 50.
70. Guion Johnson, COHP, 23–24, 46–47, 57; Young, COHP, 55; Guy Johnson, COHP, 14.
71. By request the sources for these stories are confidential.

warned his boss, Keppel, that "a foreigner could hardly afford to be fa-
cetious and breezy about the interracial matters" of the South.[72]
But the "Super-Yankee," as some southerners called him, paid little
attention to such warnings. During his southern sojourn Myrdal might
suddenly turn to a gracious host in a fine home and ask: "Why don't you
want your daughter to marry a Negro?" The Swede's behavior gave
Ralph Bunche more than one anxious moment on their 1939 tour through
Dixie. Myrdal got great pleasure from passing off the light-skinned
Bunche as a foreigner. He boldly ate with Bunche in southern restaurants and occasionally even stayed with him in the same hotels. When a
white woman joined them in their car in Mississippi, a worried Bunche
did his best to look like a chauffeur. Although Myrdal and Bunche
found themselves in some sticky situations they never, as reported in
one published work, escaped a lynch mob by speeding away in their car
amid a hail of bullets.[73]

In one case, however, Myrdal did have to flee the authorities. When
he heard about a certain Mrs. Andrews in Atlanta who headed an organization for the preservation of white womanhood, the inquisitive foreigner could not resist a little chat with her. During their conversation
the intense woman began to expound her theories on the black male's
lust for white women. Myrdal enlivened the conversation further by
asking her such questions as "Do you ever fantasize about sleeping with
a black man?" After a few such questions, Mrs. Andrews chased the
economist from her home, yelling: "Remember your race." [74] The woman
was so enraged that she swore out a warrant for indecent behavior
against Myrdal. Knowing the temper of the white South, Bunche persuaded Myrdal that the rational course was to flee across the border into
Alabama so the warrant could not be served. The Carnegie director
found all of this very amusing and repeated the Andrews story many
times. Bunche, in fact, cautioned Myrdal against such behavior, warning that if the story reached the media, the publicity might have an adverse effect on the project.[75] It was reported that some years later, when

72. Guion Johnson, COHP, 4; Robert M. Lester to Keppel, November 14, 1938; Myrdal, COHP, 102–103.
73. Myrdal, COHP, 86, 102; Young, COHP, 50; J. Alvin Kugelmass, *Ralph J. Bunche*
(New York, 1968), 88–93.
74. Myrdal, COHP, 97–99; Guy Johnson, COHP, 18–21; Arthur Raper to Myrdal,
November 15, 1939.
75. Negro Study, record of interview, Dollard and Keppel, November 20, 1939;
Bunche to Myrdal, December 2, 1939, roll 2.

Alva Myrdal visited Atlanta to make a speech, Mrs. Andrews, still seething from her humiliation by Gunnar, rudely interrupted the speaker and asked her if she had ever slept with a black man. According to the story, which may be apocryphal, Alva laid her finger alongside her nose, looked long and thoughtfully at Mrs. Andrews, and said, "Now, let me think a minute."[76]

Myrdal did not hesitate to use the "treatment" on blacks as well as whites. He assailed the affluent Spauldings, operators of one of the largest black businesses in the nation, accusing them of getting rich at the expense of the poor blacks. After a round of aggressive questioning of a southern black clergyman, the secular-minded Myrdal succeeded in getting the parson to confess that he served as "the policeman [for] the white people."[77]

After Myrdal's eye-opening southern trip in 1938, he spent the next fifteen months engaged in the planning and administration of the sprawling Carnegie project. During that time he prepared three detailed reports for Keppel, selected his permanent staff, assigned research projects to collaborators, traveled widely throughout the country, conversed with scores of racial experts, and made another extensive research tour of the South. In 1939 Myrdal would make many of the key decisions that would determine the ultimate shape of his study. But just when the director had the project in high gear and had freed himself to do some badly needed reading in the literature of race relations, World War II broke out. Because of the world conflict, the Carnegie collaboration would confront many more obstacles and extend much longer than Myrdal had ever anticipated.

76. Guy Johnson, COHP, 22; Myrdal, COHP, 100.
77. Guion Johnson, COHP, 61; Richard Sterner to Samuel Stouffer, August 27, 1940, roll 2.

II

The Ordeal of Collaboration, 1939–1943

On January 28, 1939, Myrdal sent his first outline of his proposed study on the Negro to Frederick Keppel of the Carnegie Corporation. In the sixty-three-page report, he conceded that the scope of the race problem was so great that a truly comprehensive work could not be done in two years. The race problem, Myrdal explained, could not be understood in isolation; it required a complete "observation of values and institutions prevalent in American society." To this comment, Keppel responded in the margin with an underlined "Yes." Having now measured the scope of the race problem, Myrdal wondered whether his "lack of preconception" and "nearly absolute lack of knowledge" were an advantage or a liability.[1]

Despairing of writing an original or comprehensive work, Myrdal concluded that the study had to be narrowed down either by selecting a few topics for intensive research or by writing a general treatise based on existing data but with a fresh analysis. In the end, he effected a compromise between the two alternatives, but in the meantime, he proposed to limit the study in four significant ways. First, no comparative study of blacks in other countries would be attempted. Second, insofar as possible, historical development would be eliminated in favor of present trends and extrapolations. Some historical research was necessary, Myrdal conceded, because the existing literature was such a "waste land." Third, the study would avoid purely theoretical research in favor

1. Myrdal to Keppel, January 28, 1939, 4, 7–8, 10–12, Negro Study, roll 1; hereinafter all letters, memoranda, and records of interviews and conferences in this chapter, unless otherwise stated, are from roll 1 of the microfilm.

29

of that which had "practical significance"; that is, it would be concerned with changes actually in progress or ones feasible within the near
future. Some of these changes, he added, might bring greater harmony,
but some might exacerbate "several dilemmas confronting American
culture because of the presence of the Negro." Fourth, the African heritage of blacks would be considered "insignificant" and reduced to a
short documented summary.[2] In time, critics would perceive one or
more of these omissions as a source of serious or even crucial weakness
in the *Dilemma*.

Myrdal spent the next several weeks discussing his first outline with
Keppel and Dollard at the Carnegie Corporation, with Richard Sterner,
his Swedish colleague, and with a number of social scientists. The reaction, for the most part, proved positive. Keppel, however, requested a
fuller report, which designated staff and research assignments and
specified salaries for collaborators. In a ten-page letter to Keppel on
March 8, Myrdal complained that despite the need to limit the study,
everyone he had talked to so far wanted to add something to it. Yet he
assured Keppel that the research for the project would be finished by the
spring of 1940 and that he would begin writing the main report the following summer. He wryly commented that he should begin writing
before "that naiveté which, after all, is my chief advantage," began to
erode.[3]

After completing his first report to Keppel, Myrdal turned to the task
of selecting his staff, which he wanted to consist of a sociologist, an
economist, a statistician, and a black social scientist. They would direct
the research of the various collaborators and integrate their work into
Myrdal's general framework. By the spring of 1939 he had selected as
staff members Guy Johnson, Dorothy Thomas, Ralph Bunche, and, of
course, Sterner. When Myrdal called his first staff conference at Asbury
Park, New Jersey, from April 23 to 28, he was still searching for an
American economist for his team. In addition to his staff, he invited
Thomas J. Woofter, Jr., Donald Young, Charles Johnson, and the ever-
faithful Dollard to the Asbury Park conference. Led by the whip-
cracking Swede, the group brainstormed almost without break, day and
night. The constant sessions finally provoked a minor mutiny, apparently led by Bunche, who pointed out that slavery had been abolished in
America. The conferees judged that they needed some recreation,

2. *Ibid.*, 10–11.
3. Record of conference, Myrdal, Keppel, Dollard, Sterner, and John Russell, February 10, 1939; Myrdal to Keppel, March 8, 1939.

whereupon they departed for a nearby bowling alley. As they left, someone shouted, "Come on boys, let's go." Bunche replied: "You mean,
come on 'boys' and Mr. Bunche."[4] What Dorothy Thomas said, if anything, is not known.

The Asbury Park conference seemed to add little to the ideas already
presented in the January plan. The approach remained the same. The
report was to be as comprehensive as possible, but rather than an encyclopedia, it would be an interpretive analysis. It would emphasize the
"dilemmas" in society caused by American values, be practical as opposed to theoretical, and dwell on the present rather than the past. The
main accomplishments of the conference consisted of matching specific
research topics with particular individuals and Myrdal's obtaining a
better feel for the "Negro problem."[5]

After the conference in New Jersey, the project began to move ahead
expeditiously. By June, 1939, the corporation had secured spacious
offices for twenty-two people, six private and five semiprivate, with a
grand view from the forty-sixth floor of the new and dazzling Chrysler
Building. For the next three months Myrdal and his assistants worked on
a basic plan called the "Disposition of the Study on the American
Negro." This 214-page outline issued to Myrdal's collaborators sketched
out tentative chapters and commented at length on each research project.
To this lengthy document, Myrdal attached two position papers called
Appendixes 1B and 1C. These contained the basic conceptual and value
framework for the *Dilemma*. In his first draft Myrdal incorporated much
of these very complex, academic formulations into the text of the first
two chapters of the study.[6]

In these memoranda Myrdal tried to steer his team toward practical
research that stressed dynamics, current trends, and above all, the
centrality of the "American Creed." Appendix 1B challenged the collaborators to expose the anti-Negro and conservative bias of previous
writings on the Negro. Myrdal warned that "functionalist" scholars hid
behind showy empiricism and used vague, value-laden terms to disguise
their worship of laissez-faire, do-nothing sociology. He showed equal
disdain for leftist scholars. "It should be noticed," he announced, "that
a quasi-Marxist teleology is—mostly without reference to Marx—
deeply integrated into American sociology." Both groups had in com-

4. Young, COHP, 46–47; Guy Johnson, COHP, 4–9; Dorothy Thomas to Samuel
Stouffer, November 20, 1939, roll 2.

5. Myrdal to Keppel, April 28, 1939.

6. "Disposition of the Study on the American Negro," September 10, 1939.

mon, he contended, a fatalistic and, therefore, deeply flawed approach to social change.[7]

Having argued the speciousness of American scholarship, in Appendix IC, entitled "Positive Methodology Discussion," Myrdal instructed his collaborators how to conduct their research for the purpose of "induced changes." Inasmuch as he believed that "disinterested" science was a myth, Myrdal taught that "only when value premises are stated explicitly is it possible to determine how valid conclusions are." Theoretical research could gather facts, determine their causal relationship, and determine the feasibility of a goal. But only practical research that looked to the future could lead to true "scientific planning."[8]

The problem, as Myrdal had discovered earlier in his theoretical period, revolved around the question of establishing the real values of people. In Appendix IC he held that to be conceptually useful, value premises had to be feasible, consistent, and specific or "concretized," significant, and relevant. This route, to Myrdal, constituted true realism or "scientific research." With these criteria in mind, Myrdal chose the "American state religion" or the "American Creed" as the controlling valuation. He had intuited this notion on his first trip to the South in 1938.[9]

In spite of his enthusiasm for the American creed as the key to the race problem, he knew his formulation had serious problems. He had seen that the creed did little to soften the oppressive treatment of blacks in the South. He further acknowledged the inconsistent and less than "concretized" nature of many of the elements that made up the American creed. "We do this [using the creed] in full recognition of the fact that in practice, as contrasted to ideology," he wrote, "this is really not the dominant viewpoint." But he saw little choice. "If we should not look to the American state religion for our instrumental norm," he stated, "I do not see where we should be able to localize a consistent body of valuations." Given the problematic nature of the creed and yet giving it a strategically favorable position seemed to bother Myrdal's scholarly conscience. To be fair, the Swede promised to make no final judgments until "alternative sets of value premises were applied to the analysis." In any case, his hope for racial change hinged on the proposition that future opinions of white Americans could be looked upon

7. Appendix IB, 2–5, 8–9.
8. Appendix IC, 1–4.
9. *Ibid.*, 3–4, 12; Myrdal to the author, October 1, 1982.

"as . . . if people knew as much about the Negro . . . as we will know when having completed the Study." This hopeful passage appears almost identical, if the word "Negro" is omitted, to the one in the last chapter of Myrdal's theoretical work, *The Political Element* (1930).[10]

In Appendix 2 of the *Dilemma*, Myrdal cited Louis Wirth as a notable American sociologist who supported his methodology. The Chicagoan must have winced when he read this passage. Although Wirth generally praised Myrdal's September plan, he had serious reservations about the Swede's approach to values. Indeed, he suggested that Myrdal may have stacked the deck by assuming the primacy of the American creed. Wirth queried the European: "Is this possible? Once having used every reasonable and possible device for making the collaborators explicitly aware of the premises, is it . . . possible to get them to accept even tentatively [another] set of premises, especially when these premises are those which you euphemistically call the 'American state religion'?"[11]

Wirth, moreover, pointed out that Myrdal himself had conceded that the ingredients of the state religion were ambiguous and inconsistent. To expound adequately on this ambivalence would require another book, which, Wirth surmised, Myrdal did not want to write. Nor was it prudent, the sociologist cautioned, to predicate "induced changes" on the farfetched supposition that whites would view blacks as if they had read the Carnegie study with an open and compassionate mind.[12]

Wirth was entirely correct about changing value premises once a certain set had been used from the beginning. In the *Dilemma* Myrdal admitted as much in the fine print of Appendix 2 when he wrote: "In the present volume time and space have, further, prevented the subsequent complementation of our results by applying alternative sets of value premises." Only in Section 6, Chapter 23, did he attempt to apply a set of alternative valuations, in this case southern conservative values; and, not surprisingly, he found them untenable.[13]

Neither Wirth, Young, nor other close acquaintances could persuade Myrdal to deviate from his optimistic perception of social reform propelled by the "American Creed." Young argued constantly with him about the efficacy of the creed. Myrdal asserted that if the discrepancy

10. Appendix 1C, 9–14; Myrdal, *Political Element*, 202.
11. *AD*, 1063–64; Wirth to Myrdal, September 29, 1939, roll 2.
12. Wirth to Myrdal, September 29, 1939, roll 2.
13. *AD*, 1063.

between the creed and the deed were exposed, it would die like a germ in powerful sunlight. Young parried with the idea that a strong creed on sexual behavior existed, and yet it failed to stop thousands from going out on the town on Saturday night. Furthermore, Young continued, such people could easily sit through a sermon on fornication and adultery the next morning—without changing their ways or going crazy. And Wirth suggested to the Swede that it would be rash to propose the alteration of profoundly "sacred," if "irrational," views of the people without expecting violence.[14]

In what proved to be his final pep talk to his collaborators before events unexpectedly forced Myrdal to return to Sweden in March, the director reiterated the main points of the long September disposition in a thirteen-page memorandum called "Main Viewpoints and Emphasis." The one new point he made concerned his research collaborators' almost exclusive focus on the South. Myrdal called for more information on blacks in the North and West. The final paragraph of the report, however, was an earnest plea for efforts to transcend the ordinary. "*Let us be bold!*" Myrdal implored. "It must not be said that ours is just 'another' study of the Negro, or that 'we pulled our punches,'" Myrdal coached. "Fundamental insights, bold—and at the same time—valid pronouncements of evaluation, fresh and far-reaching proposals for our social policy—these must be the distinguishing characteristics of our Study."[15]

Myrdal accomplished much in 1939, but 1940 brought disappointments, setbacks, danger, and near despair. Even as Myrdal completed his ambitious study plan in September of 1939, Hitler's legions were crushing Poland. The outbreak of general hostilities stunned the Myrdals. "We were enough rationalists," he recalled, "to feel such a silly thing could not happen."[16] In early 1940, as he worried about where the Nazis would strike next, he grew despondent about the study. On February 13, he anxiously wrote Keppel: "The whole plan is now in danger of breaking down." All of the collaborators, he complained, seemed to have overestimated their capabilities. Even the hardworking Bunche had fallen ill and was behind. Most researchers had already gone beyond their deadlines, and what had been done, he judged, was mediocre or

14. Young, COHP, 55–56; Wirth to Myrdal, critique of the February 8, 1940, memorandum by Myrdal, n.d., roll 2.
15. "Main Viewpoints and Emphasis," February 8, 1940, 3–4, 13. Harold Gosnell also found too little on the North (Gosnell to Donald Young, February 18, 1941, roll 2).
16. Myrdal, COHP, 20.

worse. On top of that, the budget surged out of control. "How to safe-guard the plan?" was a query frequently voiced by the director.[17]

Then in April the Germans suddenly ended the "phony war" and struck to the north, invading Denmark and Norway. Much to Myrdal's chagrin, Sweden allowed German troops to cross its soil to attack its neighbors. He immediately made plans to return home, feeling a strong patriotic duty to see what he could do for his country. He also feared the obvious danger of transporting his family across the ocean. On April 22, 1940, Myrdal informed Keppel that he would leave for Sweden as soon as he could do so without "undue danger" to his wife and children. As a matter of principle, he felt that he and his family should share the same destiny and dangers as the people of Sweden. Having a strong sense of family, he also vowed to keep the Myrdals together during the enveloping world catastrophe. Meanwhile, the corporation used its con-siderable connections to secure transoceanic passage for the Myrdals. Myrdal also asked help from old friends such as Sumner Welles in the State Department and acquaintances in the foreign service of the Swed-ish and British governments. By early May the Myrdals, five in all, had gotten rare permission to travel to Sweden on a Finnish freighter. Even the captain of the ship tried to dissuade Myrdal from taking his family on the perilous journey. Finally resigned to the Myrdals' trip, the Fin-nish captain joked to Gunnar that at least they would not have to worry about drowning in the cold waters. If the ship were attacked, he said, it would explode because it was crammed full of explosives.[18]

As Myrdal waited for passage abroad, he feverishly worked to wrap up the plans for the first phase of the project. Fortunately, Keppel, with Myrdal's approval, appointed Samuel A. Stouffer, a professor of sociol-ogy at the University of Chicago, to replace the Swedish scholar as gen-eral director of research. Although Stouffer's expertise was not in race relations, he possessed impressive administrative skills. He succeeded in completing about 90 percent of the research before Myrdal returned in March, 1941. He also saw to it that each research memorandum re-ceived the scrutiny of three or four experienced critics. In addition, Stouffer got permission from Keppel and Myrdal to set up a publica-tions committee to deem what pieces were worthy of publication as

17. Myrdal to Keppel, February 13, 1940, 2, 4–5, 8; Myrdal to Keppel, April 23, 1940.

18. Myrdal to Keppel, April 22, 24, 1940; Myrdal, COHP, 74–75; memorandum, Dollard to [Keppel?], April 29, 1940.

separate monographs in Myrdal's absence. The Chicago professor told Keppel and Myrdal that many of the collaborators desired to publish their research. They had vowed not to do so until the main report was finished, but now many wondered if Myrdal would return and if the Carnegie project would be completed.[19]

Actually, Myrdal's departure provided an excellent opportunity to turn the time-consuming details of the project over to Stouffer. Keppel and Dollard fretted about Myrdal's inclination to get bogged down in administrative detail and arguments with his collaborators. They hoped that Stouffer's presence would free Myrdal to begin work on the major synthesis when he returned from Sweden. Indeed, Myrdal complained in February, 1940, that traveling and encouraging tardy collaborators left him no time to read the literature on blacks, let alone draft any of the synthesis.[20]

The Myrdals got a warm send-off from Keppel and Dollard, who sweetened the event by paying wages to the departing director through September. Keppel asked the collaborators to continue with their work as if Myrdal had never left. But according to Arnold Rose, many on the project did not expect the Swede to return. Indeed, several felt he was using the war as an excuse to escape a task that had overwhelmed him. Actually, Myrdal felt miserable and described his mood about deserting the study as "heartbreaking." But he vowed to return, and soon.[21]

But he did not return as soon as he thought. Myrdal languished in Sweden for ten months and found life dull in that neutral country, rather like living on a calm island in the midst of an apocalypse. He hoped to get back to America in November at the end of the fall term, but the Battle of Britain prevented that. If he left too early, the ardent anti-Nazi feared he would play into the hands of the "defeatists." Myrdal recollected that he had nearly given up on completing the project toward the end of 1940, when a long letter from his Swedish friend Richard Sterner, who had stayed in America, persuaded him it was his duty to return and finish the project. Finally, in the late winter of 1941, he managed, again

19. Myrdal to Keppel, April 22, 1940; Dollard to Keppel, April 24, 1940; Stouffer to Myrdal, April 28, 1940; record of interview, Dollard and Stouffer, August 26, 1940.

20. Dollard to Keppel, November 29, 1940; Stouffer to Keppel, August 30, 1940; "Report of Progress," Myrdal to Keppel, February 13, 1940.

21. Record of interview, Dollard and Keppel, April 30, 1940; Keppel to staff, May 13, 1940; "Myrdal: American Dilemma," transcript of a 1963 speech by Arnold Rose, Arnold M. Rose Papers, University of Minnesota, Minneapolis; Myrdal to Keppel, April 22, 1940, 5.

with the help of the Carnegie Corporation, to arrange passage across the Soviet Union to Japan and from there to San Francisco. Because of the dangers and restrictions of wartime travel, he sadly left his family behind. He arrived in America on March 6.[22]

Thus Myrdal began the second phase of the Carnegie venture. In this phase Keppel and Stouffer conspired to keep Myrdal away from collaborators and consultants, to isolate him and prevent him from expanding the study further. By now, the cost of the study had ballooned to $245,000, no doubt alarming some of the corporation officials. Stouffer worried that Myrdal would revert to his old routine of travel and talk instead of starting to write his report. Myrdal, however, gathered up all the completed research memoranda, put them in a large trunk, and headed for Jackson, Mississippi. There in the miserable heat and humidity, he read the accumulated materials. Stouffer had warned Myrdal that in his absence the assigned research would become more sharply individualistic and less "thoroughly saturated" with his point of view. Even before his departure, he had been dissatisfied with his collaborators. In late 1939, he referred to T. C. McCormick's study on agriculture as a "dead loss." Both Myrdal and Richard Sterner judged that McCormick's work included no analysis and no "statement of dynamics" concerning the agricultural situation. Myrdal grew angry when he found that most of the research papers had no annotated bibliographies and he ordered that they be provided as a guide to his future reading. Although Myrdal praised his collaborators in the *Dilemma,* he privately condemned them. He declared that only Ralph Bunche and Arthur Raper had produced valuable contributions. In the spring of 1941 he was annoyed that Doxey Wilkerson, Sterling Brown, Charles Johnson, Guy Johnson, and others had not yet finished their studies. The Swede claimed that the Carnegie research memoranda increased the useful literature on the Negro by only a fraction of a percent.[23]

In the summer of 1941 Keppel and Dollard arranged a pleasant summer retreat for Myrdal at Dartmouth College in Hanover, New

22. Myrdal to Keppel, June 26, August 24, November 5, 1940; Dollard to Myrdal, November 28, 1940; Myrdal, COHP, 75, 120; Dollard, COHP, 76.

23. Stouffer to Keppel, August 30, 1941; Stouffer to Myrdal, April 28, 1940; Myrdal to Keppel, August 24, 1940; Myrdal to Dollard, August 28, 1940; summary of telephone call, Myrdal to Dollard, December 20, 1939; memorandum to the Carnegie Board of Trustees (Dollard?), July 9, 1941; Myrdal, COHP, 56, 61, 77; Sterner to Myrdal, comments on T. C. McCormick's "The Negro in Agriculture," December, 1939, roll 2; *AD,* xi–xv.

Hampshire. Situated in a lavish presidential office high in the bell tower of Baker Library, Myrdal plunged into the voluminous material on America and the Afro-American. Despite the idyllic setting, time dragged and Myrdal grew depressed. He missed his wife and children desperately. He displayed fits of temper, yelling at his secretary and cursing his disappointing collaborators. On July 9, he confided to Keppel a secret that every author who has ever experienced writer's block should remember. Myrdal said that he had been a "little disturbed for the last month—my subconscious, on which I always rely in work— was not in good order." He became fully aware of the stupendous burden he had taken on, and he felt shaken. He realized that he had only scratched the surface of the race problem. "This task is not only mansized," he exclaimed. "I sometimes feel it is a little super-human. The fields are too wide, and the facts are too crucially manifold." [24]

The first sketch of the report he concocted, circulated only to Keppel, Dollard, Stouffer, and Sterner, was so inferior that he destroyed the "intimate document" and apologized to his colleagues that he had been a "little crazy." Keppel was so concerned with Myrdal's state of mind that he sent Dollard to Hanover to check on the anguished writer. Dollard found him looking much less fit than before the move and concluded that his primary problem was the absence of his wife. Myrdal had, in fact, been trying to get Alva to America since early summer, but the war kept intruding. By late summer, however, she had bargained for a British military airplane to take her from Sweden to London. In return, she wrote a series of unneutral articles about Sweden and the war and made some appearances on radio talk shows in London. This task done, she got a plane to Lisbon and then at last to America. She joined her husband on October 13, 1941, for a long-awaited second honeymoon. John Russell of the corporation remembered that Myrdal "couldn't write a damned thing" until Alva returned, and then he began to produce. True, but not for a while. Myrdal confided to Stouffer that time seemed irrelevant when Alva reappeared, and he and his wife had been "rather other-worldly for a week or perhaps two weeks." [25]

By September Myrdal and his skeleton staff, consisting of Sterner and Rose, had settled down at Princeton University, where they enjoyed

24. Albert Dickerson to Walter A. Jessup, May 17, 1940; Myrdal to Dollard, July 7, 25, August 24, 1941.
25. Myrdal to Keppel, July 25, 1941, September 4, October 28, November 12, 13, 1941; record of interview, Dollard and Myrdal, August 28, 1941; Francis Keppel, COHP, 26.

excellent accommodations in the university library, arranged of course by the good offices of the Carnegie Corporation. For the next year, Myrdal worked day and night, having virtually no contact with the Princeton academic community or the outside world. He did not accept dinner invitations even when Albert Einstein was a guest. When Arnold Rose interrupted him to tell him about the Japanese attack on Pearl Harbor, they discussed it for about ten minutes. Then Myrdal returned to his all-consuming work. By late November he had written rough drafts of the first two chapters, among the most crucial of the book because they defined the "Negro problem" as a moral dilemma in the white mind. In mid-January he circulated to critics rough drafts of two chapters on race and racial beliefs, also vital and ultimately becoming most of Part II of the *Dilemma*. Myrdal readily acknowledged that Sterner and Rose wrote first drafts of several chapters, but the first compelling chapters and the last prophetic one in the book were pure Myrdal. Regardless of his tight schedule, which called for a September departure, Myrdal was determined to give the whole book his "final touch of balance and force." [26]

As the project neared completion, Myrdal grappled with the sticky problem of deciding who should read the manuscript. Early on, he picked Keppel and Dollard as representatives of intelligent, educated laymen with a sense of style. Despite his spats with Wirth, Myrdal had come to respect his editorial prowess, so he chose him as the white social science critic. Myrdal wanted a black critic, not just as a token but because he respected the minority point of view. Since blacks made up the weakest group in America, a factual or an interpretive mistake, Myrdal reasoned, would hurt them more than whites. After a great deal of deliberation, he selected E. Franklin Frazier because of his fierce independence, his lack of sentimentality, and his keen insights. Evidence suggests that Myrdal knew that the Howard sociologist felt slighted because he had not yet played a major role in the project. In this way, the Swede could make amends to this gifted Afro-American. [27]

There was also need of a white southerner as critic. The Carnegie insiders knew that the study savaged the South. Even Myrdal worried about his negativism toward the region. In Washington Keppel asked Jonathan Daniels and Will Alexander at the Cosmos Club if they knew a

26. Frank Aydelotte to Dollard, September 4, 1941; Myrdal to Keppel, November 12, 13, 1941, January 15, 1942; Myrdal, COHP, 79–80, 84; *AD*, xv–xvi.
27. Myrdal to Keppel, March 17, 1942.

good, level-headed southerner who could correct the mistakes of a foreigner. Myrdal despaired of finding a southerner who would not be romantic and defensive about his native section. He first suggested Wilbur J. Cash, for he admired the North Carolinian's book, *The Mind of the South.* One wonders what Cash might have said about the *Dilemma,* but he had died the previous year. Myrdal finally dropped the idea of a southern critic. He believed that it would be impossible to please more than a handful of people below the Potomac. "Most southerners," Myrdal predicted, "will hit the ceiling." [28]

Each of the critics performed valuable service for Myrdal. And all agreed that the manuscript was verbose, repetitive, awkward in style and organization, and far too long. Since the conference at Asbury Park in 1939, Keppel had hounded Myrdal about the primacy of writing a jargon-free book for the literate layman. Wirth worked for weeks on the manuscript and produced a hundred-page critique that focused on syntax and organization. He and Dollard together convinced Myrdal to transfer most of the tedious theoretical material in the early part, the convoluted discussions about "valuations" and "value premises," to footnotes and appendixes. Dollard also suggested that Myrdal tone down his criticism of American scholars. As it was, Dollard quipped that the book could be called "What's Wrong with the Social Sciences in America." In short, Myrdal's critics helped fashion a far more readable and balanced book. [29]

By August Myrdal could confidently say that his initial false start had been supplanted. Now he had a fresh beginning chapter called "American Ideals and the American Conscience." Revision after revision of the first few chapters finally brought satisfaction to the style-conscious Keppel. One night as Keppel lay in bed reading the huge manuscript, he exclaimed to his wife that at last the words were beginning to "march." Not that the Swede ever became a great stylist in English. Myrdal conceded that his prose had a "slight foreign touch," but he did not feel it constituted an "esthetic fault." Keppel explained in the foreword to the *Dilemma* that Myrdal was not writing in his native tongue. "As a re-

28. Myrdal to Wirth, May 11, 1942; memorandum, Keppel to Walter A. Jessup, July 27, 1942; William F. Ogburn to Dollard, July 20, 1942; Myrdal to Keppel, June 22, 1942; Jonathan Daniels, *White House Witness, 1942–1945* (Garden City, N.Y., 1975), 97.

29. Summary of conversation, Myrdal to Keppel, May 2, 1939; Myrdal to Wirth, July 2, 1942; Dollard to Myrdal, November 28, 1942; Keppel to Walter A. Jessup, July 27, 1942; Stouffer to Keppel, December 9, 1942; record of interview, Dollard and Keppel, July 6, 1942; Dollard to Myrdal, July 10, 1942.

sult," the Carnegie president announced, "there is a freshness and often a piquancy in his choice of words and phrases which is an element of strength."[30] It is not surprising that the diplomatic Keppel ended up in the State Department.

Frazier clearly was the kindest critic. He argued initially with Myrdal's use of the concept "caste" as too static to capture the changing racial situation. A return letter from the Swede, however, satisfied him that the Scandinavian did not perceive the word "caste" in a static sense. Myrdal, to be sure, saw little but dynamics. Frazier even lauded the dilemma thesis, but he thought that Myrdal had overplayed it. The Howard sociologist judged that overall the report was one of great force and timeliness. It would make, he assured Myrdal, the so-called "disinterested" social scientists rethink their position.[31]

Frazier's appraisal must have heartened Myrdal, but he had no illusions about several of the problems with his book. He pointed them out to Keppel on September 2, 1942, in what amounted to his last will and testament on the manuscript. He, like others, grew alarmed about the size of the report. He related the story to Keppel about why the English censors allowed the publication of William Godwin's *Social Justice* in the wake of the French Revolution. William Pitt the Younger reasoned that any book that cost a guinea would never spark a revolution in England. Yet Myrdal argued with Sterner and others that a book purporting to be comprehensive had to be large. In any case, size, Myrdal mused, seemed to impress Americans. Explaining further, he said the book encompassed several books about all aspects of American civilization, and he designed it so that each part or chapter could be read independently. Repetition, therefore, was necessary. He based this approach on the belief that few people would read the entire book.[32]

Another reason for the burgeoning size of the study was Myrdal's increasing emphasis on economics. Initially, he had focused on the moral aspects of the race problem and had fought a running battle against economic determinism and Marxism. In the last phase of the project, however, the Swede discovered that the "problem of breadwinning" was looming larger as an explanatory force, especially after the war began. Uncharacteristically, he rejoiced over the work of his collaborator Paul

30. Keppel to Myrdal, August 17, September 2, 1942, 6–7, March 17, 1942; *AD*, vii.

31. Frazier to Myrdal, June 24, July 1, 1942; Myrdal to Frazier, July 26, 1942; Frazier to Myrdal, July 10, September 9, 1942.

32. "Progress Report," Myrdal to Keppel, September 2, 1942, 1–2; Myrdal, COHP, 119; record of interview, Keppel and Dollard, July 6, 1942.

Norgren, an economist who had gathered material on Negro labor, gleaned in part from the 1940 census. By publication time, Part VIII on economics contained eleven chapters.[33] So great an emphasis on economics created a certain ambiguity in Myrdal's analysis. Some leftist critics would later charge that Myrdal ignored his own prodigious evidence on economics and took a safer moral approach to the race problem.

Myrdal also had qualms about his negative image of the South, although he felt it warranted. He contended that his extensive travel throughout the South and the exhaustive field research of Bunche, Raper, and others allowed him to speak forcefully and authoritatively on the region. In successive revisions, pushed by his worried critics, however, he softened the portrait of Dixie considerably. Wirth, for example, tried to steer him away from "uncomfortable conclusions" about the South. Keppel winced at Myrdal's assertion that southern conservatism rested on a foundation of "illegality." Dollard told Myrdal that some readers might think that the "smart foreigner" was trying to show up "dumb southerners." But when flattery was applied belatedly on top of the harsh descriptions of the South's treatment of blacks, the result often seemed either paradoxical or forced. On one hand, Myrdal lauded southern liberals as cultured and enlightened reformers. On the other hand, he depicted them as defensive, romantic, timid, and even irrelevant. Privately, he declared that making the study both acceptable to the South and truthful was an impossibility. Since Yankees had long left the race question to the "best men" of the South, Myrdal reasoned that perhaps only a bold foreigner could disclose the truth. But Myrdal's dark picture of the South was also difficult to reconcile with his highly optimistic prognosis. His ambiguity on this point was revealed when he asked himself: "What could I do [about the South] except stress dynamics?" He admitted that he had "gone to the limits of optimism" in finding a redeemable South, especially one that would respond to black oppression because of a guilty conscience.[34]

One issue provoked so much commotion that Myrdal backed down before his critics. In the 1962 edition of the *Dilemma*, Myrdal claimed that he had never been censured on any subject, not even after Pearl Harbor. (The State Department asked to see a copy of Myrdal's manu-

33. Myrdal to Stouffer, June 9, 1941, roll 2; Myrdal to Keppel, September 2, 1942, 3.
34. Myrdal to Keppel, September 2, 1942, 8–10; Myrdal, COHP, 69.

script, but Myrdal, on Keppel's advice, refused.) He failed to reveal, however, that he removed the analogy between racism and sexism from the text. Like many nineteenth-century abolitionists, the Carnegie liberals declined, either for tactical reasons or because of sexism, to connect the racial issue with women's rights. Myrdal thus transferred the offending analogy between racism and sexism from the text to Appendix 5, under the uninformative title "A Parallel to the Negro Problem." Despite the effort to make the comparison inconspicuous, feminists discovered it and put it to use in their cause.[35]

Myrdal, of course, failed to remedy or even recognize some of the weaknesses of his book. Despite concern by historical-minded critics, his concentration on present trends blinded him to the force of the past. But little solid history on race and race relations existed in the early 1940s. Keppel called the subject a "wasteland." Decades passed before the appearance of the brilliant revisionist works of C. Vann Woodward, Kenneth M. Stampp, Winthrop D. Jordan, George M. Fredrickson, James M. McPherson, and John W. Blassingame. Since Myrdal's initial plan of January, 1939, called for a minimum of historical research, some of the participants at the Asbury Park conference argued that history should play a larger role. Keppel suggested that they ask his old friend Charles Beard to do a study of racial ideologies, but nothing ever came of it. As Guion Johnson realized, she was assigned to do the only purely historical study because Myrdal did not consider it crucial. Even if Johnson had the talent, she did not have the time to produce a well-researched work. Critics, in fact, blasted her research. She, too, admitted that her study was not scholarly enough for publication.[36]

It has already been noted that from the beginning Myrdal considered the African heritage of the American Negro insignificant. When Bunche and Young took the Swede on a tour of Harlem, Myrdal exhibited little interest in black culture. Having dismissed Melville Herskovits as a man obsessed with "Africanisms," Myrdal wrote to Dollard that the anthro-

35. *AD*, xxv; Dollard to Myrdal, November 28, 1941; Keppel to Myrdal, July 13, 1942; Myrdal, COHP, 14. For use by feminists, see Kate Millett, *Sexual Politics* (New York, 1978), 78, 80n; Caroline Bird, *Born Female: The High Cost of Keeping Women Down* (New York, 1970), 134; Sara Evans, *Personal Politics: The Roots of Women's Liberation in the Civil Rights Movement and the New Left* (New York, 1980), 245n; William Chafe, *Women and Equality: Changing Patterns in American Culture* (New York, 1975), 45.

36. Myrdal to Keppel, April 28, 1939; Guion Johnson, COHP, 1–2, 46–47; Avery Craven to Stouffer, August 21, 1940, roll 2; Richard Shryock to Stouffer, August 28, 1940, roll 2; Myrdal, COHP, 2.

pologist "will perhaps make us some trouble." The economist, however, was confident that Guy Johnson could write a strong rebuttal to anything Herskovits produced.[37]

But Myrdal could hardly ignore black culture in a book the size of the *Dilemma*. Part IX, "Leadership and Concerted Action," contained ten chapters on such topics as Negro leadership, education, the press, and the church. Still, Myrdal continued to perceive black culture and institutions as primarily reactions to the dominant white civilization. He indicated this attitude when he suggested that Rose change the section heading from "Leadership and Concerted Action" to "Power Relations."[38]

Part X, "Negro Community," had only two chapters, which Rose drafted with only general instructions from Myrdal after the Swedish economist had departed for Europe. Although Part X dealt with black culture on its own terms, Myrdal considered the section merely "residual." In a letter of January 8, 1942, Rose mentioned Herskovits' recently published *Myth of the Negro Past*. He suggested to Myrdal that they could acknowledge the differences between black and white culture but play "agnostic" about the causes. Rose expressed a desire not to get bogged down in the "culture stuff" of the Boas School. Myrdal, however, flatly rejected the Herskovits interpretation, and he had black support in doing so. In his earlier works and in a letter to Rose, E. Franklin Frazier insisted that African survivals in American Negro culture were minimal and unimportant. In a review of *The Myth of the Negro Past*, Alain Locke, a black student of the "New Negro" of the 1920s, praised Herskovits' research and his reforming zeal, but he reached a negative conclusion about the book. The Howard professor feared that the logic of the anthropologist's position might "lead to the very opposite of Dr. Herskovits' liberal conclusions, and damn the Negro as more basically peculiar and unassimilable than he actually is or has proved to be." Myrdal and several black spokesmen feared a new round of Garvey-like black nationalism. Accordingly, the Swede dismissed the black history movement led by Carter G. Woodson as essentially propagandistic. Because Myrdal wished to heighten white guilt, he did not want the Negro viewed as an unassimilable alien but as a wronged American.[39]

37. Young, COHP, 43–44; Guy Johnson, COHP, 33–37; Myrdal to Dollard, August 28, 1940; Myrdal to Keppel, September 2, 1942; Myrdal, COHP, 77; Herskovits, *Myth of the Negro Past.*
38. Myrdal to Keppel, September 2, 1942.
39. Rose to Myrdal, January 8, 1942, and Rose to Frazier, December 8, 1942, Box

Ultimately, Myrdal thought he solved the culture problem through hard-nosed realism and common sense. In his last letter to Keppel, he explained that "American culture is the highest in America in the pragmatic and practical sense that it is advantageous for Negroes . . . to acquire so many traits as possible, which have positive value in the surrounding white culture." This line of reasoning, he felt, avoided any invidious comparisons and made no claim for the intrinsic superiority of white culture. With this qualifier, Myrdal and Rose declared that black culture was "a distorted development or a pathological condition of general American culture." The *Dilemma* avoided Herskovits almost as much as it did the analogy between racism and sexism. *The Myth of the Negro Past* was missing from Myrdal's bibliography, and Herskovits' thesis was mentioned in only two places in the text. Myrdal and Rose confined most of the discussion of Herskovits, largely negative, to footnotes.[40]

Before he left New York, Myrdal demanded that Rose be given full authority over the completion of the manuscript. He knew that neither Keppel nor Dollard had a high regard for his young assistant, so Myrdal filled his letters and conversations with lofty praise for Rose. Besides being brilliant and dependable, Myrdal pointed out, Rose was the only one besides Sterner (who was also leaving for Sweden) who knew the entire manuscript and Myrdal's intentions concerning it. The director instructed Keppel that the book should list Sterner and Rose as coauthors. Downplaying the first phase of the study, and still belittling the work of his research collaborators, he declared that the book had really taken shape in the last year at Princeton when the three authors had worked day and night to meet the September deadline. The Swedish economist entrusted Rose with safeguarding the integrity of his manuscript, and he warned Keppel to protect Rose from the prima donnas of the social science world. "This time," Myrdal pleaded with Keppel, "I believe you should rely on my judgment."[41] Keppel conceded, but he and Dollard both disliked the situation.

21, Rose Papers; Alain Locke, "Who and What Is Negro?" *Opportunity*, XX (1942), 83–87; R. Fred Wacker, "Culture, Prejudice and An American Dilemma," *Phylon*, XLII (1981), 255–61; *AD*, 753, 930.

40. Myrdal to Keppel, September 2, 1942, 12–13; *AD*, 928; Wacker, "Culture, Prejudice and An American Dilemma," 255–61.

41. Myrdal to Keppel, July 22, 1942; Myrdal to Dollard, July 17, September 2, 1942; Myrdal to Keppel, September 2, 1942; Keppel to Wirth, December 23, 1942; Wirth to Keppel, December 29, 1942.

The final days before Myrdal's departure proved to be hectic and tiring. He struggled to complete as much of the manuscript as possible while the corporation pulled strings to get him a priority flight back home. (It helped that Keppel was in the State Department now and Myrdal knew all of the people in the Swedish delegation in Washington.) Myrdal, as usual, found time to attend to important details. The public relations campaign that started in 1938 picked up again. He asked Keppel to arrange the appropriate going-away parties and luncheons in New York and at Howard University so he could pay proper tribute to the staff, collaborators, consultants, and important people who might lend credibility to the forthcoming book. In his words, he had to "create good will" and "smooth things out" before leaving. "For symbolic and personal reasons," he reported to Keppel, he would spend his last night in America at the home of Ralph Bunche.[42]

Nor did financial details escape the notice of the Swedish economist. In 1940 Myrdal's rapid departure in midstream of the project left him feeling guilty. On his return in 1941, he thus bargained less sharply. His salary dipped from $19,800 a year to $8,950 on his return in 1941. Myrdal's guilt feelings apparently evaporated rapidly, for he soon complained to Sterner and Dollard that he had made a bad bargain and was getting "poorer" in the last stage of the study. In a plaintive letter to Dollard, he reminded him about his poor state of mind in 1941 and how he had left his three children in Sweden as hostages, not to mention the great risks he had taken in traveling around the world during a war. Displaying his usual empathy and generosity, Keppel sweetened Myrdal's farewell with an additional $6,074 to atone for any underpayment. Existing records show that the corporation paid Myrdal a total of $57,729, or about $445,000 in 1986 currency—generous, to be certain, but about the going rate for a Watergate lawyer or a rock musician. In addition, the unexpected healthy sales of the giant book added about $10,000 to the Swede's bank account by February, 1946, and a small fortune thereafter.[43]

It would be remiss not to mention Rose's heroic efforts to complete and protect Myrdal's intentions for the book. True, Myrdal gave the young sociologist a long paragraph of recognition in the *Dilemma*, but it

---

42. Myrdal to Keppel, August 24, 1942; Myrdal to Dollard, August 24, 1942, roll 2.

43. Record of interview, Kepple and Dollard, March 12, 1941; Myrdal to Sterner, July 19, 1942; Myrdal to Dollard, July 22, 1942; Dollard to Myrdal, August 5, 1942; memorandum on expenses, December 15, 1944.

hardly acknowledged his full contribution. His job would have given a seasoned author pause, let alone a green graduate student. For four months after Myrdal left, Rose filled gaps in the research, checked the myriad quotations and footnotes, drafted a bibliography, checked the index for adequacy, proofread the entire manuscript, and polished and shortened it considerably. He and his assistant and future wife, Caroline Baer, kept a grueling schedule so they could deliver the 2,401-page manuscript to Harper and Brothers on January 13, 1943. Rose spent the final weeks of writing in a splendid room adjacent to the board room at Carnegie headquarters, a room reserved for special guests. It was equipped with Andrew Carnegie's desk and chair, and a huge portrait of the steel tycoon stared down upon the weary scholar as he attempted to tidy up the powerful but raw and messy report.[44]

Rose and his new bride moved to Washington, D.C., in 1943. His draft deferment arranged by the corporation had lapsed, and he went to work for the government under his old mentor, Samuel Stouffer. While working for Stouffer, Rose and his wife read the galley proofs from Harper and Brothers. In the spring of 1943 a feud that had been brewing between Rose and Ordway Tead, the editor at Harper, erupted into open warfare. As editor of a major publishing house, Tead worried about the literary quality and salability of the books he handled. Cautiously at first, then boldly toward the end, Tead began to pare down Myrdal's book. Rose responded with an angry letter to Keppel, reminding the father of the Carnegie project that Myrdal had entrusted him to protect the integrity of the manuscript. Rose charged that Tead was no longer polishing the work but distorting its substance. In some cases, Rose claimed, the changes resulted in language insulting to blacks. Keppel, though now at the State Department, still had authority over the project. With the compliance of Florence Anderson (Dollard's replacement), he backed up the irate Rose. Tead retreated and allowed Myrdal's watchdog to correct the proofs as he saw fit. All of this took considerable time, added to the expense, and delayed publication. Wartime shortages of paper and typesetters also impeded the project. Not until January, 1944, almost ten years after Newton Baker suggested the project, did the long-expected opus appear.[45]

44. AD, xvi; Rose to Keppel, January 13, 1942; "Myrdal: American Dilemma," Box 21, Rose Papers; Myrdal to Dollard, July 22, 1942, 4; Myrdal to Keppel, September, 1942, 6; Dollard to Chairman of the Draft Board, July 31, 1942.

45. Rose to Myrdal, January 14, 1943; Rose to Keppel, May 22, 1943; Florence An-

Some interesting coincidences surrounded the making of the *Dilemma*. In 1937, when Myrdal agreed to do the Carnegie study, Madison Grant, the great disseminator of "scientific racism," died. In 1942, when Myrdal completed his part of the book and returned to Sweden, Franz Boas, the guru of cultural anthropology, died. In 1944, just days after the publication of the *Dilemma*, Robert Park, the mainstay of the Chicago School, died. A new era in the study of black-white relations had begun.

Over that period Myrdal's attitude toward the Carnegie project changed considerably. By his own admission, he did not take the study too seriously at first. (Remember his remark: "These Americans are a funny lot.") But by 1940 his flippancy had been replaced by near defeatism when he realized the breathtaking scope and complexity of the race problem. When Myrdal returned from his unexpected trip to Sweden, he had a different perspective on the study. Because his country chose neutrality during the war, the Nazi-hating Swede felt a compulsion to do something important, some achievement that would facilitate postwar healing. Indeed, he came to view the Carnegie project as his unique war sacrifice. As he began to ponder the completion of the book, he searched his brain for a memorable title. One starry night as he strolled across the Princeton campus, he suddenly had it: *An American Dilemma*. On one of his final days in America, as he traveled by train to Washington, Myrdal held up a copy of the huge manuscript and said to Alva in a low, confident voice: "This is a book which will have great importance." [46]

derson to author, August 21, 1981; Anderson, COHP, 211–12; Myrdal, COHP, 81–82, 84; Keppel to Myrdal, March 3, 1943.

46. Myrdal to Frazier, May 11, 1942; "Myrdal: American Dilemma," Rose Papers; Myrdal, COHP, 87–88.

III

The Context and Content
of a Classic

Some of the most perceptive reviewers of *An American Dilemma* stressed its splendid timing. World War II sowed the seeds of profound change in American race relations. Writing in the foreword to the *Dilemma* shortly before his death in 1943, Frederick Keppel marveled at how the racial atmosphere had changed since the genesis of the Carnegie project. The president explained:

> When the Trustees of the Carnegie Corporation asked for the preparation of this report in 1937, no one (except Adolf Hitler) could have foreseen that it would be made public at a day when the place of the Negro in our American life would be the subject of greatly heightened interest in the United States, because of the social questions which the war has brought in its train both in our military and in our industrial life. It is a day, furthermore, when the eyes of all races the world over are turned upon us to see how people of the most powerful of the United Nations are dealing *at home* with a major problem of race relations.[1]

Keppel represented a small but growing minority of influential whites who understood the far-reaching implications of the global war for American black-white relations. Wendell Willkie, the presidential nominee of the Republican party in 1940, was another. In 1944 Willkie proclaimed: "Every time some race-baiter ill-treats some man in America he lessens the ability of America to lead the world to freedom."[2] After a period of diplomatic isolation and economic catastrophe in the 1930s,

1. *AD*, vii–viii.
2. Quoted in Oliver C. Cox, *Caste, Class and Race* (Garden City, N.Y., 1948), xxxvii.

many Americans once again envisioned their country as "a city upon a hill" for the postwar world to emulate. Many international-minded Americans realized that their nation's rise to world leadership necessitated changes in race relations at home. The cosmopolitan Myrdal displayed an especially keen insight into the foreign relations aspect of the race problem. In the final chapter of the *Dilemma,* he warned America that her world prestige and future secu-. rity would hinge on how the race problem was handled. Deeply suspicious of the Soviet Union, the Swedish scholar foresaw the coming of the Cold War as soon as World War II began. Owing to the international rising tide of colored peoples, the Soviets, Myrdal predicted, would woo the nonwhite nations of the world with a flood of egalitarian propaganda. If the United States hoped to make the "American Century" a reality, Myrdal maintained, she would have to persuade the world that she truly believed in equality, regardless of color.[3]

World War II fostered two trends that focused attention on America's race problem at home and abroad. The war increased black militancy and escalated racial tensions and violence. When Myrdal finished his work on the Carnegie study in the fall of 1942, he declared that the war would act as a "stimulant" to the black protest movement. Afro-Americans likewise saw the immense potential of extracting gains from a war that was being fought against Hitler, a master racist. In 1942 Myrdal commented on this point: "This War is crucial for the future of the Negro, and the Negro problem is crucial in the War. There is bound to be a redefinition of the Negro's status as a result of this War."[4]

Historians have since recognized that World War II, the once "forgotten years" of the black revolution, constituted a turning point in black-white relations. The war provided blacks with a unique opportunity to expose the gap between the American creed and the American reality. On one hand, the democratic ideology and rhetoric employed by Americans during the war aroused a sense of hope among blacks that they could make progress toward equality. On the other hand, the frustration and anger caused by the humiliating discrimination suffered by blacks during the conflict created considerable cynicism about the American Dream. In any case, the war fostered stronger feelings of black consciousness and occasioned new and more vigorous forms of civil protest. In 1941, for example, A. Philip Randolph, a black labor leader,

3. *AD*, 1015–18.
4. *Ibid.*, 756, 852, 997; Myrdal to Samuel Stouffer, June 9, 1942, Negro Study, roll 1.

threatened an all-black march on Washington to protest discrimination against blacks in employment in defense industries. The threat prompted Franklin D. Roosevelt to issue an executive order establishing the Fair Employment Practices Committee (FEPC), the president's first direct concession to the black minority. Randolph's threat foreshadowed the direct action tactics of the civil rights movement of the 1950s and 1960s.[5]

The black protest movement took many forms during the war. In 1942 in Chicago, black activists founded the Congress of Racial Equality. In the same year a group of southern blacks issued a statement in Durham, North Carolina, calling for complete equality and an end to all "compulsory segregation." In 1944 fourteen prominent blacks, ranging from conservative to radical, addressed the question: "What does the Negro want?" Their published answer unanimously demanded full equality—social, economic, and political—within an integrated society. Adam Clayton Powell, Jr., explained that Pearl Harbor marked the beginning of "Civil War II." The newly elected Harlem congressman warned whites that the war had produced a "New Negro" who was determined to fight bigotry and discrimination at all cost.[6]

The increasingly militant black press echoed Powell's call to action, demanding a dual victory, or a "Double V," in the war, against fascism abroad and against racism at home. So shrill did the black press become at times that some whites in the Roosevelt administration felt it bordered on subversion. Some army commanders banned black newspapers from military bases. The moderate and legalistic NAACP intensified its "tone of analysis" and performed the role of a fierce watchdog concerning the treatment of blacks in the armed forces. The NAACP's membership increased fivefold during the war years.[7]

Nothing unified blacks more than serving in the Jim Crow army, often under crudely racist or paternalistic white southern officers.

5. Richard M. Dalfiume, "The 'Forgotten Years' of the Negro Revolution," *Journal of American History,* LV (1968), 90–106; Neil A. Wynn, *The Afro-American and the Second World War* (New York, 1976), 102; Herbert Garfinkel, *When Negroes March* (Glencoe, Ill., 1959), 8; August Meier and Elliott Rudwick, *From Plantation to Ghetto* (New York, 1966), 222.

6. Harvard Sitkoff, *The Struggle for Black Equality, 1954–1980* (New York, 1981), 11; Charles S. Johnson, *To Stem This Tide: A Survey of Racial Tension Areas in the United States* (Boston, 1943), 131–39; Rayford W. Logan (ed.), *What the Negro Wants* (Chapel Hill, 1944); Adam Clayton Powell, Jr., *Marching Blacks* (New York, 1945), 3–6, 129, 131, 135, 182.

7. Dalfiume, " 'Forgotten Years,' " 100–101; John Morton Blum, *V Was for Victory: Politics and American Culture During World War II* (New York, 1976), 215–18.

Blacks became incensed when Secretary of War Henry L. Stimson expressed the opinion that since "leadership is not embedded in the negro race," Afro-Americans should perform the menial and inglorious chores of war. Robert Carter remembered the war as the turning point of his life. A college-educated northern black, Carter later became a brilliant lawyer who assisted Thurgood Marshall in engineering many of the legal breakthroughs of the civil rights movement. Carter said of his war experience: "I thought I was pretty well balanced regarding the race problem, but once I got in the army, the thing was ground in my face everywhere I turned: blacks acting as lackeys to whites, and whites acting oppressively toward blacks." [8] As after World War I, many black veterans returned from World War II in a fighting mood.

Predictably, the black challenge to the *status quo* caused racial tensions to skyrocket. In 1942 Myrdal observed that there was a "disturbing racial angle to the Second World War." He singled out Detroit and large areas of the South as racial powderkegs. The year after Myrdal returned to Sweden, major race riots broke out in Detroit, New York, Los Angeles, Mobile, and Beaumont, Texas. In 1944, six thousand white workers struck the Philadelphia transit system because management elevated eight blacks to the position of streetcar conductors. [9]

White southerners especially resented and feared the presence of armed black soldiers. Southern white policemen became involved in many violent altercations with black servicemen. A Texas mayor informed officials in Washington that any black soldier entering his town risked being shot. In his intriguing 1943 book, *Race and Rumors of Race,* Howard Odum reported on the fantastic wartime gossip in the South that spread tales of "Eleanor [Roosevelt] Clubs," "ice-pick conspiracies," and planned kitchen strikes by blacks against whites. The atmosphere of fear and irrationality, Odum reported, paralleled that of the years just before the Civil War. [10]

Political developments particularly disturbed those who guarded the

8. Blum, *V Was for Victory,* 185; Pittsburgh *Courier,* March 4, 1944; Richard M. Dalfiume, *Desegregation of the U.S. Armed Forces: Fighting on Two Fronts, 1939–1953* (Columbia, Mo., 1969), 89; Carter quoted in Richard Kluger, *Simple Justice: The History of Brown v. Board of Education and Black America's Struggle for Equality* (New York, 1976), 398.

9. *AD,* 517, 528–29; Philadelphia *Inquirer,* August 6, 1944, Sec. B, p. 6.

10. Dalfiume, *Desegregation of the U.S. Armed Forces,* 73; Bell I. Wiley, *The Training of Negro Troops* (Washington, 1946), 49–55; Howard W. Odum, *Race and Rumors of Race* (Chapel Hill, 1943), 74, 97, and *passim.*

status quo. In the election of 1944 both major parties included civil rights planks in their platforms, albeit weak ones. In that same year the Supreme Court invalidated the white primary, and Congress debated a constitutional ban on the poll tax, an antilynching bill, a federal soldiers' voting bill (which would have allowed many southern blacks to vote for the first time), and the highly controversial FEPC. The usually soft-spoken Senator Richard B. Russell of Georgia referred to the FEPC as "the most dangerous force in existence in the United States today," and he regarded it as a serious threat to America's war effort. Olin Johnston, the governor of South Carolina, vowed to render null and void the Court's white primary decision in any way he could; and in early 1944 the legislature of the Palmetto State passed a resolution demanding that "the damned agitators of the North leave the South alone." The editors of the choleric Charleston *News and Courier* exclaimed that the South faced a "new 'Reconstruction.'" Even the liberal journalist Mark Ethridge, one of the chairmen of the FEPC, warned: "There is no power in the world—not even in all the mechanized armies of the earth, Allied and Axis—which could now force the Southern white people to abandonment of the principle of social segregation." [11]

Although rabid proponents of the "southern way of life" in the 1940s had premonitions of a new Reconstruction, polls showed that the overwhelming majority of people in the North were racists and thought little about black rights. The blindness of northern liberals to the evils of racism and segregation, nevertheless, was coming to an end. More than half a century of calculated northern silence on the race issue had begun to erode. Liberal politicians no longer hid the Negro in the political woodpile. Even the racially moderate Roosevelt proclaimed in 1943 that racial strife "destroys national unity at home and renders us suspect abroad." Roosevelt, like Abraham Lincoln, was preparing the way for the civil rights "radicals." With vivid memories of the racial violence that followed World War I, conscientious Americans of various political persuasions sought to prevent a similar racial disaster after World War II. A special feature on blacks by the editors of the *New Republic* in 1943 attested to the renewed interest of liberals in the race issue. The editors recommended "extreme reforms" in the racial area because of

11. Russell quoted in Malcolm Ross, *All Manner of Men* (New York, 1948), 255; Charleston *News and Courier*, March 1, 24, 1944; Ethridge quoted in Buell Gallagher, *Color and Conscience: The Irrepressible Conflict* (New York, 1946), 196. See also Virginius Dabney, "Nearer and Nearer the Precipice," *Atlantic*, CLXXI (January, 1943), 94.

the threat of widespread violence and because the black cause was impeccably just.[12]

Related to the liberal awakening was the damage done in the 1940s to the massive body of pseudo-scientific racist writings, which had accumulated since the nineteenth century. Since World War I social science research, led by members of the Chicago School of Sociology and the Columbia School of Anthropology, had discredited the "scientific racism" that had worked so powerfully to the detriment of the black minority. Indeed, the situation near the end of World War II was ripe for an esteemed and politically astute scholar to popularize and synthesize the new science of race and tie it to the logic of the dynamic American creed. *An American Dilemma* appeared in propitious times.[13]

As many a reviewer of *An American Dilemma* would complain, it is almost impossible to summarize Myrdal's massive study in a way that adequately conveys its vast scope and its cumulative impact. The book consisted of eleven parts, forty-five chapters, ten appendixes, an exhaustive bibliography, voluminous footnotes, and a thorough index. The main text contained 1,024 pages, accompanied by 258 pages of footnotes in fine print. Counting the preliminaries, the Myrdal study added up to 1,535 pages. Myrdal and his associates had worried endlessly about the length of the *Dilemma*. The Swedish scholar rationalized that the book was so large because it was "actually a number of books" about an entire civilization. "The book will not be read through by practically any reader," Myrdal speculated. "As a matter of fact," he added, "few scientific books are."[14]

Hence in the following pages I attempt a short but nonsuperficial summary of a large, historic book, which I hope will enable the reader to follow more easily the subsequent discussions of the weighty work. I will concentrate on the central theme, the important subthemes, and the

12. Brewton Berry, *Race Relations* (Boston, 1951), 85; Peter J. Kellogg, "Northern Liberals and Black America: A History of White Attitudes, 1936–1952" (Ph.D. dissertation, Northwestern University, 1971), 327–42; Wynn, *The Afro-American in the Second World War*, 113; "The Negro: His Future in America," *New Republic*, CIX (1943), 535–50.

13. Stocking, *Race, Culture, and Evolution*, 300–307; Idus A. Newby, *Jim Crow's Defense: Anti-Negro Thought in America, 1900–1930* (Baton Rouge, 1965), 51, 199; Norma Jensen's "The Springfield Plan," *Crisis*, LI (March, 1944), 79, catches the liberal mood in education.

14. Myrdal to Frederick Keppel, September 2, 1942, Negro Study, roll 1.

mechanism of social change that Myrdal claimed would unravel the racial knot in America. By quoting some of Myrdal's frequent value premises (which he always italicized), some of the ideological flavor comes through. Finally, I will try to demonstrate why a generation of civil rights activists found so much appeal and utility in the Myrdal report.

Myrdal set forth his powerful central theme in the introduction:

> *The American Negro problem is a problem in the heart of the American. It is there that the interracial tension has its focus. It is there that the decisive struggle goes on. . . . Though our study includes economic, social, and political race relations, at bottom our problem is the moral dilemma of the American—the conflict between his moral valuations on various levels of consciousness and generality. The "American Dilemma" . . . is the ever-raging conflict between, on the one hand, the valuations preserved on the general plane which we shall call the "American Creed," where the American thinks, talks, and acts under the influence of high national and Christian precepts, and, on the other hand, the valuations on specific planes of individual and group living, where personal and local interests; economic, social, and sexual jealousies; considerations of community prestige and conformity; group prejudice against particular persons or types of people; and all sorts of miscellaneous wants, impulses, and habits dominate his outlook.*[15]

This statement was the Swedish economist's rather inelegant way of saying that the race problem was a conflict between verbally honored American ideals and the pervasive practice of white racism.

The gap between the democratic ideals and racial practices, Myrdal felt, bothered Americans greatly. He postulated that Americans, more than any other people, were practical idealists who wanted to be rational and just. Myrdal believed that "*people will twist and mutilate their beliefs of how social reality actually is*" to cover up their moral inconsistencies concerning blacks. The moral conflict among whites agitated not just the minds of the intellectual elite but those of ordinary people. It was an issue that people discussed "in church and school, in the family circle, in the workshops, on the street corner, as well as in the press, over the radio, in trade union meetings, in the state legislatures, the Congress and the Supreme Court." Thus Myrdal claimed at the outset that his interpretation was solidly based on "the ordinary man's own

---

15. *AD*, xlvii. In most cases, only long quotations from Myrdal will be footnoted. It is assumed that the reader can tell from the text what chapter or part of the book is being discussed.

ideas, doctrines, theories, and mental constructs." Assuming, then, that common Americans took the American creed as their highest value, Myrdal predicted that the gap between American ideals and the way whites treated Negroes would soon end. He ended his preface with the prophetic remark: "*Not since Reconstruction has there been more reason to anticipate fundamental changes in American race relations, changes which will involve a development toward the American ideals.*" [16]

Although Myrdal acknowledged that the moral issue of race affected both sides of the color line, he gave notice in the introduction that the bulk of his book dealt with the problem as it reverberated in the white mind. Myrdal declared that the "Negro problem" was really a white problem. He argued that little of importance could be understood about the race problem by studying the physical and cultural differences between blacks and whites. He stressed that the Negro's entire life was in some way or another a reaction to white pressure. In its allocations of power and prestige, the United States was truly a white man's country. Oddly, Myrdal's contention that the race problem belonged to whites was not reflected in the title of his book. In 1942 he indicated to E. Franklin Frazier that the title of his study would be *An American Dilemma: The Negro in American Democracy.* [17] But either Myrdal did not insist that his insight about the race problem be incorporated into the book's title or someone edited out the idea. In the end the subtitle reflected the orthodoxy of the time when it became *The Negro Problem and Modern Democracy.*

Nevertheless, Myrdal recognized the wide scope of the race problem. "*The Negro problem,*" he stated, "*is an integral part of, or a special phase of, the whole complex of problems in the larger American civilization.*" [18] The race problem was a national problem, Myrdal wrote. The plight of the black minority was determined by the total American setting. But the relationship between white society and blacks was not wholly one-sided. The presence of thirteen million blacks had conditioned American society more than commonly recognized. In subtle and complex ways, Myrdal pointed out, the Afro-Americans had shaped American institutions and had colored the country's world view. Myrdal ended his long introduction with an apology to Americans.

16. *Ibid.*, xlix–1, xix.
17. *Ibid.*, lii; Myrdal to Frazier, May 11, 1942, Negro Study, roll 1.
18. *AD*, liii.

He explained that they would find many of his statements distasteful because he had concentrated on the "least clean" corner of the American household. The foreigner announced that it was highly uncomfortable for him to focus on America's most glaring shortcoming. He assured Americans that they pursued a more "righteous" civic life than any other large group of people in the Western world. He premonished readers of his book to put everything in full context, saying that "*anyone who utilizes the viewpoints and findings of this inquiry of the American Negro problem for wider conclusions concerning the United States and its civilization . . . is misusing them.*"[19]

In Part I, Chapters 1 through 3, Myrdal elaborated further on the approach and theory of his study. In the first chapter, entitled "American Ideals and the American Conscience," he continued to extol the American ethos. He asserted that America had the "*most explicitly expressed* system of general ideals in reference to human interrelations." The American creed held the polyglot nation together. Even blacks were under the spell of the great "national suggestion." Myrdal quoted Ralph Bunche to make this point: "Every man in the street, white, black, red, or yellow, knows that this is 'the land of the free' and the 'land of opportunity,' the 'cradle of liberty,' the 'home of democracy,' that the American flag symbolizes the 'equality of all men' and guarantees to us all 'the protection of life, liberty and property,' freedom of speech, freedom of religion and racial tolerance." In the end, Myrdal's analysis depended heavily on the hypothesis that most blacks embraced the creed.[20]

Myrdal traced the development of the American creed to the Enlightenment, English law, the American Revolution (and its shining symbol, the Declaration of Independence), and Christianity. From these sources America constructed a government based on democracy and law. Yet Myrdal pointed out that many Americans had negative images of law. There existed in American history a "higher law" mentality that tended to undermine the rule of law. He also acknowledged that Americans had inculcated their strict Puritanical code into many laws (notably those dealing with liquor, gambling, and sex) that proved unenforceable. All of this bred disrespect for the law and a general distrust of government. These factors combined, Myrdal proclaimed, meant that Americans had a "defeatist attitude" about accomplishing social change through legislation.

19. *Ibid.*, lix.
20. *Ibid.*, 3–4.

Unfortunately, Myrdal argued, no group harbored a more negative view of induced social change than social scientists. Although his Carnegie associates Keppel and Dollard had pleaded with Myrdal to tone down his criticism of American social scientists and had persuaded him to confine most of his philippic against them to the appendixes, the Swedish economist still stridently attacked the American social science establishment. Under the heading "Intellectual Defeatism," he railed against the " 'do-nothing' tendency . . . in present-day social science in America." He directed the reader to Appendix 2, in which he elaborated on the theories about facts and valuations that he had been espousing since the 1920s. He criticized American sociologists for trying to study race relations apart from values and beliefs. Biases could not be eradicated from studies of society; rather, Myrdal argued, biases were better clearly stated than slyly hidden. Myrdal maintained that most American sociologists injected a strong but concealed bias in their work, namely the Social Darwinian thesis of William Graham Sumner, which held that "stateways cannot change folkways." In Appendix 2 Myrdal singled out sociologists such as the eminent Robert Park for chastisement. Unlike the laissez-faire American social scientists, he admitted frankly that his work was aimed at social engineering. By stressing the dynamic nature of American values and by concentrating on the moral dilemma generated by the race question, Myrdal added a new dimension to sociological literature.[21]

Despite all the drawbacks to social change, Myrdal insisted that the American creed constituted a dynamic force that would foster racial change. Because of the American creed, the status of blacks represented nothing more than "a century-long lag of public morals." The principle of racial equality, Myrdal confidently declared, had been settled long ago.[22]

In Chapter 2, "Encountering the Negro Problem," Myrdal discussed the American penchant for "explaining the problem away." White southerners claimed that blacks were content and that no race problem existed. Despite their soothing "etiquette of discussion," white southerners, Myrdal concluded, were obsessed with the race question. The Scandinavian discovered that one of the most unfortunate myths in circulation was that white southerners understood the Negro. Myrdal found that segregation in the South had increased to the point that a

21. *Ibid.*, 19–23.
22. *Ibid.*, 23–25.

white hardly ever saw a black except as a servant or in a formalized caste situation. White ignorance about blacks was even greater than might be expected because it was opportunistic, the "convenience of ignorance," in Myrdal's words.

In the North whites tended to explain the race problem away by comparing the treatment of blacks there with that in the South. Many northerners, however, seemed unaware of their discrimination against blacks. Myrdal believed that if northern whites became better informed about the plight of Afro-Americans, they would be willing to support racial reform. He even felt that many southerners would support greater justice for blacks if they knew the true situation. Myrdal therefore held that publicity about black oppression rated top priority. Concluding Chapter 2, he summed up the situation: "*The simple fact is that an educational offensive against racial intolerance, going deeper than 'glittering generalities' in the nation's political creed, has never seriously been attempted in America.*" [23]

In the third chapter Myrdal offered his main sociological theories and presented what he considered to be the strategic mechanisms of racial change. First, he held that the problems of blacks differed significantly from those of other minorities. It was true that other groups such as the Chinese and Japanese suffered because of their race. But the black minority constituted the largest group regarded as unassimilable by the white majority. And because blacks were the only Americans who had been enslaved and subjected to a rigid caste system, black-white relations, Myrdal maintained, could not be approached as a typical minority problem.

White Americans had a gut-wrenching, irrational feeling about dark-skinned people and a powerful belief in racial purity. Their refusal to accept amalgamation, Myrdal discovered, was the "common denominator" of the color problem. Even the most liberal whites frowned on race mixing. He reported that the sexual aspect of the race problem lay deep in the subconscious of whites, filling them with personal insecurities about blacks. Fear of interracial sex explained why whites condemned social equality and why they extended segregation to education, religion, recreation, and housing.

When Myrdal questioned southern whites about the priority of different forms of racial discrimination, he found that people ranked their tolerance for blacks according to the perceived amount of physical inti-

23. *Ibid.*, 49.

macy involved. Myrdal's impression was that the white man's "rank order of discriminations," or the gradation of prejudicial intensity against blacks, was from highest to lowest as follows: (1) the bar against interracial marriage and sex; (2) discrimination and segregation in public facilities such as schools, churches, transportation, theaters, and restaurants; (3) political disfranchisement; (4) discrimination in court, by the police, and by various public officials; and (5) discrimination in securing jobs, credit, property, public relief, and other means of making a living.

Myrdal emphasized that the Negro's rank order of discriminations was almost exactly parallel but inverse to the white man's. The whites resisted most strongly the desires in which the minority expressed the least interest. Blacks, according to Myrdal, wanted not interracial marriage or sex but jobs, equal opportunity, and physical security. Myrdal's impressionistic hypothesis thus contained a strong inference that grounds for racial progress existed in many areas.

Another conceptual tool for explaining racial oppression was the "principle of cumulation" or the "vicious circle." Myrdal gave credit to Knut Wicksell, his Swedish economic mentor, for the idea of "cumulative causation."[24] This hypothesis held that discrimination kept the Afro-American at the bottom of society, and his lowly position in turn gave support to the white belief in black inferiority. Myrdal, however, pointed out that a rise in black standards would bring about a corresponding decrease in white prejudice. As he did the idea of the rank order of discriminations, then, Myrdal viewed the "vicious circle" with hope. General trends, he maintained, militated against the vicious circle of black oppression. The dynamics of the American creed were gaining new strength during the war. Large institutional structures such as schools, churches, and the government were becoming more sympathetic to the Afro-American. In addition, Myrdal theorized that when Americans worked through institutions, they were more likely to adhere to the principles of Christianity and democracy than when they acted as individuals. As with the rank order of discriminations, Myrdal discovered a silver lining. The vicious circle in the Swede's eye became a wheel of progress.

In the third chapter and all through the book, Myrdal took hostile swipes at the Marxist theory of race prejudice and racial stratification.

24. Copy of unpublished manuscript by Myrdal for a seminar on the World Bank, 1983, p. 3, copy in possession of the author.

He proclaimed that the Marxist philosophy of the solidarity of the working classes was patently wrong. Race prejudice, he asserted, was strongest among the white proletariat. Myrdal claimed that whites among the higher classes were better friends for blacks than the toiling laborers.

In Part II, Chapters 4 through 6, Myrdal dealt with racial theories and beliefs. He traced historically the rationalizations that whites had used to condone slavery and the caste system. According to the Swede, white Americans' devout belief in the American creed led them to develop elaborate, if transparently expedient, theories of black inferiority, which excluded Afro-Americans from the democratic social contract. Thus racism resulted from white egalitarianism, the former a sordid perversion derived from the latter.

Myrdal cheerfully reported, however, that racial beliefs were becoming less dogmatic. Social scientists had shown that doctrines of racial inferiority were false, and educated blacks now proved willing and adept at countering white racist arguments. Unfortunately, most whites clung tenaciously to unscientific beliefs about blacks. They harbored a deep and mystical conviction about Afro-Americans. "*The 'reality' of his inferiority* [the Negro's]," Myrdal observed, "*is the white man's own indubitable sensing of it, and that feeling applies to every single Negro.*" But Americans were becoming better educated and more logical about race. "*People want to be rational, to be honest and well informed,*" he opined.[25]

Chapters 5 and 6, "Race and Ancestry" and "Racial Characteristics," represented primarily the work of the sociologist Arnold Rose, although Myrdal gave the "final touch" to all chapters. In these chapters Myrdal stressed the extensive miscegenation that had occurred in America, claiming that 70 percent of blacks had traces of white ancestry. On the delicate subject of racial characteristics, he conceded that some racial differences undoubtedly resulted from heredity. But he argued that the environment accounted for the major differences between the two races, particularly in their performance on intelligence tests. Myrdal doubted whether it could ever be conclusively determined that the Afro-American had innate psychic differences from whites. But he judged that even if psychic variances did exist, they would not be significant enough to justify discrimination against blacks in housing, education, jobs, and suffrage. Myrdal, therefore, declared that his study would be based on the premise that differences in white and black behavior were

25. *AD.*, 100, 109.

relatively insignificant and could be explained by social and cultural factors.

Having laid down the theoretical groundwork for his study in the introduction and the first seven chapters, Myrdal concentrated more heavily on facts in the remaining chapters. In Chapters 7 and 8, again largely done by Rose, the study detailed the current state of black population and migration. Not surprisingly considering his Swedish experience, Myrdal concluded that birth control was a necessary tool to fight black poverty, disease, crime, illegitimacy, and social disintegration of various sorts. He felt that the trend of northward movement was beneficial in that it lessened the chance of racial explosion in the South. It also increased black voting and bargaining power in the North, which, he forecast, would become an important element in effecting racial change in the nation.

Since Myrdal and his Swedish associate Sterner were economists, it is not surprising that the *Dilemma* devoted the next eleven chapters to the science that in this case deserved the modifier "dismal." Having explored the statistics of black economics thoroughly and having seen the urban slums and the southern agricultural system firsthand, Myrdal concluded: "The economic situation of the Negroes in America is pathological. Except for a small minority enjoying upper middle class status, the masses of American Negroes, in the rural South and in the segregated slum quarters in Southern and Northern cities are destitute." [26]

The Swedes admitted also that many economic trends worked against blacks. Mechanization in farming and industry and calamities to southern agriculture in the form of soil erosion, the one-crop system, the boll weevil, and the scourge of farm tenancy all injured blacks drastically. Even progress seemed to work against the Afro-Americans. As jobs became cleaner, safer, and better paying, whites usually replaced black workers. Myrdal pointed out that even New Deal programs often adversely affected blacks. The Agricultural Adjustment Act reduced cotton acreage and pushed black tenants off the land. The National Recovery Act threw many blacks out of work. The Works Progress Administration paid blacks lower wages than whites. And the Federal Housing Administration perpetuated segregated neighborhoods by upholding restrictive covenants.

Myrdal reported that the few Negroes who prospered, relative to other blacks, did so because they held a monopoly in some trade, busi-

26. *Ibid.*, 205.

ness, or profession that resulted from segregation. Negro ministers, doctors, lawyers, undertakers, and beauticians experienced no white competition. Other black businessmen, however, suffered greatly from white competition and a lack of venture capital, as well as from the meager purchasing power of the black masses. Myrdal estimated that black entrepreneurs held no more than 5 or 10 percent of all black trade.

The Swedish scholar warned that if discrimination persisted unabated, the black population might become "a burden on the national economy." But the Swede remained undaunted by the dire statistics, for the salutary American creed was ever at work. The most important economic fact for blacks was that "*the American Creed is changing to include a decent living standard and a measure of economic security among the liberties and rights which are given this highest moral sanction.*" [27] Additionally, labor unions were gaining strength, and the Fair Employment Practices Committee set up in 1941 held promise for the future economic well-being of the black minority. Finally, Myrdal noted, the war boom could not but help blacks.

In Parts V and VI of the book, Myrdal scrutinized politics and justice, devoting four chapters to each. In these sections he concentrated heavily on the South. In his typically blunt fashion, the Scandinavian visitor declared that southern conservatism constituted the most reactionary philosophy in the Western world. Dixie conservatives worshiped not only the *status quo* but the *status quo ante* with its heritage of slavery. "Southern conservatism," Myrdal asserted, "is a unique phenomenon in Western civilization in being married to an established pattern of *illegality.*" [28]

He viewed southern liberals more generously. They were beautiful, educated, and law-abiding advocates of slow racial change within the segregated system. But Myrdal reminded his readers that southern liberals lacked any real power and, because of local pressure, had to be exceedingly opportunistic on the race question.

Myrdal stressed the importance of black suffrage in the South. The Negro vote remained unquestioned in the North and gave the minority an increasing level of power as northward migration continued. Although the white South was determined to prevent blacks from voting there, Myrdal felt these efforts were doomed to failure. Because the Supreme Court was beginning to reinterpret the Fifteenth Amendment in

27. *Ibid.*, 212.
28. *Ibid.*, 440.

its true spirit, Myrdal predicted that black disfranchisement rested on shaky legal grounds. Indeed, he predicted that the Court would invalidate the white primary, which it did just months after the publication of the *Dilemma*.

Even more important, the Swede believed that the southern white had a split personality. The better part of the southerner belonged to the values of the American creed. *"The main thing happening in the South,"* Myrdal announced, *"is that it is gradually becoming Americanized."* [29]

In Part VI the European devoted four hard-hitting chapters to justice, southern style. He described the systematic exclusion of blacks from the legal system—the judiciary, juries, and all the law enforcement agencies. The man whom blacks most often confronted in the justice system, the white policeman, Myrdal depicted as an ill-educated, crudely racist man with a license to use a gun against minority members. He also described the notorious chain gang system, which made hardened criminals from those who committed minor offenses against the oppressive system. Lynchings and race riots, which had once been used to keep blacks "in their place," had declined. But with the rising militance of blacks, Myrdal warned that the racial situation in the South was dangerous and posed the possibility of severe race riots in the postwar period.

After his searing portrait of southern justice, Myrdal added three provocative chapters on social inequality, the part of the manuscript that critic E. Franklin Frazier found the most appealing. The Swede cavalierly pushed aside all the usual rationalizations of whites for the social inequality of blacks—that they were uncouth, uneducated, and deficient in health and morals. Instead, Myrdal claimed that the structure of segregation stemmed from sexual fears and the general desire to keep blacks down in all aspects of life. Indeed, he branded Jim Crow an unmitigated disaster. One of the most harmful effects of segregation was that whites seldom had any contact with educated Afro-Americans. The demeaning nature of segregation caused many educated and sensitive blacks to withdraw into isolation from whites. Some of the worst results of segregation could be seen in housing and education. Even the separate and inferior black schools were administered by white officials. Worst of all, legal segregation strengthened racism.

Despite the bleak picture Myrdal presented in the areas of justice and social equality, he found reason for optimism. He pointed to the de-

29. *Ibid.*, 466, 514–18.

creasing provincialism of the South, hastened by better education, urbanization, and industrialization. The Supreme Court and the executive, he pointed out, were casting a more critical eye on the denial of civil rights for blacks. He frankly proclaimed that the Jim Crow system was "flagrantly illegal" and could be so proven in court. Better-educated and determined blacks added another factor that augured well for change. Most significantly, though, Myrdal felt that southern whites, especially the young, were "*in principle . . . no longer prepared to defend racial inequality of justice.*" [30]

In Part VIII, entitled "Social Stratification," Myrdal delineated the concept of caste. He contended that blacks suffered more than other minority groups because of a rigid caste system based on color. He employed the idea of caste that had been used earlier by American social scientists in their study of ethnic relations, especially by W. Lloyd Warner, John Dollard, and others.[31] The relatively high rate of social mobility in America had enabled other minorities, in time, to move up the social and economic ladder. The caste system, however, confined most blacks to the lower rungs of the ladder. Although blacks had a class system of their own, the highest class of blacks always fell below the lowest whites in the American pecking order. For blacks, Myrdal insisted, the caste system nullified the Marxist theory of the class struggle. In a country where class was not considered paramount, the caste system supplied another powerful device to keep the Afro-American "in his place."

In Part IX, "Leadership and Concerted Action," Myrdal gave a lengthy discussion of black leadership, protest organizations, and certain black institutions (Chapters 33–42). The economist pointed out that strong impediments stood in the way of strong black leadership, especially in the South. "It is a political axiom," Myrdal counseled, "that Negroes can never, in any period, hope to attain more *in the short-term power bargain* than the most benevolent white groups are prepared to give them." Although the white-dominated system lent itself to creating accommodationist black leaders, Myrdal noted that the black protest movement had benefited from the war. He singled out W. E. B. Du Bois and A. Philip Randolph as representative of leaders who rejected the

---

30. *Ibid.*, 342, 556, 629.
31. W. Lloyd Warner, "American Caste and Class," *American Journal of Sociology*, XLII (1937), 234–37; John Dollard, *Caste and Class in a Southern Town* (New Haven, 1937); Allison Davis, Burleigh B. Gardner, and Mary Gardner, *Deep South: A Social Anthropological Study of Caste and Class* (Chicago, 1941).

style and substance of leadership exemplified earlier by Booker T. Washington. Still, the Swede admonished blacks about racial chauvinism as preached by Marcus Garvey in the 1920s. Such movements, he thought, were bound to fail without white support. He asserted that there would be no "Negro party" and added that *"only when Negroes have collaborated with whites have organizations been built up which have had any strength and which have been able to do something practical."* [32] Myrdal felt that Afro-Americans were in such a weak position that they needed all the white allies they could get.

Of all the black protest organizations, Myrdal judged that the National Association for the Advancement of Colored People was the most important and effective. He pointed out the NAACP's many limitations, such as its lack of mass appeal. But Myrdal toned down his first assessment of the NAACP. In the *Dilemma* he argued that its approach surpassed those of the more radical protest groups in effectiveness. The goal of integration within a nonrevolutionary framework was the strength of the long-established agency. "For a Negro protest or betterment organization to adopt a revolutionary program," he warned, "would be suicidal for the organization and damaging to the Negro cause." [33]

After discussing protest and betterment groups, Myrdal examined three salient black institutions: the church, the school, and the press (Chapters 40–42). The European expressed little admiration for the black church, which he judged to be passive on social issues. Escapist and otherworldly, weakened by schisms, poverty, provincialism, and inadequately educated ministers, the church to him represented in microcosm the disorganization and conservatism of the larger black community. But Myrdal suggested that as the community changed, the church would change. The secular-minded social scientist, however, hardly caught a glimpse of the vital role the church would play in the future civil rights movement.

Myrdal emphasized the long-range significance of schools in the black movement. Black schools were horribly inadequate, but at least the right of Afro-Americans to be educated went virtually unchallenged, even in the South. According to Myrdal, the rising level of black education made minority assimilation into white culture easier and rendered blacks less satisfied with the *status quo*. Curiously, in light of

32. *AD*, 740, 853.
33. *Ibid.*, 834.

the *Dilemma*'s controversial part in the school desegregation cases of 1954 (see Chapter VI), Myrdal reported that blacks were divided on the issue of integrated schools. He pointed out that some blacks such as Du Bois preferred separate schools if mixed schools entailed the humiliation of blacks and the firing of minority teachers. But he contended that most blacks desired integrated schools as the best way of improving education. In any case, Myrdal noted, many blacks demanded integrated education as a matter of principle, whatever the cost.

Myrdal found the debate about classical versus industrial education for blacks to be a phony one, for neither had truly been tried in the South. In Myrdal's estimation, *"What is needed is an education which makes the Negro child adaptable to and movable in the American culture at large."* [34] To improve black education, Myrdal called for the initiation of adult classes for blacks who had migrated to the urban centers. He also strongly advised federal aid to education. Inasmuch as black schools were unequally financed, segregated schools cost the southern states less money. But Myrdal predicted that in time increasing black demands for equal facilities would break down the segregated school system because of the financial burden. And the Swede expressed the opinion that separate schools, like everything else that was segregated by law, could be proved unconstitutional.

In conducting protest, no institution was more important than the black press, which he believed had been characterized correctly by another writer as "the greatest single power in the Negro race." [35] Few whites knew about the vehement criticism of white America to be found in black newspapers. The press therefore served as an outlet for the pent-up hostility in the black community. The press also acted as an essential unifying factor in the black community, suggesting how blacks should think and act. Myrdal complimented the black press on shrewdly exploiting the war-spawned opportunities to expose the racial hypocrisy of America. And he added that black editors seldom missed a chance to illustrate the relevancy of the colonial question in Asia and Africa to America's domestic race problem.

In Part X, mainly drafted by Arnold Rose but with coaching from Myrdal, the *Dilemma* finally took a look at black culture on its own terms. The book acknowledged that black culture differed from white culture but maintained that it had evolved under American conditions.

34. *Ibid.*, 906.
35. *Ibid.*, 924.

That is, Myrdal felt that the African heritage was of little consequence in the scheme of social causation. Thus the *Dilemma* described black culture in a way that would later incense black nationalists: *"It is a distorted development, or a pathological condition, of the general American culture."* [36] Myrdal, of course, blamed black pathology on white racism. Unfortunately, most whites attributed black cultural traits to innate racial differences. Assuming that it was the goal of blacks to join mainstream society, Myrdal felt it was practical for them to take on white cultural characteristics.

In his stirring final chapter, entitled "America Again at the Crossroads," Myrdal summarized his findings and proffered predictions based on current trends. He stressed that World War II, having been defined as a struggle for liberty and equality, would prove crucial for black progress by forcing a redefinition of the minority's place in America. Certain social trends also pointed toward change. The most significant trend involved white attitudes toward blacks. *"The gradual destruction of the popular theory behind race prejudice,"* Myrdal claimed, *"is the most important of all social trends in the field of interracial relations."* [37]

Another factor destined to hasten racial change was rising black militancy. *"America,"* Myrdal warned, *"can never more regard its Negroes as a patient, submissive minority."* [38] Equally important as black determination was a growing white willingness to extend basic rights to blacks. As the racial views in the more progressive North diverged more and more from those of the South, Dixie stood in greater isolation. Therefore, the national compromise of 1877, which woefully harmed blacks and compromised the American creed, had been jeopardized by the nationalization of the race issue. The enlarged role of the federal government in the lives of the people and the liberal thrust of Supreme Court decisions were closely related to this nationalization process.

In addition, international relations affected the American race problem. Foreseeing America's role as the major world leader after the war, Myrdal emphasized that the treatment of blacks by the United States would influence her power, prestige, and security around the globe. He reminded Americans that the nonwhite peoples of Africa and Asia constituted a large and increasing majority of the world's population. Anticipating the Cold War, Myrdal advised that the Soviet Union would

36. *Ibid.,* 928.
37. *Ibid.,* 1003.
38. *Ibid.,* 1004.

exploit any attempt by America to perpetuate white supremacy. In sum, a multitude of strong forces within and without the country would force the United States to clean up its sorriest scandal.

In the final analysis, Myrdal returned to his central theme. The most compelling force in regard to black progress was white America's sincere desire to live up to her democratic and Christian creed. "In this sense," Myrdal proclaimed, "the Negro problem is not only America's greatest failure but also America's incomparably great opportunity for the future." The Swede set the challenge for his adopted country: "*America is free to choose whether the Negro shall remain her liability or become her opportunity.*" His awesome treatise closed with a ringing affirmation of man's basic goodness. He declared that human nature was, after all, changeable; and human misery, to a large degree, could be prevented by social engineering. Not since the Enlightenment, he wrote, was there more reason for social scientists to believe in "the improvability of man and society." [39]

Myrdal saw man as a free agent who had the desire and ability to accomplish rational, orderly, and progressive change. The European Social Democrat scoffed at both those who called for revolution and those who counseled that certain eternal laws militated against equality and justice here on earth. Like Franklin D. Roosevelt's New Deal, Myrdal steered a middle course between extreme remedies offered by the left and the right. His optimism rested on a general faith in humankind, a belief in the efficacy of social engineering, and his perception of the unique vitality of the American creed. The American ideal, Myrdal insisted, could be shaped into the American reality.

39. *Ibid.*, 1021–22, 1024.

IV

First Reactions to the Myrdal Report

The casual reader of literature on race relations might get the impression that *An American Dilemma* became not only an instant but an unquestioned classic. In 1959 Myrdal told a reporter that in 1944 "there wasn't a single adverse comment on it from the South." He conceded, however, that Marxists and some Catholics took exception to his book. As for conservative southerners, the Swedish economist flippantly remarked that they simply did not read books.[1]

Although Myrdal's off-the-cuff recollections have much substance, they do not fully capture the total response to his study in all its details and nuances. The *Dilemma* was so vast and carried such an air of authority that for two decades people of various persuasions could usually find something in it, as in the Bible, to corroborate their viewpoints about black-white relations. With few exceptions, therefore, most reviewers found much to praise; few completely rejected the treatise. Most southern segregationists did not unleash their furious attack on Myrdal until the Supreme Court made his work central to the 1954 *Brown* decision. Marxist reviewers, particularly after the party line hardened in 1946, excoriated the book. Most white behavioral scientists expressed negative views about either Myrdal's methodology or his conclusions. But despite their negativism, they applauded the great amount of data gathered. Southern liberals, whether academicians or not, had views similar to those of northern white social scientists. The most favorable opinions came from liberal northern journalists, liberal clergy-

1. For example, see Elizabeth W. Miller, *The Negro in America: A Bibliography* (Cambridge, Mass., 1966), v, 3; William Brink and Louis Harris, *The Negro Revolution in America* (New York, 1964), 28–29; Myrdal quoted in the Nashville *Tennessean*, July 14, 1959; Myrdal to the author, July 1, 1968.

men, and especially Afro-Americans. But even among blacks, dissent occurred. Ralph Ellison and Carter Woodson, for example, unleashed hostile attacks on the Swede that anticipated the black nationalists of the 1960s.

Because of the large number of reviews and their often substantial length, only a few of the most representative and significant ones can be analyzed. For púrposes of clarity and style, I have set up categories of reviewers that are admittedly somewhat arbitrary and overlapping. These categories include reviewers in the popular press, white social scientists, white southerners, blacks, and liberal clergymen. Some black reviewers were, of course, social scientists, as were some white southerners. Here I have followed Myrdal's belief that all white southerners, even liberals, harbored a romantic attachment to their region and tended to put loyalty to the South first. Likewise, most blacks tended to be "race men" before anything else. Under the heading of the "popular press," I have included newspapers and periodicals like *Time, Life,* and *Saturday Review.* This categorization, too, poses problems of consistency, for Robert Lynd, a noted sociologist, wrote a review for the general reader in *Saturday Review,* and some white southerners wrote for the northern popular press.

The earliest notices of the *Dilemma* appeared in the northeastern press in late January and early February of 1944. They resembled advertisements more than critical reviews. A thorough reading and review of the book, after all, would take days, even weeks. Frederick Keppel and Charles Dollard of the Carnegie Corporation planned as early as 1942 to use their influence to generate as much editorial comment as possible on the *Dilemma* before the full-length, formal reviews appeared. In the review copies, Harper and Brothers included a substantial summary and a glowing characterization of the *Dilemma* that probably tempted those reviewers who could not find time to read the whole book. The same was true of the in-house summary done by E. Franklin Frazier that the Carnegie Corporation enclosed with the more than three hundred complimentary copies sent to important people.[2]

The *New Republic* promoted the *Dilemma* in its issue of January 24, 1944. The announcement highlighted the entire Carnegie Series but featured Myrdal's main report at the top of the page under the questions: "Race Riots or Race Unity: which shall it be America?" and "How can

2. Dollard to Keppel, September 15, 1942, Negro Study, roll 1, hereinafter all correspondence in this chapter, unless otherwise stated, is from this source; advertisement, 1944; Memorandum, January 4, 1944; Summary of discussion, Walter Jessup and Charles Dollard, November 9, 1943.

we proceed to practice democracy we profess?" The liberal journal of politics and art described the book as "exhaustive and objective" and recommended it to all serious democrats and believers in justice.[3]

On January 26 in the New York *Herald Tribune*, Lewis Gannett discussed Myrdal's study in a regular column called "Books and Things." Gannett praised the book generously and compared it to the works of Alexis de Tocqueville and James Bryce. The feature also included a flattering picture of the blue-eyed, blonde-haired Swedish economist.[4] The main review of the book for the *Tribune* did not appear until August.

A day after Gannett's advance promotion, Harry Hansen, a veteran journalist from Iowa and a writer for the New York *World-Telegram*, the Chicago *Tribune*, the *Saturday Review*, and other publications, spoke glowingly of Myrdal in his New York column, "The First Reader." The large-type subtitle captured Hansen's view: "Dr. Myrdal's Treatment of The Negro Problem And Modern Democracy Is A 'Must' Book." He fully agreed with Myrdal that racial change and progress were in the air, although he feared it might be accompanied by a cathartic explosion. Hansen also introduced Myrdal's book in a literary column in the Chicago *Tribune* and wrote a lengthy review for the *Survey Graphic* in March. Hansen's efforts essentially constituted a celebration of a publication event rather than a critical analysis of the *Dilemma*. The same was largely true of other early journalistic accounts in northern papers, which bore such titles as "Democracy's Chance: The Negro Problem" and "Comprehensive Study Of The Negro Problem: Scholar Predicts War Will Change Outlook of Negroes By Making Them Feel Entitled To Share In American Ideals of Equality." On February 2 in the Chicago *Sun*, Alan Browne wrote a short piece that introduced the Myrdal study to the Midwest. He reported that Myrdal had skillfully used his sharp ax of objectivity to cut away the confusion and underbrush. "The result," Browne concluded, "is compelling."[5]

The popular magazines *Time* and *Life* continued the early promotion of the *Dilemma*. On February 7 *Time* proclaimed: "Perhaps not since Bryce and de Tocqueville has the U.S. had such an analytical probing by a sharp-eyed foreigner." Significantly, *Time* considered Myrdal's book under the rubric "U.S. At War." It therefore stressed the relationship

3. *New Republic*, January 24, 1944, p. 121.
4. New York *Herald Tribune*, January 26, 1944.
5. New York *World-Telegram*, January 27, 1944; Chicago *Tribune*, March 19, 1944; *Survey Graphic*, XXXIII (March, 1944), 183–84. For other examples see Providence (R.I.) *Journal*, February 27, 1944; New Haven (Conn.) *Register*, March 5, 1944; Chicago *Sun*, February 2, 1944.

between the American role abroad and blacks at home, namely, Henry Luce's "American Century" idea attached to the race problem. At the end of the article, the popular weekly lifted a hopeful passage from the *Dilemma* that became one of its most-quoted parts: "The Negro is not only America's greatest failure but also America's incomparably great opportunity for the future." In short, *Time* implored the United States to set an example for the rest of the postwar world in the practice of color-blind brotherhood.[6]

In April *Time*'s sister magazine, *Life,* relied heavily on Myrdal in an editorial on black-white relations. The editors declared that the "Negro problem" had become America's number one social problem because of the increasing bitterness and militance of blacks. Despite the severity of the problem, the editors rejoiced that Myrdal had provided expert guidance. In reference to Myrdal's thesis, the editors proclaimed that America was a "psychotic case among nations." They found great confidence in Myrdal's rank order of discriminations and the declining respectability of racism among educated people. The editorial concluded with Myrdal's statement: "The Negroes are a minority, and they are poor and suppressed, but they have the advantage that they can fight wholeheartedly. The whites have all the power but they are split in their moral personality. Their better selves are with the insurgents. The Negroes do not need any other allies."[7]

Obviously, the advance editorial opinion on Myrdal proved as favorable as Keppel and Dollard could have hoped. In 1942 Dollard advised Keppel to use all his influence to see that the right people reviewed the *Dilemma* in the New York newspapers and periodicals. By the right people, Dollard meant persons with felicitous pens who could hold a general audience, not a group of jargon-addicted social scientists.[8] Although Keppel died in 1943 and Dollard went into the army before the *Dilemma* appeared, their advance work shaped the review policies of the opinion-forming New York press.

Frances Gaither wrote one of the first full-length reviews of Myrdal's book for the New York *Times* on April 2, 1944. She apparently was considered qualified to assess such an important book because she was reared in Mississippi, wrote novels about the Old South, and was married to one of the editors of the newspaper. In a relatively short review, she first expressed a complaint about the *Dilemma* that would become

6. *Time,* February 7, 1944, p. 16.
7. *Life,* April 24, 1944, p. 32.
8. Dollard to Keppel, September 15, 1942.

common: the impossibility of summarizing a book of such scope and import. She admitted that it was not easy for those with the heartiest of appetites to digest it all. "But it is a book," she asserted, "which nobody who tries to face the Negro problem with any honesty can afford to miss." [9]

Gaither stressed Myrdal's concept of the caste system and explained the many reasons for its stubborn persistence. The novelist cheerfully announced, though, that the Swede had found a way out of the racial morass through the workings of the American creed, the rank order of discriminations, and the principle of cumulation. This literary woman, however, did not use such social-science terminology as "rank order of discriminations" and "principle of cumulation." Instead, she explained in ordinary language that Myrdal had convincingly shown that black desires ran in reverse order to those of whites and that every rise in the black's status caused a more favorable attitude in the white mind toward Afro-Americans and so on toward equality.

In the last paragraph of her essay, the Mississippian voiced only three mild complaints about the book. First, she lamented that Myrdal had not relied more on firsthand experience instead of the work of sociologists; second, she felt that Myrdal should have used history more; and third, she believed that the Swede wasted too much space arguing about theories of racial differences. She proclaimed that few who read the book would believe that racial differences justified the sordid treatment of blacks.

More than four months after the *Times* review, Gerald Johnson, a highly respected journalist, discussed Myrdal's book in the *Herald Tribune*. Like his friend W. J. Cash, this North Carolinian had attended Wake Forest College, turned liberal, and grown harshly critical of his region. A great stylist with a Menckenesque vocabulary, he fled the South in his thirties and went to work for the Baltimore *Sun* and later became a regular writer for the *New Republic*. This southern liberal found many superlatives for the Myrdal study. He marveled at its scope and bulk and assured the reader that it was written in plain English. "It isn't flattering to the North or the South, to the white man or the Negro," he stated, "but it is incisive, persuasive, and brilliant." [10]

9. *Current Biography, 1950* (New York, 1951), 161–162; Frances Gaither, Review of *AD*, in *New York Times Book Review*, April 2, 1944.

10. Fred Hobson, "Gerald W. Johnson: The Southerner as Realist," *Virginia Quarterly Review*, LVIII (Winter, 1982), 1–25; Fred Hobson (ed.), *South Watching: Selected Essays of Gerald W. Johnson* (Chapel Hill, 1983), 139, 146, 157; Hobson, Review of *AD*, in *New York Herald Tribune Weekly Book Review*, August 13, 1944.

But Johnson was not convinced, for underlying his admiration for the book lurked a profound reservation. He pointed out that the study was valid only if one accepted Myrdal's basic assumption about the dilemma. To be sure, a conflict existed in the minds of white southerners, Johnson wrote, but it had nothing to do with principles of liberty and justice. Southern whites understood that the lowly position of blacks dragged the whole region down, Johnson continued, but they also knew that fairer treatment of the minority meant more power and respect for blacks. To strengthen the South without elevating the Negro, the journalist concluded, constituted the real dilemma in the southern white mind.

Robert Lynd, a professor of sociology at Columbia University and author with his wife of the famous *Middletown*, wrote a review somewhat similar to Johnson's for the *Saturday Review.* Lynd generally heaped superlatives upon the Swede. He suggested that the Carnegie Corporation had made one of the wisest foundation investments ever in Myrdal and that the *Dilemma* would stand as one of the most important books ever written on American civilization. The liberal sociologist devoted ample space to Myrdal's description of the American creed and the alleged dilemma it spawned. He quoted the long, italicized definition of the dilemma from Myrdal's introduction, a passage of more than two hundred words and destined to be one of the most-quoted passages from a work on race relations in the next quarter century. An acquaintance of Myrdal since the European had visited America in the late 1920s, Lynd had earlier attacked Sumnerian sociologists in his book *Knowledge for What?* He thus focused on Myrdal's assault on the Sumnerians in Appendix 2, and he lauded the Swede's fierce attack on Marxist thought.[11]

A more flattering review of the *Dilemma* than Lynd's would be hard to imagine. Yet he, like Gerald Johnson, expressed some doubt about Myrdal's optimistic predictions of racial change. The liberal sociologist, who with his wife had put Muncie, Indiana, under a microscope in the 1920s, wondered whether Myrdal's ideas about induced change had not been predicated on the homogeneity of Sweden rather than on the large, heterogeneous, loosely administered state of America. Lynd could only hope that Myrdal's prophecies proved true, but he had trouble with the idea that the conceptual imperative of the American creed could so easily rout the social and political forces opposing blacks.

11. Robert S. Lynd, Review of *AD,* in *Saturday Review,* April 22, 1944, p. 5; Lynd, *Knowledge for What?* (Princeton, 1939).

What seems surprising is that so many dailies outside New York and so many popular magazines and journals ignored Myrdal's book altogether in 1944. Such newspapers as the Washington *Post*, the San Francisco *Examiner*, the Minneapolis *Tribune*, the Philadelphia *Inquirer*, the Detroit *News*, and the St. Louis *Post-Dispatch* did not consider the book in their review sections. In the hinterlands of small-town America, several newspapers belatedly discovered Myrdal's book and often summarized or reprinted verbatim earlier reviews from larger papers. A number of well-known periodicals, including the *Atlantic Monthly*, the *Yale Review*, the *New Yorker*, *Harper's*, and *Current History*, initially ignored Myrdal's tome.[12]

It is clear why one of Myrdal's major aims was to destroy the "convenience of ignorance" in the North. Even New Dealers preferred to talk about economics rather than race. The historian Peter Kellogg maintains that the North had an "atrocity orientation" toward racial events. By focusing on lynchings, beatings, and the like, northern whites could evade a deeper analysis of the race issue. Race eventually came in the back door of politics when northern liberals needed black votes to defeat southern obstructionists in Washington and when the State Department figured out the relationship between race and international hegemony. Forged in the late nineteenth century, northern accommodation with the South on the race question still held sway in the mid-1940s and still included the myth of letting the "best whites" of the South take care of blacks. Thus President Roosevelt chose primarily white southerners such as Jonathan Daniels for his racial advisers, and the two major New York newspapers selected white southerners to review the *Dilemma*.[13]

And how did the "best whites" or southern liberals and moderates react to Myrdal's book? By World War II southern liberals had long accommodated themselves to a Jim Crow system that the great majority of southern whites considered indispensable to the "southern way of life." As Morton Sosna shows in his important book *In Search of the Silent South*, the most conspicuous failure of southern liberals was their reluctance to abandon segregation. As often before, race proved to be the soft underbelly of southern liberalism. Dixie progressives tended to re-

12. For example, the Willmar (Minn.) *Tribune* condensed Harry Hansen's review of the Myrdal study from *Survey Graphic*.

13. Kellogg, "Northern Liberals and Black America," 244–54, 270–72, 427–38; on Franklin Roosevelt, see Harvard Sitkoff, "Racial Militancy and Interracial Violence in the Second World War," *Journal of American History*, LVIII (1971), 676–78.

sent outside interference in racial matters and incessantly harped on the "lessons of Reconstruction," preaching that federal interference would set back race relations disastrously. They believed, Sosna argues, that a "Silent South," led by southern liberals, would eventually rise up and extricate the South from its backwardness and Negrophobia. Although southern liberals believed in progress, they also recognized the lurid depths of racism and concluded that racial change could creep in, if at all, only at a very petty pace. As educated and thinking individuals— Myrdal described them as "beautiful and dignified"—they felt a certain intellectual discomfort about the most egregious injustices of the Jim Crow system, but they felt little urgency about the Negro's plight. As Mississippian David Cohn philosophized, one simply had to endure the racial situation with "a sore heart, a troubled conscience, and a deep compassion." [14]

The race issue aside, these southerners qualified as liberals in that they generally supported New Deal reforms such as the equality of economic opportunity, improved education, collective bargaining, civil service reform, and police, court, and prison reform. Because of their criticism of the South, Myrdal pointed out, they constantly had to proclaim their orthodoxy on such issues as regional loyalty, religion, meddling Yankees, and, above all, segregation. Although southern liberals usually played down the race issue, the increasing racial tension brought by World War II not only alarmed the crude white supremacists but, as Roy Wilkins observed, caused some who were formerly considered friends of the Negro to lapse "into hysterics." Virginius Dabney, the patrician editor of the Richmond *Times-Dispatch,* seemed to be such a friend. In the 1930s he had fought for the repeal of the poll tax and in the early 1940s even advocated the ending of segregation on street cars. These acts prompted Myrdal to refer to Dabney fourteen times in the *Dilemma.* But in a 1943 article in the *Atlantic,* the Richmond liberal gave substance to Wilkins' charge about white southern apprehensions. "A small group of Negro agitators and another small group of white rabble-rousers," Dabney warned, "are pushing this country closer and closer to an inter-racial explosion which may make the race riots of the First World War seem mild by comparison." [15]

14. Sosna, *In Search of the Silent South,* 198–211; *AD,* 456; David Cohn, *Where I Was Born and Raised* (Boston, 1948), 285, 297–98. See also Anthony Lake Newberry, "Without Urgency or Ardor: The South's Middle-of-the-Road Liberals and Civil Rights" (Ph.D. dissertation, Ohio University, 1982).

15. *AD,* 466–73; Roy Wilkins, "The Negro Wants Full Equality," in Logan (ed.), *What the Negro Wants,* 113; Dabney, "Nearer and Nearer the Precipice," 94.

On March 6, 1944, Dabney discussed several new books on race relations, singling out Myrdal's for special but brief mention. The editor
referred to Myrdal as "a brilliant young Swedish economist," who had
produced a "thorough and exhaustive work" that was being compared to
the masterpieces of Tocqueville and Bryce. But Dabney did not explain
the book's thesis or describe its crucial meaning for the South. He said
only that he found the work "excessively critical" of the South.[16]
    The journalistic comments on Myrdal were confined to the Upper
South. All were brief, and none attempted extended or deep analysis of
the *Dilemma*. Douglas Southall Freeman of the Richmond *News-Leader*
found the book "comprehensive and scientific" but deplored its length.
He begged for someone to "epitomize" it for the general public. A two-
sentence notice in the Memphis *Commercial-Appeal* stated the thesis of
the *Dilemma* but gave no hint of its scope or the origin of its author. In
the Nashville *Morning Tennessean* Wayland J. Hayes, a sociologist from
Vanderbilt University, called the book a "landmark" in racial investigation, made the typical comments about its comprehensiveness, and
avoided any judgment on the book or its potential impact on the region.
In the Louisville *Courier-Journal,* Harvey Curtis Webster wrote the
most favorable review in the South. Unlike the others, he praised the
thesis as well as the factual data. "No one with a mind that can open,"
he maintained, "will argue either vehemently or long against the findings of these scholars." Jonathan Daniels, the well-known Raleigh editor and wartime adviser to Roosevelt, penned an advertisement for the
Book-of-the-Month Club News. It, too, was short and general. The editor alluded to the book's definitive nature, its provocative thesis, and its
objectivity. Daniels, however, rejected Myrdal's conclusions as too simplistic, saying the Swede seemed "almost too divinely high above the
emotions and furies of race and race feeling."[17]
    Deep South dailies, including moderate and New-Dealish news-
papers such as the Atlanta *Journal,* the Atlanta *Constitution,* the Montgomery *Advertiser,* and the Raleigh *News and Observer,* generally
ignored the *Dilemma*. In the 1940s some of the southern journalists
lionized in the North as liberals still strongly defended Jim Crow. Ralph
McGill was a case in point. In the late 1930s McGill traveled throughout
Europe on a Rosenwald Fellowship and met Myrdal in Sweden. While

    16. Richmond *Times-Dispatch,* March 6, 1944; John T. Kneebone, *Southern Liberal
Journalists and the Issue of Race, 1920–1944* (Chapel Hill, 1985).
    17. Richmond *News-Leader,* February 18, 1944; Memphis *Commercial-Appeal,*
April 23, 1944; Nashville *Morning Tennessean,* April 2, 1944; Louisville *Courier-
Journal,* April 16, 1944; *Book-of-the-Month Club News,* April, 1944.

the Swede labored on the Carnegie project, however, McGill, then editor of the Atlanta *Constitution*, railed against the FEPC, an antilynching bill pending in Congress, and any hint of race mixing. The *Dilemma* brought no commentary from McGill in 1944. Not until the 1960s did the southern liberal extol Myrdal's "world classic." [18]

If the conservative press shunned Myrdal, it did not ignore the race question. The editors of the Charleston *News and Courier*, for example, filled their pages with caustic denunciations of northern agitators, the FEPC, foes of the white primary, and Eleanor Roosevelt. In 1944 the newspaper pleaded for a slate of electors to run against Franklin Roosevelt. The editors warned that the South faced a "new 'Reconstruction.'" [19]

Liberals in academia also exhibited a growing alarm about rising black militancy and racial tensions during the war. The appearance of Myrdal's book presented campus liberals with their own special dilemma. They did not want to look backward by rejecting Myrdal's book out of hand, particularly since it was financed by a wealthy foundation. Yet most southern academics felt that the *Dilemma* presented a flawed and even dangerous analysis of the race problem. Three men from the University of North Carolina, the academic fiefdom of Howard Odum, exemplified this view. In addition to Odum, Professor Rupert B. Vance and William Terry Couch, the director of the university press, wrote lengthy and critical analyses of Myrdal's book. These reviews provide an insight into the mind of the southern liberal in the 1940s.

Odum was the most renowned sociologist in the South, and his views carried weight with southern liberals. Before writing his review of the *Dilemma* for the New York *Herald Tribune*, Gerald Johnson wrote to Odum on January 19, 1944, asking if Myrdal was "really sound." Odum responded promptly with a long letter that strongly emphasized what he deemed to be the negative aspects of the Swede's work and stressing Myrdal's ignorance of southern history and culture. Worse yet, he bristled that the European had nowhere mentioned his book *Southern Regions of the United States*. In the concluding paragraph of the letter, Odum judged that the *Dilemma* fell "in line with the common northern

---

18. Mary Ellen Parker Murray, "The South and Ralph McGill, 1945–1950" (M.A. thesis, Emory University, 1964), 26–28, 36; Wilma Dykeman and James Stokely, *Seeds of Southern Change: The Life of Will Alexander* (Chicago, 1962), 270; Atlanta *Constitution*, July 3, 12, 1962, March 31, 1968.

19. Charleston *News and Courier*, March 24, July 10, 1944. Periodicals such as the *South Atlantic Quarterly*, the *Journal of Southern History*, and the *Southwestern Social Science Review* also failed to review Myrdal's book.

level, namely everything rests upon untested moral principles." The regionalist rejected such talk as foreign naiveté. Johnson thanked Odum for confirming his suspicions. Not surprisingly, Johnson's review conspicuously reflected Odum's attitudes.[20]

Odum's review of the *Dilemma* in *Social Forces* was more positive than his private assessment, but it still came out essentially negative, if more tactful. Odum told a friend, however, that his review was "not as critical as perhaps the book deserves." The southerner praised Myrdal for his boldness, his originality, and the scope of his data. He branded it a "must" book for reformers and teachers in race relations courses. But he argued that Myrdal's work was faulty in its methodology and its major assumptions. He took offense at the Swede's sharp criticism of the Commission on Interracial Cooperation, which Odum headed. He repeated the charges in his letter to Johnson that Myrdal's excessive optimism emanated from his ignorance of southern culture. The Swede did not understand, he sniped, how the past had conditioned whites to think about blacks. "A standard saying among southern common folks," Odum explained, "is that we ought to treat the Negro as we did the Indian, kill him if he doesn't behave and, if not, isolate him and give him what we want to." The sociologist conjectured that the southern heritage ruled out rationality on the race question. In conclusion, Odum compared the *Dilemma* with two other broad-scoped books, Karl Mannheim's *Diagnosis of Our Time* and Lewis Mumford's *The Condition of Man*. "In neither Mannheim nor Mumford, or [*sic*] again in Myrdal," he complained, "does . . . specific reality offer anywhere the answer. Always there is assumed some way out; never is it pointed out." In Odum's opinion, then, Myrdal's book was better suited for graduate seminars than for real problem solving.[21]

World War II heightened the substantial differences between Myrdal and Odum. Myrdal perceived the war as a vehicle for racial change, whereas Odum saw in the global conflict the specter of racial turmoil. In his 1943 book, *Race and Rumors of Race,* he discovered a hysteria in the South that disturbed him deeply. Agreeing with Odum that *Race and Rumors of Race* contained "dynamite," Jonathan Daniels and Gerald Johnson advised against its publication. Odum spurned this advice, but he warned that the racial situation would not allow any interference

20. Johnson to Odum, January 19, 1944; Odum to Johnson, January 28, 1944; Johnson to Odum, February 7, 1944, Box 26, Odum Papers.

21. Odum to A. R. Mann, August 8, 1944, *ibid;* Odum, "Problem and Methodology in *An American Dilemma,*" *Social Forces,* XXIII (1944), 94–98.

from the outside by irresponsible militants. And his correspondence shows that the sage of Chapel Hill considered virtually every black leader north of the Potomac a dangerous radical. What few traces of modern liberalism remained in Odum's thinking seemed badly eroded by the war.[22]

Rupert Vance, a sociologist and a close associate of Odum's at Chapel Hill, firmly established his niche in social science circles with his research and publications on cotton tenancy and southern demography. Younger and less enthralled with the idea of regionalism than Odum, Vance tended to have a better grasp of the political side of the race question. This attribute, however, made him not less but more pessimistic than his older associate. According to Daniel Singal, Vance's 1929 book, *Human Factors in Cotton Culture,* carried a tone of "unrelieved pessimism." Unlike Odum, the younger sociologist was thoroughly hard-boiled and did not attempt to cover up the pathology of the South with myths and platitudes. Vance's review of the *Dilemma* differed little from Odum's. He praised Myrdal's courage for not hiding behind the "amoralistic nonconcernedness" that was common to American sociologists, but he concluded that the Swede had merely relegated the race problem to the hopeless arena of politics. Since Vance foresaw a turn toward political reaction after the war, he concluded that the European had only supplied groundless optimism "without a program of meliorism." [23]

Less guarded in his judgment of Myrdal than the liberals discussed above, William Terry Couch condemned in no uncertain terms what he considered to be the grave dangers of Myrdalism. Couch had a reputation among southern liberals for being outspoken and courageous. As the director of the University of North Carolina Press since the late 1920s, he had published a wide variety of liberal works, including sev-

22. Odum to Edwin Embree, February 7, 1944; Odum to E. Franklin Frazier, April 18, 1944; Dabney to Odum, February 7, 1944, Box 26, Odum Papers; Frank Graham to Odum, December 13, 1943, Box 25, *ibid.* For the impact of World War II on Odum, see Sosna, *In Search of the Silent South,* 112–13.

23. Singal, *War Within,* 311, 314. Some of Vance's major works are *Human Factors in Cotton Culture: A Study of the Social Geography of the American South* (Chapel Hill, 1929); *Human Geography of the South: A Study in Regional Resources and Human Adequacy* (Chapel Hill, 1932); and *All These People: The Nation's Human Resources in the South* (Chapel Hill, 1945). Vance virtually conceded the bankruptcy of regionalism in "The Sociological Implications of Regionalism," *Journal of Southern History,* XXVI (1960), 47–48. His review of *AD* was "Tragic Dilemma: The Negro and the American Dream," *Virginia Quarterly Review,* XX (1944), 440–44.

eral by black authors. Unlike Odum, Couch did not shun political action. In 1938 he helped found the Southern Conference for Human Welfare, a milestone in the history of southern liberalism. In 1943 the
southern publisher invited Rayford W. Logan, a black historian, to edit a
book of essays on the question "what the Negro wants." Long considered a friend of blacks in the South, Couch encouraged Logan to solicit
all shades of black opinion, including the views of such people as Paul
Robeson and Langston Hughes. But when the southerner found out that
all fourteen black writers—a group composed of conservatives, moderates, and liberals—demanded the end of segregation, Couch appeared
dismayed. Until reading the essays he firmly believed that blacks wanted
segregation and the preservation of "racial purity." In various letters to
friends, he commented on the "psychopathic condition the manuscript
reveals among Negro intellectuals." Couch tried to get Logan to alter
the essays drastically, lecturing the historian that blacks wanted things
"far removed from what they ought to want." When Logan refused to
modify the substance of the manuscript, Couch suggested that he seek
another publisher. At that point, the black editor threatened to consult
his attorney.[24]

Forced to publish Logan's book, Couch did something extraordinary:
he added a fifteen-page "Publisher's Introduction," which excoriated the
tone and the contents of *What the Negro Wants*. Interestingly, the white
southerner's main target proved not to be Logan's book so much as Myrdal's. Couch singled out the *Dilemma* because he judged it to be tan-
talizingly representative of majority social science thinking on race. At
the same time, it was "more comprehensive, more thorough, more readable than the mass of material sharing its attitude." Although the North
Carolinian raised some searching questions about values, science, and
social engineering in the *Dilemma*, he disingenuously confused race
and civilization. According to Couch, Myrdal's key message was that
America "must either give up the 'American Creed' or go fascistic, or
accept equality which would permit amalgamation." The publisher
laced his introduction with the specter of "biological integration." He

24. Thomas A. Krueger, *And Promises to Keep: The Southern Conference for Human
Welfare, 1938–1948* (Nashville, 1967), 22, 35; Couch to Logan, March 31, November 9,
1943; Couch to Virginius Dabney, January 14, December 20, 1944; Couch to N. C. New-
bold, November 8, 1944; Logan to Couch, November 29, December 14, 1943, in "Logan,
What the Negro Wants" file, University of North Carolina Press Records, Sub-Group 4,
Southern Historical Collection, University of North Carolina, Chapel Hill, hereinafter
cited as Logan File, Press Records.

lauded the "universal values" of the white Western world and found
them almost totally lacking in black culture. Couch admonished blacks
that, given their cultural inferiority, integration would be disastrous for
them. He worried that Myrdal had emboldened blacks to take foolish
actions. "I believe *An American Dilemma* was written under gross mis-
apprehensions of what such ideas as equality, freedom, democracy, human rights, have meant, and of what they can be made to mean," Couch
declared. "I believe the small measure of these gained by western man,"
he continued, "is in serious danger of destruction by widespread misunderstanding of the kind represented in *An American Dilemma.*" Privately, Couch wrote Dabney that, armed with Myrdal's book, blacks
"might go to the limit as the *Dilemma* does." [25] With friends like Couch,
blacks needed no enemies.

Characteristically, once aroused, Couch expressed his feelings with
abandon. Kindred southern liberals who publicly had been more cir-
cumspect toward Myrdal privately congratulated Couch for giving the
foreigner his comeuppance. Virginius Dabney, Mark Ethridge, Gerald
Johnson, and the Chapel Hill historian Fletcher M. Green praised the
southern publisher for candidly saying what they truly felt. Johnson described Couch's attack on Myrdal as the "nimblest foot-work I have seen
in a coon's age." [26]

In the main, southern liberals in the 1940s could scarcely envision
the change in the status of blacks that Myrdal foresaw. Many of them
had a visceral reaction to the idea of social equality, and they fumed at
the thought of outside coercion. Most of the gradualists were people
who, in the words of the nineteenth-century southern liberal George W.
Cable, always considered the next step in race relations to be not "logical" but "geological." [27]

A small group of southerners, including Will Alexander, Lillian
Smith, and J. Waties Waring, nonetheless endorsed Myrdal's analysis of
the race question in the 1940s. These early advocates of integration
reaped cruel abuse, not just from the masses but often from southern
liberals. Radical southerners, Marxists and socialists, had worked for
and with blacks during the 1930s, often at great risk to their physical
well-being. But because their leftist politics made them double pariahs

25. *What the Negro Wants,* ix–xxiii, quotations on pp. xiv–xv; Couch to Dabney,
February 28, 1944, Logan File, Press Records.
26. Ethridge to Couch, April 11, 1944; Johnson to Couch, October 9, 1944, Logan
File, Press Records; Singal, *War Within,* 300–301.
27. George W. Cable, *The Silent South* (New York, 1885), 102.

in the South, they were able to accomplish little in the decade after World War II. Besides, most radicals preferred to subsume race under economics, which limited their leadership role in the highly legalistic and moralistic civil rights movement.[28]

Eventually, many Jim Crow liberals, goaded by such events as the *Brown* decision, would make the transition to integration. Some, however, joined the forces of massive resistance. Others simply fell silent during the black revolution.[29]

Like most southern reviewers, the majority of northern social scientists tended to favor an evolutionary approach to race relations. The Chicago School of Sociology still dominated racial and ethnic studies in the 1940s. Although Robert Park died in 1944, his influence lingered on through a host of influential students who were positioned strategically in higher education. The evolutionist Park took a decidedly long view of black-white relations. He lectured his students against reformism and "do-gooders." He expressed disdain for the New Deal and voted Republican during the Great Depression. Park and his allies strived mightily to move their young discipline toward becoming a value-free, empirical enterprise that would merit the respectability given the hard sciences.[30]

In addition to the Chicago School, the functionalist sociologists led by Talcott Parsons engaged in a brand of social science that stressed equilibrium more than conflict and change. In 1937 Parsons published his major theoretical work, *The Structure of Social Action,* the same year Myrdal joined the Carnegie project. Parsons' version of sociology waxed in influence in the postwar years, and it showed less interest in the race problem than had the Chicago School.[31]

28. Anthony P. Dunbar, *Against the Grain: Southern Radicals and Prophets, 1929–1959* (Charlottesville, 1981), 221.

29. Sosna, *In Search of the Silent South,* 198–211; Singal, *War Within,* 301.

30. Winifred Raushenbusch, *Robert E. Park: A Biography of a Sociologist* (Durham, 1979), 96–106, 119–26; Fred H. Matthews, *Quest for an American Sociology: Robert E. Park and the Chicago School* (Montreal, 1977), 176, 183, 190–91, 258; Thomas L. Haskell, *The Emergence of Professional Social Science: The American Social Science Association and the Nineteenth-Century Crisis of Authority* (Urbana, Ill., 1977), 190–210, 242–43.

31. Talcott Parsons, *The Structure of Social Action* (New York, 1937); Tom Bottomore and Robert Nisbet, "Structuralism," in Bottomore and Nisbet (eds.), *A History of Sociological Analysis* (New York, 1978), 591–94; Matthews, *Quest for an American Sociology,* 181–83; Daniel Bell, *The Social Sciences Since the Second World War* (New Brunswick, N.J., 1982), 2–52, 55–57.

Not surprisingly, then, many sociologists expressed rather strong reservations about the Myrdal study, perhaps not only because of philosophical differences but also because of personal pique—as seemed to
be the case with Odum. Myrdal did not hesitate to name social scientists
he considered to be "laissez-faire, do-nothing" scholars ignorant about
modern social engineering. Donald Young, a friend and an invaluable
aide to Myrdal on the Carnegie project, held an attitude toward the *Dilemma* that seems fairly typical of sociologists in the 1940s. In his book,
Myrdal rightly placed Young in the laissez-faire school. Although Young
never reviewed the book, he gave his candid views about it in his memoirs. In 1944 he predicted that the *Dilemma* would become a monument
because of the data it presented and its dramatic nature, but he maintained that the study had not increased racial understanding or re-
oriented the field intellectually. Arnold Rose, one of Myrdal's coauthors,
who zealously defended the Swede's work, claimed that sociologists did
not appreciate Myrdal because he was not one of them and because several of them wanted to direct the Carnegie project. It seems, in fact, that
foreign behavioralists such as Julian Huxley were kinder to Myrdal than
most of the American ones.[32]
    White social scientists can be divided into three groups. There were
those in tune with the Chicago School, who differed with Myrdal on
methodology and disagreed with his optimistic forecast. There were liberals like Robert Lynd, who voiced basic agreement with Myrdal, even
if their optimism was not as pronounced. Finally, there were the more
radical scholars, Marxists and non-Marxists, who felt Myrdal's thesis
evaded the real source of the race problem: the economic system and the
social structure.
    E. B. Reuter represented the older view of racial liberalism that was
bound to clash with Myrdal's conceptual analysis, and Myrdal had specifically criticized his work in the *Dilemma*. A veteran writer on blacks,
Reuter labeled Myrdal's study "a mediocre performance" that might
lower the prestige of social science. He held that Myrdal's critique of
Sumner's concept of mores did not advance the argument but prejudiced
the Swede's selection of topics and biased the treatment of them. The
behavioralist explained that the brevity of his review did not allow him
to elaborate on the many underlying weaknesses of the book, but he de-

32. *AD*, 47, 50, 1048–57; Young, interview, COHP, 58–59; "Myrdal: American Dilemma," Box 21, Rose Papers; Julian Huxley, "Interracial Attitudes," *New Statesman and
Nations*, July 29, 1944, pp. 70–71.

clared that its faulty methodology resulted "in vague historical prophecies rather than tentative scientific generalizations."[33]

Other critics in tune with the Chicago School echoed Reuter but usually were less caustic and negative. At least Maurice Davie, a Yale sociologist, did not find the *Dilemma* an embarrassment for social science.
He praised its comprehensiveness and agreed that some sort of dilemma
existed in the white mind. But he disagreed with Myrdal's idea that the
dilemma would solve the race problem and quarreled with his principle
of cumulation. Overall, Davie felt that the idealistic Swede had placed
undue emphasis on the rationality and morality of the human species.[34]

Political scientists took a more positive view of Myrdal's tome. As
did Lynd in the *Saturday Review,* Harold F. Gosnell revealed an admiration and fascination with the *Dilemma* atypical of sociologists. Gosnell,
a Ph.D. from the University of Chicago and a full professor there from
1932 to 1942, took leave during the war to work for the Office of Price
Administration and the State Department until 1950. His 1935 book,
Negro Politicians, brought him accolades and awards. Gosnell described Myrdal's report as "brilliant, stimulating, and provocative" and
"one of the best political commentaries on American life" ever written.
He cheered the economist for laying bare the pretensions of value-free
social science. He pointed out that even in his criticisms of America,
Myrdal was always understanding and constructive. Unlike most reviewers, Gosnell clearly believed that the dilemma Myrdal described
existed and had the power to inspire a movement toward a more racially
equitable nation.[35]

Scholars further to the left generally took longer to get their views in
print. No doubt, it took some deep reflection by those on the left who
really cared about black rights to decide whether Myrdal's moderate,
moralistic work was good or bad for the cause. The "official" comments

33. E. B. Reuter, *The Mulatto in the United States* (Boston, 1918); Reuter, *The American Race Problem* (New York, 1927); and Reuter, *Race Mixture: Studies in Inter-marriage and Miscegenation* (New York, 1931); Reuter, Review of *AD,* in *Phylon,* V (1944), 114–18; *AD,* 1206, 1390.

34. Maurice Davie, Review of *AD,* in *Annals,* CCXXXIII (1944), 253–54; see also Kimball Young, Review of *AD,* in *American Sociological Review,* IX (1944), 327–30; Gwynne Nettler, "A Note on Myrdal's 'Notes on Fact and Valuations,' Appendix 2 of *An American Dilemma,*" *American Sociological Review,* IX (1944), 686–88.

35. Harold F. Gosnell, *Negro Politicians: The Rise of Negro Politics in Chicago* (Chicago, 1935); Gosnell, Review of *AD,* in *American Political Science Review,* XXXVIII (1944), 995–96.

of the Communist party, for example, did not materialize until 1946. In the summer of 1945 Leo Crespi, a professor of social psychology at Princeton University, produced a lengthy and sophisticated critique of the *Dilemma*. He stressed the socioeconomic factors contributing to race prejudice and played down the moral nature of the problem. Crespi worried that the *Dilemma* might tragically mislead those striving to find a solution to the racial situation. He feared that Myrdal's work might play into the hands of religious apologists, who for years had preached that the race problem was a moral one. " 'Primarily a moral issue' will be interpreted to mean that the major *determinant* and the *solution* of the problem lie in the moral realm. This is a viewpoint," Crespi argued, "that social psychologists must deplore." He insisted that the main source of prejudice lay in the "*conditions,* not in individuals—conditions which make it possible for individuals to *gain* by prejudice." To focus on the moral issue, Crespi continued, took one back to the sterile issues of human nature and evil and left the problem with Thomas Aquinas. The social psychologist felt that Myrdal had undermined his own thesis with a wealth of economic data. Crespi pointed out that Myrdal had asserted that a rise in the economic condition of blacks would decrease white racism. Why, if the problem were moral, Crespi asked, would it depend on the material status of blacks or whites? Were the consciences of the poor not as good as those of the well-to-do?[36]

If there was a conflict, the Princeton professor maintained, it was psychological rather than moral. Though Myrdal taught that segregation always entailed discrimination against blacks, he also theorized that whites had suppressed the economic motivation and had substituted more elaborate psychological rationalizations for their actions. To have a genuine moral dilemma, one must have a conscious choice between conflicting values. Since Myrdal had shown that the motivation for prejudice was often unconscious, Crespi maintained, there could be no moral issue. He conceded that if whites came to realize the real motivations for their discrimination, the race problem might become a real moral issue. Even if that should occur, he concluded, Myrdal's exuberant optimism for eliminating prejudice through education and ethical exhortation would not be warranted.[37]

36. Leo Crespi, "Is Gunnar Myrdal on the Right Track?" *Public Opinion Quarterly,* IX (1945), 201–12.

37. *Ibid.,* 210–11; see also Mordecai Grossman, "Caste or Democracy: An American Dilemma," *Contemporary Jewish Record,* VII (1944), 475–86, for a similar view by a humanist.

Crespi's skepticism about Myrdal appeared anemic compared to the stand taken by hard-line Marxists. Many black radicals such as A. Philip Randolph, Bayard Rustin, and Ralph Bunche had long ago grown suspicious of the Communist party for its many fluctuations and about-faces on the race issue. After the Popular Front period of the 1930s came the Nazi-Soviet Pact of 1939, which brought an about-face on the war. With Germany's invasion of Russia in 1941, Earl Browder became an ideological combination of Thomas Jefferson and Adam Smith. He asked blacks to suspend their civil rights activities during the war against fascism. It took some time after the war before the Soviet Union and the West declared all-out ideological and propagandistic war on each other. Thus in 1946 Herbert Aptheker, a historian and intellectual spokesman for the Communist party in America, gave Myrdal the edge of his ideological ax. In a thin book called *The Negro People in America: A Critique of Gunnar Myrdal's "An American Dilemma,"* he concluded: "In summary, we find Myrdal's philosophy to be superficial and erroneous, his historiography demonstrably false, his ethics vicious and, therefore, his analysis weak, mystical and dangerous." [38]

In his authoritative work, *The Negro and the Communist Party,* Wilson Record judged that Aptheker had reached a new low for distortion in his essay on Myrdal. Among other things, the Marxist historian accused Myrdal of holding that the race problem was insoluble. To Aptheker, the Swede's most obvious fallacy was that he was an idealist rather than a materialist and had fought a running battle with Marxism throughout the *Dilemma.* The book represented, Aptheker declared, "a classic statement of the reformist, liberal bourgeois school of moderation pleaders." Not content with ideological defamation, the spokesman for dialectical materialism denigrated Myrdal's character and country as well. "It is perhaps understandable how an adviser to an official of the government of Sweden, which treated the late war against fascism as a dilemma and preferred neutrality," Aptheker fumed, "[chose] to christen the fact of exploitation and oppression of the Negro people a dilemma." [39]

Charles Dollard happily informed Myrdal that Aptheker's book had gone practically unmentioned in scholarly journals. In the 1960s, how-

38. Wilson Record, *The Negro and the Communist Party* (Chapel Hill, 1951), 176, 216–17, 234, and *passim;* Ernest Kaiser, "Racial Dialectics: The Aptheker-Myrdal School Controversy," *Phylon,* IX (1948), 295; Aptheker, *The Negro People in America,* 66.

39. Record, *The Negro and the Communist Party,* 176; Aptheker, *The Negro People in America,* 19, 21–38.

ever, Harold Cruse, a powerful spokesman for black nationalism, lamented what he considered to have been Aptheker's influential role in shaping the Negro elite of the 1940s and 1950s.[40] One would think that such virulent attacks by Marxists in the 1940s would have exempted the *Dilemma* from red-baiting by the right, but, as will be demonstrated later, such was not the case.

By and large, the black community appreciated the efforts of Myrdal. They felt the need of white allies during the early stages of the civil rights movement. Afro-American leaders, attuned to the rising militancy of black thinking, perceived the timeliness of the *Dilemma* and quickly recognized its possible use as a reform tool. Roy Wilkins predicted the importance of the Myrdal report while it was in process and did everything possible to ensure a good press for the NAACP. Myrdal likewise stroked the black community by employing a large number of minority scholars and consulting a wide range of Negroes. Many blacks seemingly expressed more exalted opinions of the *Dilemma* publicly than they did privately. Even so, rising black pride and radical currents of thought among some blacks, not to mention in some cases personal animosity toward Myrdal, produced some highly negative responses from a minority of Afro-American spokesmen.

W. E. B. Du Bois provides a significant example of an enthusiastic endorsement by a black protest leader. A sociologist, historian, novelist, editor, and reformer since the turn of the century, Du Bois presented somewhat of a puzzle to contemporaries and to historians ever since, as he gravitated from Victorian positivism to dialectical materialism, from integration to self-determination, and from optimism to pessimism. Writing in 1944 as a professor at Atlanta University (and in the same issue of the journal in which Reuter's biting comments on Myrdal appeared), Du Bois displayed his delight with Myrdal's book. He described it as "monumental" and "unrivalled," a work that did not gag at the brutal facts or appease the South. He praised Myrdal for viewing the race problem in the total context of American civilization and for not equating "scientific" only with matters that could be quantified. The black scholar quoted long passages from the *Dilemma* to make each of his points.[41]

40. Dollard to Myrdal, December 3, 1946; Harold Cruse, *The Crisis of the Negro Intellectual* (New York, 1967), 469.

41. August Meier, *Negro Thought in America, 1880–1915* (Ann Arbor, 1966), 190–206; Cruse, *Crisis of the Negro Intellectual*, 239; Raymond Wolters, *Negroes and*

Apparently, World War II, despite the tragic aftermath of World War I, aroused Du Bois' hope for change. Myrdal's careful courting of the black sage during the study and his conspicuous use of Du Bois' writings in the *Dilemma*—the Atlantan greatly appreciated Myrdal's characterization of his nineteenth-century work *The Philadelphia Negro* as the best study on Afro-Americans—may have disposed him favorably toward the Carnegie study. Shirley Graham Du Bois claims, however, that in the early stages of the Carnegie project her husband argued against Myrdal's dilemma idea. But in 1944 he agreed heartily with Myrdal's analysis of the race problem, and near the end of his long review, he quoted a passage of nearly three hundred words which contained some of Myrdal's most idealistic pronouncements about human goodness and plasticity. One passage read: "In a sense, the social engineering of the coming epoch will be nothing but the drawing of practical conclusions from the teaching of social science that 'human nature' is changeable and that human deficiencies and unhappiness are, in a large degree, preventable." Another passage went: "People are all much alike on a fundamental level. And they are all good people. They want to be rational and just. They all plead to their conscience that they meant well even when things went wrong." [42]

L. D. Reddick, curator of the Schomburg Collection on Negro History, also found Myrdal's book heartening. Under the title "A Wise Man Writes a Book," the black archivist and scholar pronounced the *Dilemma* the "first really comprehensive survey of the Negro question" and said it represented "the sharpest break" with "anti-Negro and semi-anti-Negro tradition." He found the book a complete vindication of the idea that blacks were fit for democracy. In all, Reddick exalted the *Dilemma* as "a breath of fresh air." He confessed that the book contained flaws, but he complained only briefly that it could have paid more attention to history, that the caste-class model was questionable, and that Myrdal exaggerated the prejudice of white workers against blacks. [43]

the *Great Depression: The Problem of Economic Recovery* (Westport, Conn., 1970), 233, 329; W. E. B. Du Bois, Review of *AD*, in *Phylon*, V (1944), 118–24.

42. Myrdal to Du Bois, November 26, 1938; Du Bois to Ira De A. Reid, April 14, 1939; Myrdal to Du Bois, August 21, 1947, in Herbert Aptheker (ed.), *The Correspondence of W. E. B. Du Bois* (3 vols.; Amherst, Mass., 1973–78), II, 177, 190–91, III, 173–74; Shirley Graham Du Bois, *His Day Is Marching On: A Memoir of W. E. B. Du Bois* (Philadelphia, 1971), 67, 69; Du Bois, Review of *AD*, 123–24.

43. L. D. Reddick, Review of *AD*, in *Opportunity*, XXII (1944), 124–25; see his similar review of *AD* in the *Journal of Negro Education*, XIII (1944), 191–94.

In the *New Republic* J. Saunders Redding dwelled more on the history of black-white relations in his brief review than on the *Dilemma* itself; but throughout he maintained a reverent tone similar to Reddick's. Saunders drove home the point about the moral dimensions of the race problem and seconded the Swede's forecast that the racial *status quo* was doomed. Redding concluded with one of the familiar passages from the *Dilemma:* "America is free to choose whether the Negro shall remain her liability or become her opportunity." [44]

Charles H. Thompson, the dean of the Howard faculty, who had readily cooperated with Myrdal on the Carnegie project, stressed the practical utility of Myrdal's report in his *Journal of Negro Education*. Whether or not Myrdal's central thesis was valid, he wrote, it furnished the vehicle for protest organizations to shift from a defensive to an offensive strategy. He also pointed out that some of the book's most significant contributions resided in the methodology and conceptual framework that were explained in depth in the appendixes. [45]

Like Thompson, E. Franklin Frazier, writing in the *American Journal of Sociology,* emphasized the auspicious timing of Myrdal's book. "It might be stated," the noted and controversial sociologist judged, "that the value and significance of the study are not due so much to its unquestionably intrinsic merits as to its appearance during the present critical stage of race relations." He especially praised Myrdal for calling the white man's cry of "no social equality" a tool to keep the black man down. Frazier, however, expressed skepticism about whether blacks played on the white conscience to the extent Myrdal indicated. He explained that historical oppression and forced isolation of blacks had brought about an accommodation in many cases. This view seemingly clashed with Frazier's earlier editorial critique of Myrdal's manuscript in 1942, when he praised the Swede's sweeping thesis. But Frazier, like Du Bois, held a multitude of competing ideas, and which ones came forth depended on the situation. His background of Chicago sociology, neo-Marxism, and latent black nationalism made him difficult to decipher. [46]

For example, Frazier's review of Myrdal in the *Crisis,* the official

44. J. Saunders Redding, Review of *AD,* in *New Republic,* March 20, 1944, pp. 384–86.

45. Charles H. Thompson, Review of *AD,* in *Journal of Negro Education,* XIII (1944), 131–38.

46. E. Franklin Frazier, Review of *AD,* in *American Journal of Sociology,* L (1945), 555–57.

organ of the NAACP, differed considerably from his essay in the *American Journal of Sociology*. In the journal subscribed to mostly by blacks, he adopted a more flamboyant style and accented the significance of the *Dilemma* for Afro-Americans. Applauding the Swede's unsentimental view of black culture, he asserted that the work should bring an end to "Uncle Tomism." Frazier instructed blacks that they could learn from Myrdal the necessity of seeking full equality, including "social equality." According to the Howard professor, the *Dilemma* constituted a call to action, "a scientific charter of his [the Negro's] right to full participation in American democracy." [47]

Carter G. Woodson, a Harvard-trained historian who published the first issue of the *Journal of Negro History* in 1916, found no such charter in Myrdal's study. Although Woodson set out to review Otto Klineberg's *Characteristics of the American Negro,* he digressed into a stinging rebuke of the *Dilemma,* which he dismissed as the misguided impressions of an innocent foreigner. In addition, he leveled cryptic charges against the book without citing any specific details. The historian claimed that a citizen had initiated a lawsuit against the book and that the best part of the project lay unpublished in the New York Public Library. [48]

Most likely, in the latter case the black scholar referred either to the radical analysis by Bunche or the cultural analysis by Herskovits, which had been prepared for Myrdal's use. In truth, some people at the Carnegie Corporation tried to eliminate or restrict the circulation of certain of the Bunche memoranda. In his book Myrdal had characterized both Herskovits' "African survival" emphasis and Woodson's Negro history movement as propagandistic. In trying to compensate for the distorted view whites had drawn of the Negro past, Myrdal charged, Woodson and others had exaggerated the virtues and deeds of blacks on the historical stage. "Much of all this is zealous dilettantism," Myrdal wrote, "sometimes of a quite fantastic nature." Later, a black historian conceded that in Woodson's eagerness to reorient black students about their past, he often fell short of the canons of historical objectivity. This is not to say that criticism of Myrdal was not in order, but Woodson's remarks resembled personal pique more than scholarly analysis. With more sober reflection, Woodson seemed to retreat somewhat from his earlier judgment of the *Dilemma.* About five months later, he com-

47. E. Franklin Frazier, Review of *AD*, in *Crisis*, LI (1944), 104–106, 124.

48. Carter G. Woodson, Review of Otto Klineberg (ed.), *Characteristics of the American Negro,* in *Journal of Negro History,* XXIX (1944), 234–36.

mented on how successful the foreigner had been in focusing people's attention on the race problem. Perhaps he came to feel that, despite its flaws, the *Dilemma* could help the cause of Negro rights and the Negro history movement.[49]

Woodson's extreme suspicion of the Carnegie project was not singular given the history of black-white relations. Rumors persisted in the black community, for instance, that Bunche or Frazier had really written the *Dilemma*. Reviewing the Myrdal report in the Chicago *Defender,* Ben Burns rejoiced that Carnegie's attempt to produce a dry, bulky volume that would gather dust on the bookshelves had been foiled by the honesty and grit of Myrdal. Instead, the Swedish scholar, Burns wrote, had produced "some of the finest, enlightening prose ever written about the Negro." Most black journalists echoed Burns's conclusions without any hints of attempted sabotage.[50]

One of the most searching, and eventually one of the most influential, reviews of the *Dilemma* came from the pen of Ralph Ellison. In 1944 the future writer of the highly acclaimed 1952 novel *Invisible Man,* drafted an assessment of Myrdal for the *Antioch Review.* But for reasons unknown to me, it remained unpublished until it was reprinted in a collection of Ellison's essays called *Shadow and Act* (1964). In the 1930s the native Oklahoman journeyed to New York, where he met Richard Wright and became attracted to radical politics. He began to write regularly for the leftist *New Masses* and the *Negro Quarterly.* By 1944, however, Ellison had pretty much abandoned radical politics for art (Marxists viciously attacked *Invisible Man*), but a residue of Marxian rhetoric still adorned his vocabulary. The black artist discovered much good in the *Dilemma.* He claimed, for example, that it had destroyed the respectability of racism. What Ellison could not countenance was Myrdal's treatment of black culture. He strongly rejected the notion that black culture was "pathological" and simply an outgrowth of or reaction to white culture. He posed a question that would resonate throughout the cultural nationalist movement later on: "But can a people . . . live and develop for over three hundred years simply by reacting?"

49. Florence Anderson to L. D. Reddick, April 7, 1943; Arnold Rose to Anderson, April 12, 1943; Anderson to Rose, April 13, 1943; Earl Thorpe, *Negro Historians in the United States* (Baton Rouge, 1958), 10, 107; Woodson, "Notes," *Journal of Negro History,* XXIX (1944), 494; *AD,* 751.

50. Guion Johnson, COHP, 65; Ben Burns, Review of *AD,* Chicago *Defender,* January 29, 1944; Atlanta *Daily World,* April 22, 1944; Raleigh *Carolinian,* September 2, 1944.

Although he admitted that much in black culture was negative, Ellison accented the original and the positive. "What is needed in our country," he declared, "is not an exchange of pathologies, but a change of the basis of society." Although Ellison took no part in the militant nationalism of the 1960s and 1970s, his review would become a hallowed document for those who demanded "the death of white sociology." [51]

Race made little difference in the attitude of standard Marxists toward Myrdal. Oliver C. Cox, a native of Trinidad and a professor of sociology at Tuskegee Institute, argued that the Swede employed a "mystical approach" to the race issue so as to avoid the economic source of the problem. Cox maintained that Myrdal misled readers by focusing on the hatred between poor whites and blacks while ignoring the ruling classes' attempts to stir up racial tension to exploit the masses. The only answer to the race problem, he insisted, was the overthrow of capitalism. [52]

Although typically Marxist in his argument, Cox appeared restrained compared to Aptheker's subsequent tirade. The West Indian skillfully pointed out the apparent ambiguity in including so much on economics while castigating economic determinism. Quoting from the *Dilemma*, Cox tried to prove that Myrdal trapped himself in a contradiction when he discussed the rise of slavery in America. Here the Swede explained that when whites enslaved blacks, "*the need was felt for some kind of justification above mere economic expediency.*" When Myrdal strayed from his thesis as in the above case, Cox asserted, his mysticism about sex drives, fears, inhibitions, and the like disappeared. Torn from its ideological underpinning, Myrdal's data, Cox insisted, proved that economics led to slavery and racism. But in Myrdal's hands, Cox suggested, the data became powerful propaganda aimed at maintaining the *status quo.* [53]

Doxey Wilkerson, a former member of Myrdal's staff, blistered his former boss in the introduction to Aptheker's strident attack on the *Di-*

51. "Ralph Ellison," in James A. Emanuel and Theodore L. Gross (eds.), *Dark Symphony: Negro Literature in America* (New York, 1968), 249–50; Cruse, *Crisis of the Negro Intellectual,* 186–87, 269; Stanley M. Elkins, "The Slavery Debate," *Commentary,* LX (December, 1975), 44; Ralph Ellison, "*An American Dilemma:* A Review," in *Shadow and Act* (New York, 1964), 303–17; see the reprint of Ellison's 1944 review in Ladner (ed.), *Death of White Sociology,* 81–95.

52. Oliver C. Cox, "An American Dilemma: A Mystical Approach to the Study of Race Relations," *Journal of Negro Education,* XIV (1945), 132–48.

53. *Ibid.,* 144, 148. Cox wrote an expanded critique of Myrdal in *Caste, Class, and Race* (Garden City, N.Y., 1948), 44–98.

lemma. Less restrained in rhetoric but similar in substance to Cox's attack, Wilkerson's piece dubbed Myrdal's study another example of "crude and subtle propaganda designed to gain wide-spread acceptance of [the] 'safe' view of the Negro problem." [54]

The unmitigated economic determinism of Cox, Wilkerson, and Aptheker brought a response from Horace Cayton, a black sociologist, and Ernest Kaiser, the director of the Harlem Writers Club. Both Cayton and Kaiser rejected Myrdal's thesis, but they also excoriated what they considered the "superficial" and "un-Marxian" interpretation of Cox and Aptheker. Both accused the critics of Myrdal of adhering to an arbitrary and shifting party line on blacks. Kaiser advised the vulgar Marxists to take notice of the great strides made by sociologists, psychologists, and anthropologists on the study of race. Kaiser asked a question that would long befuddle those blacks on the left who tried to adhere to a white Communist party line. "How can Communist writers," Kaiser asked, "embrace the notion of the developing nationhood of the Negro people and yet at the same time refuse to admit that Negro psychology is unique and different from that of whites?" The problem of combining conventional Marxism and black nationalism, so artfully delineated by Harold Cruse in *The Crisis of the Negro Intellectual,* remained a continuing one for black leftists. [55]

Another group that derived sustenance from Myrdal's prescriptions was the liberal clergy. The evangelical and intellectual sectors in the religious community had, of course, played a crucial role in earlier reform movements such as the abolitionist movement and progressivism. In the 1940s the white liberal churches, Protestant, Catholic, and Jewish, displayed an increasing interest in racial matters, especially at the national level of organization. The conservative, fundamentalist faction of the church, like conservative white southerners, ignored the *Dilemma* in the 1940s. As a secular humanist, Myrdal had put little emphasis on the church as a factor in racial change, although he acknowledged religion as one of the emotional roots of the American creed. In general, he felt that the white church was not out in front on the racial issue, particularly in the South; and he criticized the black church for being an escapist institution that reveled in "other-worldliness." [56]

54. Aptheker, *The Negro People in America,* 9.
55. Horace Cayton, "Whose Dilemma?" *New Masses,* July 23, 1946, pp. 8–10; Kaiser, "Racial Dialectics," 295–302; Kaiser quoted in Cruse, *Crisis of the Negro Intellectual,* 299.
56. Frank S. Loescher, "The Protestant Church and the Negro: Recent Pronounce-

Many liberal clergymen nonetheless recognized the significance of Myrdal's study. Harold E. Fey's comments in the Protestant *Christian Century* typified the liberal, intellectual response to the church to the *Dilemma*. Fey judged Myrdal's book indispensable for anyone having pretensions to being racially informed. He also expressed strong approval that Myrdal did not retreat to "moral defeatism" but perceived that "the healing and regenerative influences of the Christian ethic now have their great chance." Fey, nevertheless, conceded that Myrdal was correct in pointing out the backwardness of the church on the race issue. Fey's review concluded by concentrating on the optimism in Myrdal's final chapter, stressing the significance of international relations, which made racial change a necessity and a great opportunity for America to set an example for the world.[57]

Similar to Fey, the eminent theologian Reinhold Niebuhr accorded Myrdal virtually unqualified praise. Once a political radical, the neo-orthodox thinker applauded the secular optimism of the *Dilemma*, but his ovation contained an irony, a device he often used. In earlier and later writings Niebuhr scolded social scientists for committing the fallacy of attributing to man the mastery of his fate. Racial prejudice, he insisted, sprang from original sin and man's inclination toward self-idolatry. Bigotry came not from ignorance (Myrdal's view) but from deep within man's soul. Despite his skepticism about man's innate goodness, Niebuhr seemed taken by Myrdal's data and logic. He lauded the economist's "total theory" and asserted that "every thoughtful student of American life ought not only to read but to possess" the *Dilemma*. Later on, he suggested that church groups should purchase copies of Myrdal's work and study and discuss it.[58]

In the ecumenical and scholarly *Christendom*, Buell G. Gallagher, a professor of social ethics at the Pacific School of Religion, also bowed reverently before the Myrdal treatise. He, too, liked the idea that a reso-

---

ments," *Social Forces*, XXVI (1947), 197–201; Ernest Q. Campbell and Thomas F. Pettigrew, *Christians in Racial Crisis: A Study of Little Rock's Ministry* (Washington, 1959). A search of several conservative church journals such as *Zion's Herald, Christian Advocate*, and the *Presbyterian South* revealed no references to Myrdal. *AD*, 9–11, 563, 936–42.

57. Harold E. Fey, Review of *AD*, in *Christian Century*, LXI (1944), 433–34.

58. Reinhold Niebuhr, "Race Problem in America," *Christianity and Society*, VII (Summer, 1942), 3–5; Niebuhr, "Christian Faith and Race," *ibid.*, X (Spring, 1945), 21–24; Niebuhr, review of *AD*, in *Christianity and Society*, IX (Summer, 1944), 2; Niebuhr, *Christianity and Crisis*, September 18, 1944, p. 2. See also Niebuhr's book, *The Children of Light and the Children of Darkness: A Vindication of Democracy and a Critique of Its Traditional Defense* (New York, 1944).

lution of the race problem was a moral imperative, and he seconded Myrdal's observation that the "Negro problem" was really a white problem. Already a veteran crusader for racial justice, Gallagher would in the future rely heavily on Myrdal, as in his book *Color and Conscience* (1946).[59]

Racial liberals in the Catholic church acknowledged the importance of Myrdal's book but were distinctly cool toward it, mainly because the Swede advocated birth control and because he paid little attention to Catholic interracial work. The liberal *Commonweal* carried but a one-paragraph review of the *Dilemma*. The journal's editor, Harry Lorin Binsse, warned readers that Myrdal seemed to be obsessed with the idea of birth control. Binsse speculated that this sinister fixation might somehow account for the European's gross neglect of Catholic writings on race relations.[60]

When Binsse spoke of neglected Catholic writers, he no doubt had foremost in mind his cousin, John LaFarge. By 1944 LaFarge, a Jesuit priest and chief editor of the influential Catholic weekly *America*, already had three decades of racial activism behind him. He had written two significant books on black-white relations, neither of which was cited in the *Dilemma*. In two reviews of Myrdal's book written for Catholic journals, LaFarge gave the *Dilemma* more favorable treatment than had *Commonweal*. The Jesuit intellectual predicted that Myrdal's treatise would become a lasting encyclopedia on race relations. But, like Binsse, he felt that Myrdal had understated the influence of religion on racial progress, and he took exception to the Swede's espousal of birth control. Despite these caveats, LaFarge concluded that the Swedish economist had produced an "admirable" and "powerful" study.[61]

In summary, in 1944 journalists gave Myrdal's book name recognition and high praise. Seemingly oblivious to the book's slant, most reviewers described the *Dilemma* as "objective" and "scientific." They proclaimed its comprehensiveness, although Myrdal rightly denied any such claims in his preface. Journalists readily compared Myrdal with Tocqueville and Bryce, and others fell into lockstep.

59. Buell G. Gallagher, "The Christian Conscience and the Crisis of Color," *Christendom*, IX (1944), 476–88.

60. Harry Lorin Binsse, Review of *AD*, in *Commonweal*, XXXIX (1944), 477.

61. John LaFarge, Review of *AD*, in *America*, LXX (1944), 496; and in *Catholic World*, CLIX (1944), 181–82. LaFarge's early books on race relations were *Interracial Justice: A Study of Catholic Doctrine on Race Relations* (New York, 1937); and *The Race Question and the Negro* (New York, 1943).

For the most part, white southern liberals and white social scientists expressed reservations about Myrdal's central thesis and his enthusiastic optimism. Still, they often concluded that the book was a classic in spite of itself. That is, even though the conceptual underpinnings of the *Dilemma* might be erroneous, its dramatic facts destined it to be an unexcelled source on race relations well into the future. Few in this grouping, however, could envision the racial ferment and change that Myrdal forecast.

Most blacks immediately grasped the timeliness of Myrdal's book. Even if they doubted the main thesis, they saw the potential utility of the *Dilemma* for the incipient civil rights movement. Utility, however, was not enough for critics such as Ellison, who took offense at Myrdal's treatment of black culture. Black Marxists such as Cox branded the Swede's approach to the race problem mystical and dangerous. White party spokesmen branded the book a tool of the capitalist classes.

After 1944 liberal church leaders often fortified their moral approach to the race problem with the authority of the secular Swede. No group, with perhaps the exception of black activists, made more use of the *Dilemma* than the liberal clergy.

It should be reiterated that many elements of American society ignored the *Dilemma*, in the North as well as in the South. Only two persons who could be classified as professional historians reviewed the book, and then in nonhistorical journals.[62] Such silence among so many Americans from important walks of life revealed much about the state of black-white relations in the mid-1940s.

Americans nonetheless launched Myrdal's bulky vessel of facts and hypotheses upon a large sea of commentary. In the year of D-Day, the *Dilemma* helped secure a strategic beachhead in the battle for racial equality. Its influence would spread quickly and widely during the formative years of the Truman era.

62. Frank Tannenbaum, Review of *AD*, in *Political Science Review*, LIX (1944), 321–40; Henry Steele Commager, Review of *AD*, in *American Mercury*, LX (1945), 751–53.

V

The Spreading of Myrdalian
Thought: The Truman Years

"The crucial turning point in viewing the problem of race as a national problem," the distinguished black historian John Hope Franklin stated in a 1968 address, "occurred when the executive branch of the federal government began actively to assume a major role." Franklin, of course, referred to Harry S. Truman's presidency. Although it has been argued that the "takeoff" period in the thinking of black activists began during World War II, many whites first responded positively to the escalating demands for black freedom in the Truman era.[1] Myrdal's ideas also probably had their most direct influence on Americans from 1945 to 1953, providing important individuals, private organizations, and government agencies with a handy and compelling conceptual framework and a wealth of data concerning the race problem.

This chapter illustrates some of the numerous ways Myrdal's thought filtered down to ordinary people through influential persons, agencies, and institutions during the eventful Truman years. In this period the groundwork was laid for more dramatic breakthroughs from the mid-1950s through the 1960s. In 1947, for example, the liberal reports of the Truman Committee on Civil Rights and the Commission on Higher Education appeared. On July 26, 1948, Truman issued Executive Order 9981, which decreed that "there shall be equality of treatment and op-

---

1. John Hope Franklin, "Civil Rights and the Truman Administration," in Donald R. McCoy, Richard T. Ruetten, and J. R. Fuchs (eds.), *Conference of Scholars on the Truman Administration and Civil Rights* (Independence, Mo., 1968), 134; Dalfiume, " 'Forgotten Years' of the Negro Revolution," 90–106; Harvard Sitkoff, "Harry Truman and the Election of 1948: The Coming of Age of Civil Rights in American Politics," *Journal of Southern History*, XXXVII (1971), 597–616.

portunity in the Armed services without regard to race, color, religion, or national origin." In 1948 the president campaigned in Harlem, the first time an American chief executive had done so. In that same year the youthful and ebullient Hubert H. Humphrey led a successful fight to include a strong civil rights plank in the Democratic platform, thereby provoking the Dixiecrat revolt. During these years the Supreme Court gradually reclaimed the original intent of the Fourteenth and Fifteenth Amendments in a series of civil rights cases, culminating in the school desegregation decision of 1954. Additionally, the Cold War provided a powerful lever for the advocates of racial change. State Department officials estimated that about one-half of Soviet propaganda focused on the American racial situation. In 1947 the black protest leader W. E. B. Du Bois discovered a new avenue of dissent when he laid the case of mistreatment of American blacks before the United Nations.[2]

Below the level of national and international politics, the "convenience of ignorance" that Myrdal spoke about began to erode as civil rights activists energetically pursued their cause. In 1947 Jackie Robinson broke the color barrier in professional baseball, and Lena Horne and other black entertainers found increased access to Broadway and Hollywood. Historians of the film point out that the racial theme came of age in the 1940s; though most celluloid productions still tended to demean Afro-Americans, stereotypes began to soften. In academia and lower levels of education, professors and teachers more frequently addressed the racial issue. In a word, the press, radio, movies, the pulpit, and ultimately television offered increasing attention to race and bigotry. Studies show that as civil rights groups proliferated, white racism became eminently less respectable. By 1946 a poll taken by the National Opinion Research Center claimed that 50 percent of whites believed Negroes were as intelligent as they.[3]

By any standards, however, racism remained a formidable force throughout the period and in all sections of the country. It was deeply embedded in the social and institutional fabric of mainstream America.

2. For the best coverage of these events, see Donald R. McCoy and Richard T. Ruetten, *Quest and Response: Minority Rights and the Truman Administration* (Lawrence, Kan., 1973).

3. Donald Bogle, *Toms, Coons, Mulattoes, Mammies, and Bucks* (New York, 1973), 158; Daniel J. Leab, *From Sambo to Superspade: The Black Experience in Motion Pictures* (Boston, 1975), 120, 125, 129; McCoy and Ruetten, *Quest and Response*, 58–59; Herbert H. Hyman and Paul B. Sheatsley, "Attitudes Toward Desegregation," *Scientific American*, CXCV (December, 1956), 35–39.

Lip service to egalitarian ideals and fair play often did not translate into meaningful action, nor did it move Congress to act. At the end of World War II, Malcolm Ross, one of the wartime heads of the Fair Employment Practices Committee, released government studies which revealed that only 7 percent of whites in the South expressed willingness to give blacks an equal chance for jobs; in the North the figure was 19 percent. A 1945 national Gallup Poll divulged that only 43 percent of whites believed that their state should enact a law requiring employers to hire qualified workers irrespective of color.[4]

Many factors accounted for the racial changes in the Truman period, many of them having little to do with attitudes or dilemmas. But as a researcher at the 1968 Conference of Scholars on the Truman Administration explained, one of the most important may have been the change in white attitudes toward blacks.[5]

What part Myrdal's book played in America's racial education is, of course, hard to judge. One clue to its impact may be found in its sales and circulation. As all academicians know, large sales do not prove influence any more than the reverse indicates a lack thereof. The Carnegie Corporation, Harper and Brothers, and Myrdal worried that the size and cost of the *Dilemma* would discourage sales. Indeed, the Carnegie Corporation had to guarantee the publisher against any financial losses on the first printing of three thousand copies.[6] By the end of 1944, however, the book had sold ten thousand copies, and by 1950 about thirty thousand. In 1962 Harper & Row brought out a one-volume hardback edition with a new author's preface and a "Postscript Twenty Years Later" by Arnold Rose. The book was still in print in 1983, selling for $25. Two-volume paperback editions came on the market in the 1960s, one by McGraw-Hill and one by Harper & Row. When Myrdal requested five copies of a paperback edition in 1973, he found that the second volume was out of print. He therefore lobbied Harper for a reissue. Pantheon Books, Myrdal's main publisher throughout the post-*Dilemma* period, brought out a paperback edition in 1975. Since Harper & Row refused to disclose sales figures on the *Dilemma*, the exact number of copies

---

4. Malcolm Ross, *All Manner of Men* (New York, 1948), 23; Louis Coleridge Kesselman, *The Social Politics of FEPC* (Chapel Hill, 1948), 176.

5. Ruetten, in McCoy, Ruetten, and Fuchs (eds.), *Conference of Scholars,* 59.

6. Ordway Tead to Charles Dollard, June 15, 1942; summary of conference, Frederick Keppel and Dollard, December 12, 1942; Tead to Keppel, December 21, 1942; all correspondence in this chapter, unless otherwise stated, is from Negro Study; Donald Young, COHP, 52.

Myrdal's book has sold over four decades is not available, but in 1975 Victor S. Navasky estimated it at approximately one hundred thousand copies.[7]

After Keppel's death in 1943 and Dollard's departure for the army, the Carnegie Corporation seemed to lose interest in Myrdal's book, and it financed little further research on blacks. Walter A. Jessup, Keppel's successor as president, entirely divorced himself from the book. "There have been many examples of a foundation turning its back on its failures," a puzzled historian wrote; "the Carnegie Corporation turned its back on a triumph."[8]

Soon after the book's publication, the corporation was inundated with requests by individuals and organizations to condense and package the *Dilemma* for the reader with a short attention span. Some even asked for foundation funds to do so. Benjamin Quarles, a black historian at Dillard University, asked for permission to write a 250-to-300-page synopsis for his classes. The corporation referred all requests to Harper and Brothers, informing the petitioners that it had no more connection with the *Dilemma*.[9]

Harper liberally granted permission for several adaptations of Myrdal's work. By 1945 various summaries of the *Dilemma* circulated about the country. The most notable condensations were *A Digest of Myrdal's An American Dilemma* by Samuel S. Wyer for the Columbus (Ohio) Council for Democracy; *A Summary of An American Dilemma: The Negro Problem and Democracy* by the historian Quarles; and *The Negro in America* by Maxwell S. Stewart for the Public Affairs Committee of New York City. Harper published the first scholarly book-length abridgment of Myrdal's study in 1948. Arnold Rose, personally chosen by Myrdal for the task, prepared a well-received condensation of slightly over three hundred pages. Entitled *The Negro in America*, Rose's book appeared in 1964 as a Harper Torchbook (paperback). Numerous civil rights groups and social science periodicals advertised these adapta-

7. Robert Lester to Myrdal, December 29, 1944; Robert G. Hawley to Robert Flexner, October 9, 1950; telephone call, Avery Russell, president of Carnegie Corporation, to author, February 17, 1983, stating that by 1983, Harper had sold 17,680 copies of the 1962 edition; Herbert Dreyer, marketing and merchandising manager for McGraw-Hill, to author, June 11, 1982; Victor S. Navasky, "In Cold Print: American Dilemma," *New York Times Book Review*, May 18, 1975.

8. Waldemar A. Nielsen, *The Big Foundations* (New York, 1972), 40.

9. Memorandum, May 5, 1944, Negro Study; A. W. Dent to Walter A. Jessup, March 1, 1944; Charles Dollard to Robert Lester, May 4, 1944.

tions. Before the year 1944 ended, twenty thousand copies of Wyer's summary had gone to colleges, schools, the armed services, government agencies, and civil rights groups. The ten-cent, thirty-two-page pamphlet by the Public Affairs Committee quickly went through four printings. The more scholarly adaptation by Rose became a staple in race relations courses that proliferated in American educational institutions after World War II.[10]

Clearly, a great number of Americans got their Myrdal secondhand. Yet observers such as Louis Wirth marveled at how many laymen, not to mention scholars, read the huge book from cover to cover. In 1946 the Riverside, California, public library reported that Myrdal's book had been checked out twice a month since its purchase. The grand initial reviews in the New York *Times, Life, Time,* and the *Saturday Review* no doubt stimulated broad interest in the book. After the war popular writers made Myrdal's name more and more familiar to Americans.[11]

In 1944 *Life* magazine used Myrdal to emphasize the moral schizophrenia of whites toward blacks. Few illustrated this personality split more vividly than the widely syndicated journalist Samuel Grafton. A native of New York City and a liberal, Grafton, according to a fellow writer, had "a passionate and feverish belief in democracy" and invariably took the side of the underdog. Grafton's reading of the *Dilemma* left him deeply troubled. In a June, 1944, column he informed the public about the provocative contents of the Myrdal study. Racial tensions, Grafton explained, had increased dangerously during the war. This fact alone, he believed, meant that the North could no longer cave in to the South on the race problem.[12]

Unsure about the issue, however, Grafton left Manhattan and took a bus to Richmond to consult Virginius Dabney about Myrdal's book. The editor of the Richmond *Times-Dispatch* was a critic of Myrdal and a Jim Crow liberal inching his way toward reaction. Nevertheless, he im-

10. "Notes," *Journal of Negro History,* XXIX (1944), 494; "Notes," *Social Studies,* XXXVI (1945), clipping in Negro Study; Ray S. Reinert to Carnegie Corporation, November 25, 1944; Peter I. Rose, *The Subject Is Race: Traditional Ideologies and the Teaching of Race Relations* (New York, 1968), 146.

11. Louis Wirth, "The Unfinished Business of American Democracy," *Annals,* CCXLIV (1946), 7n; Riverside (Calif.) *Enterprise,* March 4, 1946, clipping in Negro Study.

12. *Life,* April 24, 1944, p. 32; Charles Fisher, *The Columnists: A Surgical Survey* (New York, 1944), 251–59; Samuel Grafton, "Light on the $300,000 Race Relations Question," Chicago *Sun,* June 11, 1944, p. 14.

pressed the New Yorker. Grafton spent a large part of a subsequent column relating Dabney's plaintive story about how difficult it was to be a
southern liberal. Not one word did Grafton utter about the discrimination, humiliation, and violence suffered by blacks. Horace Cayton, a
black social scientist, acidly commented that the noted journalist had
wasted $7.50 on the *Dilemma* and the cost of the bus fare to Richmond
if all he learned concerned the perils of being a southern liberal.[13]
Whatever Grafton's slant, his writing shows how widely Myrdal's thought
spread.

In the immediate postwar period many American writers of popular
books called attention to the urgency of the race problem and sounded
praises for the prescriptions of the Swedish scholar to tens of thousands
of readers. Margaret Halsey's successful book *Color Blind: A White
Woman Looks at the Negro* (1946) provides such an example. A young
writer with two books already to her credit, Halsey astutely probed
the conscience of whites by narrating her experiences in running an
interracial canteen during the war. Published by Simon and Schuster,
Halsey's book got good reviews from a variety of critics. In the New
York *Times* the famous anthropologist Margaret Mead commended the
volume as "a straightforward, courageous and delightful book about
what Americans can do . . . to expedite the absorption of our Negro
American citizens into full membership in our democracy." In the *Saturday Review,* Harry Overstreet judged Halsey's work to be "a profoundly revealing social document" that not only was scientifically accurate but "a delight to read."[14]

Since Halsey arranged entertainment for American soldiers, particularly through dances, much of her book revolved around the problem of
interracial couples. She dwelled on black males' feelings about white
women and white males' feelings about mixed couples. Relying on revisionist social science, Halsey declared that excessive black sensuality
and the black man's consuming desire for white women were myths. She
then brought Myrdal into the discussion, pointing out that his rank order
of discriminations proved that blacks had little desire for interracial sex
or marriage. In the last chapter of the book, she suggested certain works

13. Grafton, "Light on the $300,000 Race Relations Question," p. 14; Horace
Cayton, Pittsburgh *Courier,* June 24, 1944, p. 7.

14. Margaret Halsey, *Color Blind: A White Woman Looks at the Negro* (New York,
1946); Margaret Mead, Review of Margaret Halsey's *Color Blind,* in *New York Times
Book Review,* October 13, 1946, p. 3; Harry Overstreet, Review of Margaret Halsey's
Color Blind, in *Saturday Review,* October 19, 1946, p. 14.

for further reading. Halsey recommended such racial novels as Lillian Smith's *Strange Fruit* and Richard Wright's *Native Son,* but she added that the Myrdal report was the "definitive" study to be consulted. She assured the public that despite its great length, it was easy to read. Each chapter, she instructed, could be read independently with great profit.[15]

Several books similar to Halsey's in their mixture of humor and profundity and in their Myrdalian outlook appeared right after World War II. None proved more popular than John Gunther's *Inside U.S.A.* (1947). This best-seller derived from extensive travel and hundreds of interviews with an astonishing array of people. Gunther devoted considerable space to the race problem, which he explained had become alarming because of increasing black militancy accompanied by a growing white reaction. He recounted several instances of fiendish lynchings and atrocities in the South and illustrated some of his points with quotations from the *Dilemma.* In all, he cited Myrdal fifteen times. Gunther confided that several of his friends, including a Supreme Court justice and an assistant secretary of state, insisted that Myrdal's work was the "indispensable" starting point for understanding the racial issue. The "inside" writer echoed their opinion, concluding: "Nobody has much right to discuss the Negro in America until he has looked into Myrdal's book."[16]

Stuart Chase, a veteran critic of the *status quo,* also helped to popularize the latest social science evidence on race in his 1948 book, *The Proper Study of Mankind.* More scholarly and reformist than Gunther, Chase nonetheless had paid scant attention to the race problem in his previous writings. His 1948 work illustrated a trend by the inclusion of a chapter called "Scientists Look at Race," in which he informed the reader about the increasingly familiar story of the revolution in racial thinking that started with Franz Boas and culminated in Myrdal.[17]

Such popular and semipopular books widened the circulation of Myrdal's ideas, but the Swede's thought was even more broadly disseminated through newspapers, magazines, and journals. The announce-

15. Halsey, *Color Blind,* 122, 151–52; see her foreword in Ray Sprigle, *In the Land of Jim Crow* (New York, 1949), vii.

16. For books similar to Halsey's see Benjamin C. Bowker, *Out of Uniform* (New York, 1946), 193–215; Jack Goodman (ed.), *While You Were Gone* (New York, 1946), 90–98, 100–102, 108; John Gunther, *Inside U.S.A.* (New York, 1947), 383, 654, 683–86.

17. Stuart Chase, *The Proper Study of Mankind* (New York, 1948), 50, 111, 302. See also Dennis W. Brogan, *American Themes* (New York, 1947), 269–79.

ment in early 1945 that the Myrdal study was a co-winner of the
Anisfield-Wolf Award for the best book on race relations in 1944 enhanced its prestige and recognition. Then, too, book reviewers seemed
to relate virtually every work on blacks to the *Dilemma.* Reviewers of
Wright's *Black Boy,* for instance, hailed the Afro-American's autobiography as a supplement to the Myrdal report. When *Survey Graphic* devoted its entire January, 1947, issue to the topic of racial segregation,
Myrdal's ideas permeated the articles.[18]

With the war on bigotry getting into gear, journalists often expressed
wonderment as to why certain well-fixed individuals actively joined the
fight against prejudice. A *New Republic* reporter asked a highly successful black man, who drove a Buick convertible and owned a large cabin
cruiser, why he exhibited so much concern about prejudice. The man
replied by alluding to Myrdal's observation that the "higher level" black
most resented the fact that color kept him from reaching the full potential of his education and talent. Some well-heeled white ethnics still suffered enough discrimination that they were moved to become activists in
race relations. Frank Sinatra, the singing rage of the 1940s, witnessed
so much intergroup prejudice on his tours that he decided to use his su-
perstar status to fight bigotry. Realizing his lack of education, the
crooner carried a trunk of books with him across the country. When
asked by a reporter what he had read, Sinatra reeled off the following
authors and titles: Gustav[us] Myer's *The History of Bigotry in the
United States,* Howard Fast's *Freedom Road,* and Mary Fitch's *One
God.* Although he could not recall the author of the giant, two-volume
work on the Negro, the singer claimed that he had read *An American
Dilemma* twice.[19]

Although influential individuals such as Sinatra had an effect, clearly
the burgeoning interracial organizations could reach more people. In
1945 the Julius Rosenwald Fund listed three hundred groups that dealt
with ethnic problems; in 1948 it listed over a thousand such groups.

---

18. Henry Canby, editor of *Saturday Review,* to Myrdal, February 20, 1945; Harry
Hansen, New York *World,* February 28, 1945; Lewis Gannett, New York *Herald Tribune,*
October 25, 1945; Dorothy Newman, "A World to Live In: Recent Books on Race Relations," New York *Post,* September 17, 1945; *Survey Graphic,* XXXVI (January, 1947),
21, 100, 113, and *passim.*

19. Daniel James, "Cannon the Progressive," *New Republic,* October 18, 1948,
pp. 14–15; "The Education of Frank Sinatra," *PM,* June 10, 1945, clipping in Negro Study;
John Wiener, "When Old Blue Eyes Was 'Red': The Poignant Story of Frank Sinatra's Politics," *New Republic,* March 31, 1986, pp. 21–23.

Goodwin Watson's 1947 survey revealed a nation replete with councils for democracy, councils against intolerance, and councils for unity. In 1944 Midwest activists formed the American Council on Race Relations, a consultant agency that sought to help local communities deal more fairly with minorities. Several Jewish organizations including the American Jewish Congress, the American Jewish Committee, and the Anti-Defamation League fought not only anti-Semitism but all forms of prejudice. Across the country, a host of groups waged a "war against bigotry" on a myriad of fronts.[20]

Like Myrdal, members of these agencies had faith in the use of education and the modern media to make inroads against prejudice. They pointed to the Creel Committee of World War I and the Office of War Information in World War II as examples of successful mass education. In a democracy, Edward Bernays wrote in 1947, one could not coerce people to do right, but one could practice the "engineering of consent." "The United States," the father of American public relations opined, "has become a small room in which a single whisper is magnified thousands of times." Civil rights advocates, therefore, whispered, even shouted, through the media, especially during observances like Negro History Week and Brotherhood Week. These occasions brought forth innumerable references to Myrdal and public displays of his book in schools, libraries, and city halls.[21]

Nor was the business world immune to racial pressure or the allure of Myrdal's teachings. The largely ineffective Fair Employment Practices Committee established by Roosevelt during the war had at least alerted some employers to hiring inequities. Progressive businessmen followed advice to hire more nonwhite workers and acquaint themselves with information on race relations. Fowler McCormick, chairman of the board of International Harvester, for example, reexamined his company's hiring practices and began to read widely in race literature. Soon he had

20. Brewton Berry, *Race Relations* (Boston, 1951), 122; John Hope Franklin, *From Slavery to Freedom: A History of Negro Americans* (5th ed.; New York, 1980), 421; Dalfiume, " 'Forgotten Years' of the Negro Revolution," 99–100; Goodwin Watson, *Action for Unity* (New York, 1947).

21. Edward Bernays, "The Engineering of Consent," in Theodore R. Crane (ed.), *The Dimensions of American Education* (Reading, Mass., 1974), 155; Clayton Haswell, "Father of Public Relations Going Strong at 91," St. Louis *Post-Dispatch*, November 15, 1983; "Brotherhood Week All Year Round," Chicago *News*, February 24, 1946; "Negro History Week Marked with Book, Portrait, Exhibit," Worcester (Mass.) *Telegram*, February 17, 1946; Vincent P. Franklin, *The Education of Black Philadelphia: The Social and Educational History of a Minority, 1900–1950* (Philadelphia, 1979), 165–66.

two junior executives preparing manuals and conducting seminars on intergroup relations. As one witness testified before the Truman Committee, these men did "beautiful resource reading." "I mean," she continued, "they were plowing through the whole of the *American Dilemma* . . . and they are terribly keen about it." [22]

In some cases, Myrdal's findings reached down to the local police station. The threat and reality of racial violence induced interracial agencies, as they did Myrdal, to place emphasis on police work in minority neighborhoods. By the late 1940s race relations experts commonly briefed large metropolitan enforcement officers on ethnic understanding. Gordon Allport, a noted social psychologist from Harvard University, instructed the Boston Police Department about prejudice. Members of the Cincinnati police studied the pertinent parts of the *Dilemma*. In 1947 John Lohman, a sociologist at the University of Chicago, drafted a 133-page guide for the Chicago Park District men in blue. Entitled *The Police and Minority Groups,* it served as a model for similar manuals all over America. The Lohman guide quoted Myrdal at length, particularly on the relation of segregation and restrictive housing covenants to black crime. In California the attorney general, in collaboration with the American Council on Race Relations, published a manual on race relations and established seminars for policemen in which the *Dilemma* and similar books were read and discussed. [23] Myrdal's advice that policemen working in America's complex urban scene should have college degrees rang true, if only to help them get through the sociological seminars.

Although some police departments added Myrdal to their arsenal, college students were more likely to get a dose of Myrdal than were law enforcement personnel. A dramatic increase in the teaching of the behavioral sciences occurred in American education after the war, in those very areas in which race relations courses were usually taught. In the decade after World War II, the number of teachers of sociology increased 250 percent. The wanton violence of the period created a feeling that man's survival necessitated improvement in the social sciences. [24]

22. Proceedings of the Committee, April 24, 1947, Box 13, Records of the President's Committee on Civil Rights, Harry S. Truman Library, Independence, Missouri, hereinafter referred to as Records and HSTL.

23. Watson, *Action for Unity,* 135; John Lohman, *Police and Minority Groups* (Chicago, 1947), 65–66, 68, 129; Davis McEntire and Joseph E. Weckler, A *Guide to Race Relations for Police Officers* (Sacramento, 1946); Joseph E. Weckler and Theo E. Hall, *The Police and Minority Groups* (New York, 1944), 20.

24. Hans L. Zetterberg (ed.), *Sociology in the United States of America* (Paris, 1956),

As the "sociological emphasis" gained prominence, a generation of future racial reformers in the Kennedy and Johnson administrations of the 1960s grew up on an academic diet of Myrdal. The relationship of the Swedish economist's work to academia is so significant that it will receive separate treatment later on.

As demonstrated in the previous chapter, in 1944 the liberal clergy responded enthusiastically to the *Dilemma*. During the following years, the liberal elements of the church steadily grew more involved in racial matters. Church pronouncements on race became not only more numerous but more specific and meaningful. In 1946 the Federal Council of Churches issued a landmark resolution which held that segregation violates the "Gospel of love and human brotherhood." The organization vowed to strive for a "non-segregated church and society." [25]

In the Truman period, individual theologians and ministers from various denominations devoted much of their writing to race relations. In the special March, 1946, issue of *Annals* directed at controlling group prejudice, Walter G. Muelder, professor of social ethics at the Boston University School of Theology, extolled Myrdal's dilemma thesis. One section of his article carried the heading "The American Creed." Four of his six citations referred to the *Dilemma*. Buell Gallagher, who had celebrated the Carnegie project in 1944, continued to rely heavily on Myrdal in his writing on race. This academician and Congregational minister provided a splendid example of how a liberal clergyman could integrate Myrdal's secular faith into the latest version of the Social Gospel. A Ph.D. from Columbia University, Gallagher served from 1933 to 1943 as president of a black college (Talledega) in Alabama before moving to the Pacific School of Religion in Berkeley, California. In 1952 he became president of the City College of New York. In his 1946 book with the Myrdalian title *Color and Conscience: The Irrepressible Conflict*, he freely borrowed concepts and data from Myrdal, not to mention long, hortatory quotations. In all, he cited the *Dilemma* twenty times, stressing, like Myrdal, the moral dimension of

9–20; George Lundberg, "The Senate Ponders Social Science," *Scientific Monthly*, LXIV (1947), 397–411; Judson T. Landis, "The Sociology Curriculum and Teacher Training," *American Sociological Review*, XII (1947), 113; Report by a Faculty Committee, *The Behavioral Sciences at Harvard* (Cambridge, Mass., 1954), 5, 25, 27–30; Lawrence Podell, Martin Vogefanger, and Roberta Rogers, "Sociology in American Colleges," *American Sociological Review*, XXIV (1959), 87–95.

25. Frank S. Loescher, "The Protestant Church and the Negro: Recent Pronouncements," *Social Forces*, XXVI (1947), 197–201; David M. Reimers, *White Protestantism and the Negro* (New York, 1965), 109–33.

the race problem and, above all, its urgency. Quoting the economist, Gallagher warned: "We must 'do something big, and do it soon.'" The minister vigorously maintained that religion could lead the way to an integrated society.[26]

Like Muelder and Gallagher, many clergymen, black and white alike, deftly molded the new sociology of race into their religious framework. In 1946 even the fundamentalist Southern Baptist Convention addressed the mistreatment of blacks, and in 1954 it approved the *Brown* decision. In 1947 the National Conference of Christians and Jews observed Religious Book Week by distributing a list of thirty-nine recommended works. Of the fifteen listed under "Classics," all except one dealt with intergroup relations or democracy. Myrdal's book was described as a hard-hitting, objective study that prescribed the practical steps needed to solve the race problem.[27]

The church, of course, reflected the general culture, and it responded to racial events in a variety of ways. But the liberal elements in the church, particularly those outside the South and in national and academic organizations, moved forward boldly during the Truman years. Unlike the highly religious abolitionists of the nineteenth century, the church reformers in the 1940s could use "science" as well as faith to argue that blacks were born equal. William Scarlett, an influential St. Louis bishop who integrated his Episcopal diocese in 1948, laced his "race relations" sermons with Myrdalisms, both hortatory and sociological. Though the bishop was a longtime proponent of Negro betterment, his careful reading of the *Dilemma* caused him to rethink his position on Jim Crow. By the late 1940s Scarlett was using his pulpit to laud the Swede's "monumental book" as the outstanding example of "biological equalitarianism," an idea that he claimed had brought modern science back to Jesus Christ's profound insight about the basic unity of mankind. The rediscovery of original Christian doctrine and the discovery of modern science helped move liberals such as Scarlett to condemn segregation. Other factors also tended to move church liberals in that direction in the 1940s. "It was no accident," a church historian has

26. Walter G. Muelder, "National Unity and National Ethics," *Annals*, CCXLIV (1946), 10–18; *Color and Conscience*, x, 1, 4, 23, 38–39, 223.

27. William Stuart Nelson (ed.), *The Christian Way in Race Relations* (New York, 1948), 6, 19, 29, 76, 103; Catholic Interracial Council of New York, *Catholic Statement on Negro Employment* (New York, n.d.); Reimers, *White Protestantism and the Negro*, 112–17; advertisement, May, 1944, Negro Study; "New Reading List for Democracy Book List Ready," Chicago *News*, January 23, 1946.

written, "that the call for a 'non-segregated society' came about the same time as the threatened Negro March on Washington, Myrdal's *An American Dilemma* and President Truman's Commission [*sic*] on Civil Rights."[28]

To be certain, the Truman Committee's report on civil rights represented a milestone in race relations. For nearly half a century reformers had unsuccessfully pleaded with presidents to appoint a national committee to study black-white relations. Finally, in December, 1946, Truman, who feared a racial explosion such as had occurred after World War I, selected a distinguished biracial committee of fifteen to advise him on the proper role of the federal government in racial affairs. In October, 1947, the committee, headed by Charles E. Wilson of General Electric, presented a report entitled *To Secure These Rights*, the title taken from the Declaration of Independence. The report recommended a reorganization of the Civil Rights Section of the Justice Department, the establishment of a permanent commission on civil rights, an anti-lynching law, stronger federal statutes to protect voting rights, desegregation of the armed forces, a fair employment practices law, and the denial of federal aid and grants to public and private agencies that practiced discrimination. The committee, in fact, called for the elimination of segregation in American society. The controversial report contained no footnotes, bibliography, or index.[29] The working papers of the president's committee, however, reveal a significant Myrdalian influence on the report. Indeed, *To Secure These Rights* adhered closely to the overall framework of the *Dilemma* and exhibited a similar optimism and partiality toward government action and an educational campaign against prejudice.

In 1944 L. D. Reddick commented that after Myrdal, surely no one would have the gall to ask for another study of the Negro before initiating action. Reddick, of course, was wrong. It seems logical, though, that the committee, given less than a year to study the racial situation,

28. Reimers, *White Protestantism and the Negro*, 185; William Scarlett, "Race Relations [Sermon]" and "[Notes on] Myrdal," pp. 1–14, both in the William Scarlett Papers, Box 11, Folder 205, Archives of the Episcopal Church, Austin, Texas; Robert A. Good, "An Evolution of Attitudes: The Episcopal Church of Missouri and the Problem of Race Relations During the Episcopate of William Scarlett, 1931–1951" (Senior thesis, Westminster College, Fulton, Mo., 1986), 41–51.

29. Harry S. Truman, *Memoirs: Years of Trial and Hope* (2 vols.; Garden City, N.Y., 1956), II, 180; President's Committee on Civil Rights, *To Secure These Rights* (1947), 79–87, 157–73.

could hardly ignore the work on blacks that had been constantly hailed as comprehensive and definitive. A close reading of the report shows that it began with an elaborate definition of the American creed and then contrasted it to the American practice. As had Myrdal, the committee emphasized three basic reasons for extending equal rights to blacks: the moral, the economic, and the international. "The pervasive gap between our aims and what we actually do," the report stated, "is creating a kind of moral dry rot which eats away at the emotional and rational bases of democratic beliefs." Commenting on international politics, the committee, like Myrdal, stressed how the mistreatment of blacks played into the hands of Communist propagandists.[30]

Because the report had no scholarly paraphernalia, a reader would discover only one mention of the Swedish authority in the text. In reference to economic discrimination, the committee quoted Myrdal at length to illustrate that such discrimination not only was wasteful but instilled a lingering hostility in blacks: "Not only occasional acts of violence but most laziness, carelessness, unreliability, petty stealing and lying are undoubtedly to be explained as concealed aggression. The truth is," the report continued, following Myrdal, "that *Negroes generally do not feel they have unqualified moral obligations to white people.*" The committee also spoke through Myrdal to point out that voluntary withdrawal of blacks, which increased isolation between the two castes, constituted another form of Negro protest.[31]

First, it perhaps should be pointed out that large committees do not write such reports as *To Secure These Rights;* they approve or amend them. Sometimes a minority dissents from them. Two men essentially prepared the committee report of 1947. Robert Carr, a political scientist from Dartmouth College, acted as executive secretary, and Milton S. Stewart, a sociologist from the New School for Social Research in New York City, served as research director. A very small staff of researchers and secretaries assisted them. On February 12, 1947, the day the staff began to collect resource material, Carr requested a copy of the *Dilemma* from the Library of Congress. When the full committee first met on March 6, Carr told the members that the most dramatic possible result of the proposed study would be to restate the "American creed or the American dream" as a background to serious recommendations to

30. L. D. Reddick, Review of *AD,* in *Journal of Negro Education,* XIII (Spring, 1944), 192; *To Secure These Rights,* 4–10, 133–34, 139, 146–48, 173.
31. *To Secure These Rights,* 145.

achieve those ideals. He also gave each member a copy of the special January, 1947, issue of *Survey Graphic* on segregation. Two months later a research aide sent Stewart a memorandum that expressed his idea for an introduction to the report: "The dynamics of the postwar situation with a brief statement of the American Creed, its important and international implications today. America, assuming its role of leadership, becomes the last hope of democratic ideals." [32]

Such phrases, to be sure, do not prove the influence of Myrdal. The Swede did not invent the American creed or the American dream. The memorandum cited above, however, capitalized "Creed" as Myrdal did. Additionally, the only paper prepared by the research staff exclusively on Negroes amounted to little more than a string of quotations from the *Dilemma*. On the first page of the study, the staff included a long quotation from Myrdal, indicating that the Negro was not a dying race and would continue to be a growing minority. An explanatory note at the bottom of the first page informed the reader that all subsequent quotations came from the *Dilemma*. [33]

All told, the memorandum quoted Myrdal twenty-three times, several passages running almost half a page in length. It cited Myrdal on job discrimination, segregated housing, *de jure* segregation, justice for southern blacks, lynching, Negro disfranchisement, and other topics. The paper concluded with the following lines from Myrdal: "The Negro is an integral part of . . . the whole complex of problems in American civilization. It cannot be treated in isolation." [34]

The first draft of the committee report, fortunately, included a set of footnotes; the authors cited Myrdal twenty times, but because the text had no footnote numbers, it is difficult to determine exactly what parts of the report were inspired by the Swedish scholar. It is clear, however, that the report relied most heavily on the *Dilemma* for evidence of police brutality against Negroes and the inequalities of public services for Negroes in housing, health, jobs, and education. [35]

Since the research director was not a racial expert but, as Carr put it, a sociological "quantifier," Stewart would logically have consulted the most highly recommended secondary sources like the Myrdal report.

32. Records, Box 2; "Proceedings," Box 12, pp. 3, 42; "The Report," Joseph M. Murtha to Stewart, May 19, 1947, Box 22, all in HSTL.
33. Stewart and Herbert Kaufman, "The Negro in the United States," Box 17, HSTL.
34. *Ibid.*
35. "Citations and Authorities for Statements in the Report of the President's Committee on Civil Rights," Box 14, HSTL.

He had neither time nor adequate staff to undertake original research. The executive secretary, Carr, whose expertise was in constitutional law, borrowed heavily from the yet unpublished work of his fellow political scientist Milton Konvitz, whose book *The Constitution and Civil Rights* represented yet another example of the extensive use of Myrdal in the postwar period.[36]

In the final report, the committee relied less on Myrdal. It struck out one quotation, which said in effect that a white southerner could assault and steal from a black with impunity. The discarded passage appeared near the beginning of the report and included a description of the *Dilemma* as "a monumental study of the Negro problem." Consequently, when the committee quoted Myrdal on economics later in the report, it attached neither a title nor a description of the book; it simply gave the Swede's last name.[37]

It is not surprising that the committee, or the staff, found Myrdal's work useful. It would have been negligent if it had not. But since the report was aimed at a general audience, the committee understandably did not want to burden its short length of 178 pages with scholarly attributions. Yet it seems that the committee made a calculated effort to avoid citing sociological works in the text. Criticism of J. Edgar Hoover, the U.S. Housing Authority's complicity in restrictive covenants, and the House Un-American Activities Committee also vanished from the final report. In the first draft, the text discussed the "vicious circle" as delineated by sociologists. This section was expunged from the final report. In the second draft, the committee attributed the information on the integration of American troops in the Battle of the Bulge to sociologists. The final report excised the reference to sociologists. The closest the report came to citing sociological evidence, other than the one passage from Myrdal, was its declaration that "scientific findings" had established "the equality of groups."[38]

Besides the desire to reach a wide audience, there may be other reasons for the committee's reticence about citing racial experts in *To Secure These Rights*. Before the rise of Joseph McCarthy, a budding Red

36. Robert Carr to author, January 6, 1970; Milton Konvitz, *The Constitution and Civil Rights* (New York, 1947), 62–64, 137–41.
37. Draft copy, galley proofs, "To Secure These Rights," Box 21, Records, p. 22; "Proceedings of the Committee," September 12, 1947, Box 14, HSTL; *To Secure These Rights*, 145.
38. Report of Committee's first draft, Box 19, Records; Report of the Committee's second draft, HSTL; *To Secure These Rights*, 83, 134.

Scare arose in America. Under the leadership of the anti-Negro, anti-Semitic Martin Dies of Texas, the House Un-American Activities Committee had been harassing such racial liberals as Aubrey Williams since 1938. Two members of the Truman Committee complained that they had been tagged as Communists because of their participation on the panel. A 1947 study found that the senate feared to finance the social sciences as part of the National Science Foundation because of the perceived leftism of that field. In many conservative minds, the article maintained, the difference between sociology and socialism remained blurred.[39] Considering the furor aroused by the Supreme Court's use of sociological studies in 1954, the Truman Committee may have shown remarkable prudence in downplaying the work of race specialists.

That lawyers and legalists had a major role in editing the final report, as Carr has acknowledged, also helps explain the diminution of the sociological emphasis in the published report. More important, white southerners on the committee objected to negative treatments of the South by social scientists such as Myrdal. Frank Graham, president of the University of North Carolina, led the minority southern bloc in dissent against federally coerced desegregation. A friend of southern liberals at Chapel Hill such as Howard Odum and W. T. Couch, Graham had been subjected to an anti-Myrdal line since the early 1940s.[40]

Nevertheless, the civil rights report of 1947 contained much predigested Myrdal. "We have surveyed the flaws in the nation's record and have found them to be serious," the committee declared. "We have considered what government's appropriate role should be in securing our rights," the report continued, "and have concluded that it must assume greater leadership. We believe that the time for action is now." Coming just before the committee presented its final recommendations, this strong statement bore a striking resemblance to Myrdal's conclusion. Reformers frequently used both the *Dilemma* and *To Secure These Rights* as weapons in the civil rights movement without understanding the close kinship of the two works.[41]

39. John Salmond, *A Southern Rebel: The Life and Times of Aubrey Williams, 1890–1965* (Chapel Hill, 1983), 101; "Proceedings of the Committee," June 30, 1947, Box 14, Records, pp. 255–56, HSTL; Lundberg, "Senate Ponders Social Science," 398–99.

40. Two white southerners, Graham and Dorothy M. Tilly, served on the committee. See Proceedings of the Committee, September 12, 1947, Box 14, Records, pp. 768–69, HSTL; *To Secure These Rights*, 166–68; Sosna, *In Search of the Silent South*, 150–53.

41. *To Secure These Rights*, 149. Examples of authors unaware of the relationship

With the exception of most of the South, the civil rights report received an enthusiastic welcome. The New York *Times* promoted it on the front page in a series of eye-catching headlines ranging from towering to large and carried a first-rate abridgment of it. The demand for copies of the report quickly exhausted the supply of twenty-five thousand copies. Requests poured in from professors, journalists, senators, congressmen, State Department officials, state legislators, businessmen, ministers, and others. As they had the *Dilemma,* people summarized and distributed thousands of copies, perhaps as many as half a million. The NAACP, Americans for Democratic Action, the American Jewish Congress, and a host of other liberal groups crowed about the fortitude and foresight of the committee. The report, Roy Wilkins wrote, "was a blueprint that we used for the next two decades." [42]

The report of Truman's Commission on Higher Education paralleled the themes in the *Dilemma* and *To Secure These Rights.* The two-volume *Higher Education for American Democracy* appeared about a month and a half after the civil rights report. It, too, lacked footnotes, bibliography, and index. The two volumes focused on democratic principles and the relationship of higher education to America's role in the world. "The discrepancies between America's democratic creed and how Americans live," the report stated, "are still many and serious." The commission condemned segregation by quoting Truman's civil rights report. It declared that Negro inferiority had been disproved "by authoritative scientific study in both the fields of anthropology and psychology and in the records of educational achievement itself." The report called for federal aid to education and recommended that colleges become "laboratories of inter-race and interfaith fellowship." The New York *Times* gave the report the same extensive coverage that it accorded the earlier one on civil rights. [43]

Another racially important event of the Truman administration was

are Wofford, *Of Kennedys and Kings,* 465; and Stewart G. Cole and Mildred W. Cole, *Minorities and the American Promise: The Conflict of Principle and Practice* (New York, 1954), 21.

42. New York *Times,* October 30, 1947; Box 4, Records; John B. McConaughy to Charles E. Wilson, November 24, 1947, and Nash to Francis B. Matthews, November 26, 1947, Files of Philleo Nash, Box 24, HSTL; "Requests for Copies of the Final Report," Box 22, Records; McCoy and Ruetten, *Quest and Response,* 92–93; *Standing Fast: The Autobiography of Roy Wilkins* (New York, 1982), 200.

43. President's Commission on Higher Education, *Higher Education for American Democracy* (2 vols.; 1947), I, 8, 12, 103, II, 26, 30–32, 34, and *passim;* New York *Times,* December 16, 1947, p. 1.

the desegregation of the armed forces. By the time Dwight D. Eisenhower assumed the presidency, a quiet revolution had taken place in the
military. It occurred in orderly stages and, when possible, as Chief of
Staff General J. Lawton Collins ordered, "without publicity." Officers in
the armed forces expressed mystification at the rising black militancy
during World War II. Some whites had serious problems coping with it.
Certain base commanders tried to prohibit the circulation of black
newspapers on military bases. Other military leaders undertook various
studies of the employment of black manpower, all of which automatically received classification from "restricted" to "top secret." In 1944
the government contracted with Hollywood director Frank Capra, the
top cinematic morale builder of the war, to make a movie about blacks
in the service. *The Negro Soldier,* which became required viewing for
military personnel, presented a flattering if evasive portrait of the Afro-
American in uniform. It proved to be a popular film.[44]

The humiliation blacks suffered in the Jim Crow military combined
with the democratic rhetoric common to the war made blacks alternately cynical and hopeful. Black veterans who faced Axis guns apparently lost much of their fear of the white establishment. In the postwar
period organized blacks applied unrelenting pressure on the government
to end segregation in the armed forces, even to the point of threatening a
national boycott of the military draft.[45]

A combination of black pressure, Truman's sincere belief in equal opportunity, and national and international politics compelled the executive to act. On July 26, 1948, during a heated political campaign,
Truman issued Executive Order 9981, which decreed that "there shall
be equality of treatment and opportunity in the Armed services without
regard to race, color, religion, or national origin." Although the order
did not explicitly condemn segregation, the president established a
committee, popularly known as the Fahy Committee, to examine ways
to implement his directive effectively. Truman's order set the stage for
the integration of American military forces.[46]

---

44. Collins quoted in Morris J. MacGregor, Jr., *Integration of the Armed Forces,
1940–1965* (Washington, 1981), 450; Dalfiume, " 'Forgotten Years' of the Negro Revolution," 100–101; Thomas Cripps, *Slow Fade to Black: The Negro in American Film,
1900–1942* (New York, 1977), 379–80.

45. Bowker, *Out of Uniform,* 214; Dalfiume, *Desegregation of the U.S. Armed
Forces,* 105–11; *Time,* April 12, 1948, p. 41; Charles E. Silberman, *Crisis in Black and
White* (New York, 1964), 60–61.

46. Quoted in Richard M. Dalfiume, "The Fahy Committee and Desegregation of the

Myrdal's study and social science scholarship in general did not play a direct or crucial role in the desegregation of the armed forces, but both contributed significantly. Before Truman issued his order in 1948, several individuals with awakened social consciences and social science knowledge on race had labored to change the racial configuration of the military. Donald Young, Charles Dollard, Samuel Stouffer, and Arnold Rose, among others, left the Myrdal project to study the race problem in the service. As head of the joint Army-Navy Committee on Welfare and Recreation, Young urged the desegregation of post facilities. He also collaborated with Dollard on editing the script for the film *The Negro Soldier*. Stouffer's military hitch provided the genesis of his classic sociological study *The American Soldier*.[47]

Secretary of the Navy James V. Forrestal and his able assistant Adlai Stevenson had already moved their service toward integration during the war. Lester Granger, Forrestal's civilian aide from the National Urban League and, like the secretary, an alumnus of Dartmouth College, apparently influenced the navy's course. Secretary of the Air Force Stuart Symington had also initiated an integrationist policy on his own. He, in fact, acted as a catalyst for the integration of all the armed forces. This smooth diplomat, later a senator from Missouri, had two grandfathers who fought for the Confederacy. He nevertheless helped clear the way on Capitol Hill by convincing powerful congressmen such as Carl Vinson of the House Armed Services Committee that integration of the military was practical and inevitable. According to contemporary reports, Symington often lectured the Pentagon on the necessity of integration and on the wisdom of Myrdal as well. The *Dilemma* made a deep impression on the air force secretary. "What determined me many years ago was a quotation from Bernard Shaw in Myrdal's book," he wrote David Niles, "which went something like this—'First the American white man makes the negro clean his shoes, then criticizes him for being a bootblack.'"[48]

Armed Forces," *Historian*, XXXI (November, 1968), 1; President's Committee on Equality of Treatment and Opportunity in the Armed Forces, *Freedom to Serve* (1950).

47. Ulysses G. Lee, *The Employment of Negro Troops*, in the series *The United States in World War II: Special Studies* (Washington, 1966), 159, 387–89; MacGregor, *Integration of the Armed Forces*, 613–14; Samuel Stouffer et al., *The American Soldier* (2 vols.; Princeton, 1949).

48. Lee Nichols, *Breakthrough on the Color Front* (New York, 1954), 46–47; Noel F. Parrish, "The Segregation of Negroes in the Army Air Forces" (Air University thesis, (Maxwell Field, Ala., 1947), 94–95; Dalfiume, *Desegregation of the U.S. Armed Forces*,

During the early 1940s many white officers actually doubted that blacks could fly airplanes. After studying the *Dilemma* thoroughly and consulting anthropologists from the University of Chicago, Captain Noel F. Parrish of Kentucky decided that pigmentation was no deterrent to piloting. Under the Kentuckian's guidance a newly established flight school for Afro-Americans at Tuskegee, Alabama, produced the all-black Ninety-ninth Pursuit Squadron, which gained combat distinction in Europe. When tests of Parrish's black cadets showed quicker reflex times than those of white New England cadets, a black southerner quipped: "I always knew those Yankees were slow." [49]

In 1947 Parrish, now promoted to colonel, attended the Air University in Alabama, where he wrote a 104-page thesis called "The Segregation of Negroes in the Army Air Forces." In it the officer charged that the Pentagon's preference for segregation had been based on preconceived notions rather than on the "dispassionate analysis of fact." Parrish used Myrdal's study as a model for his thesis. Although he drew upon other sociological sources, he by far resorted to the Swede most often. He cited Myrdal fourteen times, notably to debunk the popular concept of "race," to illustrate the Negro's sensitivity to discrimination, and to drive home the effects of segregation on foreign policy. He concluded his study with a quotation of almost two hundred words from the *Dilemma*. The final sentence of the passage read: "Had the improvements [in the Negro's military status] come, not mainly as a result of outside pressure from Negroes and others, but because of the action of military leaders who grasped the deeper implications of this War, they would have been much greater and more significant, not only for the Negro, but for the nation as a whole." Moved to the Pentagon in the early 1950s, Parrish found himself permanently labeled as a "Negro expert." Air force personnel used his thesis as a guide in carrying out the air force policy of desegregation in the late 1940s and early 1950s. [50]

Unlike Forrestal, Symington, and Parrish, most military officers needed a substantial shove in the direction of integration. They considered sociological studies of blacks irrelevant. The army particularly rejected the idea that the armed forces should serve as a laboratory for

178; Jean Begeman, "A Military Bill of Rights," *New Republic,* August 8, 1949, p. 11; Symington to author, May 15, 1968; quotation in MacGregor, *Integration of the Armed Forces,* 338.

49. Parrish, "Segregation of Negroes in the Army Air Forces," 9.

50. *Ibid.,* iv, 6–7, 9, 12, 24, 26, 32, 42, 61, 81, 90, 104; Parrish to author, May 18, 1970. The passage Parrish quoted comes from *AD,* 422–23.

social reform. In the hearings before the Fahy Committee in 1949, Symington and Forrestal continued to speak out forcefully for integration. As had the authors of the civil rights report, the Fahy Committee of 1950 used the data collected by sociologists on the encouraging, if unplanned, integration during the Battle of the Bulge. The work of sociologists also helped convince a recalcitrant army that desegregation would not impair "military efficiency." Social scientists soon learned that the army cared little for arguments that stressed moral, economic, or foreign policy factors.[51]

When the Korean War broke out, the army sent a team of social scientists to the Far East to analyze the crisis-inspired integration of troops. Leo Bogart, director of project Clear, has divulged the full story of his adventure with the army bureaucracy and with trying to do scientific research on the front lines. In *Social Research and the Desegregation of the U.S. Army* (1969), Bogart claimed that the army destroyed masses of documents concerning project Clear and did not declassify what remained until 1966. Because of the suddenness of the assignment and because Bogart and his assistants were not specialists in American race relations, his task proved hectic. Bogart recalled that he and his collaborators barely had time to consult a few standard sources like the *Dilemma* and Stouffer's *American Soldier.* He assessed Myrdal's book as "brilliant."[52]

In the end, two wars and political pressure, not social science findings, provided the principal levers to integrate the armed forces. The army continued to drag its feet on integration outside Korea, even though the Fahy Committee's report of 1950 concluded that segregation made equal opportunity impossible. Project Clear, however, provided evidence that integration furthered military efficiency, boosted black morale, and did not incite the feared white reaction predicted by the army. The most complete historical account of desegregation of the military to date concluded that project Clear, above all, helped absolve the traditional army and southern congressmen like Vinson from the

51. Testimony of Major General John E. Dalquist, January 13, 1949, Records of the Fahy Committee, Box 10, HSTL; *Army Talk* (Washington, 1947), Circular 170, p. 7; Leo Bogart (ed.), *Social Research and the Desegregation of the U.S. Army* (Chicago, 1969), 22; Dalfiume, "The Fahy Committee and Desegregation," 2, 5, 9, 19–20.

52. Introduction in Bogart (ed.), *Social Science and the Desegregation of the U.S. Army,* 4–5, 23–25, 35–39. The Pentagon cleared a brief article on Clear by Bogart, "The Army and Its Negro Soldiers," *Reporter,* December 30, 1954, pp. 8–11.

charge that they had made a crucial defense decision based on social and political factors rather than on "objective, scientific terms." [53]

The commander in chief of the armed forces, of course, deserved some of the credit for the racial progress brought about during his administration. How much is difficult to determine precisely. Many of Truman's political foes accused the president of expediency on civil rights. Historians have differed markedly in their assessments of Truman's motivations and accomplishments on Negro rights, not to mention civil liberties in general. [54] Alonzo Hamby, one of Truman's staunchest defenders, conceded that the Missourian's southern heritage was too strong for him to favor social integration. Hamby argued, however, that Truman's strong convictions about the Bill of Rights and equal opportunity led to considerable progress in the area of civil rights. With his eye on international politics, Truman told Jonathan Daniels, "The top dog in a world which is over half-colored ought to clean his own house." The civil rights report of 1947 was so provocative that some of the president's advisers wanted him to bury it. Truman not only gave the report his public blessing, but on February 2, 1948, he sent Congress a far-reaching civil rights bill based on its recommendations. In his last message to Congress in 1953, the man from Independence assured the nation that there had been "a great awakening of the American conscience on the issue of civil rights." [55]

Truman's deeply felt democratic convictions made him a prime candidate for the "dilemma" that Myrdal so artfully articulated. John Fischer, who as a contributing editor to *Harper's* interviewed Truman several times, claimed that the president studied Myrdal's book. The Truman scholar Richard S. Kirkendall suggested that the president's

53. MacGregor, *Integration of the Armed Forces*, 442.

54. Three of the works basically positive about Truman's civil rights efforts are McCoy and Ruetten, *Quest and Response;* Dalfiume, *Desegregation of the U.S. Armed Forces;* and Alonzo L. Hamby, *Beyond the New Deal: Harry S. Truman and American Liberalism* (New York, 1973). Works more skeptical about Truman's motives and accomplishments are William C. Berman, *The Politics of Civil Rights in the Truman Administration* (Columbus, Ohio, 1970); and Barton J. Bernstein, "The Ambiguous Legacy: The Truman Administration and Civil Rights," in Bernstein (ed.), *The Politics of Civil Rights in the Truman Administration* (Chicago, 1970).

55. Alonzo L. Hamby, *The Imperial Years: The U.S. Since 1939* (New York, 1976), 148; Truman quoted in McCoy, Ruetten, and Fuchs (eds.), *Conference of Scholars,* 82; and in David S. Horton (ed.), *Freedom and Equality: Addresses by Harry S. Truman* (Columbia, Mo., 1960), 11.

reading appetite probably had been exaggerated but conceded that aides may have briefed him on the book. It is certain, at any rate, that Myrdal, in his capacity as executive secretary of the Economic Commission for Europe, visited Truman at the White House on June 20, 1949. The foreigner autographed a copy of the *Dilemma* as follows: "To Harry S. Truman, President of the United States, Defender of Human Equality." The former Swedish senator had already struck up an acquaintance with the Missouri legislator during the Carnegie project. Myrdal remembered that in 1949 they discussed civil rights at length and agreed that "big reforms" were needed.[56]

Young Hubert H. Humphrey of Minnesota also agreed that big reforms were urgent. In 1948 this neoabolitionist electrified the Democratic Convention with an eloquent speech in which he counseled the South to step out of the shadow of states' rights and walk into the sunshine of human rights. Before entering politics, Humphrey read Myrdal and came away deeply impressed with the Swede's interpretation of the caste system's impact on blacks. Whether Myrdal's book induced his dilemma or whether he read it because he already had a dilemma constitutes a problem of cause and effect that defies an easy answer. In any case, the energetic mayor of Minneapolis exhibited the influence of Myrdal's conceptual framework and rhetoric in a 1947 speech in which he advocated a fair employment law. "Our conscience in America has become corroded and encrusted with a bitter feeling of guilt," he moralized, "because we profess a belief in justice and equality of opportunity, but we practice injustice and discrimination. . . . The outlawing of injustice in employment by adequate and effective legislation," he declared, "is a major step in lifting this burden of guilt from our American conscience."[57]

Whatever index one uses, the idea of racial equality came of age in the 1940s, affecting not only national but local, state, and international events. Congress coldly rejected Truman's request for a permanent Fair Employment Practices Committee, but by the time he left office, seven states had FEPCs. Connecticut, which passed such a law in 1947, issued

56. John Fischer, "Western Intellectuals vs. Myrdal's Brutal Facts," *Harper's,* June, 1968, p. 12; Fischer to author, June 18, 1968; Richard S. Kirkendall to author, November 7, 1969; President's Appointment File, 1945–53, vol. 5, HSTL; autographed copy of the *Dilemma* is in the Truman Library; Myrdal to author, January 29, 1970.

57. "Humphrey in Minnesota," *New Republic,* October 18, 1948, p. 8; Humphrey to author, November 13, 1969; Humphrey's speech quoted in Peter Kellogg, "Civil Rights Consciousness in the 1940's," *Historian,* XLII (November, 1979), 39.

a publication that praised the Myrdal report as "the most comprehensive and definitive study" of the race question. At the international level, in 1950 the United Nations Education, Scientific, and Cultural Organization (UNESCO), based in Paris, released a statement on race. An eight-man team of international scholars, including the former Myrdal collaborators E. Franklin Frazier and Ashley Montagu, reported that "race" was a myth and held that scientific evidence supported the "ethic of universal brotherhood." Montagu was the primary drafter of the resolution. Myrdal served as one of the international, prepublication critics of the UNESCO statement.[58]

This chapter has suggested some of the many ways that Myrdal's ideas and rhetoric spread across the land in the Truman period. One area of key importance, however, has been omitted: a decade of civil rights cases by the Supreme Court, which culminated in 1954 with the *Brown* decision. Here the Truman administration would again exert executive power on behalf of black petitioners. And here, too, Myrdal would exert a significant impact on events that warrants further treatment.

58. Leonard Broom and Norval D. Glenn, *Transformation of the Negro Americans* (New York, 1965), 49–50; Paul H. Norgren, "Fair Employment Practice Laws—Experience, Effects, Prospects," in Arthur M. Ross and Herbert Hill (eds.), *Employment, Race and Poverty* (New York, 1967), 568; Connecticut State Inter-Racial Commission, *Inter-Group Relations: Bibliography* (Hartford, 1948), 53; Leo Kuper (ed.), *Race, Science and Society* (Paris, 1975), 343–47.

VI

The Dilemma in Court:
Myrdal and the Civil Rights Cases,
1944—1954

In the historic *Brown* case of 1954, Chief Justice Earl Warren declared that segregated schools psychologically harmed black children. As evidence for this crucial assertion, the chief justice, speaking
for a unanimous Supreme Court, alluded to "modern authority." Warren
specified this authority more fully in the controversial footnote 11, in
which he cited seven social science studies. The famous footnote concluded with the words: "And see generally Myrdal, *An American Dilemma* (1944)."[1]

Although the concept and practice of "sociological jurisprudence"
had existed for roughly half a century, Warren's explicit use of extralegal
evidence in a crucial decision on the emotional issue of race set off a
heated debate about the relationship of social science to fundamental
law. Shocked and angered, segregationists lashed out at the Court. They
charged that it had replaced sixty years of legal precedents with the spu-
rious doctrines of the behavioral sciences. Senator Richard B. Russell
of Georgia characterized the Court's ruling as "a flagrant abuse of judicial power" and denounced the justices as "amateur psychologists."
Critics made snide remarks about the "nine sociologists in robes."
James Eastland of Mississippi introduced a resolution in the Senate calling for an investigation of Myrdal and his associates, whom he suggested were a part of a worldwide Communist conspiracy. Even some
liberals who agreed with the Court's ruling confided that the opinion
read more like a sociological tract than a legal document.[2]

1. *Brown v. Board of Education of Topeka*, 347 U.S. 483, 494.
2. Nashville *Tennessean*, May 18, 1954; *Congressional Record*, 83d Cong., 2d Sess.,
6748; Grover C. Hall, *U.S. News & World Report*, August 3, 1956, pp. 85–86; *Con-*

Because Chief Justice Warren dismissed much of the perplexing historical and legal evidence in the *Brown* opinion as ambiguous or inconclusive, social science evidence became, according to one scholar of the Court, not only crucial but "compelling."[3] Although that point is arguable, the *Dilemma* certainly became a formidable source for reformers in the decade of civil rights legislation. By 1954 Myrdal's name had become a household word in the halls of justice.

Regardless of the intrinsic strengths of Myrdal's study, its impact emanated in large part from its superb timing. As already shown, the publication of the *Dilemma* coincided with many factors that hastened racial change. It materialized about the time that NAACP legal strategists began an all-out effort to achieve equal rights for blacks through the courts by using sociological evidence in a more salient way.[4] Since the *Dilemma* was the best and most complete study of race relations during this period, it understandably received heavy use in the major civil rights cases.

Even judges and lawyers, as specialized as they may be, could not remain oblivious to Myrdal. In 1944 some of the legal elite undoubtedly were introduced to the Myrdal study by Charles E. Wyzanski, Jr., a federal district judge, who wrote a six-page review of the *Dilemma* for the *Harvard Law Review*. After giving proper attention to Myrdal's main theme, the jurist stressed the Swede's criticism of the courts and the police in the South. Wyzanski pointed out that Myrdal made it perfectly clear why blacks often regarded the law as the enemy. Admitting that the *Dilemma* contained no legal panaceas, the judge nevertheless announced that Myrdal had many constructive ideas such as the employment of blacks in police work and the expansion of legal aid societies. He expressed the wish that Myrdal's book would receive a wide circulation among legislators, employers, union leaders, teachers, and students. Presumably, Wyzanski did not exclude lawyers and judges from this educational opportunity.[5]

The eminent jurist Felix Frankfurter not only knew Myrdal's work

---

gressional Record, 84th Cong., 1st Sess., 6963–64. For criticism from a liberal, see James Reston, "A Sociological Decision," *New York Times,* May 18, 1954.

3. Paul L. Rosen, *The Supreme Court and Social Science* (Urbana, Ill., 1972), 151–55, 170–72.

4. Sitkoff, *Struggle for Black Equality,* 17–19; Randall W. Bland, *Private Pressure on Public Law: The Legal Career of Justice Thurgood Marshall* (Port Washington, N.Y., 1973), 38–39.

5. Charles E. Wyzanski, Jr., Review of *AD,* in *Harvard Law Review,* LVIII (1944), 285–91.

well but he knew the foreign author personally. In his book *Inside U.S.A.*, John Gunther divulged that Frankfurter swore that Myrdal's book was "indispensable" for understanding the race problem. Myrdal and Frankfurter had become fast friends during the Scandinavian's early visits to America. While directing the Carnegie project, Myrdal had carried on long discussions about the race problem with the Supreme Court justice. In 1942 Myrdal listed Frankfurter as a reference in his effort to obtain a wartime clearance from the State Department for a priority flight to Sweden.[6]

As a believer in judicial restraint and a longtime student of legal realism, the well-read Frankfurter had his own dilemma concerning the use of social science in the courtroom. He considered the relatively young behavioral sciences to be immature and untrustworthy. Yet he realized that in the fast-changing world, judicial cases could not be confined to legal precedents alone.[7] The Bostonian's mixed emotions about the social sciences and the law will get more attention when the *Brown* case is discussed. Suffice it to say here that the well-known legalist deserved primary responsibility for footnote 11 in the 1954 decision against segregation in public schools.

Had the nine men on the Court examined Myrdal's book closely, they would have found some provocative comments on the judiciary and race relations. "The Supreme Court," Myrdal wrote, "is seemingly changing its attitude and is again looking more to the spirit of the Reconstruction Amendments and not only to their possible loopholes." Emphasizing the importance of the ballot for blacks, the economist predicted that the Court would soon declare the white primary unconstitutional. Myrdal argued throughout his book that segregation kept Negroes down, but he also advised that the Jim Crow system was vulnerable. "The whole system of discrimination in education in the South," he maintained, "is not only tremendously harmful to the Negroes but it is flagrantly illegal, and can easily be so proven in the courts."[8]

As Myrdal predicted in 1942, the Supreme Court invalidated the white primary in *Smith* v. *Allwright* (1944). Although potentially strong sociological arguments for Negro enfranchisement existed— Myrdal made these points—the Court and the legal staff of the NAACP

6. John Gunther, *Inside U.S.A.* (New York, 1947), 683, 926; Myrdal to the author, February 23, 1984; Myrdal to Charles Dollard, July 7, 1942, Negro Study, roll 2.

7. Kluger, *Simple Justice*, 685; Archibald MacLeish and E. F. Prichard (eds.), *Law and Politics: Occasional Papers of Felix Frankfurter, 1913–1938* (New York, 1962), 290, 296; Rosen, *Supreme Court and Social Science*, 111.

8. *AD*, 342, 516, 629.

adhered primarily to legal reasoning in the white primary case. But they would not do so in future cases such as *Shelley* v. *Kraemer* (1948), *Henderson* v. *United States* (1950), *Sweatt* v. *Painter* (1950), *McLaurin* v. *Oklahoma* (1950), and *Brown* v. *Board of Education* (1954). In these landmark cases, social science, and therefore Myrdal, would play an increasingly significant role in legal articles, court testimony, legal briefs, and judges' opinions.[9]

By the end of World War II, demographic changes had brought a crisis in black housing in the cities, which occasioned the initiation of several court cases challenging the legality of restrictive covenants, a device that preserved segregated neighborhoods. Racially restrictive covenants, which usually stipulated that a white owner could not sell property to a nonwhite, had been upheld in 1926 by the Supreme Court. In 1948 in *Shelley* v. *Kraemer*, however, the Court decided that judicial enforcement of restrictive covenants constituted state action and thus violated the Fourteenth Amendment. Although Chief Justice Fred M. Vinson's opinion approached the subject on the narrowest of legal grounds, behavioral science, through testimony, briefs, and, particularly, the opinion of a federal judge, entered the case in a significantly new way.[10]

At first Thurgood Marshall, the head of the NAACP legal staff, hesitated to intervene in the various covenant cases at the local level. The local and state courts had all ruled against the black litigants. In addition, in 1945 the Supreme Court had refused to review a Washington, D.C., case. Marshall doubted that the Court was ready to disturb the 1926 precedent upholding restrictive covenants. But local groups continued to file suits. When a St. Louis lawyer announced plans to appeal to the Supreme Court in the *Shelley* case, Marshall decided to bring in the NAACP. He feared the case might be botched and the momentum of the movement retarded.[11]

On January 26, 1947, Marshall and other civil rights leaders met

9. *Smith* v. *Allwright*, 321 U.S. 649; *Shelley* v. *Kraemer*, 334 U.S. 1; *Henderson* v. *U.S.*, 339 U.S. 816; *Sweatt* v. *Painter*, 334 U.S. 629; *McLaurin* v. *Oklahoma State Regents*, 339 U.S. 637.

10. *Corrigan* v. *Buckley*, 271 U.S. 323 (1926); *Shelley* v. *Kraemer*, 334 U.S. 1.

11. *Mays* v. *Burgess*, 147 F.2d 869, 873 (U.S.C.A. 1945); Marshall to George Vaughn, September 23, 1947, "Restrictive Covenants—Shelley v. Kraemer," Box 144, Group II, Series B, NAACP Papers, Library of Congress; all subsequent citations from these papers are from Group II, Series B; Marshall to David M. Grant, September 23, 1947, *ibid.*; James Bush to Marshall, September 29, 1947, *ibid.*; Marshall to Herman Dreer, December 5, 1947, *ibid.*; Kluger, *Simple Justice*, 249.

at Howard University to discuss future strategy in the covenant cases. The chief attorney of the NAACP agreed that if they were to be successful, "the next record on which we apply for *certiorari* [an appeal] would have to contain something substantially stronger." That something extra turned out to be a massive infusion of social science evidence into the NAACP's arguments against segregated housing. Black planners, therefore, resolved to wage a campaign, with the help of friendly editors, to flood the legal, scholarly, and popular journals with articles condemning restrictive covenants. They selected a committee to coordinate the effort.[12]

Before long the results of the NAACP endeavor became apparent as several articles critical of housing covenants appeared in a wide variety of publications. Even before the coordination efforts of the NAACP began, Harold I. Kahen published a model article for open housing in the *University of Chicago Law Review*. Kahen attacked racial covenants on sociological grounds, insisting that they had grave social consequences for all of society. He declared that the legality of such covenants should not be decided in a "sociological vacuum." The author cited the *Dilemma* and *The Negro's Share* by Myrdal's Swedish colleague Richard Sterner as authoritative sources documenting the social harm of restrictive housing agreements. Kahen concluded that it was time for lawyers to include "relevant sociological data" in briefs to demonstrate the urgency of the situation. Many of the articles that followed Kahen's place took a similar tack and made liberal use of Myrdal and sociological arguments.[13] If the Court did not follow the election returns, civil rights advocates hoped that the nine top jurists followed the legal journals.

12. Clement E. Vose, "NAACP Strategy in the Covenant Cases," *Western Reserve Law Review*, VI (1955), 120–21, 132–33.
13. Harold I. Kahen, "Validity of Anti-Negro Restrictive Covenants: A Reconsideration of the Problem," *University of Chicago Law Review*, XII (1945), 198, 206–207. See also Clifford K. Moore, "Anti-Negro Restrictive Covenants and Judicial Enforcement Constituting State Action Under the Fourteenth Amendment," *Temple Law Review*, XXI (1947), 140–42; Notes, "Current Legal Attacks on Racial Restrictive Covenants," *University of Chicago Law Review*, XV (1947), 200–202; Irwin M. Taylor, "The Racial Restrictive Covenant in Light of the Equal Protection Clause," *Brooklyn Law Review*, XIV (1947), 82–83; Isaac N. Groner and David M. Helfeld, "Race Discrimination in Housing," *Yale Law Journal*, LVII (1948), 426. Books and nonlegal articles also addressed the topic; see Loren Miller, "Covenants for Exclusion," *Survey Graphic*, XXXVI (October, 1947), 541–59; Kenesaw M. Landis, *Segregation in Washington* (Washington, 1948), 21; Herman H. Long and Charles S. Johnson, *People vs. Property: Race Restrictive Covenants in Housing* (Nashville, 1947).

Even before the beginning of the NAACP's sociological warfare on restrictive covenants, a witness had already introduced Myrdal's name into the court record. In 1945 in the *Shelley* case, Fannie Cook testified concerning the malevolence of housing agreements. She listed her qualifications for testifying as follows: she was a member of the Race Relations Committee in St. Louis, she was involved in social work in black neighborhoods, and she had reviewed *An American Dilemma* for the St. Louis Public Library. Either the novelty of the Swedish name or a typographical error caused the court clerk to record the author of the book as "Myrdol." [14]

A few months later, in *Hurd* v. *Hodge,* a case the Supreme Court reviewed along with *Shelley,* the brilliant black lawyer Charles Houston introduced several social scientists as witnesses. Although the district and appeals courts in Washington, D.C., upheld restrictive covenants, the use of extralegal evidence impressed Judge Henry White Edgerton. In the 1945 case of *Mays* v. *Burgess,* which the Supreme Court refused to review, Judge Edgerton of the Court of Appeals in Washington, D.C., wrote a dissenting opinion in which he used government housing data to support his argument against racial covenants. Subsequently, he discovered the Myrdal report, which bolstered his sociological evidence considerably. In his 1947 dissent, Edgerton presented four pages of socioeconomic argument against restrictive agreements. He not only cited Myrdal six times, but he quoted the following passage from the *Dilemma:* "If the Court should follow up its action of declaring all local laws to segregate Negroes unconstitutional by declaring illegal also the private restrictive covenants, segregation would be nearly doomed." Additionally, the judge appended a 350-word footnote that explained the origins and the authority of the Myrdal study. Surely it was one of the most thorough introductions ever given a sociological treatise in a legal opinion. [15]

Judge Edgerton's dissent and Houston's use of sociological witnesses in the Washington cases impressed Thurgood Marshall and others involved with the civil rights cases. Loring B. Moore, a lawyer with experience in restrictive covenant cases, advised Marshall that Edgerton's dissent should be used as a model for NAACP briefs when the housing cases were appealed. Marshall ultimately selected the *Hurd* and

14. Transcript of court record, *Shelley* v. *Kraemer,* U.S. Supreme Court: Records and Briefs, Vol. 334, Pt. 1, Library of Congress, hereinafter cited as Records and Briefs.

15. Genna Rae McNeil, *Groundwork: Charles Hamilton Houston and the Struggle for Civil Rights* (Philadelphia, 1983), 178–82; *Mays* v. *Burgess,* 147 F.2d 869, 873–78; *Hurd* v. *Hodge,* 162 F.2d 242, 244–45 (1974).

Uricolo cases, which Houston had handled, for appeal to the Supreme Court. The Washington cases met Marshall's new criteria of having employed " 'socio-economic argument' . . . in the record itself and not just in the briefs." [16]

Among the many housing cases cropping up across the country, Marshall looked for a couple more that could be appealed profitably to the highest court. A case in Michigan, where the state supreme court had recently upheld the restrictive covenants, provided a likely test case. One civil rights lawyer from Chicago, however, warned Marshall that the Michigan case, *McGhee* v. *Sipes,* would not furnish a good test case because "the record was not sufficiently replete with sociological data." Similarly, Clifford Forster, the acting director of the American Civil Liberties Union, complained that the argument in the *Shelley* case in St. Louis was sociologically deficient. Forster maintained that unless the *Shelley* brief contained "sufficient sociological data, a 'Brandeis' brief approach," it would be disastrous to take it to the Supreme Court. [17]

Marshall agreed that it would be risky to take an "unqualified" case to the Supreme Court. On July 10, 1947, he requested that all the lawyers working on housing cases meet in New York on August 30 to discuss briefs and strategy. Marshall informed Charles Houston and Loren Miller, a noted black civil rights lawyer from California, that until the New York meeting, all lawyers should "do independent research on the sociological arguments, as well as the legal arguments." [18]

It is hardly surprising, then, that substantial sociological evidence appeared in the record and the briefs of the housing cases sent to the Supreme Court. The NAACP brief in the *Shelley* case, for instance, directed the Court's attention to seven works on housing which the petitioners considered to be "authoritative publications." The *Dilemma* headed the list. The brief also contained an appendix entitled "Observations of Myrdal on Housing Segregation of Negroes in the United States." The Negro litigants made like use of Myrdal in *McGhee* v. *Sipes,* a companion case to *Shelley,* which originated in Detroit, Michigan. [19]

16. Moore to Marshall, November 8, 1947, "Restrictive Covenants—McGhee v. Sipes," Box 144, NAACP Papers; Marshall to Sidney A. Jones, January 31, 1947, *ibid.*

17. Sidney A. Jones to Marshall, January 23, 1947, *ibid.;* Forster to Marion Wynn Perry, April 3, 1947, "Restrictive Covenants—Shelley v. Kraemer," *ibid.*

18. Marshall to Houston and Miller, July 10, 1947, "Restrictive Covenants—McGhee v. Sipes," NAACP Papers. See also Marion Wynn Perry to E. F. Schietinger, May 17, 1947, "Restrictive Covenants—Shelley v. Kraemer," *ibid.*

19. Records and Briefs, Vol. 334, pt. 2, pp. 54–55; *ibid.,* 35.

In the two Washington cases appealed to the Supreme Court, *Hurd* v. *Hodge* and *Urciolo* v. *Hodge,* the petitioners drafted a consolidated brief of 132 pages. The authors of the brief acknowledged the aid of the American Council on Race Relations, the Julius Rosenwald Fund, Robert C. Weaver, Charles S. Johnson, Louis Wirth (a future member of the president's cabinet and two Myrdal collaborators), and other prominent social scientists in preparing the document. Roughly half legal and half nonlegal in argument, the brief cited Myrdal six times. It included the following excerpt from Frederick Keppel's foreword to the *Dilemma:* "It is a day when the eyes of men of all races the world over are turned upon us to see how [we] are dealing *at home* with a major problem of race relations." [20]

The quotation suggests why the *Dilemma* had greater utility for civil rights litigants than did most behavioral science works. The borrowed passage from the *Dilemma* in no way drew upon empirical social science evidence but instead used the sponsor's preachy advertisement for the Carnegie project. Legal petitioners did, however, make use of the hard data in the *Dilemma*. Myrdal's study differed from other books not only because of its widespread recognition as a sociological classic but for its numerous flights of hortatory eloquence focusing on the white conscience, particularly in the final chapter, "America Again at the Crossroads." Here, in plain but moving language, the Swede shrewdly appealed to the American sense of mission. As Myrdal put it, the future international stature of the United States hinged on whether the nation solved its race problem in a fair and democratic way.

The *Dilemma* proved especially useful to the numerous civil rights organizations that filed *amici curiae,* or friend-of-the-court briefs, in the various cases. In *Shelley* alone, eighteen agencies presented briefs on behalf of blacks. So many groups submitted briefs, in fact, that the Court temporarily restricted their use in 1949. These briefs not only provide evidence of Myrdal's influence but are revealing social documents for the historian of race relations. They took on the spirit of civic pleas rather than the tenor of a legal document. Thurgood Marshall came to view them as important supplements to the normal legal briefs. The *amici* briefs, Marshall explained, emphasized the NAACP's "new angle." Charles Abrams, a coordinator of the briefs, advised the American Jewish Congress to strengthen its pleadings by appealing to the conscience of the Court. "Use the relevant references by Gunnar Myrdal," Abrams counseled. [21]

20. *Ibid.,* pp. 49, 59, 61, 75, 85–86.
21. Frederick Bernays Wiener, "The Supreme Court's New Rules," *Harvard Law Re-*

The organizations filing briefs in the various housing cases did not ignore his advice. In the *Shelley* case the American Federation of Labor, for example, drafted a thirty-seven-page brief based primarily on the 1940 census and a number of sociological works. It cited Myrdal twelve times and quoted him liberally in the text. Other sources frequently cited were Charles S. Johnson's *Patterns of Negro Segregation*, a Carnegie monograph, and the president's civil rights report of 1947.[22]

Although it is difficult to discern whether the numerous briefs affected the conscience of the Court, it is fairly certain that the justices did not ignore the friend-of-the-court brief by the United States Department of Justice. This historic brief in the *Shelley* case, signed by Tom Clark, the attorney general and a future justice of the Supreme Court, marked the first time the government had intervened in such a way for blacks in the twentieth century. Among other things, the brief indicated the growing political power of Afro-Americans and Truman's unprecedented use of executive action in the civil rights area. Important enough to enjoy commercial publication, the government's brief appealed to democratic emotions and delved deeply into the sociological arguments against segregated housing. Only one section of five in the seventy-four-page brief dealt with the constitutional issue involved. Section headings such as "Public Policy Considerations," "The Nation's Responsibility," and "Restraints and Alienation" pointed up the broad, nonlegal approach of the brief. Getting its Myrdal through Judge Edgerton's previously mentioned dissent, the brief quoted the Swede's forecast that segregated housing in the North would be virtually doomed if the Court would only act.[23]

In 1950 the NAACP won three major cases before the Supreme Court. In *Henderson* v. *United States* the Court ruled that segregation of blacks in dining cars by the use of curtains was unconstitutional on interstate railroads. In *Sweatt* v. *Painter* and *McLaurin* v. *Oklahoma*, the Court desegregated the law school at the University of Texas and a graduate school at the University of Oklahoma. As in the housing cases, social science played a prominent role. The friend-of-the-court brief by

view, LXVIII (1954), 80; Vose, "NAACP Strategy," 133, 136; Marshall to William Strong, September 23, 1947, Marshall to William K. Newman, November 20, 1947, both in "Restrictive Covenants—McGhee v. Sipes," Box 144, NAACP Papers.

22. *Shelley* v. *Kraemer*, Records and Briefs, Vol. 334, Pt. 3, *passim*.

23. Tom Clark and Philip Perlman (solicitor general), *Prejudice and Property: Historic Brief Against Racial Covenants* (Washington, 1948), 11–15, 17, 77, 81. Clark received letters from many groups asking him to file a brief in the housing cases, letters in "Restrictive Covenants—McGhee v. Sipes," Box 144, NAACP Papers.

the Justice Department in the *Henderson* case cited Myrdal seven times, more than any other source. It referred to the *Dilemma* as an authoritative source for the following assertions: racial segregation imposes a badge of inferiority on Negroes; whites' beliefs about Negro blood are mystical and irrational; social rights cannot be separated from civil rights; and segregation laws lend respectability to discrimination in the private sphere of life. The import of the brief clearly went beyond the scope of segregated dining cars.[24]

The NAACP also looked beyond the segregation of railroad cars. After World War II black strategists marshaled their forces to seek equal opportunity in professional and graduate schools. Earlier efforts by the NAACP in the 1930s had led to the establishment of some separate black graduate schools in the Upper South and border states. In the *Sweatt* case the NAACP contested whether a hastily established black law school equaled the white one in Austin. As in the housing cases, black petitioners gave free rein to the sociological emphasis in their briefs and employed several behavioral scientists to testify in court. From the beginning of the *Sweatt* case, Marshall reckoned that sociological argument would be vital. In April, 1947, Marshall wrote to William Hastie: "We are . . . contemplating putting Otto Klineberg to testify as to the . . . evils of segregation. We are also contemplating putting on anthropologists to show that there is no difference between folks."[25]

As in the housing cases, the NAACP planted articles about segregated schooling in journals that could later be cited in briefs. One such article in the *Yale Law Journal* declared that the separate-but-equal doctrine had become "untenable in light of our present knowledge of psychology and sociology." The author cited Myrdal six times.[26]

When the NAACP lost the *Sweatt* case in Texas, it appealed to the Supreme Court. The legal staff presented a seventy-five-page brief that was divided evenly between legal and extralegal argument. "Many recent studies," the document proclaimed, "have pointed up the debilitat-

24. *Henderson* v. *U.S.*, Records and Briefs, Vol. 339, Pt. 3, pp. 27, 29, 32, 43, 45, 55.

25. *Missouri ex. rel. Gaines* v. *Canada*, 305 U.S. 337 (1938); Thurgood Marshall to William H. Hastie, April 3, 1947, "Sweatt v. Painter—Correspondence," Box 204, NAACP Papers; (Marshall) Memorandum to Editors (of briefs), April 6, 1949, "Education Conferences 1948–49," Box 71, *ibid.*

26. Notes, "Segregation in Public Schools—A Violation of 'Equal Protection of the Laws,'" *Yale Law Journal*, LXI (1947), 1066. This article was often cited in *amici* briefs.

ing effect of this conflict between ideals and practices in America. See particularly," it continued, "Myrdal, *An American Dilemma* (1944) *passim* and chap. 45 for the analysis of this conflict." A few pages later the brief lifted a long excerpt from Myrdal which illustrated Booker T. Washington's remark that the white man could not keep the black man in the gutter without ending up there himself.[27]

As before, many organizations appeared as friends of the Court. The NAACP again held strategy sessions to coordinate and strengthen the sociological data in the briefs. The *amici* briefs referred to Myrdal on a number of topics, but the main contention for which he was cited concerned the allegation that segregation always brought inequality for blacks. If any of these supplementary briefs caught the eye of the justices, it might have been the one submitted by the Committee of Law Teachers Against Segregation, which Marshall held up as a model for other *amici* briefs to follow. The brief by the law teachers revealed an especially liberal use of Myrdal. The law professors described the *Dilemma* as the primary "scientific source" which proved that segregation was harmful. The pedagogues relayed Myrdal's accusation that the Supreme Court had played a part in the degradation of the Negro. The text contained a page-long quotation from Myrdal which alleged black solidarity in the detestation of segregation. The brief ended with the following observation from the *Dilemma:* "[The Negro] has in his demands upon white Americans, the fundamental law of the land on his side. He has even the better conscience of his white compatriots themselves. He knows it; and the white American knows it too." [28]

Technically, the NAACP had not challenged the separate-but-equal principle in the *Sweatt* and *McLaurin* cases, but the 1896 *Plessy* ruling had come under heavy assault for being both contrary to American ideals and practicality. Speaking for a unanimous Court in the *Sweatt* case, Chief Justice Vinson pointed out that "intangible" elements such as the reputation of a law school and its faculty could conceivably render physically equal schools unequal. Nor could a law school that was the "proving ground for legal training and practice," the chief justice continued, "be effective in isolation from individuals and institutions with which the law interacts." In both the *Sweatt* and *McLaurin*

27. *Sweatt* v. *Painter,* Records and Briefs, Vol. 339, Pt. 1, pp. 20, 28.

28. Thurgood Marshall to Galen Weaver, December 30, 1948, "Education—General," Box 71, NAACP Papers; Jerome Spingarn to Robert L. Carter, January 19, 1949, *ibid.;* Memorandum to Editors, April 6, 1949, "Education Conferences, 1948–49," Box 71, NAACP Papers; Records and Briefs, Vol. 339, Pt. 2, pp. 18, 30–31.

cases, the Court used sociological arguments to hammer away at the very basis of the separate-but-equal principle. Still, oddly enough, the Court refused to disturb the *Plessy* precedent.[29]

The path-breaking opinions by Vinson, who was not considered an advanced liberal on race, encouraged the NAACP to test the separate-but-equal formula directly, and in elementary and secondary schools. The first challenge began in South Carolina late in 1950. In *Briggs* v. *Elliott,* which in 1952 joined three other state cases under the heading of *Brown* v. *Board of Education,* senior Judge John Parker presided over a special three-man court to decide the constitutionality of South Carolina's segregation of public schools. Parker, whom the Senate had denied a seat on the Supreme Court in 1930 because of his allegedly anti-labor and anti-Negro views, expressed obvious irritation when several social scientists testified against segregation. The debate over whether a professor of political science constituted a pertinent witness on the harmfulness of segregation ended on the following note:

> Judge Parker: It seems to me that any lawyer or any man who has an experience in government would be just as well qualified as he would be to express an opinion on that. He is not a scientist in the field of education. Are you going to offer any more witnesses along this line?
>
> Mr. Marshall: No sir. The other witnesses are REAL scientists.
>
> Judge Parker: Well, I'll take it for what it's worth. Go ahead.[30]

Thurgood Marshall then brought in the behavioralists, the "real scientists" on the matter of race relations. He paraded half a dozen such witnesses before the court who attested to the harmfulness of segregation. Kenneth B. Clark, a black psychologist from Columbia University and former Myrdal collaborator, explained the results of his famous doll test to the court. By now, lawyers for the segregationists had become familiar with Myrdal. They began to search for weaknesses in the book and to question social science witnesses about their attitude toward it. In Charleston, lawyers for the defendants quizzed an NAACP witness about a passage from the *Dilemma* which, they claimed, proved that W. E. B. Du Bois opposed the integration of schools.[31] The segrega-

29. *Sweatt* v. *Painter,* 634; *McLaurin* v. *Oklahoma,* 641; Loren Miller, *The Petitioners: The Story of the Supreme Court of the United States and the Negro* (Cleveland, 1967), 340.

30. Transcript of the court record, *Briggs* v. *Elliott,* 98 F.Supp. 529, Records and Briefs, Vol. 347, Pt. 2, p. 102; see also *Davis* v. *Prince Edward County,* 103 F.Supp. 337 (E.D. Va., 1952), Records and Briefs, Vol. 349, Pt. 3, pp. 270–71.

31. *Briggs* v. *Elliott,* Records and Briefs, Vol. 347, Pt. 2, pp. 102, 144, 149–50.

tionists would improve and embellish the tactic of tearing portions of the *Dilemma* from context when they argued before the Supreme Court. As expected, the federal court in South Carolina upheld segregation. Judge Parker, speaking for the majority, sanctioned separate schools on the basis of the *Plessy* case and states' rights. He emphatically added that the court could not base decisions relating to constitutional issues on the unproved theories of sociologists.[32]

Judge J. Waties Waring, however, filed a lengthy and notable dissent designed to attract the attention of justices on the Supreme Court. When Waring was appointed as a federal district judge in 1942 at the age of sixty-one, his credentials as a segregationist were good enough for two outspokenly racist senators from South Carolina. Once a judge, however, Waring, to the dismay of everyone, acted vigorously to defend black rights. The reasons for the judge's conversion to racial liberalism are complex and cannot be fully explored here. One factor in his change of attitude, however, concerned his second marriage in 1945 to a northern divorcee just after he created a scandal by divorcing his home-town wife of more than thirty years. The second Mrs. Waring, a woman of abolitionist stock who was repulsed by southern racism, set out to do something to correct the oppressive system. First, she arranged what she called "a cram-course study of Myrdal, Cash, and all the scientific writers in the South" for the judge and herself. Waring agonized over the contents of Myrdal's study for weeks. Both the *Dilemma* and Wilbur J. Cash's *Mind of the South* strongly affected the judge's thinking. By 1950 he became a radical integrationist and a virtual exile in his home town of Charleston. *Time* magazine called him "the man they love to hate."[33]

Waring's dissent in the *Briggs* case made an elaborate legal and sociological argument for ending segregation in education. He claimed that the framers of the Fourteenth Amendment intended to eliminate racial discrimination in all public facilities. The judge maintained that the

---

Clark's doll test allegedly showed that black children preferred white dolls, indicating the damage done by segregation.

32. *Briggs* v. *Elliott*, 535–36 (E.D.S.C., 1951). George Bell Timmerman, Jr., was the other judge. He became governor of South Carolina in the mid-1950s and led the forces of massive resistance.

33. William B. Scott, "Judge J. Waties Waring: Advocate of 'Another' South," *South Atlantic Quarterly*, LXXVII (1978), 320–24; David W. Southern, "Beyond Jim Crow Liberalism: Judge Waring's Fight Against Segregation in South Carolina, 1942–52," *Journal of Negro History*, LXVI (1981), 209–27; "The Man They Love to Hate," *Time*, August 23, 1948, p. 17.

Sweatt and *McLaurin* opinions of 1950 clearly inferred that segregation denied equal protection of the laws. He stated that the social science witnesses had shown conclusively that segregation harmed blacks psychologically. Like Myrdal, the jurist also stressed the international implications of the race problem. In summation, Waring wrote with a flourish: "I am of the opinion that all of the legal guideposts, expert testimony, common sense and reason point unerringly to the conclusion that the system of segregation in education adopted and practiced in the State of South Carolina must go and must go now." A separate italicized paragraph stated the judge's opinion more concisely: "*Segregation is per se inequality.*" [34]

Counsel for the black plaintiffs in the parallel school cases in Virginia, Delaware, and Kansas likewise made wide use of social scientists. In the Delaware case, heard before the liberal Judge Collins Seitz, the NAACP mounted its heaviest sociopsychological attack yet on the *Plessy* doctrine. Fourteen expert witnesses took the stand, including Otto Klineberg and a clinical psychiatrist from Bavaria named Frederic Wertham. In Topeka the NAACP drew upon behavioralists on the staff of the Menninger Clinic. They impressed Judge Walter A. Huxman, a former Democratic governor of Kansas. Both Seitz and Huxman concluded that segregation harmed black children, but they left it up to the Supreme Court to rule on the separate-but-equal formula. A finding of the Kansas court, quoted later by the Supreme Court in the *Brown* opinion, stated: "The policy of separating the races is usually interpreted as denoting the inferiority of the negro group. A sense of inferiority affects the motivation of the child to learn. Segregation with the sanction of law, therefore, has a tendency to retard the educational and mental development of negro children and to deprive them of some of the benefits they would receive in a racially integrated system." [35]

Only in the Virginia case did the segregationists offer a social science witness of some stature. Henry Garrett, originally from Virginia and chairman of the department of psychology at Columbia University, testified to the merits of segregation. Garrett advised the court that Negroes should encourage separate schools so they could cultivate their natural skills in music, the dramatic arts, and athletics. [36]

34. *Briggs* v. *Elliott*, 529, 548.
35. Kluger, *Simple Justice*, 423–24, 440–50; *Brown* v. *Board of Education of Topeka*, 98 F.Supp. 797 (D. Kan., 1951), in Records and Briefs, Vol. 349, Pt. 2, pp. 245–46; for the Seitz opinion, see *Belton* v. *Gebhart*, 87 A.2d 862, 865 (Del. 1952).
36. Transcript of record, *Davis* v. *Prince Edward County*, Records and Briefs, Vol. 349, Pt. 3, p. 570.

Despite the success of sociological evidence in the lower courts, the NAACP legal staff still debated what role extralegal argument should play in the presentation before the Supreme Court. Social scientists and lawyers seldom seemed to work together harmoniously. The legal mind remained wary of the behavioralist. The black psychologist Kenneth Clark winced when an NAACP lawyer referred to his doll test as "crap." The staff knew, moreover, that even Justice Frankfurter held suspicions about the validity of the behavioral sciences. Marshall, in any case, had been convinced of the worth of social science evidence. The NAACP would continue with its "new angle." [37]

Briefs in the school cases by both the petitioners and the respondents contained elaborate arguments, some more then two hundred pages long. As earlier, the black plaintiffs used a wide array of extralegal sources. They not only cited Myrdal's book frequently, but they used it for dramatic effect. In the *Bolling* case from Washington, D.C., for example, the brief employed the following excerpt from Myrdal: "The spiritual effects of segregation are accumulating with each new generation, continuously estranging the two groups." "If a young student can learn in a democracy," the brief in the Kansas case went, "he must be able to do so freely—unhampered by such arbitrary and limiting factors as distinctions on the basis of race." For this statement, the authors cited "Gunnar Myrdal, *An American Dilemma, passim.*" At the last minute, the NAACP attempted to bolster its case by attaching a supplemental appendix to the *Briggs* brief. Drafted hurriedly by Kenneth Clark and signed by thirty-two prominent social scientists, it contained a concise and modest summary of the latest literature on the effects of segregation. Although thirty-five scholarly references supported the document, the only social scientist mentioned in the text was Myrdal. [38]

The chief counsel for the segregationists, however, showed little regard for extralegal evidence. John W. Davis, a southerner, 1924 Democratic candidate for president, ambassador to Britain, rich corporate lawyer, former president of the American Bar Association, and one often hailed as a "lawyer's lawyer," acted as the main attorney for the

---

37. Kluger, *Simple Justice*, 555–57; Rosen, *Supreme Court and Social Science*, 130–39; Arnold Rose, "The Social Scientist as an Expert Witness in Court Cases," in Paul Lazarsfeld, William H. Sewell, and Harold Wilensky (eds.), *The Uses of Sociology* (New York, 1967), 116.

38. *Bolling* v. *Sharpe*, 347 U.S. 497, in Records and Briefs, Vol. 349, Pt. 4, p. 37, Pt. 1, p. 8; "The Effects of Segregation and the Consequences of Desegregation," in Philip B. Kurland and Gerhard Casper (eds.), *Landmark Briefs and Arguments of the Supreme Court of the United States: Constitutional Law* (Arlington, Va., 1975), 41–66.

segregationists. The distinguished conservative, who had often argued before the Supreme Court, expressed disdain for sociological evidence. After reading Clark's supplemental brief, he exclaimed: "I can only say that if that sort of 'guff' can move the court, 'God save the state!'" The respondents, nonetheless, quoted Myrdal and Du Bois in the *Briggs* brief. The Du Bois quotation, lifted from the *Dilemma*, pointed out that integrated schools would not be desirable if blacks were subject to mistreatment and humiliation by racist whites. By taking Du Bois' words out of context, the defendants tried to make the case that most blacks preferred segregated education. Had they read the full statement in the 1935 Du Bois article, they would have encountered the following: "I know that this article will forthwith be interpreted by certain illiterate 'nitwits' as a plea for segregated Negro schools and colleges. It is not."[39]

In 1952 a deluge of *amici* briefs making the customary use of Myrdal fell upon the Court. In the *Bolling* case eighteen organizations filed a common brief and two others presented theirs separately. The other cases attracted a similar number of outside briefs. In addition to trying to divine the intent of the Fourteenth Amendment, these briefs engaged in prolonged sociological exegesis and made frequent allusions to the American creed and the American dilemma. They denounced racial distinctions as arbitrary and declared that segregation of schools caused retardation of blacks. Like Myrdal's study, the briefs collectively amounted to a compendium of the current social science knowledge about race combined with the rhetoric of the American creed and the taut drama of the American dilemma.[40]

The Justice Department filed briefs in behalf of the NAACP in 1952 and in the reargument in 1953, thereby spanning the administrations of Truman and Eisenhower. The 1952 brief held that *Plessy* was wrong as a

39. Davis quoted in Kluger, *Simple Justice*, 557; Records and Briefs, Vol. 349, Pt. 4, pp. 28–33; W. E. B. Du Bois, "Does the Negro Need Separate Schools?" *Journal of Negro Education*, IV (1935), 335.

40. Records and Briefs, Vol. 349, Pts. 3, 4. The eighteen agencies filing a common brief were the American Council on Human Rights, Americans for Democratic Action, American Jewish Committee, American Jewish Congress Commission on Law and Social Action, Catholic Interracial Council of Washington, Commission on Community Life of the Washington Federation of Churches, District of Columbia Industrial Union Council, CIO, D.C. Federation of Civic Associations, Friends Committee on National Legislation, Japanese American Citizens League, Jewish Community Council of Greater Washington, National Association for the Advancement of Colored People (D.C. branch), Unitarian Fellowship for Social Justice, Washington Bar Association, Washington Ethical Society, Washington Fellowship, Washington Interracial Workshop, and Washington Urban League.

matter of law, history, and policy. Though not emphasizing social science as conspicuously as the briefs of various civil rights groups, the Justice Department did not ignore that discipline. It included, for example, an excerpt from Judge Huxman's Kansas opinion which maintained that segregation harmed the psyche of blacks.[41]

In the oral arguments before the Supreme Court in December, 1952, the legal spokesmen for the NAACP stressed that the segregationists had offered virtually no rebuttal to their behavioral science witnesses. Marshall belittled his opponents' witnesses for their lack of recognized expertise on race relations. He scolded the segregationists for quoting such southerners as Howard Odum and Frank Graham instead of calling them as witnesses. As for the briefs of the defendants, Marshall told the Court: "I have yet to hear any one say that they denied that these children are harmed by reason of this segregation."[42]

The next day John Davis replied at length to Marshall. He denigrated the integrationist social scientists as northern professors unfamiliar with the southern situation and attacked several of the behavioral science witnesses in the South Carolina case by name. Davis also claimed that Clark's doll test proved the opposite of what the black psychologist intended. Citing figures from Clark's study, the noted lawyer pointed out that 10 percent more of the black children in the North than in the segregated South picked the white doll as the "good" doll. As in the *Briggs* brief, Davis quoted Du Bois on integrated schools. If one of the most militant blacks of the twentieth century had doubts about the desegregation of schools, surely, he implied, most blacks preferred segregation. The former ambassador took the occasion to argue that the social scientists for the plaintiffs did not speak "without contradiction from other sources." He reminded the Court that in the briefs the defendants had quoted experts on race relations including Howard Odum, Hodding Carter, Frank Graham, and, yes, Gunnar Myrdal. The latter the stately octogenarian depicted as a "Swedish scientist" but erroneously identified the sponsor of his study as the Rockefeller Foundation. Davis clearly proceeded more surely and eloquently when he stayed with legal precedents and the Constitution. Temporarily sidetracked from such argument at one point by Frankfurter's questions, Davis struck an emotional tone that sprang from deep within his heritage. Quoting Benjamin

41. *Brown* v. *Board of Education,* Records and Briefs, Vol. 349, Pt. 3, pp. 2–6, 8, 12–13, 17, 24, 32.

42. Leon Friedman (ed.), *Argument: The Oral Argument Before the Supreme Court in Brown v. Board of Education of Topeka, 1952–55* (New York, 1969), 39, 47.

Disraeli, he intoned: "No man will treat with indifference the principle of race. It is the key to history."[43]

Davis' use of Du Bois and Myrdal in the *Briggs* argument plainly irritated Marshall. He countered by explaining to the justices that the overwhelming majority of social scientists backed his claims about the harmfulness of segregation. He wondered out loud why the state of South Carolina could not afford more acclaimed witnesses. This observation brought a question from Frankfurter and an ironic exchange with Marshall:

> Justice Frankfurter: Can we not take judicial notice of writings by people who competently deal with these problems? Can I not take judicial notice of Myrdal's book without having him called as a witness?
>
> Mr. Marshall: Yes, sir. But I think when you take judicial notice of Gunnar Myrdal's book, we have to read the matter, and not take portions out of context. Gunnar Myrdal's whole book is against the argument.
>
> Justice Frankfurter: This is a different point. . . . How to inform the judicial mind, as you know, is one of the most complicated problems. It is better to have witnesses, but I did not know that we could not read the works of competent writers.[44]

On one hand, Frankfurter let it be known that the justices, especially a well-versed one like himself, would not hide from social science facts, even those not presented in the courtroom. On the other hand, Marshall pointed out the deceptive use the segregationists had made of works by people such as Du Bois and Myrdal; and he correctly charged that the segregationists had trouble getting prestigious social scientists to testify for them.[45]

When the *Brown* opinion came down in May, 1954, the new chief justice rushed into the sociological thicket where Chief Justice Vinson had only lightly trod. With a wave of the hand, Earl Warren dismissed the question of the intent of the Fourteenth Amendment as inconclusive with regard to public schools. He then followed a sociological argument designed to show that segregated schools deprived black children of equal opportunity in education and that segregation placed a badge of inferiority on the minority. After explaining the sociological import of the *Sweatt* and *McLaurin* cases and those in the lower courts in Kansas and Delaware, Warren concluded: "Whatever may have been the ex-

43. *Ibid.*, 58–61; Brief in *Briggs* v. *Elliott*, Records and Briefs, Vol. 349, Pt. 4, pp. 28–32.

44. Friedman (ed.), *Argument*, 63, 216.

45. Kluger, *Simple Justice*, 343–44.

tent of psychological knowledge at the time of *Plessy* v. *Ferguson,* this finding [that segregation is harmful to blacks] is amply supported by modern authority." [46]

Then came the controversial footnote, specifying the Court's "modern authority." The six sources cited in the footnote besides the *Dilemma* referred to scholarly essays or brief portions of books. But in the case of Myrdal, the note instructed the reader to see the entire voluminous study.[47] The Court had been subjected to a steady diet of Myrdal since the covenant cases of the 1940s, and the blanket reference to the *Dilemma* most likely was made because so many briefs over the period had advised, "see Myrdal, *An American Dilemma, passim.*" The inclusive reference to Myrdal's book also indicated that it, unlike the other sources cited in the footnote, had not been used solely to document the allegation that segregation was deleterious. Rather, the petitioners had employed Myrdal repeatedly to heighten the American dilemma in the Court's mind.

As more information has become available to historians on the strategy involved in the *Brown* opinion, one can understand better why social science played a prominent part. According to Richard Kluger, the author of the fullest account on the *Brown* case, Warren considered unanimity of the Court crucial for such a historic decision. The chief justice, therefore, sacrificed depth and subtlety for a short, simple opinion that did not condemn the South. Tom Clark and Hugo Black, both from the Deep South, feared violent resistance to the ruling unless the opinion was flexible and as palatable as possible to Dixie. Justice Robert Jackson argued in conference that there was no legal basis for overturning segregation. Thus he would vote to reverse *Plessy* only if the Court confessed that it was making new law. Despite their differing legal views, all of the justices agreed that times had changed drastically since 1896 and that the social facts of the nineteenth century no longer applied to current matters of education and race. The Court hesitated to de-

46. *Brown* v. *Board of Education,* 347 U.S. 483, 493–95.

47. The other sources, in the form the Court cited them, were K. B. Clark, "Effect of Prejudice and Discrimination on Personality Development" (Midcentury White House Conference on Children and Youth); Witmer and Kotinsky, *Personality in the Making* (1952), c. VI; Deutscher and Chein, "The Psychological Effects of Enforced Segregation: A Survey of Social Opinion," 26 *J. Psychol.* 259 (1948): Chein, "What are the Psychological Effects of Segregation Under Condition of Equal Facilities?" 3 *Int. J. Opinion and Attitude Res.* 229 (1949); Brameld, "Educational Costs," in *Discrimination and the National Welfare* (MacIver, ed., 1949), 44–48; Frazier, *The Negro in the United States* (1949), 674–681.

nounce *Plessy* as wrong in the context of its time but stated that the psychology of 1896 simply was not relevant in 1954. Unlike John Davis, the justices did not accept the permanence of the American dilemma. They favored movement that would narrow the gap between ideals and practice. The opinion, as approached by Warren, revolved around crucial facts and the existence of new knowledge and new conceptions concerning Afro-Americans. To make the decision seem less arbitrary, Chief Justice Warren drew upon "modern authority" to document the brute facts about education and race in an advanced industrial society.[48]

The reaction of rigid segregationists to *Brown* seemed fairly predictable, but many liberals expressed substantial reservations about Warren's opinion. Even many of those who thought that the *Brown* case involved a question of "simple justice" found the opinion less than a legal *tour de force*. Law professor Herbert Wecksler criticized the subjectivity of the opinion and called for a return to principles of "neutral law." Edmond Cahn, another such professor, maintained that the Court's decision had been based on common sense. The introduction of "flimsy" social science evidence, he charged, presented a needless and "bizarre" spectacle in the courtroom. In the late 1970s J. Harvie Wilkinson said of the *Brown* opinion: "It was, with the pardonable exception of a footnote, a great political achievement." The chief justice simply explained: "It was only a note, after all." Warren did not even broach the subject in his memoirs.[49]

Understandably, liberals, for pragmatic reasons, lamented the inclusion of a footnote that subjected what seemed a necessary decision to vitriolic attack. But to deny the influence of social science in the *Brown* case or to talk vaguely about neutral law and common-sense evidence distorts history. Louis H. Pollack reminded his colleague Wecksler that the framers of the Fourteenth and Fifteenth Amendments did not intend neutrality on race. To those who argued that common sense was just as enlightened as social science on race relations, the counter question

48. Kluger, *Simple Justice*, 678–99, 706, 711–13; Rosen, *Supreme Court and Social Science*, 151–55, 170–72.
49. Herbert Wecksler, "Toward Neutral Principles of Constitutional Law," *Harvard Law Review*, LXXIII (1959), 31–35; Edmond Cahn, "Jurisprudence," *New York University Law Review*, XXX (1955), 158–60; J. Harvie Wilkinson III, *From Brown to Bakke: The Supreme Court and School Integration, 1954–1978* (New York, 1979), 39; Kluger, *Simple Justice*, 706; *The Memoirs of Earl Warren* (New York, 1977). For a representative conservative critique of the *Brown* opinion, see Ernest van den Haag, "Social Science Testimony in the Desegregation Cases: A Reply to Professor Kenneth Clark," *Villanova Law Review*, VI (1960), 69–79.

was: If so, why had the democratically elected officials of America not acted on common sense to end racial discrimination in public institutions? Or if social science evidence was flimsy, as Cahn claimed, why did it agree with liberal common sense about segregation?[50] Common sense might also tell one that had Warren based the decision on legal precedents and historical interpretation, both of which were ambiguous and conflicting, the rabid segregationists would have reacted no less strongly.

Many of the critics of *Brown* did not seem to realize that Warren's opinion represented not an aberration but the culmination of sociological jurisprudence. Long before modern liberals resorted to social science in court, conservative behavioral science had seeped into many of the most important high court rulings. When Chief Justice Roger Taney remarked in the *Dred Scott* case that "the unhappy black race" had been separated from whites by "indelible marks," he not only stated what passed for common sense by whites in that time but also echoed the racist anthropology of Josiah Nott and the American School of Ethnology. The 1896 Court that sanctified segregation in *Plessy* not only interpreted law but made it. It also handed down a decision that fairly bristled with the social science of Adam Smith, Herbert Spencer, and William Graham Sumner—all of course without a footnote.[51] Had Warren eliminated footnote 11 from the *Brown* opinion, it would not have lessened the impact of social science on the decision any more than the absence of a footnote in *Plessy* expunged the influence of Smith, Spencer, and Sumner.

In the twentieth century, liberals found that they too, could use social science. In *Muller* v. *Oregon* in 1908, Louis Brandeis persuaded the Court to take "cognizance of all matters of general knowledge" in a case that upheld the limitation of working hours for certain women. To cope with the extensive legislation passed by progressives to prevent industrial injustices, the Court formulated a doctrine known as the "rule of reason." Because the Constitution threw no light on what was reason-

50. Louis H. Pollack, "Racial Discrimination and Judicial Integrity: A Reply to Professor Wecksler," *University of Pennsylvania Law Review*, CVIII (1959), 24–32; Kenneth B. Clark, "The Desegregation Cases: Criticism of the Social Scientist's Role," *Villanova Law Review*, V (1959–60), 232.

51. *Dred Scott* v. *Sandford*, 19 Howard 393, 410 (1857); George M. Fredrickson, *The Black Image in the White Mind: The Debate on Afro-American Character and Destiny, 1817–1914* (New York, 1971), 71–96; Barton J. Berstein, "Plessy v. Ferguson: A Conservative Sociological Jurisprudence," *Journal of Negro History*, XLVIII (1963), 196–205.

able in complicated economic cases, jurists had to rely increasingly on social science for facts and theories as they related to changing public priorities.[52]

To be sure, strong forces resisted the trend toward legal realism. Conservative members of the bar regretted the tendency to stray from law books for information to decide cases. Unlike Europeans, most American lawyers thought of the law as a vocation and not an intellectual pursuit closely related to other disciplines that dealt with man's behavior. Even so, sociological jurisprudence made steady inroads into the process of law before World War II. It was not until after the war, however, that social science acquired a prominent and overt role in civil rights cases. And not until the postwar period did law schools place sociologists and psychologists on their staffs. Scholarship from a burgeoning new field of study labeled the "sociology of law," of course, now informs law students on the most prestigious campuses in America.[53]

The sociological influence on law nonetheless has not created a runaway Court propelled by avant-garde social scientists. The case of Felix Frankfurter illustrates why the Court has been restrained in its use of social science evidence. Possessing a voracious intellectual curiosity, Frankfurter was keenly interested in the social sciences. His searching questions on extralegal evidence during the civil rights cases placed him a notch above his colleagues on the bench. His question in the oral arguments in *Brown* about how to inform the judicial mind was one over which the learned jurist truly agonized.

Yet the Bostonian believed in judicial restraint. Moreover, he cast a suspicious eye on the "still unshapen" social sciences, which he felt were characterized by "inherent vagueness." "But such as they are," he explained, "we must apply them." Frankfurter was enough of a realist to know that judges did not "find" law but made it. Indeed, Frankfurter had cited his friend Myrdal in a 1950 case dealing with race. Yet his

52. *Muller* v. *Oregon,* 208 U.S. 412, 420–21; Alfred H. Kelly and Winfred A. Harbison, *The American Constitution: Its Origins and Development* (3d ed.; New York, 1963), 522–23.

53. Rosen, *Supreme Court and Social Science,* 115; Richard D. Schwartz and Jerome H. Skolnick (eds.), Introduction to *Society and the Legal Order* (New York, 1970), 3–6; J. Willard Hurst, *The Growth of American Law* (Boston, 1950), 185–89; Alfred W. Blumrosen, "Legal Process and Labor Law," in William E. Evans (ed.), *Law and Sociology* (New York, 1962), 191; Philip Zelznick, "The Sociology of Law," in Robert K. Merton, Leonard Broom, and Leonard S. Cottrell (eds.), *Sociology Today: Problems and Prospects* (New York, 1959), 115–27; Lawrence M. Friedman and Stewart McCaulay (eds.), *Law and the Behavioral Sciences* (Indianapolis, 1969), viii.

inclination was to be very selective and to use social science evidence only when it coincided with his common sense and his feel for justice. It is often forgotten that in the second *Brown* case in 1955, the Court ignored social science testimony that called for a strict time schedule for desegregation. Instead, Frankfurter inserted into the implementing decision the phrase, "with all deliberate speed." This phrase, as Justice Hugo Black admitted in 1969, allowed the segregationists to "stonewall" it for fifteen years. Certainly *Brown* II weakened *Brown* I much more than did footnote 11. A close look at Frankfurter suggests, furthermore, that the Court can and will occasionally use social science, but that social scientists can seldom use the Court.[54]

Actually, the Warren Court used social science modestly in the *Brown* case. The decision simply applied the obvious conclusion that forced segregation was harmful to blacks, a conclusion on which over 90 percent of behavioral scientists agreed. Footnote 11 provided an alternative to the antiquated social science used in the *Plessy* case. *Brown* qualified as a "legal" decision because it was based on the constitutional principle of the "equal protection of the laws." It illustrated, nevertheless, that such abstract legal principles necessarily received new meaning as society changed. Less squeamish liberal realists such as Archibald Cox and Randall Bland candidly conceded that judges, for better or worse, inevitably made law or restructured the Constitution to meet the perceived needs of the time. They did not try to deny the obvious: that social science significantly affected the *Brown* opinion.[55] As it was, social science provided that extra boost, or according to Marshall, the "new angle" the NAACP needed for the civil rights cases.

Myrdal's study, of course, was only one of many significant forces impinging upon the Supreme Court after World War II. Had no other powerful forces been working to undermine the caste system, the opinions of social scientists would probably have meant little. The fortuitous timing of Myrdal's work, however, enhanced its impact. As a social science work, the Myrdal report had the requisite qualities for gaining in-

54. Frankfurter, in MacLeish and Prichard (eds.), *Law and Politics,* 290; *Hughes* v. *Superior Court,* 339 U.S. 460, 463; Rosen, *Supreme Court and Social Science,* 111, 225; Kluger, *Simple Justice,* 938–39; Friedman (ed.), *Argument,* 172–73; Leo Katcher, *Earl Warren: A Political Biography* (New York, 1967), 324; Atlanta *Constitution,* September 6, 1969, p. 1.

55. Deutscher and Chein, "Psychological Effects of Enforced Segregation," 259; Archibald Cox, *The Warren Court: Constitutional Decision as an Instrument of Reform* (Cambridge, Mass., 1968), 22, 26; Bland, *Private Pressure on Public Law,* 84.

fluence.[56] With the dilemma model, the Swedish economist proffered a seductive metaphor for a Court resolved to reduce the gap between American ideals and practices.

Although white segregationists in the South and the Radical Right had largely shunned Myrdal's book before the *Brown* decision, after 1954 the Swede's work attracted intense interest from these sectors of society. Southerners and ultraconservatives, who directed much of their frustration at the Warren Court, would see fit to render Myrdal more than just a footnote.

56. Philip W. Semas, "How Influential Is Sociology?" *Chronicle of Higher Education,* September 19, 1977, p. 4.

Gunnar Myrdal in 1938, the year he began the Carnegie study.
Courtesy of UPI/Bettmann Newsphotos.

Gunnar and Alva Myrdal in Frankfurt am Main, West Germany, in 1970.
Courtesy of Anna Britta Jansson.

The segregationist view of the *Brown* decision, in *Citizens' Council,*
November, 1955, p. 1.

By permission of the Citizens Councils of America, Jackson, Mississippi.

SUPPLYING THE EVIDENCE

Subversive evidence gleaned from *An American Dilemma,* a white supremacist view, in *Citizens' Council,* March, 1956, p. 1.

By permission of the Citizens Councils of America, Jackson, Mississippi.

VII

The White South and the Far Right Respond to Myrdal

Racial tensions and violence escalated markedly during World War II, and the end of the war brought little relief to the anxious white South. The civil rights activism of President Truman, blacks, and northern liberals helped spur the Dixiecrat revolt of 1948 and the growing conservatism that engulfed the South after the war. All that was needed for race to supplant all other issues was a direct challenge to segregation. In 1954 the Supreme Court released the racial genie from the bottle. For the next decade or more, the racial question dominated and solidified a majority of white southerners as it had not done for half a century.[1]

If most whites below the Potomac interpreted events as threatening the "southern way of life," those on the extreme right of the political spectrum throughout the nation perceived national and international trends as conspiring against the "American way of life." In Cold War America a brand of politics emerged (or reemerged) which Richard Hofstadter has labeled the "paranoid style." The political paranoiac, Hofstadter demonstrated, suspected that titanic forces plotted to destroy a nation, a culture, a way of life. Reducing all political questions to one of good versus evil, the practitioner of the paranoid style of politics sought to preserve a fundamentalist Christianity, economic orthodoxy,

1. On racial fear, see Dabney, "Nearer and Nearer the Precipice," 94; and Odum, *Race and Rumors of Race*. A classic work on southern politics in the 1940s is by V. O. Key (who correctly said, "Of books about the South there is no end"), *Southern Politics in State and Nation* (New York, 1949). A more recent scholarly work to consult is Numan V. Bartley, *The Rise of Massive Resistance: Race and Politics in the South During the 1950s* (Baton Rouge, 1969), 3–57.

and the fabled virtues of the original republic.[2] Sometimes called the Far Right or the Radical Right, this small but influential minority tended to perceive liberals as fellow travelers of the Soviet Union and centrists such as President Dwight D. Eisenhower as Communist dupes.

Although southern segregationists at first concentrated on the politics of color in the desegregation crisis, they quickly broadened their approach until they became virtually indistinguishable from the Far Right.[3] McCarthyism, which had been relatively weak in the South, gained a new lease on life in Dixie in the late 1950s. By then, segregationists not only attacked integration but also, like the Radical Right, aimed their barbs at the countless ramifications of modernism, big government, and "atheistic" communism.

By the 1960s one could scarcely differentiate between the views of the John Birch Society of New England or southern California and the White Citizens' Councils of the Deep South. Both groups stressed the alleged threat the behavioral sciences posed to American values and institutions. In so doing, they frequently singled out Myrdal as a whipping boy. The two groups applied a dazzling assortment of epithets to the foreign economist. They dubbed him the "notorious Swedish Communist," the "Red psychologist," or the "alien anthropologist." Both Radical Rightists and segregationists stereotyped Myrdal as an integral part of a sinister Communist conspiracy. Whereas many liberals underplayed Myrdal's role in the *Brown* case, the ultraracists and rightists wildly exaggerated the Swedish economist's impact on the Court and the civil rights movement. By the 1960s they even blamed Myrdal for igniting "the intellectual fuse of Black Power," paying no mind to the black militants' constant flagellation of the Scandinavian as an enemy and an implicit racist.[4]

2. Richard Hofstadter, *The Paranoid Style in American Politics and Other Essays* (New York, 1965), vii–xiv, 23–26, and *passim;* see also Daniel Bell (ed.), *The Radical Right* (Garden City, N.Y., 1963); Harry Overstreet and Bonaro Overstreet, *The Strange Tactics of Extremism* (New York, 1964); Mark Sherwin, *The Extremists* (New York, 1963); J. Allen Broyles, *The John Birch Society* (Boston, 1964); Benjamin R. Epstein and Arnold Forster, *Danger on the Right* (New York, 1964).

3. Neil R. McMillen, *The Citizens' Council: Organized Resistance to the Second Reconstruction, 1954–64* (Urbana, Ill., 1971), 191–98. The terms "Far Right" and "Radical Right" have been capitalized to denote the extreme right of the political spectrum. These terms do not refer to the majority "right," which has not been capitalized. For variety, I have also used "extreme right," "ultra right," and "radical conservatives" to refer to the Far Right. The Far Right, of course, is related to the more recent New Right.

4. Wilmot Robertson, *The Disposed Majority* (rev. ed.; Cape Canaveral, Fla., 1973), 211.

Since most of the segregationists and radical conservatives paid
scant attention to Myrdal before 1954, southern liberals initially provided the bulk of the commentary on the *Dilemma*. As shown in Chapter IV, most southern liberals gave Myrdal a polite public reception, but
they rejected the major thrust of his book. Privately they applauded
W. T. Couch's venomous attack on the European egalitarian. Most
southern liberals considered the Swede a well-meaning but impractical social engineer with a woefully inadequate understanding of their
region.[5]

As Myrdal well knew, the Dabneys, the Odums, the Couches, the
Johnsons, and the Ethridges had their dilemmas too. As southern progressives, they had qualms about the South's treatment of blacks. But
they also feared class and racial conflict, constantly conjured up the
"tragic era" of Reconstruction, and warned against federal interference
in southern racial affairs. From 1944 to 1954 Myrdal's contention that
southern liberals had more in common with Edmund Burke than with
modern liberals throughout the rest of the Western world still rang true.[6]

Many southern liberals recognized their increasing intellectual isolation in the 1940s and 1950s. Even the fiery Couch ruefully conceded
that his views on blacks were no longer "intellectually respectable." Although Couch never retracted his acerbic attack on Myrdal, the southerner confessed that he would rather not have made battle with the
Swede. In a letter to Jackson Davis, he characterized the *Dilemma* as "a
magnificent piece of work" which was beneficial because it would make
whites think.[7]

Despite the coolness toward Myrdal's study by the notables at Chapel
Hill, it did provoke them to thought and even action. Although Odum
freely hurled barbs at Myrdal, he nonetheless sent a copy of the *Dilemma* to the governor of North Carolina, advising him to dip into it
here and there when he had time. He also requested twenty-five copies
of a pamphlet based on the Swede's book, and he told Guy Johnson that
the Southern Regional Council (SRC) should distribute copies of it.[8]

But Odum could never eradicate a certain residue of bitterness to-

5. For Couch's comments, see Logan (ed.), *What the Negro Wants*, xiv–xv.
6. *AD*, 470.
7. Logan (ed.), *What the Negro Wants*, ix–x, xv; Couch to Jackson Davis, February
4, 1944; Couch to Dabney, February 15, 1944, in Logan File, Press Records; Couch to the
author, July 21, 1984; Sosna, *In Search of the Silent South*, 114–15, 156.
8. Odum to Governor J. M. Broughton, March 23, 1944, Odum to Guy Johnson, September 6, 1944; Johnson to Odum, September 8, 1944, Box 26, Odum Papers.

ward Myrdal. The Scandinavian had incensed Odum and the staff of the Commission on Interracial Cooperation (CIC) in August, 1942, when he sent a first draft report on the southern organization to his friend Will Alexander in Washington and to Arthur Raper, one of his collaborators on the Carnegie project. Raper sent his copy to Odum, who shared it with his subordinates at the CIC. The Swede ignited a firestorm of controversy with his comments on the CIC. Odum immediately fired off a telegram to Princeton, informing Myrdal that the report—based on the research of the then-leftist Ralph Bunche—was replete with errors and "inexcusably inadequate" in every way. The CIC president quickly followed up his cable with an indignant six-page letter to the European vigorously defending his organization. Other officers of the CIC also responded in mass and in kind. After venting his anger on Myrdal, Odum told Will Alexander: "I am hoping that . . . tomorrow will be better because of having thrown a lot of bile out of the system." [9]

Since Myrdal had tried to appease the Chapel Hill School from the start, he moved rapidly to try to repair the damage he had done. A telegram, a letter, and a long memorandum by Myrdal explained to the southerner that the draft was only preliminary and torn out of a larger context. The economist confessed that it did not contain current data on the CIC. Judging from Odum's return letter, Myrdal's deferential tone had mollified the North Carolinian somewhat. In any case, the portrait of the CIC in the *Dilemma* was much more positive than the original assessment. In the final chapter of Myrdal's book, however, the Swede quoted a "prominent white Southern liberal" who expressed a very pessimistic forecast for race relations south of the Potomac. The anonymous quotation actually came from Odum's 1942 response to Myrdal's critique of the CIC, in which he had warned about "a crisis greater than we have had in many years." Myrdal removed Odum's name from the long quotation because he did not want to engage in another letter-writing spree with the southerner and his supporters. The Swede also realized that despite Odum's growing pessimism about race relations, the regionalist wanted to be known as a hopeful liberal. [10]

Actually, research shows that Myrdal's trenchant criticism of the CIC in 1942 hastened the reorganization of that agency. In 1944 it became

9. Odum to Myrdal, August 7, 13, 1942, Box 24, Odum Papers; Emily Clay to Myrdal, August 18, 1942; Jesse Daniel Ames to Myrdal, August 31, 1942, Negro Study, roll 1.

10. Myrdal to Charles Dollard, August 7, 1942; Myrdal to Odum, August 19, 1942; Odum to Myrdal, August 13, 21, 1942; Myrdal to Dollard, September 4, 1942, in Negro Study, roll 1; *AD*, 842–50, 1013.

the Southern Regional Council. Internal documents indicate that many of Myrdal's complaints about the CIC had hit close to home. The foreign social scientist (and Bunche) had branded the CIC as a mainly white, paternalistic, highly centralized organization not sustained by dues-paying members but by foundations from the North. The CIC, Myrdal had charged, avoided taking stands on social, economic, and political equality for blacks. The critique contended that the CIC had elevated opportunism from a means to a principle. Above all, Myrdal pointed out, blacks had lost faith in the CIC. The validity of the last charge seemed borne out by the "Durham Statement" that came two months later. In this 1942 declaration, southern blacks called for an end to the poll tax, the white primary, and segregation. An in-house study by the CIC also showed that blacks viewed Odum's organization as "static and colorless," even "Uncle Tomish." [11]

The establishment of the Southern Regional Council, however, did not alter Odum's course. As the first president of the SRC, he chose to continue to work, as one observer put it, "for racial harmony without effecting fundamental change in the social order." But blacks and white liberals such as Will Alexander and Lillian Smith argued that the SRC would be of no consequence unless it officially repudiated segregation. Far from being the grand council envisioned by Odum, which would scientifically study all aspects of the South, the SRC essentially continued in the path of the earlier CIC. Indeed, the organization spent much of its time between 1944 and 1949 in acrimonious debate over segregation. Odum, with Virginius Dabney and Guy Johnson as allies, resisted attempts to make the SRC integrationist. In 1944 a frustrated Odum wrote to John Temple Graves: "If we could just stop talking about social equality and segregation and go to work, it would be a day for us, wouldn't it?" [12]

The Chapel Hill social scientist had come a long way from his racist attitudes of earlier years. Yet he never lost his ambivalence about blacks or completely shook the "consciousness of kind" theory taught by his

11. Critique of CIC, August, 1942, Box 24, Odum Papers; William Clifton Allred, "The Southern Regional Council" (M.A. thesis, Emory University, 1966), 14–15; Krueger, *And Promises to Keep,* 119–20; Raymond Gavins, *The Perils and Prospects of Southern Black Leadership: Gordon Blaine Hancock, 1884–1970* (Durham, N.C., 1977), viii, 145.

12. Henry Allen Bulloch, "Urbanism and Race Relations," in Rupert B. Vance and Nicholas J. Demerath (eds.), *The Urban South* (Chapel Hill, 1954), 225; Odum quoted in George B. Tindall, *The Emergence of the New South, 1913–1945* (Baton Rouge, 1967), 720.

influential teacher, Franklin H. Giddings. And seldom did he miss a chance to take a verbal swipe at Myrdal and other foreigners. In 1951 he wrote: "Weber never understood America. No more did Myrdal." Shortly before his death in late 1954, Odum declared that in the *Brown* case a "naive and amateurish" Supreme Court had handed down an opinion of tragic proportions. Both Odum and Guy Johnson had to relinquish leadership of the SRC before it took a strong stand for integration. In 1949 the new leadership of the SRC proclaimed that segregation was a "constitutional anachronism" that hurt both blacks and whites. Under Jim Crow, the statement pointed out: "The white person must adjust himself to the hypocrisy of a double standard violating the American creed." [13]

In the decade preceding *Brown*, many southerners, often hailed as risk-taking liberals by the northern press, continued to villify the national black leadership and warn white northern liberals about the futility of meddling in the South's racial affairs. David Cohn, for example, argued that "racial purity" constituted a primordial force in southern society and could not be remedied. Ralph McGill flayed the Truman Committee on Civil Rights for suggesting that toleration could be legislated. Although Hodding Carter advocated full economic and political rights for blacks in his 1950 book, *Southern Legacy,* the Mississippi editor also made it clear that his racial strategy was designed to accord blacks more dignity so they would have greater respect for their "ethnic integrity." [14]

To gain better perspective, one must remember that Odum, Cohn, Carter, and McGill grew up in an era when paternalism or "accommodationist racism" was considered a less vicious alternative in race relations than so-called "neo-Darwinist" racism. The latter, elaborately formulated in 1896 in Frederick L. Hoffman's *Racial Traits and Tendencies of the American Negro,* forecast the extinction of blacks because of

13. Odum to Hawkins Brown, February 4, 1944, Box 26, Odum Papers; Odum, *American Sociology: The Story of Sociology in the United States Through 1950* (Chapel Hill, 1951), 429; "The Supreme Court Considers Segregation," *New South,* IV (November–December, 1949), 4–6. On Guy Johnson's inactivity during the civil rights movement, see John Ehle, *The Free Men* (New York, 1965), 202–13, 316–17.

14. David Cohn, "How the South Feels," *Atlantic,* CLXXIII (January, 1944), 47–51; and *Where I Was Born and Raised* (Boston, 1948), 185; John Hope Franklin, "Civil Rights and the Truman Administration," in Donald R. McCoy, Richard T. Ruetten, and J. K. Fuchs (eds.), *Conference of Scholars on the Truman Administration and Civil Rights* (Independence, Mo., 1968), 139; Hodding Carter, *Southern Legacy* (Baton Rouge, 1950), 10–11, 48–63, 89–91, 181–82.

genetic weaknesses. Around the turn of the century, demagogues such as Benjamin Tillman and James Vardaman called for more oppressive treatment of the minority. Some worked for the repeal of the Fourteenth and Fifteenth Amendments, the termination of black education, or a ban on the ownership of land by Afro-Americans. Others renewed the idea of colonizing blacks abroad. Southern liberals of the 1940s rejected such extreme measures, but they had little to offer blacks.[15]

Myrdal made plain that whatever substance white paternalism had held in previous times, it evaporated with World War II. A small minority of southern whites readily recognized this fact and acted boldly on its implications. Like an impassioned abolitionist of another era, Lillian Smith had been denouncing the caste system since the late 1930s. In 1944 the novelist and editor turned down an invitation to join the board of directors of the Southern Regional Council because it refused to condemn segregation. In a letter to Guy Johnson of the SRC and an essay in the *New Republic,* the Georgia writer scolded southern liberals for not targeting Jim Crow for extinction. She described segregation as the "spiritual lynching" of blacks and "a menace to the health and culture of our individual souls." "I believe the time has come," she lectured Johnson, "when we must take our stand."[16]

Although Smith's views stemmed primarily from her strong religious beliefs, she was conversant with modern social science. Indeed, she probed the psychological origins of white racism as no other southerner had ever done. Smith met Myrdal several times and had frank discussions with him about the race problem. At a 1948 NAACP dinner honoring Myrdal, she sat on the dais as a special guest. Later Smith cited the *Dilemma* as one of the most influential books of the twentieth century. She judged that it served as "an excellent compendium of social-science thinking of the Forties, with some very keen, terse insights of [its] own."[17]

Will Alexander, another member of this notable minority, exempli-

15. Fredrickson, *The Black Image in the White Mind,* 228–319; Robert C. Bannister, *Social Darwinism: Science and Myth in Anglo-American Social Thought* (Philadelphia, 1979), 190–200; John W. Cell, *The Highest Stage of White Supremacy: The Origins of Segregation in South Africa and the American South* (New York, 1982), 171–80.

16. Lillian Smith to Guy B. Johnson, June 12, 1944, quoted in Allred, "Southern Regional Council," 39; Smith, "Addressed to White Liberals," *New Republic,* CXI (1944), 331–33.

17. Paula Snelling (Smith's longtime companion), to the author, September 29, 1969; folder, "Gunnar Myrdal Dinner," in Group II, Series B, Box 14, NAACP Papers; Smith quoted in Rochelle Girson, "Mutation in the Body Politics," *Saturday Review,* August 27,

fied the way some liberals changed with the times. The founder of the CIC in 1919, Alexander publicly announced his desire for integration in *Harper's* in January, 1945. After being away from Atlanta for years serving as the head of various New Deal agencies, he began to see the race problem in a larger context. He also became a close acquaintance of and an adviser to Myrdal. A deeply religious man and an ordained Methodist minister, Alexander helped persuade the Federal Council of Churches to condemn segregation officially in 1946.[18]

While Alexander exercised his influence in the executive branch of the federal government and the church, J. Waties Waring tried to point the federal judiciary toward a new racial path. Deeply influenced by Myrdal and Wilbur Cash late in life, the district judge from Charleston, South Carolina, preached equality with the intensity of a new convert. The judge damned all Jim Crow liberals. More striking, he preached that the South needed outside help to cure its racism, and he used his position to invite federal intervention.[19]

Southern liberals who crossed the Rubicon early suffered mightily for it. Ralph McGill, for example, described Lillian Smith as the "ex-missionary who has made a profession of writing stuff that purposely sets out to debase the South." The Atlantan characterized Smith as a zealot in a hair shirt who was given to the "pouring of ashes on her head and rubbing salt in her own psychiatric wounds." Odum sneered at her "cosmic causes." When Will Alexander retired from his long activist career to a farm near Chapel Hill after World War II, he found that many members of the liberal establishment at the nearby university shunned him. Emily Clay, a longtime secretary for Alexander at the CIC, now viewed him as a traitor. Blacks notwithstanding, the city of Charleston, including close relatives, ostracized the Warings. Night riders burned crosses on their lawn and fired shots into their home. Mounds of scurrilous letters and constant obscene telephone calls descended upon the couple. In 1952 Judge Waring retired and moved to New York City. As

---

1964, p. 76. Smith's psychological insight into the race problem was illustrated in her *Killers of the Dream* (New York, 1949).

18. Will Alexander, "Our Conflicting Racial Policies," *Harper's*, January, 1945, pp. 173–78; Alexander to Myrdal, May 1, 1940, Negro Study, roll 2; Wilma Dykeman and James Stokely, *Seeds of Southern Change: The Life of Will Alexander* (Chicago, 1962), 278, 299; Sosna, *In Search of the Silent South*, 160.

19. William B. Scott, "Judge J. Waties Waring: Advocate of 'Another' South," *South Atlantic Quarterly*, LXXVII (1978), 320–34; Southern, "Beyond Jim Crow Liberalism," 216, 218–21.

one white southerner said of Waring: "We all can't do like him. We all can't be crucified."[20]

Nevertheless, in the decade and a half after *Brown* a number of southern whites stepped forth to brave the wrath of the segregationists. Although there were many glaring exceptions such as Alexander and Waring, younger southerners who came of age in the Great Depression or later made the transition to integration with greater ease. By the 1960s McGill, born in the same year as Myrdal, informed his readers that his old Swedish acquaintance of the 1930s had been right after all.[21]

Since the Supreme Court put the burden of implementing the *Brown* decision on federal district judges, southern jurists found themselves in a sticky situation. Judge Waring's retirement removed the only avowed integrationist from the federal bench in the South. Rigid segregationist judges, usually appointed before 1954, often found ways to render the *Brown* decision meaningless. Moderate judges at least tried to follow the letter of the law, if with deliberate slowness. Only a handful of jurists acted forthrightly in the spirit of the law. By so doing, Frank M. Johnson, an appointee of President Dwight D. Eisenhower, gained notoriety in the South and fame elsewhere. The thirty-seven-year-old Johnson came from northern Alabama, which had a heritage of pro-Union, pro-Republican sympathies. A classmate of George C. Wallace in law school, Johnson sat on the special three-judge court that ordered the desegregation of Montgomery city buses. Wallace, the future governor of Alabama, called the Republican judge "an integrating, race-mixing, scalawagging liar."[22]

20. McGill quoted in Redding S. Sugg, Jr., "Lillian Smith: A Prophecy of Strange Fruit," *Atlanta,* IX (February, 1970), 42; Odum to Guy Johnson, June 22, 1944, Odum Papers; Sosna, *In Search of the Silent South,* 154, 160, 170; Southern, "Beyond Jim Crow Liberalism," 217; quote on Waring in Carl Rowan, "How Far from Slavery?" *Look,* January 15, 1952, p. 22.

21. Atlanta *Constitution,* July 12, 1962, March 31, 1968; Harold Martin, *Ralph McGill: Reporter* (Boston, 1973), 133. For another skeptical liberal who made a quick commitment to integration after 1954, see Harry Ashmore, *An Epitaph for Dixie* (New York, 1958).

22. Wallace quoted in Earl Black, *Southern Governors and Civil Rights: Racial Segregation as a Campaign Issue in the Second Reconstruction* (Cambridge, Mass., 1976), 221; Kenneth N. Vines, "Federal District Judges and Race Relations Cases in the South," *Journal of Politics,* XXVI (1964), 337–57; Jack W. Peltason, *Fifty-Eight Lonely Men: Southern Federal Judges and School Desegregation* (New York, 1961), xii, 6–7, 244–54; Walter F. Murphy and C. Herman Pritchett, *Courts, Judges and Politics: An Introduction to the Judicial Process* (New York, 1961), 591; Jack Bass and Walter Devries, *Transformation of Southern Politics: Social Change and Political Consequence Since 1945* (New

If Johnson received the bulk of the publicity for his liberal stance, Richard Taylor Rives, a native Alabamian and a Democrat, actually wrote the majority opinion concerning Montgomery buses for the three-judge court under the Fifth Circuit Court of Appeals. Until about 1950, Rives held fairly conventional southern views about the Negro. In 1949, however, a personal tragedy changed his life. In that year his son, Richard, Jr., died in an automobile accident. The son, who had been educated in the North, at Exeter and Harvard, and was a student at the University of Michigan Law School at the time of his death, had acquired more liberal views on race than his father. Serving in World War II, he had become acquainted with black soldiers while in a military hospital. He had also devoured Myrdal's book as a student. Deeply affected by the *Dilemma*, the young law student discussed its contents with his father and encouraged the judge to read it.[23]

While trying to recover from the loss of his son, the elder Rives plunged into Myrdal's tome. As a result, his racial views became decidedly more liberal. With Rives and Johnson sitting on many three-judge courts in Montgomery (which then heard cases involving the constitutionality of state laws) and with the former presiding over the Fifth Circuit Court of Appeals in New Orleans, these judicial bodies not only dutifully followed Supreme Court guidelines but blazed a new path of jurisprudence along liberal lines. Sadly, both judges suffered cruel abuse for their courage, the worst incident perhaps being the desecration of the grave of Judge Rives's son.[24]

Few southerners were in a position to effect social change as could a tenured judge. In the Bible Belt of America, however, one might hypothesize that the clergy would wield some power. A sociological study of Little Rock ministers during the desegregation crisis of 1957 concluded that many pastors experienced a Myrdalian dilemma and that the Protestant ministry was "potentially the most effective agent of social change in the South in the decade ahead." Southern preachers hardly

---

York, 1976), 81–83; Tinsley E. Yarbrough, *Judge Frank Johnson and Human Rights in Alabama* (University, Ala., 1981), 1–17, 49.

23. *Browder* v. *Gayle*, 142 F.Supp. 707; Jack Bass, *Unlikely Heroes: The Dramatic Story of the Southern Judges of the Fifth Circuit Who Translated the Supreme Court's Brown Decision into a Revolution for Equality* (New York, 1981), 70; Yarbrough, *Judge Frank Johnson*, 52–53.

24. Bass, *Unlikely Heroes*, 70, 78–79; Stephen Wasby, Anthony A. D'Amato, and Rosemary Metrailer, *Desegregation from Brown to Alexander* (Carbondale, Ill., 1977), 444; see also references in note 22.

lived up to their alleged potential as agents of racial adjustment. By the 1940s, however, the leaders in various churches had become more aware of the contradictions in Jim Crow Christianity. In that decade some seminaries and divinity schools began to integrate. Southern Presbyterians held their first desegregated General Assembly in 1950. In 1954 not only the relatively small and liberal southern Presbyterian church approved the *Brown* decision but also the largest and most conservative denomination, the southern Baptists. Passing resolutions, however, proved easier than implementing them. The liberal pronouncements from on high obviously did not reflect the attitudes of most southern Protestants, many of whom stoutly resisted desegregation.[25]

But the leaders of the church often forged ahead of the religious masses. A significant minority of ministers constituted what Robert Penn Warren called a "fifth column of decency" in racial affairs. Younger ministers particularly had gained more exposure to the sociology of race in their religious education. Most southern clergymen, however, tended to stick closely to biblical references to support their racial directives. This position was prudent when social scientists, especially Myrdal, had become synonymous with the Devil. Many southern pastors, moreover, denounced modern social science at the same time they castigated racism and segregation. Giving the prestigious Rauschenbusch Lectures at the Colgate Rochester Divinity School in the late 1950s, Kyle Haselden displayed a deep knowledge of the social sciences when he spoke on the race problem. He denounced racism and segregation as strongly as any northerner had. The South Carolinian, however, found the social science explanations of racism to be erroneous. Like Reinhold Niebuhr, the famed leader of neo-orthodoxy, Haselden fixed the origins of prejudice in man's self-idolatry. Racism was an independent variable, inherent in the "primordial nature of man."[26] Although Haselden and some other ministers favored the civil rights movement, their analysis of the race problem did not lend itself to the easy optimism of Myrdal and likeminded social scientists. If Myrdal's forecast depended on the idealistic

25. Ernest Q. Campbell and Thomas F. Pettigrew, *Christians in Racial Crisis: A Study of Little Rock's Ministry* (Washington, 1959), viii; E. Terry Prothro and John A. Jensen, "Interrelations of Religious and Ethnic Attitudes in Selected Southern Populations," *Journal of Social Psychology*, XXXII (1950), 45–49; Reimers, *White Protestantism and the Negro*, 107–108, 112–17, 126, 133; Kenneth Bailey, *Southern White Protestants in the Twentieth Century* (New York, 1964), 137–51.

26. Robert Penn Warren, *Segregation: The Inner Conflict* (New York, 1956), 93; Kyle Haselden, *The Racial Problem in Christian Perspective* (New York, 1959), 74–89.

American creed, Haselden's hope hinged on the prospect that millions of whites would be born again into a divine state of color-blindness.

In any case, most southern ministers often approached the race question obliquely. A collection of Presbyterian sermons indicates that pastors employed such refrains as "not race but grace" and "there are no back doors in heaven" when speaking of the race issue. Even so, unrepentant congregations forced many of them into exile or retirement. Occasionally, a preacher such as Carl R. Pritchett would volunteer to his congregation that he had steeped himself in the literature of race. This native North Carolinian, however, served as a pastor in Bethesda, Maryland, on the very fringe of the South. In 1963, on the heels of the massive civil rights march on Washington, Pritchett declared in Myrdalian tones to his congregation: "This is the time. Now we have a great opportunity to live up to the American creed." Liberal preachers and influential laymen such as James McBride Dabbs, who became president of the Southern Regional Council in 1957, had faith that Myrdal's insights and the South's religiosity, combined with the region's much advertised contact between the races, would allow Dixie to solve its race problem more quickly than the North.[27]

Such faith was not restricted to ministers of the gospel. In the decade after *Brown*, liberal scholars, especially historians and political scientists, expressed great hope for the South's racial prospects. They found in Myrdal's thesis a captivating forecast of race relations. They labeled the *Dilemma* a "basic book" on race relations, which furnished a reservoir of factual information about the South, especially on the New Deal period.[28] Exemplifying this use of Myrdal was the work of the noted historian and liberal activist C. Vann Woodward. Coming of age in the 1930s, Woodward had found a reformist hero in 1938 when he wrote a biography of Tom Watson, the Georgia Populist. The *Brown* decision of 1954 further strengthened the young historian's hope that the Jeffersonian, Populist soul of the South was about to be born again. Right after the historic Court decision, the Arkansas scholar reminded Americans

27. Donald W. Shriver, Jr. (ed.), *The Unsilent South: Prophetic Preaching in Racial Crisis* (Richmond, 1965), 34, 49, 58, 95, 99–108; James McBride Dabbs, *The Southern Heritage* (New York, 1958), 68–69.

28. For examples of historians' use of Myrdal, see Tindall, *Emergence of the New South*, 565–66, 571, 633, 636, 762; Thomas B. Clark and Albert A. Kirwan, *The South Since Appomattox* (New York, 1967), 191, 351–52; John Samuel Ezell, *The South Since 1865* (New York, 1963), 356, 476. Even the conservative Francis B. Simkins found use for Myrdal in *The Everlasting South* (Baton Rouge, 1963), xi, 29, 41, 43–44.

in his timely book, *The Strange Career of Jim Crow,* that *de jure* segregation was of recent origin and was therefore not immutable. At the point in the book at which he presented his influential thesis purporting that segregation increased racism, Woodward alluded to the authoritative findings of Myrdal. Unlike his Chapel Hill professors, Odum and Vance, Woodward believed that stateways could change southern folkways. When he sent a draft of his manuscript on the origins of Jim Crow to Vance for criticism, the liberal activist predicted that his former teacher, close friend, and fellow Arkansan would think him "a shallow optimist." In any case, Woodward no longer looked to Chapel Hill for sustenance but to hopeful sources like the *Dilemma,* a book he had eagerly read while on naval duty in World War II. "It did have a strong impact," Woodward recalled, "since it lent support to views I already had." In *The Strange Career of Jim Crow,* he listed Myrdal's book first in his bibliography and described it as "a most useful synthesis of modern scholarship." [29]

In 1958 Woodward published a moving article called "Equality: America's Deferred Commitment." In this essay, he suggested that Afro-Americans could confidently expect full citizenship because the promise of equality had been made long ago. For more than a decade after *Brown,* Woodward exhibited a Myrdalian faith in rational, peaceful, and far-reaching racial change within the system. Like the Swede, he hardly ventured a peek beyond the issue of legal equality. Nor did he seem to doubt that blacks would remain patient and continue to champion a common culture and value system with whites. [30]

Another work that illustrated how liberal historians applied Myrdal's insights to their interpretation of the past can be found in an anthology of essays entitled *The Southerner as American* (1960). In "The Travail of Slavery," Charles G. Sellers virtually ignored the suffering of blacks. Instead he stressed the ordeal of whites under slavery. "Like no other Americans before or since," Sellers sympathized, "the white men of the ante-bellum South drove toward catastrophe by doing conscious violence to their truest selves." In another essay in the collection entitled

29. C. Vann Woodward, *The Strange Career of Jim Crow* (New York, 1955), 94, 104, 153; Woodward's reference was to *AD,* 580; Woodward to Vance, September 14, 1954; Vance to Woodward, September 21, 1954, Rupert B. Vance Papers, Southern Historical Collection, University of North Carolina, Chapel Hill; Woodward to the author, August 12, 1984.

30. C. Vann Woodward, "Equality: America's Deferred Commitment," *American Scholar,* XXVII (1958), 459–72.

"The Central Theme Revisited," George B. Tindall maintained that the white southerner's staunch belief in the American creed represented the "larger Southernism." Had not Myrdal demonstrated, Tindall asked rhetorically, that southern whites could not think "constructively along segregation lines" because "this would imply an open break with the principles of equality and liberty"?[31] If some Myrdal-influenced judges shaped the future, Myrdal-influenced historians inspired change in thinking about the southern past.

Liberal political scientists shared a similar attitude about the South and Myrdal. Professors William G. Carleton and William H. Nicholls, for example, foresaw a progressive future for the South because of the implacable forces of industrialism and the truth of Myrdal's insights. "It now seems fairly certain," Carleton wrote in 1957, "that the American Dilemma posed by Gunnar Myrdal will be resolved in favor of democracy by the fusion of America's traditional ethos with the dynamic, integrating, and leveling forces of industrialism." The revolution in intellectual thinking about race that started with Franz Boas and culminated with Myrdal, Carleton rejoiced, had now spread to the masses. The second Reconstruction, he predicted, would not bog down as the first had.[32]

Liberal professors seemed especially prone to underplaying the realities of the southern past. Myrdal himself confessed that he had "gone to the limits of optimism" when facing the dark facts about Dixie. Similarly, liberal historians emphasized the "forgotten alternatives," "deferred commitments," "travail of slavery [for whites]," and "truest selves" to accentuate the positive. Immensely irritated by all this, the conservative historian Francis B. Simkins countered: "There is a reality about the South which historians with egalitarian standards find hard to understand or appreciate." Simkins lectured liberals that they should learn to "tolerate" the real South that had been aristocratic, fundamentalist, and segregationist.[33]

David M. Potter, a brilliant student of southern history and a native of Georgia, observed that Woodward had constantly been engaged in

31. Charles G. Sellers, "The Travail of Slavery," v–vi, 40, 51; George B. Tindall, "The Central Theme Revisited," 105–106, 116–17, 128–29, in Sellers (ed.), *The Southerner as American* (Chapel Hill, 1960).

32. William G. Carleton, Introduction to Hugh D. Price, *The Negro and Southern Politics* (Washington Square, N.Y., 1957), xv–xvi; William Nicholls, *Southern Tradition and Regional Progress* (Chapel Hill, 1960), xii, 183.

33. Myrdal to Frederick P. Keppel, September 2, 1942, Negro Study, roll 2; Francis B. Simkins, "Tolerating the South's Past," *Journal of Southern History*, XXI (1955), 5.

"an inner struggle in which his historical realism was pitted against his liberal urge to find constructive meaning in the past for the affairs of the present." Though inclined to give his southern colleague the benefit of the doubt, Potter closely scrutinized Woodward's writing in a 1969 biographical essay. In his article "The Search for Southern Identity," Woodward had warned that "if Southernism is allowed to become identified with a last ditch defense of segregation, it will increasingly lose its appeal among the younger generation." From a professional standpoint, Potter found the implications of that statement disturbing. He perceived that Woodward "could not," whatever the evidence, accept Ulrich B. Phillips' thesis concerning the centrality of white supremacy to southern history. Such an admission would diminish Woodward's attempt to find a usable southern heritage for the nation (and perhaps eliminate Woodward as a real southerner). Interestingly, Myrdal and V. O. Key, both liberal observers of the South, had no trouble accepting Phillips' thesis. But, unlike them, Woodward felt that he had to right the past before the present could change. He therefore lauded the early, Populist, pro-Negro Tom Watson and tried to explain away the later Georgia politician who turned reactionary and Negrophobic.[34]

In short, Woodward exhibited the "presentism" that traditional historians found so distasteful in the New Left historians of the 1960s. But because of his graceful prose, his adroit hedging, and his avoidance of stern moral judgments in favor of deft ironies, the southern historian escaped sharp criticism for many years. By the 1970s, however, critics less friendly than Potter pored over Woodward's every word. Some detractors believed that Woodward's assumption of "the burden of southern liberalism" adversely affected his historical judgment. That is, they charged that in looking for a distinctive, liberal, nonracist South, he blinded himself to certain negative realities of his native region. Enthralled by the civil rights crusade, Woodward, Robert Westbrook opined, temporarily dispensed with his usual liberal realism. David A. Hollinger suggested that Woodward spoke more as a southerner than as a historian. He claimed that the influential professor initially praised *Time on the Cross*, a highly controversial and suspect work on slavery, because it tended to vindicate the South.[35]

34. David M. Potter, "C. Vann Woodward," in Marcus Cunliffe and Robin W. Winks (eds.), *Pastmasters: Some Essays on American Historians* (New York, 1969), 392–93, 398; Charles Crowe, "Tom Watson, Populists, and Blacks Reconsidered," *Journal of Negro History*, LV (1970), 99–116; Key, *Southern Politics*, 665.
35. Michael O'Brien, "C. Vann Woodward and the Burden of Southern History,"

In any event, the burden of southern liberalism, not to mention liberalism in general, grew heavier in the late 1960s. Woodward began to lose some of his Myrdalian optimism in the wake of racial violence, black nationalism, and the white backlash. As Potter put it, Woodward's hope for peaceful change had given him "a perfect affinity for the civil rights movement but found him far less compatible with the impulses toward Negro revolution." The Arkansas historian seemed as perplexed by the black revolution as he had been by the transformation of Tom Watson. In a 1969 review of six books on the Civil War and Reconstruction period, which documented the depths of past racism, Woodward conceded that there had been no earlier commitment to racial equality, deferred or otherwise. Although he refused to bow to "cheap fatalism" and fashion facile analogies between the first and second Reconstructions, he acknowledged that the climate had changed drastically in the late 1960s. He now posited the idea that a third and more radical Reconstruction was needed, but he doubted the nation's willingness to undertake it. In the second and third revised editions of *The Strange Career of Jim Crow,* Woodward had much less hope that the democratic creed would bring forth a liberal South. By 1966 he no longer described the *Dilemma* as "modern scholarship" but cited it as "scholarship of its time." [36]

If Woodward's optimism lost some of its edge in the late 1960s, those who had their fingers on the racial pulse of America questioned the prospects of the future even more. Lewis Killian and Charles Grigg, two liberal southern sociologists and racial experts, characterized the southern liberal as a "deviant" in a society that accepted as normal the inferiority of the Negro. Equally somber was the assessment of southern politics at the end of the 1960s. In an impressive statistical study of the state of Georgia, Numan V. Bartley, the liberal political scientist from Texas, concluded: "The best that can be hoped is that Georgia politics will not become substantially more conservative than it has been in the

American Historical Review, LXXVII (1973), 589–604; Allan Peskin, "Was There a Compromise of 1877?" *Journal of American History,* LX (1973), 63–75; Robert B. Westbrook, "C. Vann Woodward: The Southerner as Liberal Realist," *South Atlantic Quarterly,* LXXVII (Winter, 1978), 67–68; David A. Hollinger, "History and the Social Sciences," *Chronicle of Higher Education,* September 29, 1977, pp. 15–16.

36. Potter, "C. Vann Woodward," 404; Woodward, "What Happened to the Civil Rights Movement?" *Harper's,* CCXXXIV (January, 1967), 29–37; and "White Racism and Black Emancipation," *New York Review of Books,* February 27, 1969, pp. 5–11; Woodward, *The Strange Career of Jim Crow,* 2d rev. ed. (1966), 193, 3d rev. ed. (1974), 221.

past."[37] These liberals, like the Jim Crow liberals of the 1940s, judged Myrdal a false prophet who had greatly underestimated the tenacity of racism in the South.

The white supremacists' reaction to Myrdal's book made clear how tenacious that racism was. One of the first efforts to refute the sociology of equality came from the pen of Stuart Omer Landry. In *The Cult of Equality* (1945), this sixty-one-year-old Louisiana banker and advertising agent complained about how unpleasant it was to make "invidious comparisons" between the races. Landry displayed no crude invective or open hate in his attack on Myrdal, as others would often do after 1954. Indeed, he presented Myrdal's book as essential for serious students of race relations. But at the same time, he held that the Swede's interpretations were hopelessly warped. Landry argued that the fate of Western civilization depended upon white supremacy. The only permanent solution to America's race problem, he counseled, entailed sending blacks back to Africa or to some other sparsely populated and remote spot.[38]

In 1947 a broader and more significant book than Landry's appeared: *Whither the Solid South?* by Charles Wallace Collins. An influential Alabama lawyer who practiced in the nation's capital, Collins, like a modern John C. Calhoun, laid down a theoretical and practical framework designed to preserve southern orthodoxy. Widely read and circulated among southern politicians, *Whither the Solid South?* provided a blueprint for the States' Rights party of 1948. Collins not only expressed his alarm about creeping "statism" but also delineated his racial fears under the heading "Second Reconstruction in the Offing." He singled out the *Dilemma* as a book of "ominous prophecy." The Alabama conservative pointed worriedly to a long passage from Myrdal's book that said, in part, that "the North is getting prepared for a fundamental redefinition of the Negro's status in America."[39]

Collins devoted a full page to describing Myrdal's central thesis. He argued, however, that practically no whites, not even liberals like W. T.

37. Lewis Killian and Charles Grigg, *Racial Crisis in America* (Englewood Cliffs, N.J., 1964), 16, 94–95; Numan V. Bartley, *From Thurmond to Wallace: Political Tendencies in Georgia, 1948–1968* (Baltimore, 1970), 109.

38. Stuart Omer Landry, *The Cult of Equality: A Study of the Race Problem* (New Orleans, 1945), vii, xii, 324–28, 345.

39. Robert A. Garson, *The Democratic Party and the Politics of Sectionalism, 1941–1948* (Baton Rouge, 1979), 236–38; Charles Wallace Collins, *Whither the Solid South?* (New Orleans, 1947), 20.

Couch, endorsed Myrdal's extreme ideas. Yet the conservative strategist warned that Myrdal's influence should not be underestimated. Indeed, he seemed to attribute the rising race consciousness among blacks to the Carnegie project. He forecast that "practically every educated Negro and every intelligent radical Negro protagonist among the white people will use this source for support and propaganda in every aspect of the Negro's struggle against every form of segregation and discrimination.'" Like Landry, Collins felt that a possible answer to the race problem was the formation of a forty-ninth state in Africa.[40]

In contrast to the books by Landry and Collins, Theodore G. Bilbo's *Take Your Choice: Separation or Mongrelization* ranked as an exercise in political demagoguery. In 1911, the state senate of Mississippi censured Bilbo and declared him "unfit to sit with honest, upright men in a respectable legislative body." This fiery politician nevertheless later became governor and senator. An inveterate race-baiter, Bilbo characterized the Fair Employment Practices Committee of World War II as "nothing but a plot put niggers to work next to your daughters and to run your business with niggers." In *Take Your Choice,* Bilbo excoriated the egalitarian behavioral scientists from Franz Boas to Myrdal. He cited the *Dilemma* as the "most comprehensive and elaborate" book of its kind, but he argued that it differed from other books promoting race mixing only in its collaborative method and its verbosity. The senator, however, did not accuse Myrdal of being a Communist subversive.[41]

Such restraint would not continue after the Supreme Court ruled against segregation in schools. Although parts of the South took the *Brown* decision fairly calmly, the response in the Deep South was immediate and defiant. On May 17, 1954, Senator James Eastland of Mississippi declared: "The South will not abide by nor obey the legislative decision by a political court." Governor Herman Talmadge of Georgia exclaimed: "The fact that the high tribunal has seen fit to proclaim its views on sociology as law will not make any difference." Talmadge promised there would be no race mixing in Georgia schools. The powerful Senator Richard B. Russell of Georgia branded the justices "amateur psychologists." Other southern politicians registered their disdain for the Court in the *Congressional Record.*[42] But the angry legislators

40. Collins, *Whither the Solid South?* 62.
41. James W. Silver, *Mississippi: The Closed Society* (New York, 1963), 19; New York *Times,* June 30, 1946; Theodore G. Bilbo, *Take Your Choice: Separation or Mongrelization* (Poplarville, Miss., 1947), 170–72.
42. New York *Times,* May 18, 1954; *Christian Science Monitor,* May 18, 1954; *Congressional Record,* 83d Cong., 2nd Sess., 6742–49.

made no mention of Myrdal's name. Footnote 11, which encouraged the reader of the *Brown* opinion to see "generally" the *Dilemma*, had not yet received the intense scrutiny of the segregationists.

Many, however, would soon attack the social scientists whose work had buttressed the *Brown* opinion. Judge Tom P. Brady launched one of the earliest and most significant assaults on the Court's decision and its social science references. In late May, 1954, Brady, a state circuit judge in Brookhaven, Mississippi, delivered a speech entitled "Black Monday" to the Sons of the American Revolution in the town of Greenwood. Implored by his enthusiastic audience to put his thoughts in a book, the judge published *Black Monday* the following month. This brief and hastily written book proved to be the catalyst in the formation of the trend-setting White Citizens' Councils. *Black Monday*, in fact, elevated Brady to the position of metaphysician of the master racists.[43]

The judge's book typified the flood of segregationist tracts spawned by the *Brown* decision. Brady blurred the lines between the civil rights crusade and the international communist movement. He asserted that inferior Negro blood had always acted like a cup of hemlock to white civilization. Unlike the genteel Landry, Brady did not flinch from making invidious comparisons of the races. The scion of the Magnolia Jungle compared Negroes to chimpanzees in contrast to "the loveliest and purest of God's creatures . . . a well-bred, cultured white woman or her blue-eyed, golden-haired little girl."[44]

Brady argued that the Supreme Court had been "socialized and psychologized." Even Myrdal had acknowledged, the judge explained, that Negroes did not desire integrated schools. For this specious use of Myrdal, the judge, no doubt, had perused the briefs by the segregationists in the *Brown* case. Like them, Brady quoted Myrdal's discussion of W. E. B. Du Bois out of context, making the black leader appear to favor segregated schools. Despite this appeal to Myrdal, Brady condemned the Swedish economist as follows: "Gunner [*sic*] Myrdal (who probably had never seen a dozen negroes in his life until the Carnegie Foundation brought him to this country) wrote a volume on the racial problem. . . . It is based on a few uncorrelated facts, impersonally obtained, together with much theory, 'full of sound and fury signifying nothing.' Such nonsense could have been the reservoir from which our Supreme Court obtained some of its conclusions."[45]

43. Hodding Carter III, *The South Strikes Back* (Garden City, N.Y., 1959), 26–27, 30–31; Silver, *Mississippi*, 25.
44. Tom P. Brady, *Black Monday* (Winona, Miss., 1955), 7, 12, 45.
45. *Ibid.*, 30–34, 47, 63.

The Mississippi judge felt that the racial situation demanded drastic action to save the white race and American capitalism. He suggested the abolition of public schools, economic coercion of Negroes to keep them from pressing for desegregation, the establishment of a national federation of sovereign states, and creation of a forty-ninth state outside the United States for Afro-Americans. In addition, he warned that the shrewd communist leaders knew that "a mongrelized race is an ignorant, weak, easily conquered race."[46]

If Brady helped spark massive resistance in Dixie, Senator Eastland used his leverage in Washington as chairman of the Senate Judiciary Committee to wage a heroic one-man resistance to civil rights legislation. Numerous civil rights bills met their death in his committee, if he even allowed them a hearing. Moreover, he helped etch into the brain of every segregationist worth his salt the image of Myrdal as a diabolical foreigner who worked inside the international communist conspiracy to subvert Anglo-Saxon America. About a year after the first *Brown* decision, Eastland aimed a barrage of charges at the "modern authority" cited by the Court in the 1954 ruling. On May 25, 1955, the Mississippian introduced a lengthy resolution into the Senate, parts of which bear repeating:

Whereas, The book, *An American Dilemma*, was prepared by a Swedish Socialist who declared in the book that the United States Constitution was "impractical and unsuited to modern conditions" and its adoption was "nearly a plot against the common people"; and

Whereas, This book was the result of collaboration between Myrdal and certain alleged "scholars and experts" assigned him by the Carnegie Corp., of Alger Hiss fame; and

Whereas, Sixteen of these so-called scholars and experts, who contributed to no less than 272 different articles and portions of the book, have been cited numerous times as members of communist and subversive organizations; and

Whereas, The citation of these authorities clearly indicates a dangerous influence and control exerted on the Court by communist-front pressure groups and other enemies of the American republic and individual members thereof that is inimical to the general welfare and best interest of the Republic; and. . . .

Resolved, That it is the sense of the Senate that the Senate Committee on the Judiciary should proceed under its presently constituted powers to investigate the extent and degree of participation by individuals and groups iden-

46. *Ibid.*, 67, 78, 84.

tified with the communist conspiracy, communist-front organizations, and alien ideologies, in the formation of the "modern scientific authority" upon which the Supreme Court relied in the school integration cases.[47]

Apparently, Eastland had already carried out his investigation. The next day he had entered in the *Congressional Record* five pages of allegations concerning the works and authors cited by the Court. The senator described Myrdal as a "Socialist who had served the Communist cause" and had "utter contempt for the principles on which America was founded." After a brief respite, the spirit of Joseph McCarthy stalked Capitol Hill once more.[48]

The Eastland resolution became a prime source for leading segregationists, especially politicians. Governor Herman Talmadge, for example, launched his race-baiting Senate campaign with a booklet called *You and Segregation* (1955). In the section "Court Trusts Foreign 'Experts,'" Talmadge filled two pages with quotations from Eastland. For the next two decades, Senator Talmadge would bewail the "un-American" revolution wrought by the Supreme Court and Myrdal. At all levels of government—whether it be Governor James F. Byrnes of South Carolina, a former Supreme Court justice, or Leander Perez, the boss of Plaquemines Parish in Louisiana—politicians echoed Eastland's allegations over and over, often in identical language. Senators and congressmen filled the *Congressional Record* with character assassinations of the "Swedish Carpetbagger." Debunkers sometimes referred to "Dr. Karl Gunnar Myrdal," a version of the European's name technically correct but one the subject never used.[49] The segregationists most likely reasoned that "Karl" sounded more Marxian.

Members of the legal profession seldom displayed any better grasp of Myrdal's work and his politics than did the politicians. In a desegregation case in South Carolina, Judge Armistead M. Dobie, appointed by

47. *Congressional Record*, 84th Cong., 1st Sess., 6963–64.
48. *Ibid.*, 7120–24.
49. Herman Talmadge, *You and Segregation* (Birmingham, Ala., 1955), 58, 74, 78; see Talmadge's comments in the *Congressional Record*, 86th Cong., 1st Sess., 5421; James Graham Cook, *The Segregationists* (New York, 1962), 113, 198–99. For attacks on Myrdal by various congressmen and senators, see *Congressional Record*, 84th Cong., 2nd Sess., 8758; *Congressional Record*, 85th Cong., 1st Sess., 557; *Congressional Record*, 85th Cong., 2nd Sess., 452; *Congressional Record*, 88th Cong., 1st Sess., 23252; *Congressional Record*, 88th Cong., 2nd Sess., 9600. For provocative vignettes of the reactionaries, see Robert Sherrill, *Gothic Politics in the Deep South: Stars of the New Confederacy* (New York, 1969).

Herbert Hoover to the Fourth Circuit Court of Appeals, lectured Thurgood Marshall that the Court should rely on sound evidence and not on "foreign communistic anthropologists." The obvious dig at Myrdal (and perhaps Boas) would be repeated, with slight variations, again and again by southern federal judges, state supreme court justices, attorneys general, state judges, and prosecuting attorneys. When the supreme court of Florida refused to integrate the state university as ordered by the high tribunal, Justice C. J. Terrell said he could not follow an opinion based "solely on the writing of Gunnar Myrdal." In a trial of whites who had lynched a Negro in Mississippi, the prosecuting attorney refused to read an FBI report that incriminated the defendants. Judge Sebe Dale backed up the prosecuting attorney and told the members of the all-white jury that they were like soldiers battling for the southern way of life. "We should have the backbone to stand against tyranny," he declared, "even including the board of sociology, sitting in Washington . . . and dishing out the precedents of Gunnar Myrdal." [50]

Southern journalists also found Myrdal an inviting target. In a 1956 article, Grover C. Hall, editor of the Montgomery *Advertiser*, castigated the "nine most puissant sociologists in the republic—proteges grateful of the Swede Myrdal." Ross Valentine of the Richmond *Times-Dispatch* began one of his anti-Court columns with the phrase, "All for Sweden and the Constitution Well Lost!" The Richmond journalist commented that desegregation never had a chance to pass in Congress, but the Court did the trick with "Dr. Myrdal's distorting mirrors." [51]

Myrdal's position in the hierarchy of demons can be seen in the attitude of the White Citizens' Councils. In the second issue of its official journal, the *Citizens' Council*, a cartoon on page 1 showed a malicious-looking judge pounding his desk with a gavel marked "Black Monday Decision." Below the bench looking up at the judge was a youth labeled "The Innocent South." Leering over the judge's shoulder was a satanic character representing the NAACP. To complete this poignant scene, a large book marked *An American Dilemma* lay beside the judge. Similar

50. *Southern School News*, II (August, 1955), 7; Peltason, *Fifty-Eight Lonely Men*, 23; Murphy and Pritchett, *Courts, Judges and Politics*, 614; *Florida ex rel. Hawkins v. Board of Control*, 93 So 2d 354 (1957); U.S. Civil Rights Commission, *1961 Report*, Vol. 5, *Justice* (1961), p. 42.

51. Grover C. Hall, "Alabama's Bus Boycott: What It's All About," *U.S. News & World Report*, August 3, 1956, pp. 85–86; Richmond *Times-Dispatch*, April 13, 1955, July 18, 1956; see also Thomas R. Waring, "The Southern Case Against Desegregation," *Harper's*, CCXII (January, 1956), 37.

cartoons appeared regularly in later issues of the journal. In the March, 1956, issue, a six-frame sequence cartoon, designed to reveal how the NAACP won legal cases, included one scene that had little men poring over a gigantic, opened copy of the *Dilemma*. Presumably, they searched for passages to beguile the Supreme Court.[52]

In the 1960s some less shrill and more scholarly southern segregationists dealt with Myrdal. Two works stand out in particular: William D. Workman, Jr.'s *The Case for the South* (1960) and James J. Kilpatrick's *The Southern Case for School Segregation* (1962). The South they spoke for was the white South, but they strived, albeit not always successfully, to present their arguments in a fair and scholarly way. Employing relentless logic and starting from the Calhounian premises of state sovereignty and Negro inferiority, they presented a more formidable case for segregation than the Eastlands, the Talmadges, and the Bradys.

Workman criticized the integrationists for posing the race question as a moral issue. When issues became enmeshed in moral values, he argued, the possibility of peaceful change diminished. The subject of moral values served to bring Myrdal into the picture. Using statistics from a much used article in the *Scientific American,* attesting to declining racism, Workman claimed that no moral dilemma existed in the white mind. He demonstrated that polls over the previous fifteen years indicated that two-thirds of whites nationally believed that the Negro was treated fairly. The figure was even higher in the South. All of this proved, Workman insisted, that Myrdal had recorded what people ought to think rather than what they thought. Since Myrdal's main thesis was unsubstantiated by empirical data, such an attack on him raised serious questions about the *Dilemma*. Indeed, radical scholars outside the South and black nationalists often used this line of attack on Myrdal in the 1960s.[53]

James Kilpatrick, who succeeded Douglas S. Freeman as editor of the Richmond *News-Leader,* relied more on antebellum constitutional theory than Workman did to make his case. He revived the nineteenth-century doctrine of interposition for use against the federal government. Although the Virginia conservative did not criticize Myrdal's central thesis, he sniped hard at the Swede's intellectual flanks. On the subject

52. *Citizens' Council,* I (November, 1955), 1; *ibid.,* II (March, 1956), 4; *ibid.* (June, 1956), 2.

53. William D. Workman, *The Case for the South* (New York, 1960), 121–23; Herbert H. Hyman and Paul B. Sheatsley, "Attitudes Toward Desegregation," *Scientific American,* CXCV (December, 1956), 35–39.

of Negro crime, for instance, Kilpatrick accused Myrdal of relying on "scoffs, sneers, apologies, high-blown fabrications and wildly speculative generalities, all intended to whitewash the Negro record." In reading the statistics on Negro crime, he concluded that only genetics satisfactorily explained the higher incidence of lawlessness among the minority. In a sarcastic aside, the journalist speculated that only eleven men south of the Potomac had ever completely read Myrdal's "monumental and monumentally unreadable work." Kilpatrick did not include himself among the courageous few, but he admitted to have "ploughed through most of it."[54]

Extreme right-wingers added little new ammunition to the southern segregationist attack on Myrdal, and they certainly read less of the *Dilemma* than had Kilpatrick. Nonetheless, they contributed mightily to the sound and the fury. Since the Radical Right had almost no national organization before the late 1950s, no official statements issued forth on Myrdal as from the Communist party in America. The initial reactions from ultraconservatives, like those of the southerners, emanated from scattered individuals. The early responses thus varied more than the later ones. After the *Brown* decision and the formation of the John Birch Society in 1959, however, the Far Right churned out greatly distorted and highly stereotyped portraits of Myrdal and the *Dilemma*.

Even before the desegregation decree, Congressman George A. Dondero of Michigan had defamed Myrdal in a fashion not unlike that of his midwestern colleague, Senator Joseph McCarthy. In reference to a 1950 bill that supported the United Nations International Children's Emergency Fund (UNICEF), Dondero asked his fellow congressmen if Alva Myrdal would have anything to do with the distribution of UNICEF funds. His anxiety about Mrs. Myrdal became evident when he described her husband as "a prominent Swedish Communist who introduced Trygve Lie to Stalin recently." Dondero not only fought Communist phantoms, but he also campaigned against such assorted evils as cubism, surrealism, and futurism.[55]

In the early 1950s A. H. Hobbs, a professor of sociology at the University of Pennsylvania, also began a crusade against several of the mod-

54. James J. Kilpatrick, *The Southern Case for School Segregation* (New York, 1962), 66, 69–70, 216; see also Peter Carmichael, *The South and Segregation* (Washington, 1965), 147, 151–52, 308.

55. *Congressional Record*, 81st Cong., 2nd Sess., 7532; Congressman James F. Fulton of Pennsylvania corrected Dondero's impression of Myrdal on p. 7534; Richard Hofstadter, *Anti-Intellectualism in American Life* (New York, 1964), 14–15.

ern isms. He selected "liberal scientism" or the "sociological empha-sis" as his primary target. With the growth of the teaching of sociology in the schools after World War II, Hobbs grew alarmed about what he perceived as the brainwashing of the young. In *The Claims of Sociology* in 1951, the professor complained that the textbooks were ignoring he-redity in favor of environmentalism. Two years later, in *Social Problems and Scientism*, Hobbs blamed modern education for fostering divorce, juvenile delinquency, dope addiction, and homosexuality. Because of books like the *Dilemma*, he groused, teachers had eradicated the idea of racial differences. Without mustering any evidence, Hobbs caricatured the Myrdal study as a heap of ludicrous inconsistencies.[56]

In the early 1950s an increasing demand arose in some circles for such thinkers as Hobbs. In the eventful spring of 1954, he turned up in Washington, along with several other radically conservative witnesses, to testify before the ad hoc House committee set up to investigate tax-exempt foundations. Known as the Reece Committee after its Republi-can chairman, B. Carroll Reece of Tennessee, this legislative device provided the southern congressman with a chance to lambast philan-thropic agencies thought to be liberal or left-leaning. Riding the crest of the McCarthy wave, in 1953 Reece charged that foundations had given grants and aid to numerous Communists and un-American types. In hearings that began one week before the *Brown* decision, Reece's staff unveiled a report so ill-documented and one-sided and witnesses so far to the right that the minority Democrats mutinied. Although the staff report reeked with insidious innuendo about the nature of the Carnegie-Myrdal project and many witnesses accused it of sinister tendencies, the charges ultimately boiled down to the allegation that the Swedish scholar was very liberal, highly prejudiced, and severely critical of the Constitution. The hearings terminated prematurely because of the Democratic revolt, but foundation heads, who received no opportunity to testify, were belatedly invited to send written statements to the com-mittee. Charles Dollard, who had welcomed Myrdal off the ship from Sweden in 1938 and who now held the presidency of the Carnegie Cor-poration, defended Myrdal in a strong letter to the committee. Dollard reminded the committee that Myrdal was vehemently anti-Communist, had made that fact central in his study of blacks, and had been roundly condemned by the Communist party for doing so. The McCarthy-army

56. A. H. Hobbs, *The Claims of Sociology* (Harrisburg, Pa., 1951), 1, 5, 8–13; *So-cial Problems and Scientism* (Harrisburg, Pa., 1953), iii–v, 183.

hearings and the *Brown* decision overshadowed the Reece Committee in
1954, but several scholars have since looked closely at the Tennessee
congressman's efforts. They basically judged the Reece Committee to be
"crudely prejudiced" and "inept." It turned up no persuasive evidence
against the large foundations.[57]

The *Brown* opinion, of course, only provoked the Radical Right to
more frenetic activity. By the late 1950s numerous John Birchers had
authored an avalanche of books and articles warning of internal subversion in America. The works of E. Merrill Root, a former professor of
English at Earlham College, typified this genre. Two of his books, *Collectivism on Campus* (1956) and *Brainwashing in the High Schools*
(1959), served as guidebooks on education for the Far Right. After examining numerous textbooks, Root concluded that Communist influence
in the schools had reached frightening proportions. In both of his books,
Root labeled Myrdal as one of the "tainted sources" eagerly employed
by the modern educational establishment.[58]

The man most identified with the Far Right, of course, was Robert
Welch, the founder of the John Birch Society. In the 1950s the candy
baron from Massachusetts privately circulated a provocative manuscript
about American politics; it was finally published in 1963 in a somewhat
expurgated form as *The Politician*. In this volume few officials of any
stature in the American government escaped the Red smear, including
George Marshall, John Foster Dulles, and President Eisenhower. The
paladin of the Far Right asserted that the civil rights movement was a
nefarious plot that went "as far back as when Gunnar Myrdal [was]
brought over here to write his mammoth book."[59]

With the tighter organization under Welch, radical conservatives
spread cloned indictments of Myrdal throughout the land. In the Southwest Dan Smoot and other evangelists enlisted the support of right-wing
oilmen such as H. L. Hunt to indict the Scandinavian author as a

57. *Hearings, Special Committee to Investigate Tax-Exempt Foundations and Com-
parable Organizations*, 83d Cong., 2nd Sess., Pt. 1, pp. 167–72, *passim; Congressional
Record*, 83d Cong., 1st Sess., Pt. 3, pp. 3726–28; John Lankford, *Congress and Founda-
tions in the Twentieth Century* (River Falls, Wis., 1964), 69; Waldemar A. Nielsen, *The
Big Foundations* (New York, 1972), 86; Warren Weaver, *U.S. Philanthropic Foundations:
Their History, Structure, Management and Record* (New York, 1967), 175.

58. E. Merrill Root, *Collectivism on Campus* (New York, 1955), 255; and *Brainwashing in the High Schools* (New York, 1959), 249; Overstreet and Overstreet, *Strange
Tactics of Extremism*, 252–56.

59. Robert Welch, *The Politician* (Belmont, Mass., 1963), 15, 66–67, 291.

communist-fronter. Westbrook Pegler, a former liberal journalist turned reactionary, referred regularly to the *Brown* decision as the "Myrdal edict." Earl Lively perhaps disclosed his contempt for Sigmund Freud as well as for the Swede when he wrote: "The Gunnar Myrdal thesis that segregation injures the Negro's *id* has no bearing." [60] All of these critics exaggerated the influence of Myrdal and displayed a superficial grasp of the *Dilemma*.

Even those who were considered members of the responsible right could not resist the broadside approach of the radical conservatives when considering Myrdal. An editorial in the *National Review* by William F. Buckley, Jr., resorted to sarcasm, innuendo, and *ad hominem* arguments to burlesque the Swedish scholar. A 1957 editorial, entitled "Dr. Gunnar Twistmaul," introduced Myrdal as an economist who had taken a little time off to become "the world's greatest authority on the American Negro." The article also charged that Myrdal had been fired as Swedish minister of trade for making an economic agreement too favorable to the Soviet Union. Buckley used similar tactics when he interviewed the globetrotting Swede on his television show, "The Firing Line." After introducing Myrdal as "the most-hated social scientist in conservative circles" and as an expert on practically everything from bridge to blacks, Buckley asked the European to elaborate on his belief that capitalism caused racism. In the ever voluble and now indignant Scandinavian, Buckley clearly met his verbal match. Myrdal correctly told his host in a torrent of words and in the bluntest terms that he had never held such a belief, and he bellowed at Buckley that it was nowhere to be found in the *Dilemma*. The interview showed that the conservative pundit, like the more radical right-wingers, had not read Myrdal's classic with care. [61]

Whether from the responsible right or the irresponsible right, the brush that smeared Myrdal followed Arnold Rose. The Far Right converged on Myrdal's chief assistant on the Carnegie project when he won

60. *Dan Smoot Report,* June 30, 1965, p. 5; *American Opinion,* VI (March, 1963), 16; Earl Lively, Jr., *The Invasion of Mississippi* (Belmont, Mass., 1963), 43–44, 115; for some other examples, see Rosalie M. Gordon, *Nine Men Against America: The Supreme Court and Its Attack on American Liberties* (New York, 1958), 92; Harold Lord Varney, "Who and What Is Ralph Bunche?" *American Mercury,* LXXXII (May, 1956), 29–34; Alan Stang, *It's Very Simple: The True Story of Civil Rights* (Boston, 1965), 227; *White Sentinel,* IX (April, 1959), 8.

61. *National Review,* III (January 26, 1957), 78; "Firing Line" on Public Television Station, Channel 8, Athens, Georgia, December 21, 1969.

election to the Minnesota legislature in 1962. At that time Gerda Koch, the publisher of a radical sheet called *Facts for Action*, stepped up her attack on the Jewish sociologist, charging him with subversion. Rose sued Koch for libel. The subsequent three-week trial presented a bizarre spectacle, beautifully captured in Rose's book *Libel and Academic Freedom: A Lawsuit Against Political Extremists*. In his opening remarks to the jury, Koch's lawyer, Jerome Daly, charged that Rose was "one of the most resourceful Communists in the whole United States with reference to the Communist conspiracy as it exists today." The defense then paraded a horde of conspiratorial-minded witnesses before the jury. It introduced as evidence a small library of publications which alleged that Myrdal was "a notorious Swedish Communist" who had "blueprinted the whole race-equality policy" in America and the United Nations. Between sessions of court, Koch sold copies of Senator Eastland's 1955 resolution for twenty cents. In his final words to the jury, Daly maintained that Myrdal had merely been a front man for Rose and other American conspirators. Daly described Rose as a "Jewish-Shylock-usury" element. Surprisingly, Daly acknowledged that the American Communist party had villified Myrdal in the 1940s, but he explained that it was a clever ruse to divert attention away from the *Dilemma's* collectivism.[62]

In preparing Koch's defense, Daly undoubtedly perused *The Great Deceit: Social-Pseudo Sciences* (1964). In fantastic detail, this work outdid all the others in attempting to demonstrate that the Communist conspiracy had totally subverted American social sciences. Published by the Veritas Foundation under the direction of Archibald Roosevelt and Zygmund Dobbs, *The Great Deceit* devoted almost twenty pages to the Carnegie-Myrdal project. According to Veritas, the project was a conspiracy that began in the 1920s, when the socialist Frederick Keppel became president of the Carnegie Corporation. Keppel then collaborated with the Social Science Research Council, described as a "holding company" for radical anthropology, to concoct a racial Bible for the left. The book maintained that Americans such as Arnold Rose, Otto Klineberg, Gordon Allport, and Arthur Schlesinger, Jr., collected and organized the material for the "gigantic anthropological device" known as the *Dilemma*. These native scholars attached Myrdal's name to

62. Arnold Rose, *Libel and Academic Freedom: A Lawsuit Against Political Extremists* (Minneapolis, 1968), 11, 16, 181, 238, 241, 250, 281, and *passim;* see *Time,* December 10, 1965, pp. 67–68, for a brief description of the trial.

the book for prestige and to hide the truth that it constituted a "major Communist-Socialist joint effort."[63]

Carleton Putnam could hardly enhance the exotic conspiracy theories the Far Right used to explain the course of racial events in America. He did, however, devise a new strategy for the southern segregationists. A New Englander by heritage and a southerner by adoption, Putnam became the foremost popularizer of "neo-scientific racism" in the 1960s. He also represented an important link between the Far Right and southern segregationists. After the publication of his *Race and Reason* in 1961, the prosperous airline executive replaced Judge Brady as the metaphysician of the White Citizens' Councils. Provoked into political activism by President Eisenhower's use of troops in Little Rock in 1957, Putnam delved deeply into the *Brown* case and the literature on race. He found to his dismay that social science had changed dramatically since his undergraduate days at Princeton University. The more he read, the more indignant and alarmed he became about the dominance of equalitarian social science in the schools. He singled out the *Dilemma* as "an open threat to the pillars of the American way of life." He contended, however, that Myrdal did not create the threat but only popularized the "insidious propaganda" of Franz Boas, who as a German Jew he linked with Karl Marx.[64]

In 1961 Mississippi Governor Ross Barnett proclaimed October 26 Race and Reason Day. On that day Putnam appeared in Jackson to speak before five hundred of the state's most illustrious members of the White Citizens' Council at a $25 a plate dinner. The Yankee orator warmed up his southern audience by telling them that they need not succumb to world opinion as long as their capital was in Jackson and not in the Congo's Leopoldville. To the delight of his listeners, Putnam soundly thrashed the "pseudo scientists" on the left. Then the Madison Grant of the 1960s thundered in a manner befitting William Jennings Bryan: "You don't crucify the South on a cross of equalitarian propaganda."[65]

More significantly, Putnam coaxed southerners to abandon their rigid

63. Archibald Roosevelt and Zygmund Dobbs, *The Great Deceit: Social-Pseudo Sciences* (West Sayville, N.Y., 1964), 195–211.

64. Idus A. Newby, *Challenge to the Court: Social Scientists and the Defense of Segregation, 1954–1966* (Baton Rouge, 1967), 146–70; Silver, *Mississippi*, 25; Carleton Putnam, *Race and Reason: A Yankee View* (Washington, 1961), 22–23, 111; see also Putnam, *Race and Reality* (Washington, 1967), 14, 17, 21–23, 67, 69–70.

65. *Citizen*, VI (November, 1961), 13–33, carried Putnam's speech and devoted the entire issue to the Yankee racist; Silver, *Mississippi*, 26.

constitutional defense of segregation. He advised them to fight the *Brown* decision with inequalitarian sociology. Putnam assured his hosts that the evidence to overturn *Brown* and restore legal segregation in the schools was nearly ready and would come from a scientist of unimpeachable reputation. The segregationists, the Yankee entrepreneur counseled, must take a new case to the Supreme Court, one showing that integrated schools harmed the superior white race. Governor Barnett felt that Putnam's speech marked "a turning point in the South's struggle to preserve the integrity of the white race."[66]

The great white hope of science to whom Putnam alluded turned out to be Wesley Critz George. A retired chairman of the anatomy department at the University of North Carolina in Chapel Hill, George received direct sponsorship and financial aid from the governor of Alabama for his racial research. His 1962 booklet, *The Biology of the Race Question*, resorted to the old and discredited practice of comparing the sizes of Caucasian and Negroid brains. Essentially, though, George's attack on equalitarian social science and Myrdal more resembled the work of the antebellum Thomas R. Dew than that of a modern natural scientist.[67]

Encouraged by Putnam and George, the segregationists took a new case to court. In 1963 they initiated legal action in Savannah, Georgia. Their case directly challenged footnote 11 in the *Brown* opinion with the works of neoscientific racists. The segregationists won at the district level. But the Fifth Circuit Court of Appeals, under the Myrdal-influenced Judge Rives, refused to encourage another lost cause. It reversed the lower court and foiled Putnam's grand strategy to preserve the integrity of the white race.[68]

With the convergence of the southern segregationists and the Radical Right, the criticism of Myrdal became highly stylized and outlandish. By the 1960s the conventional wisdom among white supremacists was that the *Brown* decision had been masterminded in the Kremlin with an assist from the Swedish radical. Myrdal became one of the primary demons upon which frustrated southerners and the Far Right vented their

66. *Citizen*, VI (November, 1961), 32–33; Silver, *Mississippi*, 26.
67. Wesley Critz George, *The Biology of the Race Problem* (N.p. [Montgomery, Ala.?], 1962), 56, 78, and *passim*. See McMillen, *Citizens' Council*, 169; and Newby, *Challenge to the Court*, 110, 115, for criticism of George.
68. *Stell v. Savannah-Chatham County Board of Education*, 315 F.2d 425 (1963); for the facts of the case, see *Race Relations Law Reporter*, VIII (1963), 514–18.

collective spleen.[69] The Swedish economist provided a convenient symbol who represented both the alleged Communist conspiracy and the civil rights plot in one person, one book. Members of the segregationist tribe seemed to differ only on whether Myrdal constituted a powerful and corrupt source in his own right or whether he simply posed as a front man for such indigenous subversives as the Klinebergs, the Frankfurters, and the Schlesingers.

Obviously, almost none of the rabid segregationists or the radical conservatives read the *Dilemma* closely, much less with an open mind. Among other things, they blindly ignored Myrdal's prescience about the Soviet Union and his fervent anticommunism.[70] For a more informed, judicious, and interesting view of the *Dilemma,* one had to go to the academic world from whence Myrdal came.

69. Charles O. Lerche, Jr., *The Uncertain South* (Chicago, 1964), 245; James W. Vander Zanden, *Race Relations in Transition* (New York, 1965), 19, 24; Francis M. Wilhoit, *The Politics of Massive Resistance* (New York, 1973), 122, 130.

70. In addition to *AD,* see *Challenge to Affluence* (New York, 1963), 122–24, 306.

VIII

Myrdal, Academia, and the Race Problem, 1945–1965

In his review of the twentieth-anniversary edition of the *Dilemma,* Oscar Handlin declared that Myrdal's study had been a "magnet" to scholars, who had spread and enhanced his influence through their constant emulation, criticism, and confirmation of his findings. One such example occurred in 1955, when many luminaries of the social science world gathered at Fisk University in Nashville, Tennessee, to dedicate a building to the late Robert E. Park. Professor Ernest Burgess, one of a series of speakers, told his audience that the last fifteen years had brought tremendous breakthroughs in the study of race relations. "Of first importance in the forward movement," he stated, "was the publication of the book *An American Dilemma.*" [1]

Some of the listeners must have sensed the irony as Burgess, a long-time colleague of Park at the University of Chicago, gave such exalted praise to the Swedish economist. Myrdal's *Dilemma* had lumped Park with the "laissez-faire, do-nothing" social scientists. Burgess conspicuously ignored the intellectual chasm between Myrdal and Park and simply recited their respective contributions to the advancement of race studies. Burgess explained the astounding success of Myrdal's report in the following words: "The combination of the facts and its value-orientation has made *An American Dilemma* the most powerful instrument of action in the field of race relations since Harriet Beecher Stowe's *Uncle Tom's Cabin.*" He added that the Myrdal study appealed

1. Handlin, Review of *AD,* 1; Ernest W. Burgess, "Social Planning and Race Relations," in Jitsuichi Masuoka and Preston Valien (eds.), *Race Relations: Problems and Theory* (Chapel Hill, 1961), 20.

187

to "the hearts of men by evoking the American Creed and also to their minds by its ordering of the facts."[2]

This chapter investigates this dual appeal of Myrdal's work to the academic world. It also deals with the many modifications and denunciations of the *Dilemma* that steadily accumulated from 1945 to 1965. As Burgess stated, Myrdal struck an emotional chord in people, but the Swede had less success in capturing the minds of scholars when they considered his ordering and interpreting of the facts. At the same Nashville meeting at which Burgess so effusively praised Myrdal, Samuel Stouffer, for instance, expressed regret that Myrdal had affected the thinking of so many professors. Another product of the University of Chicago, Stouffer had served as an indispensable staff member for Myrdal on the Carnegie project. In 1949 he produced his own classic, *The American Soldier.* Myrdal's old friend, however, was a quantifying sociologist, who felt that the Scandinavian economist had deflected attention away from the most crucial forces shaping American race relations. He complained that the Swede had overemphasized vague ideological factors at the expense of more measurable economic and political forces, particularly the all-important black political activity.[3]

Although Stouffer disagreed with Myrdal's emphasis in the *Dilemma,* he confessed that the American creed affected and strengthened all other forces bearing on racial change. Stouffer, like many liberal scholars, wanted to believe in the moral suasion of the American ethos as enunciated by Myrdal. Yet in their quest for academic respectability through hard empiricism and disinterested research or through grandiose theory, many social scientists tended to shy away from the value-oriented social engineering of the Swede. As discussed in Chapter IV, the Chicago School showed little enthusiasm for Myrdal's methodology or his rosy conclusions. Nor did the rising school of functionalism under the tutelage of Talcott Parsons express an interest in the race question comparable to that of the waning Chicago School. Marxists and some radical scholars of the left thought racism simply a product of capitalism, "race" a "false consciousness." They vehemently denounced Myrdal's analysis of race relations as romantic nonsense served up to preserve the capitalistic system. Even many black scholars, who immediately grasped the

2. *Ibid.*, 21, 13–25; Appendix 2 in *AD.*
3. Samuel A. Stouffer, *The American Soldier* (2 vols.; Princeton, 1949); Stouffer, "Quantitative Methods in the Study of Race Relations," in Masuoka and Valien (eds.), *Race Relations,* 209–10.

potential of the *Dilemma* for the black rights movement, had been profoundly influenced by an economic-class model of black-white relations; and in the 1940s, a few blacks such as Ralph Ellison dissented vigorously from Myrdal's depiction of Afro-American culture as pathological.

The greatest quantity and the most direct comments on Myrdal's book came from sociologists and social psychologists. But academics in all disciplines in the social sciences and the humanities responded to Myrdal in some fashion, directly or indirectly. In the field of psychology several modes of thought, especially those connected with the "authoritarian personality" model, had implications for Myrdal's research. Much of the work done by psychologists, anthropologists, and political scientists, however, only tangentially touched on the *Dilemma's* hypotheses. Historians found much use for Myrdal's work and tended to treat it less critically than social scientists. Until the mid-1960s, historians generally embraced the optimistic outlook of the *Dilemma*. Its insights, in fact, helped inspire significant revisions of the American past.

In any event, the tremendous amount of writing about race in the two decades after the *Dilemma's* publication is intimidating. This chapter, therefore, can present only a small sampling of the voluminous discussion of Myrdal's work in various academic disciplines and put them into the context of the changing times. Despite sneers about the ivory tower mentalities of academicians, racial events in the turbulent period after World War II noticeably affected scholarship on race relations. The numerous racial breakthroughs after 1944 elevated Myrdal to the status of a prophet in his own time. Hope sprang forth like flowers in spring with the integration of the armed forces, the Supreme Court's ruling on the desegregation of schools, the sit-ins, the freedom rides, and the first significant civil rights legislation in Congress since Reconstruction. Events lured many former skeptics into Myrdal's do-something-big, social engineering camp. Pierre van den Berghe, a profound scholar of international race relations, observed that in the area of race, "social science theory is little more than a weathercock shifting with ideological winds." [4]

Van den Berghe disliked such academic fickleness. He complained that the study of race relations had been excessively dominated by moral rhetoric. C. Wright Mills also excoriated the "utopian and progressive style of thought" involved with the concept of "cultural lag."

4. Pierre L. van den Berghe, *Race and Racism: A Comparative Approach* (New York, 1967), 8.

He perceived liberals as impressionistic Pollyannas who assumed that the American system was benign and that the people were good, rational, and plastic. They believed that integration and assimilation could be achieved without radical change in the system. Van den Berghe, too, dissented from such optimism. If Myrdal stood virtually alone in predicting the black revolution in the 1940s, in the early 1960s a minority of perceptive scholars predicted a deterioration of race relations. By the mid-1960s van den Berghe noted that as race relations soured and violence mounted, the reputation of liberal social scientists such as Myrdal declined markedly. By then many scholars characterized the *Dilemma* as having only "historical interest." [5]

Among academics, sociologists performed most of the exegesis on the famous Myrdal text. This fact evokes in me a certain amount of trepidation. It seems that most historians, like the lawyers discussed in Chapter VI, persist in harboring a certain skepticism about the behavioral sciences, despite the fruitful mixing of the behavioral sciences and history that has produced some remarkable scholarship. The results, of course, have not always been benign, and many historians remained unconvinced that the disciples of Clio should be casually browsing among the social sciences, as David P. Thelen put it, for "methodological windfalls." In 1962 the historian Arthur Schlesinger, Jr., told an assembly of sociologists that he doubted that scholars could expect to discover universal laws of human behavior. The Harvard historian maintained in addition that the most important questions about human society could not be answered by quantification or grand theories. Insofar as the historian retains a deep reverence for the unique event, the charismatic leader, and the varied human experience in time and place, he naturally winces at statements like the following from a book called *Group Dynamics:* "The ultimate goal is the discovery of general laws about groups . . . that can be shown to hold for a great variety of groups in widely different social settings." Such sweeping quests for the calculus of human behavior provoked the historian Joyce Appleby to write that social scientists habitually erred in "assuming uniformities, reducing real complexity to artificial simplicity, treating fragments as independent parts of an indivisible whole . . . and reifying obfuscating abstractions in words that torture

5. *Ibid.* For examples of relegating Myrdal's work to history, see John Madge, *The Origins of Scientific Research* (Glencoe, Ill., 1962), 272; Brink and Harris, *Negro Revolution in America,* 28; and Samuel Lubell, *White and Black: Test of a Nation* (New York, 1964), 197.

the English language."[6] Appendix 2 notwithstanding, the Swede's plain talk certainly posed no problem of comprehension for the historian, but the same can scarcely be said for a great deal of the social science commentary on race relations.

Harsh criticism of behavioralists by historians, who for many years have loitered outside the corridors of power while social scientists have commanded lucrative grants and consulting fees from private and public policy makers, might be written off as sour grapes. One need not, however, go outside the social sciences for awareness of the problems of the behavioral sciences. In *The Sociological Imagination* in 1959, C. Wright Mills, the maverick sociologist and hero of the New Left, submitted the theory that sociologists had apparently fallen prey to two dreadful maladies. One group suffered from the affliction of the "grand theory," which, Mills noted, caused the stricken academician to lapse into "cloudy obscurantism." The other group of victims had contracted "abstracted empiricism," whose symptoms consisted of collecting trivial facts unaccompanied by meaningful interpretation. Over on the right, the neoconservative Robert Nisbet also decried the pretensions of his quantifying, overtheorizing cohorts. A man of keen insights into the nature of the history of social change, Nisbet insisted that sociology was an art form rather than a science. Like Mills, he lampooned "abstracted empiricism" as devoid of passion, insight, or historical perspective. Pitirim Sorokin, a Harvard sociologist with more than twenty books to his credit, spoke of the "speech disorders" of his profession and mocked the debates over methodology "as finicky as the angelology of the medieval Scholastics."[7]

The substance and goals of the young discipline also posed problems. Sociology in the United States swung from one extreme of the con-

6. David P. Thelen, "Social Tensions and the Origins of Progressivism," *Journal of American History*, LVI (1969), 324; Arthur Schlesinger, Jr., "The Humanist Looks at Empirical Research," *American Sociological Review*, XXVII (1962), 768–71; Darwin Cartwright and Alvin Zander, *Group Dynamics* (Evanston, Ill., 1953), 4; Joyce Appleby, "Social Science and Human Nature," *Democracy*, I (January, 1981), 125. Two works that show especially strong feelings on the historical misuse of social science are David Stannard, *Shrinking History: On Freud and the Failure of Psychohistory* (New York, 1980); and Herbert G. Gutman, *Slavery and The Numbers Game: A Critique of Time on the Cross* (Urbana, Ill., 1975).

7. C. Wright Mills, *The Sociological Imagination* (New York, 1959), 6, 23, 26–31, 75, 146–64; Robert A. Nisbet, *Sociology as an Art Form* (New York, 1976); Pitirim Sorokin, *Sociological Theories of Today* (New York, 1966), 3–7, 649.

tinuum to the other in the first half of the twentieth century. Most of the early giants of sociology, including Albion Small, Frank Lester Ward, and Edward Ross, actively engaged in reform. They saw sociology as a problem-solving discipline to guide society along progressive lines. The second generation of sociologists retained humanitarian sympathies but gave top priority to empirical research and "value-free science." By the 1940s the early dominance of the Chicago School had suffered a marked decline. By then, the functionalist-structuralist sociologists, more prevalent in the East, gained momentum in the profession. Such activist liberals as Robert Lynd and most black social scientists charged that both the Chicagoans and the functionalists employed a raw empiricism and a false neutrality, which, wittingly or not, lent legitimacy to the unjust *status quo*. Thus in 1951 Ernest Burgess, Alfred McClung Lee, and others more in tune with Myrdal's social activism formed the Society for the Study of Social Problems and began publishing the journal *Social Problems*. The twentieth century, unfortunately, produced no behavioral Newton or Einstein with a unifying paradigm for the study of human society, least of all in the field of race relations. Nor did any discredited or declining social science models, like the once-revered Ptolemaic system in the natural sciences, ever vanish entirely. Even "scientific racism" had a revival in the 1960s. The hopeful racial events of the 1950s and early 1960s, however, created a growing and powerful school of optimistic Myrdalians.[8]

For all its foibles, internal divisions, and problems, sociology and the related behavioral disciplines rapidly gained power and respect in academia after World War II. The frightful explosion at Hiroshima convinced many intellectuals that the study of mankind had to approach more nearly the accuracy of the natural sciences if the planet were to survive. Foundations poured money into research on human behavior. The number of sociology teachers nearly tripled in the first decade after the war. Their subject became a staple in the undergraduate curricula of colleges and universities. The behavioral emphasis received expanded use in the teaching of politics, law, religion, and history. In rare agreement, C. Wright Mills and Talcott Parsons declared that the "socio-

8. Charles H. Page, *Fifty Years of Sociological Enterprise: A Lucky Journey* (Amherst, Mass., 1982), 9–11. Many good articles on trends appear in Tom Bottomore and Robert Nisbet (eds.), *A History of Sociological Analysis* (New York, 1978); Matthews, *Quest for an American Sociology*, 163–65, 183, 189–93; Haskell, *Emergence of Professional Social Science*, 190–210, 242–43; R. Fred Wacker, *Ethnicity, Pluralism and Race: Race Relations Theory in America Before Myrdal* (Westport, Conn., 1983).

logical era" had begun. All over the West, sociology gained notable re-
pute, but in America, as one British sociologist commented, it became
a "thriving industry."[9]

No part of that industry thrived more than the teaching of race relations. Such studies, interdisciplinary in nature but usually assigned to
the sociology department, became commonplace in the years following
World War II. In his excellent survey on the teaching of race relations in
colleges and universities, Peter I. Rose disclosed that by the mid-1960s
the number of courses on race had increased fivefold and continued to
grow rapidly.[10]

Frequently, whole chapters or sections of books designed for these
courses consisted of little more than paraphrases of Myrdal. As Thomas
Kuhn has brilliantly demonstrated in his work on scientific revolutions,
"normal science," at least in the natural sciences, mostly amounts to
"mopping up" or fleshing out an accepted paradigm. Raymond Murray's
textbook for college students, *Sociology for a Democratic Society,* exemplified Kuhn's point. In what was tantamount to a ten-page condensation of Myrdal's book, the chapter headed "The American Dilemma"
aimed its message not only at white racism but at Soviet imperialism. The Notre Dame sociologist, like Myrdal, clearly set forth his
value premises, which unabashedly extolled the verities of the Judaeo-
Christian-democratic ethos. He pronounced the Myrdal report unexcelled because, unlike positivistic science, it incorporated religious and
philosophical values into its analysis. The nationalistic Murray saw in
the Swede's moral teachings and in such Cold War warriors as Dean
Acheson and John Foster Dulles the salvation of the West. The "American Dilemma," he warned, represented the "achilles heel of Western
Democracy."[11]

The most popular textbooks and supplementary readings in courses
on race and intergroup relations frequently drew from the well of Myrdal's data and concepts and from his central theme. According to Peter
Rose, professors used George E. Simpson and J. Milton Yinger's 1953

9. Zetterberg (ed.), *Sociology in the United States of America;* Sorokin, *Sociological
Theories of Today,* 3; A. Duncan Mitchell, *A Hundred Years of Sociology* (Chicago,
1968), 216, 224–32; Page, *Fifty Years of Sociological Enterprise,* 3; Madge, *Origins of
Scientific Research,* 566.

10. Rose, *The Subject Is Race,* 5, 95.

11. Thomas S. Kuhn, *The Structure of Scientific Revolutions* (Chicago, 1962), 24;
Raymond Murray, *Sociology for a Democratic Society* (New York, 1950), 39–49,
373–74.

volume, *Racial and Cultural Minorities,* as a textbook in about one-fourth of the college race relations courses. Simpson and Yinger cited Myrdal seventy-seven times in their popular book, although they differed with him on several important matters. They doubted his faith in the rationality of man, and they pointed out new research that had rendered some of his hypotheses suspect. Nevertheless, they adopted unquestioningly many of Myrdal's views and illustrated many of their points with lengthy quotations from the *Dilemma.* They also took a generally optimistic, problem-solving approach to the race issue. Avoiding historians—not necessarily an error at this time—the authors cited Myrdal for historical interpretations of abolition, Reconstruction, the New Deal, and other events.[12]

Other influential textbooks also borrowed freely from Myrdal's study. In a virtual second-place tie for classroom usage after Simpson and Yinger came Charles F. Marden's *Minorities in American Society* (1952), Gordon Allport's *The Nature of Prejudice* (1954), and Brewton Berry's *Race Relations* (1951), each commanding around 10 percent of the market. Marden cited Myrdal twenty-two times, and in the introduction he stated: "In this book wherever a 'problem' . . . is discussed without reference to any other value system, the reader may assume the 'American Creed' as Myrdal has popularized the term, as our value frame of reference." Berry lauded Myrdal's "brilliant insights," but he disclaimed any intention of social engineering; he nonetheless praised Myrdal's dictum that a scientist should state his value premises and discussed approvingly the optimistic implications of Myrdal's rank order of discriminations, a topic considered in more detail below.[13]

Scholars usually ranked Allport's *The Nature of Prejudice* as one of the two or three top books on that subject that appeared in the decade or so after World War II. Although the Harvard social psychologist leaned toward a psychological explanation of prejudice, his keen mind brought the best of several disciplines to bear in his well-received work. Allport artfully incorporated Myrdal's main thesis into his own eclectic framework. Since he not only used Myrdal's ideas but made some salutary

12. George E. Simpson and J. Milton Yinger, *Racial and Cultural Minorities: An Analysis of Prejudice and Discrimination* (New York, 1953), 88–89, 109, 159, 416–17, 420, 428, 659; Rose, *The Subject Is Race,* 146.

13. Rose, *The Subject Is Race,* 146; Charles F. Marden, *Minorities in American Society* (New York, 1952), x, 238, 309, 438, 458; Brewton Berry, *Race Relations* (Boston, 1951), 16, 18, 263–64.

modifications of them, Allport will receive fuller attention later on in this chapter.[14]

Myrdal also entered the classroom through Arnold Rose. In 1948 Myrdal's former chief collaborator brought out the long-awaited scholarly condensation of the Myrdal study, *The Negro in America*. It kept Myrdal's ideas before the academic establishment, and as Peter Rose has documented, professors of courses on race relations frequently used it as a textbook or for supplementary reading in their classes. Additionally, Rose fought Myrdal's academic battles against dissenting sociologists while the economist pursued his career in Europe.[15]

In addition to undergraduate and graduate courses in race relations, many courses aimed at training teachers for elementary and secondary schools. Books designed to inform those who would deal with young and impressionable minds emphasized the intercultural movement that flourished after the world war. The Bureau of Intercultural Education, for instance, supported Ina Corrine Brown's 1949 book, *Race Relations in a Democracy*, and Stewart G. Cole and Mildred W. Cole's *Minorities and the American Promise* (1954). Brown lent support to Myrdal's thesis on page 2 of her book and on the last page ended with a hopeful allusion to the Swedish scholar's work. She agreed wholeheartedly with Myrdal that history and racial change could be engineered. The Coles' book, which carried the subtitle *The Conflict of Practice and Principle*, constantly exhorted the American creed. Early in their book, which included a foreword by a Columbia professor of education, the authors referred to "The American Dilemma" [*sic*] several times before attributing the concept to Myrdal.[16]

Besides textbooks, professors used a variety of monographs, anthologies, and journal articles as supplementary reading material. The most frequently used journals were sociological. In these, too, Myrdal's book received vast exposure. A team of quantifiers has provided statistical

14. Gordon Allport, *The Nature of Prejudice* (Cambridge, Mass., 1954), 329–31, 501–507.

15. Arnold Rose, *The Negro in America* (New York, 1948); see also his other works, with Caroline Rose, *America Divided: Minority Group Relations in the United States* (New York, 1948); *Race Prejudice and Discrimination: Readings in Intergroup Relations in the United States* (New York, 1951); with Caroline Rose, *Minority Problems* (New York, 1965); Peter Rose, *The Subject Is Race*, 145–47.

16. Ina Corrine Brown, *Race Relations in a Democracy* (New York, 1949), 2, 89, 194; Stewart G. Cole and Mildred W. Cole, *Minorities and the American Promise: The Conflict of Practice and Principle* (New York, 1954), 4, 19, 21.

evidence of Myrdal's impact. Three sociologists examined ten major sociological journals between 1944 and 1968 to ascertain which works scholars most often cited on the Afro-American. The results showed that Myrdal's study was accorded more than twice as many references as any other work. As the authors worded it: "The dominant position of Myrdal's *An American Dilemma* is obvious." Myrdal, stationed in Geneva from 1947 to 1957 as executive secretary of the Economic Commission for Europe, was informed by his many American contacts that his book had influenced "a whole college generation in America."[17]

In his examination of race relations courses, Peter Rose unhappily discovered that few of them had an integrating framework, theoretically or methodologically. Their approach typically leaned toward eclecticism and meliorism. Indeed, Rose lamented, students preferred even less theory and more practical ideas on how to resolve the race problem. Rose pointed out that it was common for professors to assign papers and essay questions on Myrdal's book. These questions usually involved a discussion of Myrdal's central theme, often requiring arguments for and against the Swede's dilemma thesis.[18]

To be sure, a generation of college students, race relations specialists, and broadly read academics in many disciplines employed the word "dilemma" as a metaphor for America's most troublesome social problem. In a special 1946 issue of *Annals*, which was devoted to "controlling group prejudice," the first sentence of Helen V. McLean's article read: "The word dilemma is being used frequently these days in regard to racial matters." Writers on race routinely used the term "American Dilemma" either preceded by "an" or "the," sometimes capitalized and sometimes not.[19]

The high recognition of Myrdal's book combined with its extraordinary breadth also gave it influence beyond strictly racial matters. It may be recalled that early commentators on the *Dilemma* most often com-

17. Howard M. Bahr, Theodore J. Johnson, and M. Kay Seitz, "Influential Scholars and Works in the Sociology of Race and Minority Relations, 1944–1968," *American Sociologist,* VI (1971), 296–98; Myrdal to the author, February 24, 1983.

18. Rose, *The Subject Is Race,* 102–103, 153–55, 164–69.

19. Helen V. McLean, "Psychodynamic Factors in Racial Relations," *Annals,* CCXLIV (1946), 159; for some examples of the unattributed use of Myrdal's title, see Paul A. F. Walter, Jr., *Race and Culture Relations* (New York, 1952), 261, 289; John D. Lohman and Dietrich C. Reitzes, "Note on Race Relations in a Mass Society," *American Journal of Sociology,* LXVIII (1952), 240; Robin M. Williams, Jr., and Margaret W. Ryan, *Schools in Transition* (Chapel Hill, 1954), 24; Cole and Cole, *Minorities and the American Promise,* 4, 19.

pared Myrdal to Alexis de Tocqueville and James Bryce rather than to racial specialists. When in the early 1940s a blue-chip faculty committee at Harvard University set out to determine the best curriculum for a general education, it recommended a required course in American democracy for all students. The committee, selected by President James B. Conant and chaired by Paul Buck, included several esteemed academicians such as Arthur Schlesinger, Sr., Benjamin Wright, and George Wald. The group spent almost two years and $60,000 to complete the widely hailed "Harvard Report," in which it suggested that the course on American democracy should include material on American institutions and values examined from a detached point of view. According to the committee, the best prospects for such a point of view would be found in the works of Tocqueville, Bryce, and Myrdal. The report conceded that the Carnegie study encompassed a more limited subject than the works of the other illustrious foreigners, but it concluded that the *Dilemma* "approaches [American democracy] with such breadth that his method indicates the possibilities for a study of current problems which draw upon relevant material in all of the social sciences and which also transcend the contemporaneous." [20] Not only did Myrdal provide a model for the holistic approach to the social sciences, but a close reading of the report demonstrated that Cold War academicians employed the Scandinavian's flattering perspective on American democracy as a weapon against the Soviet Union.

It is clear that Myrdal appealed to a broad sector of the academic world for a variety of reasons. What it less certain is whether his book actually stimulated original research on the race question. Some felt it did, but others argued that it actually slowed down basic research. Many writers, such as the authors of the popular textbook on minorities, Simpson and Yinger, held that the *Dilemma* occasioned new interest and publication in the racial field. [21] Early critics of Myrdal feared his study would spawn a school of misguided efforts, and later in the 1960s many felt it had. Myrdal recollected that at scholarly meetings in the late 1940s and early 1950s, social scientists told him that research on race had dwindled. The reason, they speculated, stemmed from the belief

20. Harvard Committee on the Objectives of a General Education in a Free Society, *General Education in a Free Society* (Cambridge, Mass., 1946), 219.

21. Simpson and Yinger, *Racial and Cultural Minorities*, 121; Louis Wirth, "The Unfinished Business of American Democracy," *Annals*, CCXLIV (1946), 7n.; Paul Kecskemeti, "The Psychological Theory of Prejudice: Does it Underrate the Role of Social History?" *Commentary*, XVIII (1954), 359.

that Myrdal had written the definitive work on the race question. It is true that the Carnegie Corporation invested no significant funds in racial research after the Myrdal success. It is also true that almost every scholar who wrote after the Swedish economist felt the need to justify his work vis-à-vis the *Dilemma*. In the important book *The Negro in the United States* (1949), the author E. Franklin Frazier and Louis Wirth, who wrote the introduction, stressed the volume's differences from Myrdal's tome. Wirth insisted that the black writer had avoided the Swede's policy-making approach and employed an international aspect missing in Myrdal's study. In an equally significant book called *The Mark of Oppression* (1951), Abram Kardiner and Lionel Ovesey confessed that "strong justification" was required to write another book on blacks after the Myrdal report.[22] Such deference indicates that Myrdal may have intimidated some social scientists from attempting ambitious projects about black-white relations.

Myrdal's book both stimulated and stifled research and writing on the race question. Myrdal may have been correct when he stated that his book hindered "deeper" research. The *Dilemma* certainly steered research in directions that were not always salutary. When Paul B. Sheatsley, a longtime student of racial attitudes, was asked in 1984 why so little study of black attitudes had been done in the early postwar period, he replied: "It never occurred to us when we wrote the questions in the Forties and Fifties to ask them of blacks because Myrdal's dilemma was a white dilemma and it was white attitudes that demanded study." The *Dilemma* undoubtedly helped produce more literature on race overall, though much was unoriginal in character, and no small part of it was imitative of Myrdal. Textbooks and readers for classrooms, for example, fitted into this category. The locus of racial studies, furthermore, was shifting from Chicago to new centers at Harvard, Columbia, the University of California, and elsewhere. This decentralization perhaps served to make the output of racial writing seem less than it was. Some sociologists pointed out that the leaders in the discipline displayed less interest in the race problem than had the prominent sociologists of the 1920s and 1930s.[23] Whatever the case, after the mid-1950s racial

22. Myrdal to the author, December 2, 1981, February 24, 1983; Florence Anderson, COHP, 71; Charles Dollard, COHP, 242; E. Franklin Frazier, *The Negro in the United States* (New York, 1949), vii–x, xiii–xv; Abram Kardiner and Lionel Ovesey, *The Mark of Oppression: A Psychological Study of the American Negro* (New York, 1951), xiv–xvi.

23. Sheatsley quoted in Howard Schuman, Charlotte Steeh, and Lawrence Bobo, *Racial Attitudes in America: Trends and Interpretations* (Cambridge, Mass., 1985), 139; Ed-

events sparked new interest in race and resulted in a flood of writings on the topic. Whether or not Myrdal's study helped or hindered original research, it definitely spread broadly and reinforced the then current social science idioms on race. The renowned *Columbia Encyclopedia* of 1950, for example, proclaimed that race was an "obsolete division of humanity." In the same year the United Nations issued a statement declaring that race was a "myth" and that "universal brotherhood" was a scientifically valid concept. In 1946 a Yale study concluded that children under ten were "catholic and cosmopolitan in their interracial contacts." The smash hit *South Pacific* instructed tens of thousands that children had to be carefully taught to hate because of racial differences.[24]

By the late 1940s the term "race" was practically taboo among many behavioralists. They preferred to discuss intergroup relations. Though never dismissing race as cavalierly as did Boas or Ashley Montagu, Myrdal exposed the ghastly imprecision of the biological concept of race. At the same time he recognized that white beliefs about race gave the concept a reality as social fact. Some white liberals apparently believed, however, that color prejudice would disappear if race were expunged from the academic vocabulary.[25]

Whatever their attitude toward Myrdal, the vast majority of sociologists believed in racial equality and endorsed civil rights activity. A poll of "racial experts" conducted by Arthur Kornhauser of the Bureau of Applied Science in 1945 claimed that everyone questioned rejected the idea of black inferiority. Among those polled, 93 percent believed that racial prejudice was not inborn. Even though about half of the respondents were black, most racial scholars from all backgrounds clearly leaned toward Myrdalian equalitarianism. As has already been suggested, many racial specialists simply assumed Myrdal's main thesis and moved on. One critic scolded the authors of *A Manual of Intergroup Relations* (1955) for presupposing that the moral climate in America

ward Shils, "Tradition, Ecology, and Institution in the History of Sociology," *Daedalus*, XCIX (1970), 807–809; Blackwell and Janowitz (eds.), *Black Sociologists*, xx; Howard Odum, *The Story of Sociology in the United States Through 1950* (Chapel Hill, 1951), 23, 325.

24. William Bridgewater and Elizabeth J. Sherwood (eds.), *The Columbia Encyclopedia* (2d ed.; New York, 1950), 1632; Leo Kuper (ed.), *Race, Science and Society* (Paris, 1975), 343–47; Arnold L. Gesell and Frances L. Ilg, *The Child from Five to Ten* (New York, 1946), 338, 356–57.

25. R. Fred Wacker, "An American Dilemma: The Racial Theories of Robert E. Park and Gunnar Myrdal," *Phylon*, XXXVII (1976), 117.

was conducive to racial change. Like Myrdal, the authors presumed that the moral commitment to racial equality had been settled long ago.[26]

Although some writers borrowed heavily from the Swedish economist, they sometimes conspicuously avoided any mention of Myrdal's name. Carey McWilliams, for instance, published a book in 1943 entitled *Brothers Under the Skin*. His views roughly resembled Myrdal's, except that McWilliams emphasized economic-class factors more heavily. The second edition of his book in 1951 contained not a trace of recognition of the Carnegie project, unless one counts the two sections headed "The Discovery of the Dilemma" and "Resolution of the Dilemma." It seems that those who had written books about race relations and had been eclipsed by Myrdal rendered little public appreciation for the foreigner's work.[27]

Unlikely as it may seem, most of the praise and criticism of Myrdal in the first two decades by sociologists had little or no empirical basis. By and large, they either supported or condemned Myrdal with impressionistic judgments. This proved more true of pro-Myrdal scholars than those who were critical. Those who believed in the possibility of substantial racial change, for example, accepted Myrdal's untested hypothesis that interracial contact decreased prejudice; they downplayed resistance to racial change; they felt that the white and black rank orders of discrimination boded well for the future; and, above all, they perceived race prejudice as a cultural lag from a pre-industrial era, now doomed by "modernization." Many social scientists continued to consider the *Dilemma* one of the top two or three relevant works on race relations well into the 1960s. In 1962 the biographers of the southern liberal Will Alexander described the Myrdal report as "the capstone of interracial investigation, social science surveys, statistical studies, and psychological explorations."[28]

Interestingly, some of the liberal sociologists who tried to find empirical evidence for Myrdal's analysis failed to make the Swede's dilemma thesis more secure. In *Strangers Next Door* (1964), Robin Williams, Jr.,

26. Arthur Kornhauser, "Should Negroes Have Equal Rights?" *American Magazine*, CXL (August, 1945), 32–33; John Dean and Alex Rosen, *A Manual of Intergroup Relations* (Chicago, 1955). See the trenchant criticism of this *Manual* by James McKee, "Community Power and Strategies in Race Relations," *Social Problems*, VI (Winter, 1958–59), 197–98.

27. Carey McWilliams, *Brothers Under the Skin* (2d ed.; Boston, 1951), 256, 262.

28. Quoted in Wilma Dykeman and James Stokely, *Seeds of Southern Change: The Life of Will Alexander* (Chicago, 1962), 276.

reported the results of studies of several cities throughout the country undertaken between 1948 and 1956. He found that 33 percent of the white adults in Savannah, Georgia, admitted that they "sometimes" felt guilty about the treatment of blacks. Only 8 percent said they "often" felt guilty. By a two-to-one margin, whites in the Georgia city expressed the opinion that blacks were better off in the South than in the North. Testing the western city of Phoenix, Williams discovered that about 64 percent "sometimes" had guilt feelings about blacks. Williams put great hope in such statistics. He especially took comfort in the ones which indicated that people tended to underestimate the guilt feelings of other people. According to Williams, if education revealed the truth, those with guilt feelings would no longer feel so isolated. He asserted that many secretly wanted to do right and abide by the American creed and would therefore change. Although Williams examined cities outside the South, his thesis sounded remarkably similar not only to Myrdal's but to the concept of the "Silent South" whose realization has been awaited by southern liberals since the Civil War.[29]

In spite of the *Dilemma*'s prestige, or perhaps because of it, a sizable amount of social science writing aimed at undermining the powerful appeal of the book. As explained in Chapter IV, the most belligerent attacks on Myrdal came from Marxists and the radical left, and after the *Brown* decision, from the Far Right and southern segregationists. The Old Left's line followed the familiar groove and need not be repeated here. The Marxist view of the race problem and Myrdal was so rigid that it caused many defections from the Communist ranks, especially among militant blacks who had not already deserted in the late 1930s.[30]

Myrdal's book, however, not only elicited acerbic attacks from radicals of the left and right. Large numbers in the middle also expressed concern about its widespread appeal. Although the Chicago School of Sociology had paved the way for the repudiation of biological racism, its adherents maintained a somewhat deterministic posture, a kind of Darwinian progressivism, which made them cool toward the Swede's work. As a European Social Democrat, Myrdal had chastised both the Chicago School and the rising functionalists who stressed stasis and equilibrium and exhibited little urgency about racial matters. Several

29. Robin Williams, Jr., *Strangers Next Door* (Englewood Cliffs, N.J., 1964), 9, 34, 70–71, 386; Sosna, *In Search of the Silent South.*
30. Kaiser, "Racial Dialectics," 295–98; Horace Cayton, "Whose Dilemma?" *New Masses,* July 23, 1946, pp. 8–10; Cruse, *Crisis of the Negro Intellectual,* 218.

American sociologists retaliated in kind. E. B. Reuter, a veteran scholar on blacks, branded the *Dilemma* so poor a performance that it might become an embarrassment for the profession. Methodological purists like the functionalist Gwynne Nettler railed against Myrdal's value-oriented research in several articles. Sociologists such as Nettler seemed more appalled by Myrdal's methodology than by his conclusions. Others damned the Swede with faint praise. Maurice K. Davie scorned Myrdal's optimistic forecast in his 1948 book *Negroes in American Society.* The Yale sociologist predicted that only an exceedingly slow advance toward racial democracy could be expected. At the same time Edward Shils praised the breadth of Myrdal's perspective but added that the European had made no "theoretical or technical advances" in his celebrated work.[31]

Liberal sociologists, who, as Ernest Burgess speculated, had their hearts touched by Myrdal, tended to give the economist his due. But if they loudly sang his praises, they also engaged in critical scrutiny of many of Myrdal's most vaunted hypotheses. For example, Robert K. Merton, one of the most noted sociologists of his time, wrote an article in 1949 called "Discrimination and the American Creed." According to Peter Rose, it became one of the most widely read pieces of racial literature and served as a model for discussion in race relations courses. Merton did not deny that the American creed acted as a dynamic factor in American society, but the Harvard professor felt that the Swedish scholar's version might be "seriously misleading for social policy and social science." As a sacred tradition the American creed escaped direct attack, but people violated it so often that the transgressions became what Merton called "institutionalized evasion of institutional norms." The creed, he pointed out, was also unevenly distributed throughout the country. Merton explained that when peace of mind was threatened, as in the case of southern whites, individuals deviated from the creed for reasons of "psychological equilibrium." Further to complicate matters, the functionalist announced that attitudes and behavior often differed significantly, making prediction difficult.[32]

31. Gwynne Nettler, "A Note on Myrdal's 'Notes on Facts and Valuations,'" *American Sociological Review,* IX (1944), 686–88; and "Toward a Definition of the Sociologist," *ibid.,* XII (1947), 553–60; see Arnold Rose's reply to Nettler in "Communication and Opinion," *ibid.,* X (1945), 560–61; Maurice Davie, *Negroes in American Society* (New York, 1959), 503–507; Edward Shils, *The Present State of American Sociology* (Glencoe, Ill., 1948), 28.

32. Robert K. Merton, "Discrimination and the American Creed," in Robert M.

Hence Merton divided people into four categories: the unprejudiced nondiscriminator, the unprejudiced discriminator, the prejudiced nondiscriminator, and the prejudiced discriminator. Because of the differing relationships between attitudes and behavior, people in each category needed different forms of social therapy. The unprejudiced nondiscriminator or the "all-weather liberal" adhered religiously to the creed in belief and practice. This relatively small group, unfortunately, lived in isolation from mainstream society and talked only among themselves, indulging in the "fallacy of unanimity." [33]

The two groups in the middle presented a similar problem. The unprejudiced discriminator or "fair-weather liberal" and the prejudiced nondiscriminator or "fair-weather illiberal" both led expedient and conformist lives. One believed sincerely in the American creed, the other did not; but both conformed to the local folkways. The fair-weather liberal might be somewhat vulnerable to ethical exhortation because he showed some signs of conscience. If pressured, the fair-weather illiberal would conform to racially liberal law despite his lack of principle. Merton theorized that both groups would cease their discrimination if institutional changes made it unprofitable, unpopular, or both. [34]

Finally, the prejudiced discriminator or all-weather illiberal was immune to education and propaganda. These people, heavily concentrated in the South, could be changed only by forceful legal and administrative pressure over a sustained period of time. In the tradition of the patient, disinterested social scientist, Merton called for careful, wide-scale research to determine the proportion of the four categories of individuals in all localities. Social therapies tailored to suit the various circumstances could then be devised. [35] The foregoing discussion is a somewhat simplified presentation of Merton's views, so one can easily see why civil rights activists might favor Myrdal's simpler thesis over that of the elaborate, if deeply insightful, theories of the prestigious Harvard scholar.

In his excellent work of social psychology, *The Nature of Prejudice,* Gordon Allport, like Merton, conceded the substance of the American creed as a sociological factor in racial affairs. Although Allport emphasized the psychological origins of prejudice, he did not ignore American

MacIver (ed.), *Discrimination and National Welfare* (New York, 1949), 100–102; Rose, *The Subject Is Race,* 75.

33. Merton, "Discrimination and the American Creed," 104–105.

34. *Ibid.,* 106–109.

35. *Ibid.,* 109–26.

ideals and socioeconomic factors. As for the creed, the Harvard social psychologist quoted Myrdal to stress that facts must be organized around "relevant value premises." He championed the idea that the democratic ethos acted as a dynamic force in the nation's behavior. Allport speculated that the quickest way to deflate a bigot was to show him that his prejudice violated the Christian-democratic creed. In a 1953 letter to the black psychologist Kenneth B. Clark, Allport opined: "People really know that segregation is un-American, even the masses in the South know it." He confidently predicted that if the Supreme Court would take a decisive stand against segregation, those timid souls who lived in conflict with their consciences would conform to democratic standards.[36]

Despite his basic agreement with Myrdal, Allport notably modified one of the *Dilemma's* main concepts: the proposition that interracial contact reduced prejudice. Allport counseled that contact between two people from different races would bring about a reduction of prejudice only under four conditions: that the two individuals hold equal status; that they sought common goals; that they were independent rather than in competition; and that they interacted with the positive support of authorities, customs, and law. Without such favorable circumstances, Allport suggested, interracial contact might actually increase prejudice.[37]

One of the most debated of Myrdal's concepts involved his rank order of discriminations. This hypothesis embodied an idea that gave social reformers hope, and scholars began to test it regularly in the 1950s. Put simply, the idea held that the things that blacks wanted most, such as jobs, whites seemed most willing to countenance. The things that whites most staunchly resisted, such as miscegenation and social equality, blacks wanted the least. In short, the inverse order of desires and dislikes of the two races implied that racial change could occur without conflict.[38]

The first empirical test of Myrdal's rank order took place in Columbus, Ohio, in 1950. W. S. Banks concluded that Myrdal's model proved valid in that midwestern city. He pointed out, however, that blacks truly resented all forms of discrimination against them, if in different degrees. In 1952 Irwin D. Rinder found that whites expressed much more

36. Allport, *Nature of Prejudice*, 329–32, 501–507; Allport to Kenneth Clark, August 4, 1953, quoted in Clark, "Desegregation: An Appraisal of the Evidence," *Journal of Social Issues*, IX (November, 1953), 75.
37. Allport, *Nature of Prejudice*, 261–81.
38. *AD*, 60–67.

opposition to black employment than Myrdal had indicated. His re-search also disclosed a considerable overlap between the economic, so-cial, and political spheres, which Myrdal had not detected. Subsequent studies revealed more discrepancies in Myrdal's rank order. In 1954, for example, Edwin R. Edmunds published an in-depth study of the rank orders of the two races in Texas and Oklahoma. As had Rinder's, his findings differed most significantly from Myrdal's in the area of white perceptions about black economics. In the ten years since Myrdal had recorded his impressions, jobs had moved from sixth place to fourth on the white rank order. That is, when the war boom ended and the first of several postwar recessions ensued, whites exhibited increasing sensi-tivity to competition for jobs. In 1948 Malcolm Ross, a wartime head of the Fair Employment Practices Committee, released the results of sev-eral government reports in his memoirs, *All Manner of Men*. Studies of several cities in the North and South strongly indicated white hostility to black economic gains. In the South, only 7 percent favored giving better jobs to blacks. In the North the figure inched up to 19 percent. Research also divulged that most whites would refuse to work for a black super-visor under almost any circumstances. Edmunds concluded that a dec-ade had changed the racial configuration in the Southwest so much that the Swede's hypothesis no longer had relevance there.[39]

Not only had whites grown less generous in their views about black economic advancement but blacks had changed their rank order—and in a way that presaged racial conflict. Although Edmunds' analysis still found that Afro-Americans ranked jobs first on their rank order of de-sires, only 42 percent did so. Significantly, over 30 percent ranked pub-lic services, politics, or legal equality as of primary importance. An exhaustive study of the South in the early 1960s by Donald R. Matthews and James W. Prothro also claimed that Myrdal's impressionistic judg-ments about rank orders had been rendered tenuous by changing cir-cumstances. Large majorities of blacks demanded equality of treatment in every sphere of life. The only part of Myrdal's concept that seemed to hold up involved the Afro-American's declaration that he desired no

39. W. S. Banks, "The Rank Order of Sensitivity to Discriminations of Negroes in Columbus," *American Sociological Review*, XV (1950), 529–34; Irwin D. Rinder, "Some Observations on the Rank Order of Discriminations Hypothesis," *Journal of Negro Education*, XXI (1952), 541–45; Edwin R. Edmunds, "The Myrdalian Hypothe-sis: Rank Order of Discrimination," *Phylon*, XV (1954), 297–303; Malcolm Ross, *All Manner of Men* (New York, 1948), 23; Melvin M. Tumin, *Desegregation: Resistance and Readiness* (Princeton, 1958), 43.

breaking of the color line on sex and marriage. Even here, Matthews and Prothro suspected that blacks who no longer denied their desire for social equality were being less than candid (see Chapters IX and X). In the black mind, they felt, the prohibition of interracial sex meant only that the minority demanded the end of the white exploitation of black women. In another test Lewis Killian and Charles Grigg studied Jacksonville, Florida, and discovered "no significant inverse relationship" between the white and black scales. All signs, the authors said, pointed to future strife.[40]

Above all, such studies uncovered whites' monumental ignorance of black attitudes and feelings. In *Negroes and the New Southern Politics,* Matthews and Prothro reported that only 22 percent of whites believed that blacks wanted integration. But, in fact, most did. Of ninety white youths interviewed at Little Rock High School in 1955, 83 percent thought that blacks preferred segregated schools. Interviews of black youths disclosed that three-fourths desired to desegregate, despite all the white threats about the wrath attempted integration would bring upon black heads. A similar study by Melvin Tumin in Greensboro, North Carolina, a town considered liberal compared to those inside the Magnolia Jungle of the Deep South, turned up ominous evidence. Tumin found that three-fourths of the whites felt that blacks were morally less responsible than whites; 65 percent thought Afro-Americans lacked normal ambition, and 60 percent judged them intellectually inferior. Finally, more than 80 percent of whites totally rejected the idea of integration.[41]

These figures did not necessarily dampen Tumin's spirits. A liberal activist who singled out the *Dilemma* as the best guide to race relations,

40. Edmunds, "Myrdalian Hypothesis," 300–301; Donald R. Matthews and James W. Prothro, *Negroes and the New Southern Politics* (New York, 1966), 332–36, 339, 351; Lewis M. Killian and Charles Grigg, "Rank Orders of Discrimination of Negroes and Whites in a Southern City," *Social Forces,* XXXIX (1961), 235–38. See also similar rank orders for the North in Frank F. Lee, *Negro and White in a Connecticut Town* (New York, 1961); Arthur Katona, "Community Services and the Negro: A Survey of Discrimination in a Northern Town," *Social Forces,* XXVI (1948), 443–50; and William K. Ming, Jr., "The Elimination of Segregation in Public Schools of North and West," *Journal of Negro Education,* XXI (1952), 265, 274.

41. Matthews and Prothro, *Negroes and the New Southern Politics,* 357; Tumin, *Desegregation,* 34–38. Other studies showed strong white resistance to racial fairness or cooperation: Martin M. Grossack, "Attitudes Toward Desegregation of Southern White and Negro Children," in Grossack (ed.), *Mental Health and Segregation* (New York,

Tumin stressed the alleged dynamics of the situation. He disregarded the hardened attitudes of whites and asked the people of Greensboro how they would actually behave if a black person infringed upon the racial mores of the area: what would a white do if a black sat down beside him in a restaurant or on a bus? In their responses, Tumin found whites unlikely to react negatively or violently. Yet, whether a seat in a restaurant or a seat on a bus was involved, a majority of whites said they would physically remove themselves or resist the intrusion. Tumin, nevertheless, felt that enough nonextremists, albeit racist ones, existed to lead the city toward substantial racial change. The "middle group," he contended, would follow strong, sensible leadership. As Tumin looked for the silver lining in 1958, a ranting segregationist defeated George C. Wallace for the governorship of Alabama. Wallace, who had run a moderate campaign by Alabama standards, vowed that he would never be "out-niggered" again. In 1962 he was elected governor, and his promise was segregation now and forever.[42]

Not surprisingly, however, many sociologists read the signs differently from Tumin. In 1950 a prescient Jesse Bernard asked: "Where is the sociology of conflict?" Bernard complained that American sociologists had fallen prey to a static view of society, neglecting the theory of competition and conflict. Bernard speculated that the reasons were, first, because conflict was associated with Marxist philosophy. Second, American scholars harbored a deep fear that the study of conflict might be interpreted as advocating it—not an unfounded fear in the age of McCarthyism. Third, Americans had an ingrained faith in natural, orderly change. Bernard urged more research on conflict so it could be better understood and channeled toward constructive ends when it threatened.[43]

Bernard's call did not go unheeded. In the 1950s Kurt H. Wolff translated into English the seminal works on conflict theory by the nineteenth-century German sociologist Georg Simmel. In 1956 Lewis Coser's book *The Foundations of Social Conflict* gave new life to Simmel's ideas. More important perhaps, "massive resistance" in the South against inte-

---

1963), 7–13; Daniel C. Thompson, *The New Negro Leadership Class* (Englewood Cliffs, N.J., 1963), 168; and Bartley, *Rise of Massive Resistance*, 14.

42. Tumin, *Desegregation*, xi, 43, 199; Robert Sherrill, *Gothic Politics in the Deep South: Stars of the New Confederacy* (New York, 1969), 314.

43. Jesse Bernard, "Where Is the Modern Sociology of Conflict?" *American Journal of Sociology*, LVI (1950), 11–16; Bernard cited one modern German sociologist as having written on conflict: Kurt Lewin, *Resolving Social Conflict* (New York, 1948).

gration made the subject of conflict inescapable. Thus the moral dilemma model received a strong challenge from the conflict model of race relations in the late 1950s and 1960s. In reference to race relations, some simply called this model the power-relations approach.[44]

In his popular textbook in race relations courses *These Our People* (1949), Richard A. Schermerhorn focused on power relations as the key to the race issue. Although Schermerhorn did not dismiss the dilemma thesis out of hand, he attributed little importance to "the veneer of ideal." Joseph Roucek deplored the talk about creeds and normative behavior; he maintained that Myrdal's analysis changed nothing in the power base of the organized purveyors of white racism. In a similar vein, Herbert Blumer's 1957 article "Race Prejudice as a Sense of Group Position" presented one of the most important short statements of the power-relations model in the 1950s. Though Blumer came from the University of Chicago group, his formulations proved highly useful to radical anti-Myrdalians in the 1960s. Blumer was reacting in part to the "authoritarian personality" school with its emphasis on the individual. His thesis stressed that prejudice emerged from a historical sense of a group's overall position in society, from a process in which a group like whites in America felt at once superior to and fearful of an opposing group. In short, racism was historical and collective, and it dealt with group image. Blumer felt the disease could not be cured by moral preaching or psychotherapy. Blacks as a group had to change their position and image by acquiring power.[45]

Clearly, sociologists suffered from a split personality. Some stressed conflict and pointed to the massive resistance and slow progress of blacks in the 1950s. The Myrdalians emphasized the Supreme Court decisions, the decline in intellectual racism, and the civil rights legislation of Congress in the late 1950s. The Cassandras felt that the moral dilemma approach only built up false hope that would be dashed by reality. In 1951 a teacher of race relations in Washington, D.C., polled her white students about Myrdal's dilemma thesis. They concluded that the

44. Kurt H. Wolff, *The Sociology of Georg Simmel* (Glencoe, Ill., 1950); and *Conflict* (Glencoe, Ill., 1955); Lewis Coser, *The Functions of Social Conflict* (Glencoe, Ill., 1956).

45. Richard A. Schermerhorn, *These Our People: Minorities and American Culture* (Boston, 1949), 14–15, 168, 559, 570; Joseph Roucek, "Minority-Majority Relations in Their Power Aspects," *Phylon*, XVII (1956), 24–30; Herbert Blumer, "Race Relations as a Sense of Group Position," *Pacific Sociological Review*, I (1958), 3–7.

American creed was "right but not realistic." The teacher surmised that intellectuals like Myrdal suffered from an ailment common to reformists: they judged others by their own dilemmas and their thirst for abstract justice. One pessimistic sociologist phrased it this way: "What Myrdal failed to comprehend is that for most Southern whites there is no . . . moral dilemma. The doctrine of Negro inferiority or 'differences' serves to place the Negro beyond the pale of the democratic creed." To be certain, the decade of the 1950s spawned many well-argued denials of the efficacy of the American creed.[46]

Sociologists, of course, stressed groups and social-economic conditions; psychologists focused on individuals and espoused highly imaginative ideas about how the mind responded under certain conditions. Despite the hope in the late nineteenth and early twentieth centuries that an interdisciplinary social science would develop with great problem-solving capabilities, fragmentation and isolation of the various behavioral sciences became the rule.[47] Psychologists, social psychologists excepted, seldom spoke as directly or as extensively on Myrdal's book as did sociologists. Cornelius Golightly provided an exception. In a 1947 article entitled "Race, Values, and Guilt," he used the figures from the National Opinion Research Center in Chicago that some liberal social scientists had employed to demonstrate the decline of white racism. Golightly, however, pointed out that no matter what the condition of Afro-Americans at any particular time, most whites expressed the opinion that blacks were either treated fairly or were satisfied. The implication of the polls, Golightly submitted, was that whites felt they treated blacks "fairly as Negroes or as *fairly as they deserve to be treated.*" Whites, in fact, sanctioned the caste system as an outlet for "aggressiveness lingering in the unconscious," Golightly claimed. Indeed, he felt

46. Sophia Fagen McDowell, "Teaching Note on the Use of the Myrdal Concept of 'An American Dilemma' with Regard to the Race Problem in the United States," *Social Forces,* XXX (1951), 87–91. See, for example, James W. Vander Zanden, "The Ideology of White Supremacy," *Journal of the History of Ideas,* XX (1959), 399; Ralph H. Turner, "Value-Conflict in Social Disorganization," *Sociology and Social Research,* XXVIII (1954), 301–308; Marie Jahoda, "The Problem," *Journal of Social Issues,* V, No. 3 (1949), 4–11; Muzafer Sherif and Carolyn Sherif, *Groups in Harmony and Tension* (New York, 1953).

47. See Irving L. Horowitz (ed.), *The Use and Abuse of Social Science: Behavioral Research and Policy Making* (2d ed.; New Brunswick, N.J., 1975), 125, for dreams in the 1930s about a unified social science.

that whites suffered guilt feelings primarily when they violated the rigid race etiquette of the South.[48]

The most influential publication on prejudice by psychologists in this period, *The Authoritarian Personality* (1950), made no reference to the Scandinavian economist and scarcely mentioned blacks. This huge book by Theodore Adorno and others presented a model of prejudice that offered little of the hope for substantial racial change envisioned by Myrdal. The theme of the book held that prejudice stemmed from deeply and universally rooted mechanisms within the human personality. Education and propaganda simply bounced off the authoritarian mind. Inspired by the rise of Nazism and the anti-Semitism of the 1930s and 1940s, the "authoritarian school" fixed its gaze on the supposedly universal tendency of mankind to "scapegoat," transfer hostility, rationalize value dissonance, and the like. It evinced no apparent relevance in the dynamics of a national creed in the matter of bigotry.[49]

Psychologists manufactured a vast body of literature in the late 1940s and 1950s which cast doubt on several of Myrdal's pet ideas. Two social scientists affirmed that three hundred studies on the psychological bases of prejudice had been written between 1950 and 1964. Many of these reiterated the belief that bigots competently resisted rational change. Gerhart Saenger's *The Social Psychology of Prejudice* (1953) typified many of the studies. Under the heading "Feelings of Guilt," Saenger mentioned Myrdal only to say that guilt, if not rationalized away, increased aggression and irrationality toward minority groups. Such logic seemed to say that racial reformers courted disaster when they pointed out the blatant discrepancy between the democratic creed and racial practice. Another work in psychology, *A Theory of Cognitive Dissonance* (1957), by Leon Festinger, illustrated the myriad ways an individual could reduce dissonance caused by conflicting values, without of course actually making the values reconcilable.[50]

48. Cornelius L. Golightly, "Race, Values, and Guilt," *Social Forces*, XXVI (1947), 125–39.
49. Theodore Adorno *et al.*, *The Authoritarian Personality* (New York, 1950), 103; see Naomi Goldstein, *The Roots of Prejudice Against the Negro in the United States* (Boston, 1948), for a typically cool reception to and limited use of Myrdal by a psychologist.
50. Bruno Bettelheim and Morris Janowitz, *Social Change and Prejudice* (Glencoe, Ill., 1964), 77; Gerhart Saenger, *The Social Psychology of Race Prejudice* (New York, 1953), 120; Leon Festinger, *A Theory of Cognitive Dissonance* (Evanston, Ill., 1957), 7. The following works are just a few that supported the limited effect of exhortation and

In 1961, in a thorough investigation of the pitfalls of informational campaigns against racism, Charles Stember disputed Myrdal's claim that the educated were not as racist as the less educated. Stember discovered that the effect of education on an attitude as deep-seated and emotional as racism often proved superficial. He conceded that if schooling did not cause people to reject stereotypes, it did make them more likely to favor nondiscrimination as an official policy and approve contact with minorities. But he continued: "As we go up the educational ladder, old images of minorities are replaced by new ones, often no less harmful. Covert discrimination continues to be acceptable and, most important perhaps, the desire to keep minorities at some social distance remains." Education, therefore, served only to reduce "traditional provincialism" and to lessen the fear of casual intergroup contact. *"But the limits of acceptance,"* Stember warned, *"are sharply drawn; while legal equality is supported, full social participation is not."*[51]

If educated whites rejected full participation of blacks in society, Myrdal did not exactly qualify as an equal opportunity employer when it came to hiring historians. In his public relations campaign designed to charm various factions within the social science community, he tended to slight the past masters. Among his collaborators only Guion Johnson could be considered a professional historian, and Myrdal allowed Johnson only a brief period of time to research the vast subject of the history of racial ideologies in America. In the *Dilemma* Myrdal flatly stated that he had no interest in the "uniquely historical datum." He vowed to use history only when absolutely necessary for ordinary comprehension of a topic. In a 1965 pamphlet on blacks for the American Historical Association, Louis R. Harlan charged that Myrdal's attitude inadvertently harmed black history by casting it in a "presentist framework."[52]

Yet despite Myrdal's lack of interest in pure history, the *Dilemma* ulti-

education on bigotry: Eunice Cooper and Marie Jahoda, "The Evasion of Propaganda: How Prejudiced People Respond to Anti-Prejudice Propaganda," *Journal of Psychology,* XXIII (1947), 15–25; Samuel H. Flowerman, "Mass Propaganda in the War Against Bigotry," *Journal of Abnormal and Social Psychology,* XLII (1947), 429–39; Herbert Hyman and Paul B. Sheatsley, "Some Reasons Why Information Campaigns Fail," *Public Opinion Quarterly,* XI (1947), 412–23; and Jeanne Watson, "Some Social and Psychological Situations Related to Attitude Change," *Human Relations,* III (1950), 15–56.

51. Charles H. Stember, *Education and Attitude Change: The Effects of Schooling on Attitude Change* (New York, 1961), 168–73.

52. *AD,* lvii; Louis R. Harlan, *The Negro in American History* (Washington, 1965), 3.

mately included a considerable amount of it. To establish the pre-eminence of the American creed, Myrdal had to look far back into the American past. His entire thesis hinged on the view that the national character had been nurtured by a democratic creed. The dilemma Myrdal described existed not only in the present but in the American past. Myrdal also made the historical case that the presence of blacks had shaped the whole of American culture. Unlike most white historians of the 1930s, Myrdal had no qualms about using legitimate black sources; for example, he borrowed heavily from the work of W. E. B. Du Bois, which in effect made him a revisionist on Reconstruction in advance of most American historians. Probably because Frederick Keppel of the Carnegie Corporation was a close friend of Charles Beard, Myrdal relied almost exclusively on the progressive historian's interpretation of the Constitution—which infuriated the right. Despite his Beardian view of the Constitution, Myrdal judged that America was a consensus society. He judged that the people were fundamentally conservative, but what they conserved, he added, was liberal in principle. The Swede thus anticipated the Consensus School of History.[53]

Although historians did not exploit Myrdal's work as quickly or to the degree that social scientists did, they soon discovered its value as a repository of facts, ideas, and inspiration. Initially, only two historians reviewed the *Dilemma*. One of them, Frank Tannenbaum, generally approved of Myrdal's book. A professor at Columbia University, Tannenbaum held views similar to those in the Chicago School of Sociology. He believed in the inevitability of black assimilation because of evolution, the race relations cycle, and the catchall: modernization. Time, not social engineering, would solve the race problem. Another Columbia professor, Henry Steele Commager, gave Myrdal's book a glowing review. Writing in the *American Mercury,* the intellectual historian stated that the dilemma described by Myrdal had always plagued Americans. Commager, like Myrdal, felt confident that America would soon close the gap between the idealistic creed and its discriminatory practices toward blacks.[54]

Perhaps Myrdal's book served no greater utility for historians than in furnishing a social scientific basis for the reinterpretation of Negro slav-

53. *AD,* xlvi–xlvii, 3, 6–7, 12–13, 16, 19–20, 38, 251–78, 406, 431–35, 451, 709–11, and *passim.*
54. Frank Tannenbaum, Review of *AD,* in *Political Science Quarterly,* LIX (1944), 321–40; Henry Steele Commager, Review of *AD,* in *American Mercury,* LX (1945), 751–53.

ery. In 1944 Richard Hofstadter, an inveterate borrower of social science concepts and methods, advised historians to familiarize themselves with "modern cultural anthropology" and "social psychology." A professor at Columbia who had just finished a book on Social Darwinism, Hofstadter no doubt got his cultural anthropology firsthand from Boas and his disciples. In any case, the historian made his challenge to his colleagues about social science in an article that called for a reassessment of Ulrich B. Phillips' racist interpretation of American slavery.[55]

In short order, Kenneth M. Stampp met Hofstadter's challenge. In a 1952 article in the *American Historical Review,* Stampp leveled his academic guns at Phillips' *American Negro Slavery* (1918); this work by a white Georgia racist had long been considered the standard volume on the topic. Stampp admitted that it was difficult to counter the racist arguments of George Fitzhugh and Phillips with pronouncements of faith in the equality and the goodness of all mankind. But the historian rejoiced that he could prove that Phillips had erred egregiously when he claimed that Africans were born to be slaves. "Scientific" evidence now showed, Stampp asserted, that the races had approximately equal intellectual capacity. On this crucial point, Stampp cited the chapter of the *Dilemma* called "Racial Characteristics."[56]

In 1956 Stampp published *The Peculiar Institution,* which replaced Phillips' book as the standard work on slavery in the United States. In the preface of his book, Stampp spoke the language of equalitarian social science popularized by Myrdal. "I have assumed that slaves were merely ordinary human beings," he wrote, "that innately Negroes *are,* after all, only white men with black skins, nothing more, nothing less." As he had in his earlier article on slavery, Stampp supported this strategic assumption by citing Myrdal's study. The eminent Berkeley professor had bought a copy of the *Dilemma* soon after its publication and read it from "cover to cover." He remembered that he was most impressed by Myrdal's comments that "no convincing evidence" indicated "any significant differences in the intellectual capacities . . . of Negroes and whites."[57]

At the very time Myrdal was criticizing American historians for adjusting so comfortably to the Compromise of 1877, revisionists like

55. Richard Hofstadter, "U. B. Phillips and the Plantation Legend," *Journal of Negro History,* XXIX (1944), 124.
56. Kenneth M. Stampp, "The Historian and Southern Negro Slavery," *American Historical Review,* LXII (1952), 620.
57. Kenneth M. Stampp, *The Peculiar Institution: Slavery in the Ante-Bellum South*

Stampp had begun to test the conventional views about blacks, the Civil War, Reconstruction, and so on. Just as it had for the Supreme Court and the civil rights movement, Myrdal's study proved timely for historians. It provided what Alvin W. Gouldner called the "domain assumptions" that shape interpretations and grand theories. After the rise of Myrdalian sociology, historians could no longer consider blacks a low-priority issue. Nor could Reconstruction be regarded as a complete failure brought about by avenging Yankees. It was demonstrated in the previous chapter that C. Vann Woodward cited Myrdal's study to support his influential thesis about segregation in 1954. Other southern liberal historians followed Woodward's lead in searching for the long "Silent South."[58]

I cannot begin to illustrate fully the use of Myrdal by historians here. Suffice it to say that almost all works from massive studies of American civilization to thin monographs showed the impact of the Swede. In a long survey of American thought called *America as a Civilization* (1957), for example, Max Lerner enumerated several factors such as the New Deal, World War II, the Supreme Court decisions, black migration, and the Cold War to explain the civil rights revolution. But he added: "More powerful than any of them, and what gives them their momentum, is the American conscience." Myrdal, of course, was his evidence for such a judgment.[59]

The increasingly optimistic and equalitarian attitude of historians could be seen in Carl N. Degler's important text on American history, *Out of Our Past* (1959). The young Stanford professor, who became one of the most notable members of his craft, prominently featured the race issue in his history. More than once he expressed his basic agreement with Myrdal. To Degler, the South was becoming more American, and America was becoming more equalitarian. The trends pointed to inevitable progress. In addition to Myrdal's study, Degler cited Gilberto Freyre's research on Brazil, which supposedly bolstered the proposition that two races could live in harmony and equality, even if one of them had been enslaved in the past.[60]

(New York, 1956), vii, 10; additionally, Stampp cited Myrdal's collaborator, Otto Klineberg (ed.), *Characteristics of the American Negro* (New York, 1944), which was one of the Carnegie monographs; Stampp to author, December 27, 1982.

58. *AD*, 431; Alvin W. Gouldner, *The Coming Crisis of Western Sociology* (New York, 1970), 29–35, 196–97.

59. Max Lerner, *America as a Civilization: Life and Thought in the United States Today* (New York, 1957), 67, 520–21, 981.

60. Carl N. Degler, *Out of Our Past: Forces That Shaped Modern America* (New York, 1959), 27–28, 39, 185–86.

Because Myrdal observed the New Deal years firsthand and collected mountains of data on the period, his work has special meaning for historians of the era of Franklin D. Roosevelt. Every New Deal historian wrestled with Myrdal's observation that the Roosevelt administration "changed the whole configuration of the Negro problem." John B. Kirby pointed out that Myrdal's comment sparked his interest in writing his excellent book, *Black Americans in the Roosevelt Era* (1980). Generally, in the first two decades after Roosevelt's death, liberal historians treated the New Deal as a boon to blacks. Myrdal acknowledged that New Deal programs gave material aid to blacks but charged that many of the Roosevelt alphabet agencies practiced blatant discrimination against the minority. He demonstrated that such major programs as the Agricultural Adjustment Administration in agriculture and the National Recovery Administration in industry often penalized the deprived Afro-American. He revealed that the Federal Housing Agency perpetuated segregated housing and that the Works Progress Administration paid blacks less than whites. William E. Leuchtenburg, the author of the best one-volume work on the New Deal, was one of the first liberal historians to criticize at length the shortcomings of the New Deal in regard to blacks. Not surprisingly, he made good use of the *Dilemma*.[61]

Not all historians, of course, accepted Myrdal's sunshine sociology. In 1959 Stanley M. Elkins wrote a controversial book called *Slavery* in which he made the provocative analogy between plantation slavery in the South and Nazi concentration camps. He reasoned that if concentration camps could reduce intelligent Jews to infantilism, the brutal slavery of the South could have rendered black slaves somewhat less than normal. Elkins postulated that a "Sambo" personality developed among the oppressed slaves. In the introduction to *Slavery,* Elkins explained that he wanted to move the question of slavery beyond the moral debate of Phillips and Stampp. He wished to discern the impact of slavery on blacks and to analyze the failure of American institutions in ending the peculiar institution without internecine bloodshed. To attack Stampp, with whom he agreed on the immorality of slavery, Elkins felt it was necessary to undermine the Myrdalian approach to race on which *The Peculiar Institution* was based. He therefore deprecated the Carnegie project. Elkins declared that the Myrdal study sounded too much like the abolitionist literature of the pre–Civil War period. To him the *Di-*

61. *AD*, 256–66, 349, 359, 361, 412, 418–22; John B. Kirby, *Black Americans in the Roosevelt Era: Liberalism and Race* (Knoxville, 1980), x; Harvard Sitkoff, *A New Deal For Blacks: The Emergence of Civil Rights as a National Issue* (New York, 1978), 59; William E. Leuchtenburg, *FDR and the New Deal* (New York, 1963), 141, 187, 322.

lemma contained too much mushy "*obiter dicta* on the functional inter-
changeability of the human race."[62]

Elkins accused Stampp of allowing a Myrdalian mind-set to blind
him to the "scientific" possibilities about the effects of slavery on
blacks. In effect, as one historian has persuasively argued, all Elkins did
was replace Stampp's social science model with a functionalist one. In
any case, Elkins' environmentalism told him that the oppressive system
of American slavery had forced a unique psychology on blacks. He
more or less repeated what several behavioralists felt Myrdal had not
emphasized adequately in his work: "the mark of oppression." They
reasoned that the brutal passage of the Afro-American from the seven-
teenth to the twentieth centuries might have handicapped many blacks
with a debilitating culture and an injured psyche. Elkins and other social
scientists believed that the Afro-American past had produced a distinct
black problem in addition to the white one that Myrdal defined, at least
with regard to assimilation.[63]

To say the least, neither Stampp nor Elkins pleased those who were
looking for a usable black past. In the 1960s and 1970s many black militants and some white radicals fiercely attacked both Stampp and Elkins
for their views of slavery. They vehemently rejected not only Elkins'
highly questionable "Sambo" image but Stampp's idea of slaves as a
"troublesome property." Prideful blacks demanded that historians find
derring-do freedom fighters, efficient workers, and successful culture
and family builders minimally scarred by the yoke of human bondage.
And many historians did.[64] After the mid-1960s the slightest mention by
whites of pathology in the black community (past or present) for whatever reasons brought angry retribution from militant blacks. (As will be
shown later, Daniel P. Moynihan suffered in the extreme for being the
proverbial messenger of bad news.)[65]

62. Stanley M. Elkins, *Slavery: A Problem in American Institutional and Intellectual
Life* (Chicago, 1959), 19–20, 22–23, 83n.

63. *Ibid.*, 81–139; William Issel, "History, Social Science, and Ideology: Elkins and
Blassingame on Ante-Bellum Slavery," *History Teacher,* IX (1975), 81–139.

64. For example, see John W. Blassingame, *The Slave Community: Plantation Life in
the Ante-Bellum South* (New York, 1972); Robert W. Fogel and Stanley L. Engerman,
Time on the Cross: The Economics of American Negro Slavery (2 vols.; Boston, 1974);
Herbert G. Gutman, *The Black Family in Slavery and Freedom, 1750–1925* (New York,
1976); Lawrence W. Levine, *Black Culture and Black Consciousness: Afro-American Folk
Thought from Slavery to Freedom* (New York, 1977).

65. An instructive example of a strident attack on a well-known novelist is in John
Henrik Clarke (ed.), *William Styron's Nat Turner: Ten Black Writers Respond* (Boston,
1968).

In the 1970s a reaction to what appeared to some as an ill-advised attack on environmentalism, the very idea that had academically destroyed biological racism, began to emerge. In 1978 Barry D. Adams exclaimed in the journal *Social Psychology:* "It is as if mention of the 'demoralizing and brutalizing consequences of exploitation' somehow impugns the humanity of the sufferers." The black psychologist Kenneth Clark sarcastically quipped that current literature suggested that perhaps slavery was not so bad after all. When the white Marxist historian Eugene Genovese blurred his usual ideological focus to glorify black culture under slavery in *Roll, Jordan, Roll* (1974), the ever-salty David Donald accused him of trying to be the "house Honkey." In the 1980s Peter Kolchin and Laurence Shore mounted formidable attacks on the proliferation of black "celebratory" history and the motives behind it. In a prize-winning essay in the *Journal of American History,* Kolchin amassed impressive evidence to suggest that revisionist scholars had replaced the Sambo myth with the equally misleading myth of the "idyllic slave community." Shore brilliantly upbraided "revolutionary posturing" historians who drained Negro slavery of its tragic content. He charged that present-minded revisionists treated the exceptional slave as average and viewed accommodation and survival as heroic, an extreme position that earlier and more objective writers such as Frederick Douglass and W. E. B. Du Bois had avoided. Both Kolchin and Shore rejected Elkins' idea of a slave community consisting primarily of "depersonalized Samboes" and gave due praise to revisionists such as Genovese, John W. Blassingame, Herbert G. Gutman, and Lawrence W. Levine. But they also rightly maintained that the desire to put the past to work for contemporary causes had resulted in a profusion of exaggerated black history.[66]

In a 1975 article Elkins admitted that he had some regret about his rough treatment of Stampp in the 1950s. He evidently felt more empathy for his colleague after he had received a heavy dose of abuse from many quarters. Elkins admitted that he and Stampp stood in the same

66. Barry D. Adams, "Inferiorization and 'Self-Esteem,'" *Social Psychology,* XLI (1978), 49; Kenneth Clark's comment is in Elkins, "Slavery Debate," 52; David Donald, "Writing About Slavery," *Commentary,* LIX (January, 1975), 89; Peter Kolchin, "Reevaluating the Antebellum Slave Community: A Comparative Perspective," *Journal of American History,* LXX (1983), 579–601; Laurence Shore, "The Poverty of Tragedy in Historical Writing on Southern Slavery," *South Atlantic Quarterly,* LXXXV (1986), 147–64. For another provocative critique, see the black sociologist Orlando Patterson, "Toward a Future That Has No Past—Reflections on the Fate of Blacks in the Americas," *Public Interest,* XXVII (Spring, 1972), 25–62; see also his *Slavery and Social Death: A Comparative Study* (Cambridge, Mass., 1982).

camp. Both were conscience-stricken white liberals who wanted to reveal the horrors of slavery. Elkins failed to realize, however, that he
could have criticized Stampp without scourging Myrdal, who, after all,
recognized the damage of slavery and racism. He, too, opened himself
to attack by describing blacks as "exaggerated Americans" and by de-
picting black culture as an unhealthy outgrowth of white racism. And
long before Elkins stressed it, Myrdal pointed out that the absence of a
national church and other strong national institutions hindered the
peaceful abolition of slavery. Ironically, the controversial historian even
rejected the Herskovits thesis about African cultural survivals just as
pointedly as had Myrdal.[67] In short, it seems that Elkins attacked the
Swede to undermine Stampp.

Unfortunately for scholarship, the events of the 1960s caused many
historians to change moods frequently. The decade brought both profound hope and disillusionment. Oscar Handlin, a giant in the field of
historical ethnicity, seemed to change his opinion with the headlines. In
his 1957 book, *Race and Nationality in American Life*, the Harvard historian asked in mock horror: "What ever happened to race?" He rejoiced that the latest "scientific" findings had all but destroyed the idea
of race. Echoing C. Vann Woodward on segregation, Handlin asserted:
"The origins of racism lie in the comparatively recent past and we may,
in our lifetime, see it run its full course." He felt that blacks, like other
ethnic groups, would move steadily up the ladder to equality. By 1963,
however, Handlin suggested that Myrdal's cheerful analysis might no
longer prove reliable as a guide to race relations. In 1964, in *Fire-Bell in
the Night*, he inched toward alarmism. "Only the most cynical or the
foresighted could have foreseen," Handlin exclaimed, "that the circumstances would give racism an ominous new birth." Still, at a special
conference of the Academy of Arts and Sciences on the Negro held in
May, 1965, Handlin derided the deepening pessimism expressed by a
large number of the participants and huffily remarked that many social
scientists now found it fashionable to scoff at Myrdal's thesis. He counseled them that the era of racism had been but a short and passing inter-
lude in American history.[68]

67. Elkins, "Slavery Debate," 40–41.
68. Oscar Handlin, *Race and Nationality in American Life* (Boston, 1957), xii, 187;
Handlin, Review of *AD*, in *New York Times Book Review*, April 21, 1963, pp. 1ff; Hand-
lin, *Fire-Bell in the Night: The Crisis in Civil Rights* (Boston, 1964), 73, 109; Handlin,
"The Goals of Integration," in Kenneth B. Clark and Talcott Parsons (eds.), *The Negro
American* (Boston, 1966), 659, 663–64.

Scholars nonetheless continued to pile up evidence that rendered more and more of Myrdal's main ideas supsect. Whether "cynical" or "foresighted," they dredged up sobering facts about America's racial situation. Two articles in *Social Forces* are exemplary. In 1961 Ernest Q. Campbell examined Myrdal's main thesis empirically by testing 275 southern college students outside the Deep South. His conclusion was blunt: "Myrdal performed a disservice to our understanding of segregated social systems by his drastic simplification of the normative dimensions of the issue." In a 1962 article, Nahum Medalia argued vigorously, if in painfully abstruse language, that white Americans, particularly southerners, held other values that rivaled or surpassed the American creed. He maintained that there were no signs that they would change these other values to bring them into line with the idealistic creed. Facing blacks in a new urban, industrial setting, Medalia speculated, would further threaten white dominance and create a dilemma rather than dissolve one.[69]

Not only did Myrdal's thesis come under repeated attack, but the very idea that a consensus existed on the democratic American creed incited strong doubt in some scholars. In this case political scientists uncovered much of the negative evidence. In a 1960 study James Prothro and Charles Grigg discovered a consensus on broad, abstract principles, but they added that specific application of the principles brought almost total discord. In a stimulating book on community leaders in 1961, Robert Dahl asserted that political stability in America happily did not depend on widespread belief in democratic and constitutional principles, for he found very little belief in them. A select few at the top of the political stratum, he wrote, resolved conflicts over democratic principles, and the common people acquiesced in their decisions. Dahl found less consensus on the issue of minority groups than on any other.[70]

In 1964 Herbert McClosky's extensive study of forty-five hundred people concluded that the American consensus on democratic ideals and practices had waned. The people, he wrote, were "sharply divided"

69. Ernest Q. Campbell, "Moral Comfort and Racial Segregation: An Examination of the Myrdal Hypothesis," *Social Forces,* XXXIX (1961), 228–34; Nahum Medalia, "Myrdal's Assumptions on Race Relations: A Conceptual Commentary," *ibid.,* XL (1962), 223–27.

70. James Prothro and Charles Grigg, "Fundamental Principles of Democracy: Bases of Agreement and Disagreement," *Journal of Politics,* XXII (1960), 276–94; Robert A. Dahl, *Who Governs?* (New Haven, 1961), 322–25 and *passim.*

on the basic principles of the American system. He also found an alarming authoritarian strain running through the masses. About 47 percent
agreed with the following statement: "If congressional committees
stuck strictly to the rules and gave every witness his rights, they would
never succeed in exposing the many dangerous subversives they have
turned up." About 35 percent felt that force was necessary to save "the
true American way of life," and 58 percent nodded affirmatively to the
idea that "the main trouble with democracy is that people don't really
know what's best for them." McClosky divulged that roughly half of the
population vowed that the races were not equal in the "things that count
most." The primary bright spot in the study appeared to be that the political elite and well educated tended to believe in the creed. As long as
the masses were placid, the elite would adhere to American principles.
But McClosky warned that prolonged strife or crisis could exacerbate
dangerous ideological differences and unleash authoritarian tendencies
in grass-roots America.[71]

By the early 1960s a troubled minority of social scientists began to
look beyond the "post-bigotry" era. That is, they pondered the racial
problem after legal segregation and bald individual prejudice declined
or disappeared. Their troubling conclusion was that the second phase of
the race problem would prove far more difficult than the first. As Earl
Raab said in 1962, the movement would be from "simpler problems to
more complex problems." Participating in a conference in Detroit in
connection with the one hundredth anniversary of the Emancipation
Proclamation, James Q. Wilson summed up his extensive research on
blacks and politics. Sharing the platform with the honored guest, Gunnar Myrdal, the Harvard political scientist denied the Swede's belief that
blacks could gain very much from political activity. Wilson declared:
"The problems which confront the masses of American Negroes will
·. . . remain for many years even if every major political goal of Negroes
is attained tomorrow." Referring to Myrdal's book, Wilson contended
that years of bitter oppression for the minority meant that there was a
"Negro problem" apart from white racism.[72]

In 1962 Dan W. Dodson suggested that the new era of race relations

71. Herbert McClosky, "Consensus and Ideology in American Politics," *American
Political Science Review*, LVIII (1964), 361–79.

72. Introduction in Earl Raab (ed.), *American Race Relations Today* (Garden City,
N.Y., 1962), 11, 15; James Q. Wilson, "The Changing Political Position of the Negro," in
Arnold Rose (ed.), *Assuring Freedom to the Free* (Detroit, 1964), 182–83; see also
Wilson's *Negro Politics: The Search for Leadership* (Glencoe, Ill., 1960), 6–7, 295–315.

would have to discard the idea of color-blindness that had been so sacred among white liberals and black activists. Blacks, he argued, needed and deserved special help from white society to help them enter the mainstream that centuries of abuse had denied them. Another factor eroding Myrdal's analysis involved the rise of black pride and nationalism. One social scientist suggested the concept of "ethnogenesis" to describe what was happening in the black community. Even if Myrdal had been correct on the absence of African survivals, some held that the Swede's "exaggerated Americans" would become even more exaggerated in the future. In the 1962 edition of *Black Metropolis,* a book first issued in 1945, the authors retraced the path of Afro-American culture: "Changes have been in the direction of a more intensive elaboration of Bronzeville's separate culture, not toward its disappearance." Few scholars agreed with Everett C. Hughes, a veteran scholar on race, when he said in 1963 that the Negro wanted "to disappear as a defined group." [73] In short, an outspoken minority of academics predicted in the early 1960s that the "strange career" of the Afro-Americans would become stranger, and they forecast that the changes would be accompanied by significant conflict and much confusion.

In 1964, the year that Congress passed the most comprehensive civil rights bill of the twentieth century, several books appeared which attested to the changing perspective on race relations. Two of the most provocative of these had the term "crisis" in their titles. In *Crisis in Black and White,* Charles Silberman reminded his readers that twenty years earlier Myrdal had implored the nation "to do something big, and do it soon." According to Silberman, Myrdal's plea had gone unheeded. Furthermore, the situation had changed so much that more extreme measures than Myrdal imagined were now needed. Silberman's assessment of the racial situation was grim. He claimed that America had not begun to face the depths of its racism. "Twenty years ago, Gunnar Myrdal concluded that the American Negro problem is a problem in the heart of the American. . . . Myrdal was wrong," Silberman lamented. "The tragedy of race relations today is that there is no American Di-

---

73. Dan W. Dodson, "Can Intergroup Quotas Be Benign?" in Raab (ed.), *American Race Relations Today,* 125–33; Lester Singer; "Ethnogenesis and Negro Americans Today," *Social Research,* XXIX (1962), 419–32; St. Clair Drake and Horace Cayton, authors of *Black Metropolis,* quoted in Louis L. Knowles and Kenneth Prewitt (eds.), *Institutional Racism in America* (Englewood Cliffs, N.J., 1969), 175; Everett C. Hughes, "Race Relations and the Sociological Imagination," *American Sociological Review,* XXVIII (1963), 883.

lemma." Silberman conceded that whites had Afro-Americans on their mind, but they suffered no psychic anguish borne of principle. They were bothered only because their peace and businesses had suffered. Like James Q. Wilson, he maintained that a separate black problem existed and would continue for years even if white racism miraculously vanished overnight. In sum, Silberman felt that the tremendous oppression of the past necessitated "a radical reconstruction of society" that would bring blacks into the mainstream of American life.[74]

The same year Silberman's book appeared, Lewis M. Killian and Charles Grigg, both experienced students of southern race relations, raised the specter of imminent conflict in *Racial Crisis in America*. The result of five years of research, this book by two southern sociologists averred that all the social indicators presaged an era "in which neither good will nor mutual understanding, but impersonal power will be the most significant factor in race relations." The trouble for blacks was that they had little power. The authors pointed out that relative to whites, blacks had been losing ground economically since World War II, and they were demanding more than white liberals were willing to give. Indeed, the authors concluded that "the decision of 1954 may prove to be not the beginning of the resolution of 'a struggle in the hearts and minds of white Americans' but the opening battle of a race war."[75]

Killian and Grigg not only tore into the laissez-faire functionalists but soundly castigated the moral dilemma school of thought as well. The latter, they charged, glibly assumed that people chose to be rational and good. The authors chided Myrdal and company for insisting that all men were "brothers under the skin" and that prejudice was highly unnatural and easily unlearned. The southerners asked sarcastically: "Had not Myrdal provided a cogent argument for the proposition that the race problem arose not from a conflict between whites and Negroes but from a conflict within the hearts and minds of white people?"[76]

Ernest Burgess notwithstanding, Myrdal did not always persuade academics, even those who were liberals. By 1965 many liberals complained that Myrdal's thesis greatly oversimplified the race problem by downplaying the real problem, which was the social and economic

74. Silberman, *Crisis in Black and White*, 4–14, 132–33, 193, 354, 358.
75. Killian and Grigg, *Racial Crisis in America*, 1, 8, 79, 91–92, 99, 128. See also Sidney M. Wilhelm and Edwin H. Powell, "Who Needs The Negro?" *Trans-Action*, September–October, 1964, pp. 3–6.
76. Killian and Grigg, *Racial Crisis in America*, 15–26.

origins of racism. This racism, they pointed out, included not only personal prejudice and discrimination but seemingly intractable institutional racism as well. The latter was more subtle, insidious, and tenacious. Thus, they argued, substantial changes in socioeconomic conditions were required before attitudes and behavior could be altered. They feared that Myrdal's moral approach would play into the hands of gradualists like President Eisenhower, who felt that legislation and court rulings could not change the hearts of people.

Throughout the 1950s the popular "authoritarian personality" school of psychology and the functionalist brand of sociology worked against Myrdal's view of race relations. Their faith shattered by World War II and the Holocaust, many psychologists proclaimed that the authoritarian personality dampened hopes of an easy victory over racism. Social scientists also produced abundant research that proved that people could live comfortably with conflicting values, especially when part of the conflict involved racial values.

In the 1960s empirical research by political scientists raised serious doubt about the solidity of the American democratic consensus. Historians did their part by digging into the past. There they found pervasive racism in both the North and the South. Howard Zinn, a white civil rights crusader who taught history at a black college in Atlanta, said in 1964 that the question was not whether white supremacy was the central theme of southern history but of American history in general. On the disease of racism, he wrote: "Physical difference is so gross a stimulus to human beings that once it is latched onto as an explanation for differences in personality, intelligence, demeanor, it is terribly difficult to put aside." Charles Silberman concluded that color consciousness would cease only when men lost their color or their eyesight.[77]

Unfortunately, critics of Myrdal who called for drastic structural changes in American society to solve the racial problem offered no plausible way to accomplish that goal. How could one even interpret polls that indicated declining racism but also showed that whites always felt that blacks were "moving too fast" or were basically satisfied? If racism were as deep and widespread and exhortation and education as ineffective as scholars said, how could racism be ended? What therapy could a government design to deal with the collective authoritarian personality? How could officials in a majority-rule society institute changes deemed

77. Howard Zinn, *The Southern Mystique* (New York, 1964), 10–11; Silberman, *Crisis in Black and White,* 166.

necessary for minority justice? How could a small, poor, and often-despised minority work its will in a power relations framework, the model so favored by Myrdal's critics?

Despite repeated assaults on Myrdal, his authority remained formidable until about the mid-1960s. The Swede's high visibility on American campuses helped strengthen his influence. He received an honorary degree from Columbia University a few days after the historic *Brown* decision. The university cited him as "a man of gifted energy, at home on two continents." Myrdal took the occasion to remind the academic world that he had predicted the opinion and that he had influenced the Court. Howard University bestowed a degree upon the Swede in 1962. His commencement speech at Howard, which was widely circulated, predicted more racial breakthroughs in the near future. In 1963 Myrdal published a highly respected economic appraisal of America called *Challenge to Affluence*. Hardly a year passed that the Swedish celebrity did not grace American shores. Some hailed him as proof that the Renaissance Man still lived. And when England acknowledged in the early 1960s that it had an ominous race problem, the London Institute of Race Relations searched for "a Myrdal for Britain while there is still time." [78]

The march of events from 1954 to 1965, of course, persuaded many of Myrdal's prescience. In those years blacks largely achieved legal equality and a new group pride. The year 1964 brought enactment of a far-reaching civil rights bill, followed in 1965 by the crucial Voting Rights Act. It seemed like a time to celebrate. A national catharsis of racial liberalism occurred when in March, 1965, President Lyndon B. Johnson implored legislators to enact the voting bill. Speaking before a joint session of Congress and millions of television viewers, the southern leader brought Congress to its feet when near the climax of his moving address, he dramatically paused and repeated the words from the civil rights theme song: "And we *shall* overcome." [79]

78. New York *Times*, June 2, 1954, p. 34; Myrdal's 1962 commencement speech at Howard University was published in the *New Republic*, July 9, 1962, pp. 11–12; Gunnar Myrdal, *Challenge to Affluence* (New York, 1963), v, 51; Edwin L. Dale, Jr., Review of *Challenge to Affluence*, in *American Scholar*, XXXIII (1963), 145.

79. Lyndon B. Johnson, quoted in New York *Times*, March 16, 1965, p. 30.

IX

The *Dilemma* and the Civil Rights Movement, 1954–1965

In his 1964 book *Portrait of a Decade,* Anthony Lewis labeled the period between 1954 and 1964 "the revolutionary decade." The Washington correspondent for the New York *Times* subtitled his widely read book *The Second American Revolution.* Americans, it seems, have a tendency to dilute the meaning of the word "revolution." Perhaps the inclination stems from the partial nature of all American political and social revolutions. Lewis acknowledged that what he described as revolutionary was actually conservative. "The race-relations revolution in the United States," the journalist wrote, "has so far been a unique effort to join a society rather than overthrow it." [1]

Myrdal's study seemed especially fashioned for the conservative revolution sought by most white liberals and black activists in the decade after the *Brown* decision because Myrdal envisioned a peaceful, orderly, and limited revolution in racial arrangements. The battle would not be one of raw power, group against group, culture against culture, but a struggle within the white conscience. The movement did not concern itself with affirmative action but with legal equality and equal opportunity. In *Portrait of a Decade,* Lewis followed Myrdal's precepts closely. The first sentence of his book quoted from the "great study" by the Swedish economist. The quotation explicated Myrdal's theme that the "Negro problem" constantly plagued the white mind and conscience. The reporter ended his first chapter with a full paragraph ex-

1. Anthony Lewis, *Portrait of a Decade: The Second American Revolution* (New York, 1964), 14. Lewis wrote and edited part of this volume using material gleaned from the New York *Times,* including articles by James Baldwin and John Oliver Killens.

225

cerpt from the *Dilemma*, quoting the oft-cited passage of Myrdal's final chapter, which ended with the sentence: "*America is free to choose whether the Negro shall remain her liability or become her opportunity.*" In the same chapter, Lewis claimed that the civil rights movement had advanced as far as it had because the American conscience finally had been touched. Even in the paperback edition of *Portrait*, which appeared in late 1965, Lewis remained optimistic about the future, although he warned that all revolutions had a tendency to lapse into irrationality and hatred. Despite the Watts riot of 1965, the rising white backlash in the North, and Lewis' recognition that the civil rights movement had entered a new and precarious phase, the liberal journalist kept the faith. "The commitment of the American people and their government to progress," he maintained, "had not weakened and the vital thread of hope was still intact."[2]

Although Lewis' book attested to Myrdal's impact on the liberal mind, he made almost no effort to demonstrate how the *Dilemma* affected the civil rights movement. In the second chapter, on school desegregation, he mentioned only that the Supreme Court had cited Myrdal's study in the *Brown* opinion. Actually, Myrdal's influence on liberals such as Lewis was so basic that it never occurred to them to detail how the Scandinavian's work related to people and events. They considered Myrdal's impact to be self-evident. Moreover, as the *Dilemma* aged, its influence, though still important, became more diffuse. According to Arthur Schlesinger, Jr., by the 1960s Myrdalism had been "generally absorbed into the [liberal] bloodstream." Harry McPherson, a bookish young racial adviser to Lyndon Johnson, observed that Myrdal's ideas provided "a kind of background music for the civil rights effort." Frederick G. Dutton, who advised both Presidents Kennedy and Johnson on racial matters, recalled that Myrdal and his book "were so towering in the intellectual and . . . political climate of that period and the preceding years that its influence [was] more fundamental than just immediate policy decisions." Dutton correctly pointed out that the *Dilemma* affected "attitudes and premises of action, which are a more important way to effect the public course in the long run."[3]

This chapter shows that the period from *Brown* to Watts marked an era when white liberals and most black leaders believed that Myrdal's

2. *Ibid.*, 3, 13–14; *ibid.* (New York, 1965), xiii.
3. *Ibid.*, (1965), 26–27; Arthur Schlesinger, Jr., to the author, October 5, 1981; Harry McPherson to the author, July 8, 1981; Frederick G. Dutton to the author, July 7, 1981.

analysis of the race problem had special relevance. The year 1965, however, constituted a turning point. At that time the civil rights movement fell into confusion and acrimony, and Myrdal's study ceased to have much meaning for the rapidly changing racial situation. Earlier, though, the black rights movement reflected, directly or indirectly, many of Myrdal's ideas. Just as Truman's Committee on Civil Rights began its work with a copy of the *Dilemma,* ten years later the Commission on Civil Rights of the Eisenhower era did likewise. When events forced the aloof and pragmatic Kennedy to move boldly on civil rights in 1963, he dramatically framed the issue in Myrdalian terms. Before a national television audience, the president proclaimed, as no other had, that the race question was, above all, a moral issue.[4] Kennedy's emotional words emanated from the felicitous pen of the Myrdal-influenced speechwriter Theodore Sorensen. And Martin Luther King, Jr., who shared many of Myrdal's views on race relations, admired the work of the Swedish economist. The charismatic black leader not only used Myrdal's *Dilemma,* but he also struck up a warm friendship with the Swede. King's books and speeches illustrated just one of the various ways in which Myrdalian logic and language seeped into the heart and soul of the civil rights movement.

As shown in previous chapters, most blacks viewed Myrdal's book as a positive contribution to their cause, despite initial skepticism and even some hostility toward Myrdal. In the 1940s blacks as different as W. E. B. Du Bois, E. Franklin Frazier, Richard Wright, and Adam Clayton Powell, Jr., lauded the *Dilemma.* Coming out of World War II with a new determination to achieve freedom, Afro-American spokesmen recognized the superb timeliness of Myrdal's study. They saw the potential of the *Dilemma* as a guide for protest action throughout the country. In the 1940s and 1950s most black activists sought integration into the American mainstream, as Myrdal claimed. Their outlook was pragmatic and eclectic. As the Swede had advised, they took their allies where they could find them. Black protest leaders were not quick to criticize the well-meaning, if perhaps obtuse, white liberals who joined their movement for racial justice. Most blacks also counted, at least in part, on the existence of a Myrdalian dilemma as a significant factor in their deliverance.[5]

4. New York *Times,* June 12, 1963.
5. Du Bois, Review of *AD,* 118–24; Frazier, Review of *AD,* 555–57; Richard Wright, Introduction to St. Clare Drake and Horace Cayton, *Black Metropolis: A Study of Negro*

Still, it should be repeated, many blacks did not swallow Myrdal's analysis of race relations whole. Several blacks were antagonistic to the Myrdal report. The eminent black sociologists Charles S. Johnson and E. Franklin Frazier emerged from the Chicago School of Sociology, which Myrdal had roundly condemned as being laissez-faire in outlook. In the 1930s a substantial part of the black intelligentsia fell under the sway of some form of Marxist thinking, which Myrdal had also loudly repudiated. Generally speaking, black leaders put less emphasis on white guilt feelings as a factor in racial change than did Myrdal. They tended to put more stress on power and class solidarity, particularly Frazier and Ralph Bunche, who had prepared voluminous memoranda for the Carnegie project. Before World War II, Bunche's reasoning followed a rigid economic determinism. He castigated the "myth of race" and the "false consciousness" of the masses. Many felt that Bunche had been closer to the truth than Myrdal. In 1951 Wilson Record, a black political scientist, declared that the one "glaring shortcoming" of Myrdal's study was its failure to incorporate Bunche's findings. By 1951, however, the radical Bunche had moved to the center and joined the political establishment. To meet the shifting circumstances between the Great Depression and the 1950s, many Afro-American leaders, including Bunche, adjusted their thinking considerably. Once a severe critic of the NAACP, the diplomatic Bunche worked closely with the senior protest agency in the 1950s.[6]

The NAACP and Myrdal had always been essentially in accord. In the *Dilemma*, Myrdal expressed basic approval of the strategy and tac-

---

Life in a Northern City (New York, 1945), xxxix; Adam Clayton Powell, Jr., *Marching Blacks* (New York, 1945), 141–42, 148, 197; *AD*, 794, 799, 853. For optimism among blacks in this period, see also Rayford W. Logan, *The Negro and the Post-War World: A Primer* (Washington, 1945); Spencer Logan, *A Negro's Faith in America* (New York, 1946).

6. For examples of Frazier's changing views, compare "The Status of the Negro in the American Social Order," *Journal of Negro Education*, IV (1935), 293–307; *The Negro in the United States* (New York, 1949); *Black Bourgeoisie* (Glencoe, Ill., 1957); and *Race and Culture Contacts in the Modern World* (New York, 1957). For an assessment of Frazier, see John Bracey, August Meier, and Elliott Rudwick, "The Black Sociologist: The First Half Century," in Ladner (ed.), *Death of White Sociology*, 13–19; and G. Franklin Edwards, "E. Franklin Frazier," in Blackwell and Janowitz (eds.), *Black Sociologists*, 85–117. On Ralph Bunche, see his "A Critical Analysis of the Tactics and Programs of Minority Groups," *Journal of Negro Education*, IV (1935), 308–20; see also John B. Kirby, "Ralph J. Bunche and Black Radical Thought in the 1930's," *Phylon*, XXXV (1974), 129–41.

tics of the New York–based organization but encouraged it to become more militant and to recruit more heavily among the black masses. Because Thurgood Marshall, the head of the NAACP's legal staff, adopted a sociological approach to the civil rights cases in 1947, Myrdal's name echoed across the land in 1954. The Swede achieved both acclaim and notoriety when the chief justice cited the *Dilemma* in the crucial footnote 11 to the *Brown* opinion. Myrdal's ties with the NAACP, however, went beyond a footnote. While undertaking the Carnegie study, the European became close friends with Walter White and Roy Wilkins, the two major officers of the NAACP in that period. In 1948 Walter White arranged a dinner to honor Myrdal at the Waldorf-Astoria Hotel in New York City. The guest list read like a *Who's Who* of the early civil rights movement. Eleanor Roosevelt delivered the main tribute to the Swedish visitor. White advertised the *Dilemma* as "beyond doubt one of the greatest socio-economic studies" ever done in America.[7] Esteem for Myrdal remained extremely high at the NAACP during the quarter century following the publication of the *Dilemma*.

The NAACP and the Supreme Court worked together in 1954 to precipitate the great catalytic event of the 1950s: the school desegregation decision. Revolutions and movements require galvanizing symbols. The *Brown* decision provided one for the civil rights movement and its opponents. No other event in the twentieth century so greatly aroused the hopes of blacks or alarmed white supremacists.[8] Whereas southern segregationists reacted fiercely to the *Brown* ruling, blacks delighted in its promise. A doctoral candidate at Boston University named Martin Luther King, Jr., hailed the decision as a "world-shaking decree." It made the aspiring minister look forward to returning to Dixie. Sheer jubilation reigned at the NAACP headquarters in New York. Thurgood Marshall predicted that in five years all schools would be integrated and by 1963, the hundredth anniversary of the Emancipation Proclamation, all forms of segregation and discrimination would be eliminated. Walter White recorded his thoughts about that day in his last book, *How Far the Promised Land?* (1955). He perceived the *Brown* decision as the methodical working out of the American dilemma and, like Marshall, predicted the abolition of all overt forms of discrimination by 1963. In his

7. *Brown* v. *Board of Education of Topeka*, 347 U.S. 483; "Gunnar Myrdal Dinner," Group II, Series B, Box 14, NAACP Papers.

8. Lewis, *Portrait of a Decade* (1964), 5–6; all subsequent citations are from the 1964 edition.

autobiography, Roy Wilkins remembered May 17 as the "sweetest day of his life." Around the country, black hopes rose markedly. Ralph Bunche, reverting to his old habit of minimizing color, proffered that racism was "more veneer than deep grain" and it would be peeled off "with little damage or pain." In 1954 a national poll indicated that 64 percent of blacks forecast a brighter future for themselves. In his memoirs, Wilkins confessed to his naïveté in the premature celebrations of 1954. Neither he, Bunche, nor White anticipated the decades of litigation, struggle, and violence that lay ahead.[9]

Some have suggested that blacks in Harlem, on Beale Street in Memphis, or in similar places remained more dubious about the outcome of the *Brown* decision. They had been deceived by white men before. The ever-skeptical E. Franklin Frazier looked at the motivation behind the opinion by saying, "The white man is scared down to his bowels, so it's be-kind-to-Negroes decade at last."[10]

Whether there has yet been a decade that was truly kind to American blacks is questionable. It is certain, however, that Martin Luther King dramatically put the American creed before the American people from 1955 until his death in 1968. For about a decade, the spellbinding minister from Atlanta dominated the racial scene. The well-read King drew his philosophy from such sources as Henry David Thoreau, Mohandas Gandhi, Walter Rauschenbusch, G. W. Friedrich Hegel, and Reinhold Niebuhr. Although he admired the work of Niebuhr, he ultimately rejected the pessimism of neo-orthodoxy. Rather, from the liberal Social Gospel of Rauschenbusch and the idealistic philosophy of Hegel and Gandhi, King concluded that the universe was on the side of justice. More down to earth, King believed that the American creed constituted a dynamic factor that worked against the racial *status quo*. In his first book, *Stride Toward Freedom* (1958), he wrote: "Indeed, as the Swedish economist Gunnar Myrdal has pointed out, the problem of race is not a political but a moral issue." The 1957 charter of King's Southern Christian Leadership Conference stated: "SCLC believes that the American dilemma in race relations can best and most quickly be re-

9. Stephen B. Oates, *Let the Trumpet Sound: The Life of Martin Luther King, Jr.* (New York, 1982), 50; Kluger, *Simple Justice*, 714; New York *Times*, May 18, 1954; Walter White, *How Far the Promised Land?* (New York, 1955), 26–27, 232; Roy Wilkins, *Standing Fast: The Autobiography of Roy Wilkins* (New York, 1982), 214–15; Bunche quoted in *ibid.*, 216.

10. Kluger, *Simple Justice*, 710, 714; Frazier quoted in Harold R. Isaacs, *The New World of the Negro Americans* (New York, 1963), 332.

solved through the action of thousands of people, committed to the philosophy of non-violence, who will physically identify themselves in a
just and moral struggle." And in his historic speech in Washington in
1963, King thundered in Baptist cadences the litany of the American
creed: "I have a dream that one day this nation will rise up and live out
the true meaning of its creed: We hold these truths to be self-evident,
that all men are created equal." [11]

I do not know when King first became familiar with Myrdal's book,
although it seems likely that he encountered it early in his life. In 1944,
the year Myrdal's study appeared, King entered Morehouse College in
Atlanta at the age of fifteen. As a sociology major, he surely heard about
or read some of Myrdal's book or a condensed version of it. His schooling at Crozier Theological Seminary in Pennsylvania (B.D., 1951) and
at Boston University (Ph.D., 1955) coincided with the spread of the
sociological emphasis in higher education and the inculcation of Myrdal's ideas into American liberal thought. In any event, King's personal
secretary recalled that the black leader considered Myrdal one of the
"truly great contemporary scholars." The two men corresponded occasionally, and when King traveled to Sweden in 1964 to accept the Nobel
Peace Prize, he dined at Myrdal's home. The Swedish scholar also es-
corted the American to several official functions connected with the
event. [12]

Myrdal and King shared many basic beliefs about the race issue beyond the idea that it was a moral question. Although the Baptist minister
felt that the universe was in lockstep with the march of justice, he saw
the necessity of social engineering. In his famous 1963 letter from the
Birmingham jail, an impatient King told the so-called southern moderates that "time itself was neutral." Because progress was not automatic,
King stressed the need for leadership, education, and federal action. On
the efficacy of legislation and law, he proclaimed in a Myrdalian accent:
"Judicial decrees may not change the heart, but they can restrain the
heartless." Indeed, King believed that laws could alter habits and eventually lead to fundamental changes in attitude. Also, like Myrdal, he

11. Martin Luther King, Jr., *Stride Toward Freedom: The Montgomery Story* (New
York, 1958), 106, 205; Oates, *Let the Trumpet Sound*, 24–26, 31–35; August Meier,
Elliott Rudwick, and Francis L. Broderick (eds.), *Black Protest Thought in the Twentieth
Century* (2d ed.; Indianapolis, 1971), 303; Brink and Harris, *Negro Revolution in Amer-
ica*, 26.

12. David L. Lewis, *King: A Critical Biography* (New York, 1970), 18–21; D. Mc-
Donald to the author, October 28, 1969.

asserted: "The Negro is an American." King told Robert Penn Warren: "We know nothing of Africa." Additionally, King echoed Myrdal's cardinal rule: blacks needed white allies. They thus needed to appeal to the white conscience. As August Meier has pointed out, King "unerringly knew how to exploit to maximum effectiveness their [whites'] growing feeling of guilt." Both men heartily endorsed the idea of the basic goodness and rationality of mankind. In 1970 Myrdal said of King: "There was a deep understanding between us." [13] Perhaps too much has been made of King's exalted philosophical undergirding and not enough of his initial interest in sociology or his experiential knowledge about people and politics.

Although King retained his belief in nonviolence and progress throughout his life, the events of the 1960s saddened and sobered him. Recognizing the growing impatience of blacks, King acknowledged that he had to move resolutely to keep the leader's baton. In 1963 he quoted Gandhi to describe the paradoxical situation. "There go my people," King explained, "I must catch them, for I am their leader." By moving as fast as he did, however, he managed to appear revolutionary to many whites. Indeed, in the 1960s "moderate" black leaders such as King positioned themselves significantly to the left of most white liberals. In 1964 King called for a multi-billion-dollar compensatory program for Afro-Americans, which he labeled a "Bill of Rights for the Disadvantaged." After taking his movement to Chicago in 1967 and witnessing the seething hate and explosive violence of a northern city, he spoke of congenital racism. In an article concerning social science and the race question, which was written shortly before his assassination, King declared that events from 1955 to 1965 had misled everyone. "Everybody, activists and social scientists," he wrote, "underestimated the amount of violence and rage Negroes were suppressing and the amount of bigotry the white majority was disguising." [14] Experience proved to be a troubling teacher for King. By the mid-1960s he knew that it was prob-

13. King, "Letter from Birmingham Jail," in Ronald Lora (ed.), *America in the '60's: Cultural Authorities in Transition* (New York, 1974), 59; King, *Stride Toward Freedom,* 197–98; King, "A Challenge to the Churches and Synagogues," in Mathew Ahmann (ed.), *Race, Challenge to Religion* (New York, 1963), 166; Robert Penn Warren, *Who Speaks for the Negro?* (New York, 1965), 216; Martin Luther King, Jr., *Where Do We Go From Here: Chaos or Community?* (New York, 1967), 94; August Meier, "On the Role of Martin Luther King," in Bracey, Meier, and Rudwick (eds.), *Conflict and Competition,* 86; Myrdal to the author, January 29, 1970.

14. Daniel C. Thompson, *The Negro Leadership Class* (Englewood Cliffs, N.J., 1963), x; Martin Luther King, Jr., *Why We Can't Wait* (New York, 1964), 143–44,

lematic whether his approach would work as well in the future as it had in the past.

Although there was rising consternation among certain blacks in the early 1960s, most minority activists still remained primarily nonviolent, integrationist, and hopeful. But the strong determination of Afro-Americans to make integration happen faster was clearly evident. Thus the decade of the 1960s began with sit-ins, freedom rides, and widespread demonstrations designed to quicken the pace of change. In 1960 four black college freshmen in Greensboro, North Carolina, initiated a trend. They sat down at a dimestore lunch counter and asked for service. They got none, but they received extensive media attention. From Greensboro, the sit-in spread across the South. When a reporter asked the original instigators of the sit-in why they had decided to brave the wrath of the whites in Greensboro, they replied that they had been inspired by reading the works of Lillian Smith, Gandhi, and Myrdal.[15]

The sit-in movement led to the formation of the Student Nonviolent Coordinating Committee in 1960. SNCC looked back to the idealism of King's SCLC, as it had looked back to the idealism of the Congress of Racial Equality. Founded in 1942, CORE had strived to end discrimination in public places through "inter-racial, non-violent direct action." In 1943 James Farmer organized sit-ins at Chicago restaurants, and blacks in other northern cities adopted his tactics during World War II and after. The 1957 charter of King's organization stated that its ultimate goal was the "beloved community," which would be characterized by "genuine intergroup and interpersonal living." The 1960 SNCC charter dripped with moral fervor. It gave currency to King's idea that violence was not only impractical but immoral. It centered on the lofty principles of Christian love, peace, and racial integration. James M. Lawson, Jr., a student who was expelled from Vanderbilt University three months before getting his degree because of civil rights activity, provided some of the inspired leadership for SNCC in its early years. From a lunch counter in Raleigh, North Carolina, in 1960 Lawson said: "We are demonstrators trying to raise the 'moral issue.' That is, we are pointing to

149–55; and *Where Do We Go From Here?* 83; Lewis, *King,* 364–65; King, "The Role of the Behavioral Scientist in the Civil Rights Movement," *Journal of Social Issues,* XXIV, No. 1 (1968), 3; see the similar economic ideas of Whitney Young, Jr., of the National Urban League in *To Be Equal* (New York, 1964); and *Beyond Racism: Building an Open Society* (New York, 1969).

15. Clayborne Carson, *In Struggle: SNCC and the Black Awakening in the 1960s* (Cambridge, Mass., 1981), 12–18; Pat Watters, *Down to Now: Reflections on the Southern Civil Rights Movement* (New York, 1971), 73; Sosna, *In Search of the Silent South,* 197.

the viciousness of racial segregation and prejudice and calling it evil or sin." The young black man predicted that the sit-ins would sensitize and attract white support. But even the idealistic Lawson complained that the pace of change was so slow that if it did not speed up, African natives would be free before American blacks.[16]

Although there was a huge reservoir of respect for King in the black community, it began to diminish as the decade progressed, especially among the young. In the early 1960s more and more blacks began to attack King's philosophy and tactics. In a 1961 radio broadcast, Kenneth Clark, a black social psychologist who had worked under Myrdal on the Carnegie project, suggested that there was something pathological in King's philosophy. "It would seem," Clark argued, "that any demand that the victims of oppression be required to love those who oppress them places an additional and probably intolerable psychological burden upon the victims." In a television interview in 1963, James Baldwin expressed the opinion that King was "a rare person, a real Christian," but one, he felt, who had reached "the end of his rope." Baldwin swore that King had utterly failed to awaken the conscience of white America. He speculated that Malcolm X had more support among the black masses than did King. Malcolm X's judgment of King was blunt: "King is the best weapon that the white man, who wants to brutalize Negroes, has ever gotten in this country." The black nationalist denounced King's "foolish philosophy," which did not permit blacks to defend themselves against white violence.[17]

Even those black writers who emphasized the importance of the American creed often seemed ambivalent about its potential for solving the race problem. In his instructive volume *The Negro Revolt* (1962), Louis E. Lomax theorized that blacks could not make "the slightest compromise with the American creed as stated by the founding fathers." Yet Lomax relied more heavily on appeals to white fears than to their democratic consciences. Like Madison Grant and Lothrop Stoddard, the great white alarmists of the early twentieth century, Lomax raised the specter of international race war. He emphatically reminded

16. Quoted in Meier, Rudwick, and Broderick (eds.), *Black Protest Thought in the Twentieth Century,* 239, 312, 314–15; August Meier, *CORE: A Study in the Civil Rights Movement, 1942–1968* (New York, 1973).

17. Kenneth B. Clark, "The Negro in the North," in Mathew Ahmann (ed.), *The New Negro* (New York, 1969), 37; James Baldwin, interview in Leslie H. Fishel, Jr., and Benjamin Quarles (eds.), *The Negro American: A Documentary History* (Glenview, Ill., 1967), 352–53; Malcolm X quoted in John Henrik Clarke (ed.), *Malcolm X: The Man and His Times* (New York, 1969), 177.

the reader that colored people had a numerical superiority in the world. The black writer advised the white man to learn to love nonwhites before the majority got guns.[18]

Nobody expressed the pent-up rage of blacks more eloquently than did the novelist James Baldwin. Because of the treatment blacks received during World War II, Baldwin had become pessimistic about white America's ability to render justice to Afro-Americans. "To put it briefly," he wrote, "a certain hope died, a certain respect for white America faded." In 1955 Baldwin stated that no black had not felt "naked and unanswerable hatred" for whites or had not wanted at some time "to smash any white face" he happened to encounter. In *The Fire Next Time* in 1963, he ridiculed the idea that whites suffered from a moral dilemma concerning blacks. Only the Cold War and political necessity, he declared, had brought about the *Brown* decision. "Had it been a matter of love or justice," he explained, "the 1954 decision would surely have occurred sooner; were it not for the realities of power, it might not have occurred yet." Baldwin submitted that the "sloppy and fatuous nature" of whites would never enable them to deal justly with the race problem. He lamented that Negroes could never assume that the humanity of whites was more real than their color.[19]

Studies in the early 1960s suggested that bitterness among blacks was not restricted to writers such as Baldwin, Lomax, or Malcolm X. By 1963 moderate blacks demanded "freedom now." "Race men" replaced the old accommodationist leaders. The new leaders directed their appeals less to the white conscience than to white fears. They focused their attention more on black identity and economics and less on integration. "White liberal" joined "Uncle Tom" as epithets in the militants' lexicon.[20] Finally, many black leaders no longer ruled out violence as a tactic or an inevitability. In 1959 Baldwin predicted race riots in the major cities. In that same year Robert Williams of Monroe, North Carolina, began arming the local chapter of the NAACP for defense against the marauding Ku Klux Klan, an act that brought his expulsion by the national board of that civil rights organization. In 1964 Williams fore-

18. Louis E. Lomax, *The Negro Revolt* (New York, 1962), 81, 241–47.
19. James Baldwin, *Notes of a Native Son* (Boston, 1955), 38, 45, 97; and *The Fire Next Time* (New York, 1963), 68, 101.
20. Jack L. Walker, "The Functions of Disunity: Negro Leadership in a Southern City," in Bracey, Meier, and Rudwick (eds.), *Conflict and Competition*, 54–64; Thompson, *Negro Leadership Class*, 58–79, 161–63, 165–71; Pat Watters and Reese Cleghorn, *Climbing Jacob's Ladder: The Arrival of Southern Negroes in Southern Politics* (New York, 1967).

cast that the "storm of violence" would reach "hurricane proportions by 1966." [21]

In the early 1960s even many blacks considered moderates began to express their resentment against the usual liberal approaches to the race problem. In 1962 Loren Miller, a noted black civil rights lawyer and NAACP leader, accentuated this mood when he bade "farewell to [white] liberals" in the pro–civil rights journal the *Nation*. At the March on Washington in 1963 John Lewis, the chairman of SNCC, prepared a blistering speech to deliver at the Lincoln Memorial. Never before had the nonviolent philosophy been expressed in such violent rhetoric. The SNCC leader lambasted President Kennedy's civil rights bill as "too little and too late." He proclaimed, however, that the masses would force the necessary changes. "We will march through the South, through the heart of Dixie, the way Sherman did," Lewis warned. "We shall pursue our own 'scorched earth' policy and burn Jim Crow to the ground—non-violently." Moderate black leaders such as Martin Luther King persuaded Lewis to tone down his speech for the sake of black and white unity. [22]

Every civil rights victory seemed to make blacks more impatient. As the movement became more inclusive and massive, it became less civil. After 1963, SNCC caromed off intransigent racism in the Deep South toward disillusionment, radicalism, and separatism. Although Congress enacted a strong civil rights bill in July, 1964, SNCC workers keenly remembered the rebuff of the Mississippi Freedom Democratic party at Atlantic City, when the pro-black Mississippi delegation failed in its bid to be seated at the Democratic Convention. According to James Forman of SNCC, "Atlantic City was a powerful lesson. No longer was there any hope . . . that the federal government would change the situation in the Deep South." His colleague Cleveland Sellers wrote: "We left Atlantic City with the knowledge that the movement had turned into something else. After Atlantic City, our struggle was not for civil rights, but for liberation." [23]

The idealism and the integrationist posture of SNCC eroded not only

21. Watters, *Down to Now*, 52; Meier, Rudwick, and Broderick (eds.), *Black Protest Thought in the Twentieth Century*, 360–72.

22. Loren Miller, "Farewell to Liberals: A Negro View," *Nation*, October 20, 1962, pp. 235–38; Watters and Cleghorn, *Climbing Jacob's Ladder*, xiv–xv.

23. Sara Evans, *Personal Politics: The Roots of Women's Liberation in the Civil Rights Movement and the New Left* (New York, 1980), 89–91; Mary A. Rothschild, *A Case of Black and White: Northern Volunteers and Southern Freedom Summers, 1964–1965* (Westport, Conn., 1982), 71.

because of events like Atlantic City but also because of interracial hostility and sexism among the crusaders themselves. In 1963 a vocal minority of blacks in SNCC called for the exclusion of whites from the Mississippi summer projects. The majority prevented this action, but it did not obviate the resentment felt by many blacks toward the often better-educated and sometimes paternalistic whites who came to Dixie from Ivy League schools. Stokely Carmichael broadcast the sexist nature of SNCC with his widely quoted remarks: "The position of women in SNCC should be prone." The memoirs of SNCC workers subsequently disclosed that white female volunteers had to pass a "sexual test" administered by black men before they were considered serious workers and nonracists. According to historian Allen J. Matusow, "The most serious obstacle to healthy race relations inside SNCC was sex." SNCC fell victim to a long history of twisted race relations and sexual fantasies that left Americans, white and black alike, with bizarre sexual hangups when race was involved. This persistent problem, which one sociologist labeled "sexual racism," was more broadly studied after 1965 and will be discussed at greater length in the next chapter. It is enough here to say that Myrdal clearly erred in downplaying the barrier to integration presented by the combined forces of racism and sexism in American society. Like virtually all white and black liberals, Myrdal understandably tried to assure fearful whites that racist stereotypes about the black man's sexuality had absolutely no validity.[24]

Despite many ominous signs in the civil rights movement, Myrdal's optimism never faltered. The European visited America regularly, giving speeches and participating in discussions on race relations in virtually every year of the 1960s. In all of his comments, he never wavered from his theme of 1944. But blacks, who once tended to be exceedingly deferential to the foreign scholar, openly began to take issue with Myrdal. In a 1964 roundtable discussion on black-white relations that involved several white liberals and Kenneth Clark and James Baldwin, Myrdal received some exposure to changing black attitudes toward white liberals. An extremely agitated James Baldwin, after assailing many of Myrdal's pet ideas, branded white liberals an "affliction." Nor

24. Carson, *In Struggle,* 100–101, 144, 148, 196–97; Rothschild, *Case of Black and White,* 21–22, 73, 136–49, 153; Evans, *Personal Politics,* 78–82, 88–89; Alvin Pouissant, "The Stresses on White Female Workers in the Civil Rights Movement in the South," *American Journal of Psychiatry,* CXXIII (1966), 401–407; Allen J. Matusow, "From Civil Rights to Black Power: The Case of SNCC, 1960–1966," in Barton J. Bernstein and Allen J. Matusow (eds.), *Twentieth Century America: Recent Interpretations* (2d ed.; New York, 1972), 508.

did the more restrained Clark, the integrationist who had worked for
Myrdal and for the NAACP in the school cases, come to Myrdal's defense. Instead, the black psychologist turned to the Scandinavian and
said: "With all due respect to my friend and former colleague and boss,
I have come to the conclusion that so far as the Negro is concerned, the
ethical aspect of American liberalism or the American creed is primarily verbal." Clark complained that the ambivalence of verbal liberalism was illustrated by illiberal action. "I am forced to agree with
James Baldwin," he continued, "that . . . liberalism as it is practiced
. . . is an affliction. It is an insidious type of affliction because it attempts to impose guilt upon the Negro when he has to face the hypocrisy of the liberal." [25] In other words, black leaders announced that white
liberals were now fair game.

To be sure, black nationalists saved their choicest words for white
liberals, not to mention integrationist blacks. For many reasons, one of
them being the constant rejection of blacks by white society, there has
always been a strain of black nationalism in Afro-American thought.[26]
Some blacks, like Du Bois, seemed to combine like amounts of integrationist and separatist sentiment in the same breast. The closer blacks
moved to the threshold of integration, the more some feared that white
culture would swallow up Afro-American identity. Nationalists of all
stripes stressed that greater group identity, group pride, and group ac-
complishment had to occur before blacks could hope to assimilate on
their own terms. Malcolm X popularized this concept. He taught that a
race had to affirm its "selfhood" before it could advance. "The cultural
revolution," he maintained, "will be the journey of our rediscovery of
ourselves." In 1963 Malcolm X appeared on television more than any
other black leader. Many blacks who rejected his black separatism still
greatly admired his pitch for racial pride. The black historian Lerone
Bennett, Jr., for example, stressed the wholesome distinctiveness of
black culture and boldly suggested that it might yet save Western white
culture from its crass materialism and self-idolatry.[27] Activist nation-

25. The discussion is in "Liberalism and the Negro," *Commentary*, XXXVII (March,
1964), 25–42.
26. The literature on the historical roots of black nationalism has proliferated. Some
examples are Theodore Draper, *The Rediscovery of Black Nationalism* (New York, 1970);
Edwin S. Redkey, *Black Exodus: Black Nationalist and Back-to-Africa Movements,
1890–1910* (New Haven, 1969); and Rodney Carlisle, *The Roots of Black Nationalism*
(Port Washington, N.Y., 1975).
27. Clarke (ed.), *Malcolm X*, 341; Lerone Bennett, Jr., *The Negro Mood* (New York,
1964), 115.

alists such as the Black Muslims largely ignored white literature like Myrdal's study. Not until the late 1960s, when academia began to recruit nationalist intellectuals, would they turn their attention to the Swede's book.

Meanwhile, liberal black scholars stepped up their criticism of Myrdal's study. Samuel DuBois Cook, a schoolmate of Martin Luther King and a political scientist at Atlanta University, exemplified the mixed feelings of many black thinkers about the *Dilemma*. In 1964 Cook reviewed Arnold Rose's paperback abridgment of the *Dilemma*. The black political scientist announced that Myrdal's study had been "the most influential and exhaustive description and analysis of race relations ever written in America." He applauded the enormous good that the book had done, and he characterized some of the Swede's insights as brilliant. He concluded, nevertheless, that the vague and ambiguous American creed did not provide enough substance on which to hang a race's destiny. Myrdal's analysis, Cook complained, had been woefully incomplete and misled a generation of liberals. Cook charged that Myrdal had missed the "tragic dimension" of the race problem. One passage of the review deserves quoting:

> The "American Creed" has been twisted, distorted, and mutilated in such a manner that it has been, generally, ruled inapplicable or irrelevant to the Negro. Exclusion of the Negro was not even admitted as an exception. Racism is an ontological principle, a religion, a philosophy of history and culture, and an ethical, social and political theory. Because of the ideology of racism, the Negro has been dehumanized and robbed of his intrinsic dignity, promise, selfhood, and nobility. Only the whites of the most sensitive consciences have been, in the least, troubled by the degradation, suppression, and humiliation of the Negro. On the whole, white Americans have had an easy and complacent conscience about slavery and its progeny, the caste system of segregation and discrimination. Only a handful of whites have shown any sustained and genuine moral indignation and outrage over the plight of the Negro. Indeed, many whites have accepted the caste system with a sense of moral righteousness and ethical duty—as though it were the institutional translation of the Kingdom of God (which some really believe).[28]

Black pessimism can be exaggerated by focusing on spokesmen such as Clark, Baldwin, Malcolm X, or even Samuel Cook. Between World War II and 1965 the black masses displayed less sensitivity (or knowledge) than black activists about such events as Atlantic City, California's 1964 referendum against open housing, or the growing white backlash

28. Cook, Review of *AD*, 207–209.

exploited by the 1964 presidential candidates Barry Goldwater and George Wallace. They were perhaps less aware than the elite that the average black family income had dropped from 58 percent of the average white family's income in 1952 to 54 percent in 1962. By 1962 black unemployment had increased to two and a half times that of whites. An extensive polling of blacks for *Newsweek* magazine in 1963, however, showed that it was still the era of Myrdal, the NAACP, and Martin Luther King. Sixty-three percent of blacks believed that whites could be won over to their cause without violence. Seventy-three percent thought white attitudes toward blacks would continue to improve in the future. The poll also revealed that the black movement was deep, militant, and authentic. Skepticism about white moderates and liberals was on the upswing. As one woman put it, "All Negroes are tired of waiting for the white man to get ready to give him something that is his." [29] But on the whole, polls indicated that in 1963 the black community still viewed the American dilemma with hopeful eyes.

Although most blacks retained their optimism, before 1963 the national government moved at a snail's pace to meet the rising expectations of its largest minority. Even the Supreme Court, the boldest of the three branches of government, doomed school desegregation to years of litigation and turmoil when it announced its "with-all-deliberate-speed formula" in 1955. The Court, which had drawn upon modern social science in *Brown* I, ignored it in *Brown* II. It instead accepted the course preferred by southern attorneys general. The New Confederacy of the Deep South, therefore, managed to stave off significant desegregation of schools for over a decade. The 1954 decision remained but a statement of principle, a distant goal.

To be sure, President Dwight D. Eisenhower did not feel enough moral urgency about the race issue to use his popularity and the tools of his high office to challenge southern defiance of the law. In the 1940s General Eisenhower had opposed the desegregation of the armed forces. As president, he privately referred to the *Brown* decision as a blunder and described his appointment of Earl Warren as chief justice as the "biggest damfool mistake I ever made." Never fully understanding the meaning of *Brown*, Eisenhower was often heard to say: "I don't believe you can change the hearts of men with laws or decisions." Shortly

29. August Meier and Elliott Rudwick, *From Plantation to Ghetto* (rev. ed.; New York, 1970), 265; "The Negro in America," *Newsweek*, July 29,1963, pp. 15–34; Brink and Harris, *Negro Revolution in America*, 129–30, 136, and *passim*.

before the *Brown* decision, the president invited Warren to a White House dinner. Near the end of the affair, Eisenhower took Warren by the arm and told him: "These [white southerners] are not bad people. All they are concerned about is to see that their sweet little girls are not required to sit in school alongside some big overgrown Negroes." Presidential adviser Arthur Larson judged that Eisenhower was neither intellectually nor emotionally in favor of desegregation.[30] Not surprisingly, given Eisenhower's reading habits and his feelings on race, there is no evidence that he ever heard of Myrdal or the *Dilemma*.

Although Eisenhower received no stimulus from the social science of the day, events and momentum from the previous administration forced him to move forward in several areas. The Republican leader completed the desegregation of the armed forces, for example. Attorney General Herbert Brownell of New York continued the precedent set by Truman in submitting an *amicus curiae* in the 1953 reargument of the *Brown* case. Philip Elman, a former law clerk for Felix Frankfurter, wrote most of the brief, as he had done for the Truman administration. And the document contained just as much sociological argument for desegregation. The attorney general displayed a knowledge of the *Dilemma* in Senate hearings on the 1957 Civil Rights Act. The subject arose when Senator Thomas A. Hennings of Missouri quizzed Brownell about the necessity of the Civil Rights Commission. Hennings wondered why a commission was needed to make more studies when the Truman Committee's report and the Myrdal study were available. The attorney general replied that Myrdal's valuable and exhaustive study consisted of many "opinions." A commission, he counseled, could take sworn testimony and establish irrefutable facts.[31]

Clearly Brownell involved himself in most of the positive steps the administration took to advance black rights, if often for the reason of political expediency. He persuaded Eisenhower to send a civil rights bill to Congress after the 1956 election, arguing that the proposal would strengthen the Republican party in key northern states and divide the Democratic party along regional lines. Actually, Brownell devised a

30. Robert F. Burk, *The Eisenhower Administration and Black Civil Rights* (Knoxville, 1984), 142, 172, 263, 266; Sitkoff, *Struggle for Black Equality*, 25; Earl Warren, *The Memoirs of Earl Warren* (Garden City, N.Y., 1977), 29; Arthur Larson quoted in Charles C. Alexander, *Holding the Line: The Eisenhower Era, 1952–1961* (Bloomington, Ind., 1975), 119.

31. Lewis, *Portrait of a Decade*, 24–28, 107–108; U.S. Senate, Subcommittee on Constitutional Rights, *Civil Rights 1957*, 85th Cong., 1st Sess., 203–204.

much stronger civil rights bill than Eisenhower desired or even realized. The president's public comments on the bill revealed that he had a limited understanding of its contents. Title Three of the bill would have given the government the power to initiate action in the courts on behalf of civil rights plaintiffs, including those contesting school segregation. Lyndon Johnson, the Democratic Senate majority leader, capitalized on the civil rights bill as an opportunity to enhance his national stature and to keep blacks from deserting the Democratic party. To avoid a southern filibuster, however, the Texas senator agreed to a watered-down bill that focused narrowly on voting. Title Three was removed from the bill. Senator Richard Russell of Georgia considered its removal the "sweetest victory" of his long Senate career. Weak as it was, the Civil Rights Act of 1957 was the first civil rights legislation since 1875, and it helped to legitimize the black movement. Most black leaders reluctantly endorsed the half loaf. The bill upgraded the civil rights section in the Justice Department to a division. More important, it established for two years the Civil Rights Commission.[32]

Eisenhower's enforcement of the loophole-filled 1957 Civil Rights Act was spotty at best. The conservative president clearly did not have the stomach for intruding the federal government into areas that brought conflict with the states. Still, when Governor Orval Faubus expressed calculated contempt for a federal court order, Eisenhower sent troops to Little Rock to desegregate Central High School. The president justified his action on the grounds of upholding the integrity of the federal courts and preserving order. In addition, he alluded to foreign affairs as a factor in his decision to use force. "Our enemies are gloating over this incident," Eisenhower told the public, "and using it everywhere to misrepresent our whole nation." Not once, however, did the president raise the moral aspects of the race issue in the Little Rock crisis.[33]

The moral dimension of the race problem nevertheless began to bother some members of Congress. After the *Brown* decision, elected officials proposed scores of civil rights bills. More than fifty bills went

32. Sitkoff, *Struggle for Black Equality*, 33–35; Lewis, *Portrait of a Decade*, 111–12. For a detailed view of the civil rights bill, see J. W. Anderson, *Eisenhower, Brownell and Congress: The Tangled Origins of the Civil Rights Bill of 1956–1957* (University, Ala., 1964). See also Alexander, *Holding the Line*, 119, 200–201; and Carl M. Brauer, *John F. Kennedy and the Second Reconstruction* (New York, 1977), 3–11.

33. Lewis, *Portrait of a Decade*, 113; Eisenhower quoted in John Hope Franklin and Isidore Starr (eds.), *The Negro in the 20th Century: A Reader on the Struggle for Civil Rights* (New York, 1967), 290.

to House committees in 1955 alone. The major arguments for the bills paralleled those made by Myrdal for government action. Proponents contended that there was a moral imperative to close the yawning gap between creed and practice. And they stressed the economic waste caused by discrimination and its harmful effect on American foreign policy. In the 1950s legislators had another reason for forward movement. The legislature appeared backward compared to the executive and judicial branches. On July 27, 1955, Congressman David Rose of Massachusetts, in testimony before a House committee, characterized the various civil rights bills as follows: "All these are sound measures that would be good for America as a whole—for its spiritual, economic, and diplomatic well-being." In 1957 Senator Hubert Humphrey, an enthusiastic reader of the *Dilemma,* advocated passage of civil rights legislation to remedy America's greatest shortcoming. "No conscientious observer who has ever examined the American scene," Humphrey instructed, "has failed to put his finger on our great national weakness—the gap between our pretensions and our performance in the field of civil rights." [34] In some cases, political factors no doubt explained the action of legislators. But in most cases, the moral discomfort in the white lawmakers' minds appeared genuine and was often expressed in Myrdalian rhetoric.

In the hearings on the various civil rights bills, southern segregationists often singled out Myrdal for verbal abuse. The attorneys general of almost every southern state decried Myrdal's role in fashioning "Black Monday" in 1954. Charles Block, the attorney general of Georgia, called for a return to the Constitution "in lieu of psychological principles of Myrdal and other similar Swedish investigators." Other southern officials focused on the allegedly subversive record of those associated with the "modern authority" the Supreme Court cited in the *Brown* case. The testimony of Leander Perez, the flamboyant boss of Plaquemines Parish in Louisiana, included a long harangue on the Myrdal study. Even the liberal Senator J. William Fulbright, a Rhodes Scholar from Arkansas, derided Myrdal and referred to the social sciences as the "socialistic sciences." The Myrdal-hating southern bloc in the Senate showed that it could kill or gravely weaken any civil rights bill put before Congress, at least before 1964. This was true of the 1957

34. *Hearings,* Subcommittee No. 5 of the Committee on the Judiciary, House, 85th Cong., 1st Sess., 349, 406, 440; *Hearings,* Subcommittee on Constitutional Rights, Judiciary Committee, Senate, 85th Cong., 1st Sess., 164; *Hearings,* Committee on the Judiciary, Senate, 84th Cong., 2d Sess., 4, 77.

and 1960 bills, both of which focused primarily on voting and contained many loopholes. The liberal Senator Paul Douglas of Illinois summed up the situation when he said: "I think the Senate is the South's revenge for Appomattox."[35]

The civil rights hearings in Congress in the 1950s and early 1960s showed that although liberals used Myrdalian ideas and language in their advocacy of civil rights, they seldom referred directly to the findings of social scientists, especially sociologists and psychologists. Nor did civil rights proponents in Congress normally respond to the exaggerated and simplistic accusations leveled at the Swedish scholar by southerners. The residue of McCarthyism and the adverse reaction to footnote 11 in the *Brown* opinion made liberal politicians extraordinarily cautious about supporting their beliefs with evidence from behavioral science. Indeed, as in the case of Truman's Committee on Civil Rights, the climate of fear and hesitancy resulted in the conspicuous absence of Myrdal where one would most expect to find his name.

The 1957 Civil Rights Commission provides a case in point. In time the commission became a fierce and independent watchdog on civil rights. It gathered invaluable evidence and kept pressure on Congress and the executive in the civil rights area.[36] Not until the 1980s did a president dare to counter its criticism by wholesale removal of its personnel. Yet in its first report of 1959, the commission purposefully avoided the mention of Myrdal's name.

As critics pointed out, the Civil Rights Commission of 1957 seemed designed for stalemate. It consisted of two northern Republicans, three southern Democrats, and one independent Catholic priest. Eisenhower picked John Hannah, a Republican and president of Michigan State University; Ernest Wilkins, a dour black Republican with no civil rights experience; Theodore Hesburgh, president of the University of Notre Dame; John Battle, former governor of Virginia and a Dixiecrat walkout in 1948; Doyle Carlton, former governor of Florida; and Robert Storey,

---

35. *Hearings,* Subcommittee on Constitutional Rights, Judiciary Committee, Senate, 85th Cong., 1st Sess., 114, 336–67, 458–59, 625; *Hearings,* Committee on the Judiciary, Senate, 84th Cong., 2d sess., 178, 333; *Hearings,* Subcommittee No. 5 of the Committee on the Judiciary, House, 85th Cong., 1st Sess., 974; *Congressional Record,* 88th Cong., 2d sess., 9600–9601; Fulbright quoted in Steven Wasby, Anthony D'Amato, and Rosemary Metrailer, *Desegregation from Brown to Alexander: An Explanation of Supreme Court Strategies* (Carbondale, Ill., 1977), 423.

36. Foster Rhea Dulles, *The Civil Rights Commission, 1957–1965* (East Lansing, 1968), x–xi.

dean of the Law School at Southern Methodist University. J. Lindsay Almond, the attorney general of Virginia, warned in congressional hearings that if the commission were given the power of subpoena and the resources to compensate witnesses, the result would be "a legion of that variety which produced Gunnar Myrdal's *American Dilemma.*" Bombarded by broadsides against the Swede since 1954, southerners on the commission insisted that Myrdal's name not be mentioned in the first report. They even excluded sociologists from their major investigation of school desegregation. Eager not to repeat the Supreme Court's controversial use of social science, the northern commissioners acquiesced in the prohibitions on Myrdal and sociologists.[37]

That is not to say that Myrdal did not figure in the first report by the Commission on Civil Rights. In the early part of 1958, as the commission awaited discrimination complaints to investigate, the members of the group studied as basic textbooks the *Dilemma* and the report of Truman's Civil Rights Committee. The latter used the *Dilemma* as a basic though largely unacknowledged source. According to Harris Wofford, who served as legal counsel for Father Hesburgh, the commission used Myrdal's rank order of discriminations to pick out black voting as a strategic priority, a goal Myrdal indicated to be within the realm of the most possible.[38]

Harris Wofford not only introduced the *Dilemma* to the commission, but he also participated in some of the most dramatic and significant events of the civil rights movement. This civil rights crusader was born in the South and spent his first six years of life in Tennessee before moving to New York. His family roots reached back into the Deep South. His ancestors fought for the Confederacy in the Civil War. When his family returned to the South to visit relatives, young Wofford experienced hostility and ridicule for his liberal views on blacks. The taunts of his kinfolk motivated Wofford to go into civil rights law. Before attending law school, however, he traveled to India and became an avid student of the subcontinent and Gandhi. In a 1950 book called *India Afire,* coauthored by his wife, Clare, Wofford pleaded with Afro-Americans to adopt Gandhi's tactics for their movement. In 1950 Wofford entered Howard University Law School, the first white male ever to do so. As a law student and a lawyer, he continued to advocate Gandhi's nonviolent,

37. Wofford, *Of Kennedys and Kings,* 463, 482; *Hearings,* Subcommittee No. 5 of the Committee on the Judiciary, House, 85th Cong., 1st Sess., 1243.
38. Wofford, *Of Kennedys and Kings,* 465; Wofford to the author, July 28, 1981.

direct-action approach as a model for the Negro rights movement. Martin Luther King read a speech he gave on Gandhi shortly before the Montgomery bus boycott and was highly impressed by it. Wofford became a good friend as well as an adviser to the rising black star. King once quipped that Wofford was the only white lawyer who understood why he wanted to go to jail.[39]

The transplanted white southerner thus had intellectual affiliations with Myrdal and Gandhi and personal ties with Martin Luther King and, by 1959, with John F. Kennedy. In that year Senator Kennedy asked Wofford to join his staff. Theodore Sorensen, Kennedy's chief aide, had become acquainted with the young lawyer and had informed his boss about Wofford's knowledge on foreign affairs and civil rights. He did not, however, join Kennedy's staff until the 1960 campaign because of his prior commitment to Father Hesburgh to teach at the University of Notre Dame Law School. In 1960 it was Wofford who suggested the famous telephone call that Democratic candidate Kennedy made to Coretta King. This event, which some have interpreted as a vital factor in Kennedy's razor-thin victory, came after Mrs. King had worriedly called Wofford about her husband's incarceration in a Georgia jail. The enterprising legalist also contributed the campaign slogan "with a stroke of a pen," which became an acute embarrassment to him later on. In the campaign Kennedy promised to end discrimination in federal housing with a stroke of his presidential pen. The promised stroke did not occur until November, 1962. In the meantime, Wofford received many pens from his friends in the civil rights movement.[40]

In his recent book *Of Kennedys and Kings,* Wofford disclosed some of the inside details about the operation of the first Civil Rights Commission. Wofford recounted how the regionally divided panel quarreled and deadlocked on many issues. Yet the commission put forth a remarkably strong proposal on voting rights. A common interest in fishing and bourbon, Wofford believed, alleviated some of the differences on race relations between the northern and southern members. Myrdal's rank order of discriminations seemed validated when the commission, with only one southern dissent, called for temporary federal registrars in elections. But as Myrdal had hypothesized in his rank order, when

39. Wofford, *Of Kennedys and Kings,* 109–10, 112.

40. *Ibid.,* 11–28, 36–38, 58, 85; Brauer, *John F. Kennedy and the Second Reconstruction,* 36, 43, 47–48, 50; Harris Wofford, interview, May 22, 1968, pp. 46, 48, Oral History Program, John F. Kennedy Library.

southerners got beyond voting, they strongly resisted government action in such areas as schools and housing.[41]

For reasons discussed earlier, the commission studiously avoided references to Myrdal or to sociologists. Even when I.Q. tests or the *Brown* case were debated, the panel cited only general works by historians and political scientists. Wofford, Hannah, Hesburgh, and other liberals on the commission and its staff nevertheless slipped Myrdal's ideas into the report, consciously or unconsciously. As Wofford noted in his memoirs, by the late 1950s some simply took Myrdal's main thesis for granted. Although the report of 1959 did not refer to Myrdal or to the term "dilemma," on page 3 it made a statement that, at least in scholarly circles, would usually be attributed to Myrdal. "The gap between the great American promise of equal opportunity and equal justice under the law and its at times startling inadequate fulfillment in practice has thus been a major—and probably a creative—factor in American history from the beginning of the Nation," the report declared. "The conflict between those who would extend the republican principle to all men and those who would delay its application," it continued, "has produced a tension in the minds and hearts of Americans and in American laws that is with us still."[42] Like the Myrdal-laced report of Truman's Civil Rights Committee, the major thrust of the 1959 report concerned the gap between the exalted ideal and the brutal reality.

Father Hesburgh, who served on the Civil Rights Commission for fifteen years before being forcefully retired by President Richard M. Nixon, recalled that he often "used Myrdal's book to great advantage." Myrdal's moral framework was well suited to Hesburgh's spiritual approach to the race problem. In 1959 the Catholic priest attached a personal statement to the commission's report, a practice that became almost habitual in subsequent reports. The president of Notre Dame felt compelled to add a little spiritual "fire" to the heavily factual reports turned out by the commission. In his 1959 statement, Hesburgh discussed the philosophical, theological, and sociological bases for his liberal position on the race question. He stressed the theme that all human life was sacred and that all men were equal before God and should be before the law. Sociologically, he agreed with Eisenhower that laws

---

41. Wofford, *Of Kennedys and Kings,* 461–83; U.S. Commission on Civil Rights, *Report of the United States Commission on Civil Rights 1959* (1959), 156, 275.

42. Wofford to the author, July 28, 1981; *Report of the United States Civil Rights Commission 1959,* 3.

alone would not solve the race problem. But, like Myrdal, he emphasized the importance of legislation. Law, Hesburgh held, defined "the
goals and standards of the community" and as such was one of "the
great changers of minds and hearts." With Myrdalian confidence he
claimed that if blacks achieved equal opportunity, "the problem of civil
rights would solve itself." [43]

Hesburgh's colleague and chairman of the Civil Rights Commission,
John Hannah, also found Myrdal's study a handy source. In a speech
before the Anti-Defamation League in New York in 1959, Hannah referred to the writings of three foreign observers: Tocqueville, Bryce,
and Myrdal. The latter's work he described as "monumental." "Because
of the recency of the [Myrdal] study and because the disinterested
though friendly analysis he makes is so appropriate," the chairman told
the congregation, "I will draw heavily upon his report." Hannah maintained that the Civil Rights Commission would be a success only if it
could arouse the "national conscience and undermine the moral lag in
America." [44] Before a friendly northern crowd, the Michigan State University president disclosed his sources on race relations with greater
candor than he did as a member of the commission.

After Kennedy became president, he made appointments that tilted
the Civil Rights Commission toward a decisively liberal position. As
white southerners grew less powerful on the commission, Myrdal was
brought out of the closet. The commission's 1961 report on employment,
for example, included Myrdal's study in the bibliography and cited it in
a footnote. Senator Eastland of Mississippi, however, had not been ap-
peased or fooled by the absence of Myrdal's name in the first report of
the commission. When the senator castigated the report, he noted the
omission of any references to the Scandinavian's name. Eastland knew
Myrdalian talk when he read it, disguised or not. "My conclusion,"
Eastland pronounced, "is that the U.S. Supreme Court has more courage than did the Civil Rights Commission." [45]

Courage was a trait John Kennedy admired greatly. His popular book
Profiles in Courage celebrated politicians who displayed courage, or

43. Theodore Hesburgh to the author, July 9, 1981; *Report of the United States Civil
Rights Commission 1959*, 551–55; see also U.S. Commission on Civil Rights, *1961
United States Civil Rights Commission Report* (5 vols.; 1961), 5: 166–70.

44. Reprinted in the *Congressional Record*, 86th Cong., 2d Sess., 448–51.

45. U.S. Commission on Civil Rights, *1961 Report*, 3: 128, 243; see also *1963 Report
of the United States Civil Rights Commission* (1963), 171; Wofford, *Of Kennedys and
Kings*, 482.

"grace under pressure." One of Kennedy's favorite quotations was Dante's statement that assigned the hottest places in hell to those who remained neutral in a moral crisis. Yet the historical evidence shows that as a congressman, senator, and for much of his tragically abbreviated presidency, Kennedy exhibited precious little courage, passion, or deep knowledge about the race issue. Until events forced him to move more resolutely in 1963, the Bostonian did not view the race problem as an urgent moral problem. To him it was a political problem to be managed. His main interest and forte lay in foreign policy. He also had higher priorities in domestic affairs than race relations. He considered the civil rights plank in the 1960 Democratic platform, largely written by Chester Bowles and Harris Wofford, to be too strong and too specific. Carl Brauer, the author of the best historical work on Kennedy and civil rights, pegged the charismatic Irish-American "a moderate in moderate times." [46]

Kennedy apparently applied none of his celebrated speed-reading skills to Myrdal's huge compendium or to anything else of importance on race relations. Although John Fischer, a longtime editor at *Harper's* magazine and an interviewer of the president, claimed that Kennedy had read the *Dilemma,* no other source suggests that he did. In the 1960 campaign Kennedy realized that he needed more education on the race issue. One day in August the Democratic nominee gave Harris Wofford a ride in his car on the way to the Senate. As soon as Wofford got into the vehicle, the senator gave his aide a command. "Now, in five minutes," Kennedy barked, "tick off the ten things that a President ought to do to clean up this goddamn civil rights mess." As in everything else, Kennedy wanted quick, and preferably witty, answers from the "best and the brightest." In early 1962 David Donald, a noted American historian, led an after-dinner discussion on Reconstruction for the president and some of his staff and friends. Afterward, Donald wrote in a personal letter that Kennedy's knowledge about Reconstruction was scanty and outdated. When Kennedy dealt with Mississippi governor Ross Barnett in 1962, he remembered Donald's talk on how the white South twisted the truth of Reconstruction. After the 1963 murder of Medgar Evers in Mississippi, the president told Arthur Schlesinger:

46. Arthur Schlesinger, Jr., *A Thousand Days: John F. Kennedy in the White House* (Boston, 1965), 86–87; John F. Kennedy, *Profiles in Courage* (New York, 1956); Brauer, *John F. Kennedy and the Second Reconstruction,* 11, 35–36; Sitkoff, *Struggle for Black Equality,* 106.

"I don't understand the South. I'm coming to believe that Thaddeus
Stevens was right."[47] Only when Kennedy began to shed his jaundiced
view of the first Reconstruction could he envision the necessity for a
second.

Before June, 1963, Kennedy merely reacted to civil rights events and
tried to contain them by executive action. The center of racial activity,
therefore, lay with the Civil Rights Division in the Justice Department
under Robert Kennedy. The president once entertained the idea of
making Harris Wofford an assistant attorney general to his brother, but
he decided that his aide was too much of a crusader. Instead he kept
Wofford in the White House to serve as a buffer between himself and
blacks. In 1962 Kennedy sent Wofford off to the Peace Corps in
Africa.[48]

Several of Kennedy's advisers besides Wofford had grown up on the
teachings of Myrdal. Among these relatively young men were Burke
Marshall, Nicholas Katzenbach, Lee White, Frederick G. Dutton,
Arthur Schlesinger, John Kenneth Galbraith, and special counsel to the
president Theodore C. Sorensen. According to Burke Marshall, the courageous assistant attorney general, Myrdal's influence in the Kennedy
administration was pervasive though hard to measure. "Everyone, including myself, [who] had any responsibility for, or any interest at all
in, the American racial problem," Marshall recalled, "was influenced
by Myrdal in ways that cannot be identified."[49]

Although there is no conclusive evidence that John Kennedy read
Myrdal's book, he apparently kept abreast of the Swede's periodic economic assessments of America. At a press conference on July 23, 1962,
a reporter asked the president to comment on Myrdal's charge that
America had too many slums for a rich country, a reference to an interview with Myrdal in the New York *Times* on the previous day. Kennedy
expressed regret that his administration had not found the formula for
economic growth to eliminate slums. Showing his familiarity with the

47. John Fischer, "Western Intellectuals vs. Myrdal's Brutal Facts," *Harper's*, June,
1968, pp. 12–13; John Fischer to the author, June 18, 1968; Wofford, interview, p. 10,
November 29, 1965, Kennedy Library; Brauer, *John F. Kennedy and the Second Reconstruction*, 153, 204, 240.
   48. Wofford, *Of Kennedys and Kings*, 93–94.
   49. Burke Marshall to the author, July 14, 1981. Other letters from Kennedy advisers
confirm their awareness of Myrdal's study: Katzenbach to the author, July 14, 1981; Dutton to the author, July 7, 1981; Schlesinger to the author, October 5, 1981; Sorensen to the
author, June 19, 1981. Galbraith recounts his experience with Myrdal in *A Life in Our
Times: Memoirs* (Boston, 1981), 66, 82–83.

Myrdal interview, the president added that Myrdal had demonstrated that a stagnant economy hurt blacks more than any other group. He also acknowledged that he was exploring Myrdal's contention that the traditional budget system had served America badly.[50]

Circumstances finally forced Kennedy to abandon his executive-action-only strategy and request strong civil rights legislation. Slowly the president came to realize the depth and urgency of the race problem. Criticism from Martin Luther King, James Reston, and other liberals of both races, charging that Kennedy was too cold-blooded, calculating, and timid on the race issue, stung the chief executive. More important, events in Birmingham, Alabama, in the spring of 1963 galvanized the nation and the president to demand action from Congress. After Governor George Wallace stood in the doorway of the University of Alabama on June 11, Kennedy decided the time was ripe. Well into the afternoon he informed the networks that he planned to go on the air that night. His hurriedly prepared address, which asked Congress for comprehensive civil rights legislation, turned out to be one of his most eloquent speeches. After citing the familiar economic, sociological, and international reasons for granting civic equality to blacks, Kennedy stressed the moral reason for acting. The issue, he exclaimed, was "as old as the scriptures . . . and as clear as the American Constitution."[51]

Kennedy made his decision to go on television so late in the day that Ted Sorensen barely had time to write one draft of the speech. Even then, the president had to extemporize the ending. A brash Nebraska populist with a keen sense of human rights, Sorensen had helped prepare an *amicus* brief for the Americans for Democratic Action in one of the school segregation cases in the early 1950s. He remembers that Myrdal's influence on him in race relations was "pervasive." This statement seems demonstrably true considering his unwarranted optimism about the South. In 1952 Sorensen wrote in the *New Republic* that significant integration of schools was taking place in the South already, not just in higher education but in secondary schools as well. His early im-

---

50. Werner Wiskari, "Myrdal Terms U.S. 'Stagnant': Urges Wide Economic Reform," New York *Times,* July 22, 1962; Harold W. Chase and Allen Lerman (eds.), *Kennedy and the Press: The News Conference* (New York, 1965), 294. Myrdal's views on Kennedy and the economy were summed up in *Challenge to Affluence.*

51. Brauer, *John F. Kennedy and the Second Reconstruction,* 25, 258–62; William V. Shannon, *The Heir Apparent: Robert Kennedy and the Struggle for Power* (New York, 1967), 141; Sitkoff, *Struggle for Black Equality,* 156–58; Chase and Lerman (eds.), *Kennedy and the Press,* 291.

mersion in Myrdal prepared him for the hurried drafting of Kennedy's June address. A learned liberal such as Sorensen could readily call on his memory to produce a short, convenient version of Myrdal's report. Just as the Swede found "America again at the crossroads" in his conclusive chapter of 1944, two decades later Kennedy and Sorensen placed the nation in that same perilous and opportune spot.[52]

Although Kennedy's speech seemed refreshingly spontaneous, his new course had been thoroughly discussed within the administration. Several of Kennedy's advisers urged caution on civil rights, but Robert Kennedy opted for decisive action. Having dealt more often and more directly with blacks and southern white supremacists as attorney general, Robert better understood the growing impatience of Afro-Americans and the intransigence of the white South than did the president. The attorney general even found time to read the provocative works of James Baldwin and other black writers. Of the two Kennedys, Robert more likely read, or was briefed on, the *Dilemma*. Whatever the case, the younger Kennedy became an effective spokesman for the administration on Capitol Hill. At the hearings on the 1963 civil rights bill, the younger Kennedy held his own against such constitutional experts as Senator Sam Ervin of North Carolina. He, in fact, had an edge over legalistic, segregationist senators because he unabashedly resorted to moral exhortation on the subject of racial discrimination. Before the Senate Judiciary Committee, Kennedy described the outcome of racial injustice in a typical sentence: "Great moral damage is done to individuals, to communities, to states, and to the very fabric of our Nation." Color discrimination in public places, the attorney general declared, was "plainly wrong, and must be corrected." [53]

Southern segregationists in Congress preferred not to discuss the morality of discrimination. They tended to confine the debate to political and constitutional questions. Senator Russell of Georgia maintained repeatedly that the race question "is not and cannot be a moral question." But northern legislators felt otherwise. Senator Everett M. Dirksen of

52. Brauer, *John F. Kennedy and the Second Reconstruction*, 259; Wofford, *Of Kennedys and Kings*, 35; Sorensen to the author, June 19, 1981; Theodore C. Sorensen, *Kennedy* (New York, 1965), 493–96; Sorensen, "School Doors Swing Open," *New Republic*, December 15, 1952, pp. 16–17.

53. Brauer, *John F. Kennedy and the Second Reconstruction*, 242–45; *Hearings*, Committee on the Judiciary, Senate, 88th Cong., 1st Sess., "Civil Rights—The President's Program, 1963," 94; *Hearings*, Committee on the Judiciary, House, 88th Cong., 1st Sess., "Civil Rights," Pt. 4, p. 2662.

Illinois, the leader of the Republican minority, asserted that "we are confronted with a moral issue." Emanuel Celler, the dean of the House and the chairman of the powerful Judiciary Committee, congratulated civil rights activists appearing before his committee. He submitted that they had awakened the "conscience of the nation." [54] In general, southerners took a defensive stance on the moral aspects of discrimination.

Lyndon Johnson seemed less defensive on racial matters than most southerners. He was one of a handful of southern senators and representatives who did not sign the Southern Manifesto in 1956. The rangy Texan had a genuine sympathy for Negroes, Hispanics, and the poor. His Populist roots and his New Deal experience, moreover, inclined him toward a belief in government solutions to problems. Johnson accurately thought of himself as a liberal "doer" rather than a liberal "thinker." He had little respect for intellectuals or the force of abstract ideas. He felt, as did most New Dealers, that the race problem was primarily an economic issue. Johnson believed that white southerners would respond to pleas to obey the Constitution and the laws of the land. Feeling that the country wanted no debate on fundamental issues, he hoped as president to move the nation forward under a broad, pragmatic consensus. [55]

The outpouring of sympathy for the martyred Kennedy and Johnson's renowned political skill in handling Congress enabled the new president to enact the civil rights bill in July, 1964. Soon thereafter Johnson engineered an overwhelming election victory in November over archconservative Senator Barry Goldwater. The Arizona Republican, who voted against the Civil Rights Act of 1964, became the first post–World War II presidential nominee of the two major parties to cater to the white backlash. Once elected in his own right, Johnson reacted to the Selma voting rights march by proposing a far-reaching bill to guarantee the ballot to blacks. On March 15, 1965, the president spoke on television. Before the cameras and a joint session of Congress, Johnson threw the complete moral weight of his office behind the most elemental civil right. Dra-

54. Senators Russell and Dirksen quoted in Lester A. Sobel (ed.), *Civil Rights, 1960–1966* (New York, 1967), 233; *Hearings*, Subcommittee No. 5 of the Committee on the Judiciary, House, 88th Cong., 1st Sess., Vol. 2, Pt. 3, p. 2214; see Senator William Proxmire's comments on Myrdal, *Congressional Record*, 88th Cong., 1st Sess., 29713.

55. Doris Kearns, *Lyndon Johnson and the American Dream* (New York, 1976), 152–53; interview, George Reedy, June 7, 1975, Oral History Program, Lyndon Johnson Library; Jack Bass and Walter De Vries, *The Transformation of Southern Politics: Social Change and Political Consequence Since 1945* (New York, 1976), 9–10.

matically using the movement's theme song, "We Shall Overcome," near the conclusion of his speech, Johnson brought the Congress and the nation to its feet; some openly wept at the climax of the address.[56]

If President Johnson got any ideas from Myrdal, it was secondhand and unintentional. As vice-president in 1963 he did share the same platform with the Swedish economist at the hundredth anniversary celebration of the Emancipation Proclamation at Wayne State University. At some point, holdover advisers from the Kennedy administration, such as Fred Dutton and Lee White, may have impressed some of their Myrdalian ideas upon the president. Bill Moyers, the young Baptist preacher whom Johnson treated like a son until the Vietnam War drove them apart, read Arnold Rose's condensation of the *Dilemma* with great interest while he was in college. When he became deputy director of the Peace Corps, he gave each volunteer worker a copy of the Myrdal study. In all probability, however, no erudite scholar, foreign or native, measurably influenced Johnson's thinking on civil rights. In race relations his beliefs and actions came from firsthand experience.[57]

A touch of Myrdal nonetheless found its way into one of the most profound speeches on race relations ever made by an American president. In a commencement address on June 4, 1965, at Howard University, where Myrdal had spoken three years earlier, Johnson opened a new phase of the civil rights movement. The president told the Howard graduating class that "freedom was not enough." Johnson argued that the scars of centuries could not be wiped away by saying that blacks were now free to integrate and compete. Someone who for years had been hobbled by chains could not be placed on the starting line of a competitive race and think that justice was complete. America, the president announced, had to strive for equality of condition. Johnson admitted that clear-cut answers to the problem of real equality were not yet known. He promised, however, to call a White House conference in the fall and invite every black and white spokesman and every racial expert to seek answers to the problem. The theme of the conference would be "To Fulfill These Rights."[58]

56. Eric F. Goldman, *The Tragedy of Lyndon Johnson* (New York, 1969), 322; New York *Times,* March 16, 1965, p. 30.

57. Moyers to the author, July 13, 1981. Father George H. Dunne of Georgetown University tried to arrange a meeting between Myrdal and Johnson to discuss the "war on poverty," but Moyers replied that the president's schedule would not permit it (Dunne to Moyers, January 13, 1964; Moyers to Dunne, January 14, 1964, "Gunnar Myrdal Name File," White House Central Files, Lyndon Johnson Library).

58. Johnson's speech in Franklin and Starr (eds.), *The Negro in the 20th Century,* 225–31.

If one looks closely at Johnson's cogent speech, the hand of Daniel P. Moynihan is evident. In 1965 Moynihan, a Harvard urbanologist and an official of the Labor Department, completed a study for the government called *The Negro Family: The Case for Action*. From this controversial and initially secret study, President Johnson got the gloomy content and the paradoxically hopeful conclusion for his Howard speech. In the first sentence of his study, Moynihan had written: "The United States is approaching a new crisis in race relations." From studying the ghetto family, the social scientist concluded that the relative position of many blacks was worsening. Moynihan perceived a massive breakdown in the Negro family. He believed that only a major compensatory program by the government could counteract the social disintegration. The Moynihan Report echoed the words of E. Franklin Frazier and Myrdal by focusing on the social and economic problems of the black underclass. In its pessimistic tone and its recognition of the crisis, the study only reiterated what many social scientists had been saying for some time. American liberals, however, seldom saw a gathering cloud without a silver lining. Thus Moynihan injected a familiar passage from the *Dilemma* into the president's speech to hold out a ray of hope: "*America is free to choose whether the Negro shall remain her liability or become her opportunity.*" To Moynihan, as to Myrdal, the solution to the race problem required only choice and will. The sad racial affair in America could be transformed into a magnificent national redemption. Near the end of the Howard address, Moynihan, with an assist from speechwriter Richard Goodwyn, paraphrased Myrdal. "It is a glorious opportunity of this generation to end the one huge wrong of the American Nation," the historic speech went, "and, in so doing, to find America for ourselves, with the same immense thrill of discovery which gripped those who first began to realize that here, at last, was a home for freedom." [59] No doubt totally unknown to the president, his historic address had incorporated a large dose of Myrdalism.

The idea of national redemption through racial justice appealed to no group more than theologians and ministers. As illustrated in earlier chapters of this study, American church leaders favored the moral framework of Myrdal's study over the other sociological models of race relations. The liberal elite of the church played an increasingly impor-

59. Harry McPherson, *A Political Education* (Boston, 1972), 339; Lee Rainwater and William L. Yancey (eds.), *The Moynihan Report and the Politics of Controversy* (Cambridge, Mass., 1967), 43. Rainwater and Yancey include a copy of the Moynihan Report in their volume. Johnson's speech in Franklin and Starr (eds.), *Negro in the 20th Century*, 231.

tant role in the civil rights movement after World War II. Senator Russell complained that the 1964 Civil Rights Act became law because "those damned preachers got the idea that it was a moral issue." The ecumenical gathering of church leaders at the National Conference on Religion and Race in Chicago in January, 1963, demonstrated the aptness of Russell's remark. The 637 delegates representing some seventy different religious groups passed a resolution called "An Appeal to the Conscience of the American People." It branded racial discrimination as an "insult to God" and called for its immediate eradication. These delegates, too, saw racist blight as opportunity. It is difficult to tell whether Rabbi Abraham J. Hershel was being Jobian or Myrdalian when he observed that "*the Negro problem is God's gift to America,* the test of integrity, a magnificent spiritual opportunity." [60]

By 1965 the time was fast approaching when it would be hard to find a white or black racial spokesman who counted America's race problem as a blessing. As scholars began to put the race problem in a world perspective, they found that providence had similarly "blessed" other countries besides America with racist societies. In retrospect, one wonders why anyone ever viewed the race problem as an opportunity to precipitate utopia, especially when one realizes that the liberal solutions to the race problem, not to mention the radical ones, were so improbable. One example is the compensatory programs prescribed by Moynihan, Martin Luther King, and Whitney Young, Jr., of the National Urban League. Moynihan admitted that such programs did not necessarily square with the creed of the white majority. When one went beyond legal equality to equality of condition, Moynihan confessed that middle-class support rapidly began to dissipate, principles became unclear, and consensus vanished. [61]

Actually, a consensus did exist among whites on many issues regarding Afro-Americans; and this consensus did not bode well for blacks. For instance, at any point in the civil rights movement, a majority of whites disapproved of specific black actions, even if nonviolent. In 1961 64 percent of whites expressed negative feelings toward the "freedom riders," those blacks and whites who tested the enforcement of the de-

60. Robert S. Spike, *The Freedom Revolution and the Churches* (New York, 1965), 108; Mathew Ahmann (ed.), *Race, Challenge to Religion* (Chicago, 1963), 68, 171–72.

61. Transcript of the Conference on the Negro by the Academy of Arts and Sciences, May 14–15, 1965, *Daedalus,* XCV (1966), 288–89; Daniel P. Moynihan, "Employment, Income and the Negro Family," in Kenneth B. Clark and Talcott Parsons (eds.), *The Negro American* (Boston, 1966), 135.

segregation of interstate bus travel in the Deep South. The extensive polling of white attitudes toward blacks by Louis Harris for *Newsweek* magazine in 1963 disclosed that most whites still held rigid stereotypes of Afro-Americans: 71 percent believed that Negroes smelled worse than whites; 69 percent thought blacks had looser morals than whites; and 49 percent felt that blacks had less native intelligence. Nor did whites want to live next to Afro-Americans. California voters dramatically illustrated this point when in 1964 they repealed, by a two-to-one margin, an open housing law. That same year Alabama's governor George Wallace ventured out of the Deep South into the border states and the North. In the Democratic primary in Maryland, the arch segregationist received 43 percent of the vote, and he received over 30 percent in Wisconsin and Indiana.[62]

Despite the palpable racism of whites, the editors of *Newsweek* chose to put the most optimistic interpretation on the Harris polls. Throughout the highly acclaimed issue of October 21, 1963, the editors emphasized the idealism of Americans. The editors judged that America had arrived at "the acute crisis in the American dilemma which Gunnar Myrdal identified . . . as the U.S. failure to live up to 'the century-old dream of American patriots, that America should give the entire world its own freedoms and its own faith.'" *Newsweek* confidently submitted that the American penchant for fair play would bring a just resolution to the race problem.[63]

Perhaps no one illustrated more vividly the white idea of fair play toward blacks than Eric Hoffer. A former longshoreman, an author, a self-made philosopher, and a television personality in his old age, Hoffer expressed publicly what cartoonist Al Capp believed white Americans were saying privately "through clenched teeth." In an article in the New York *Times* on November 29, 1964, Lyndon Johnson's favorite philosopher blasted blacks for what Hoffer considered their inability to help themselves. No people, Hoffer complained, had ever been "so deficient in the capacity for mutual aid and cooperation." As to white guilt feelings that Myrdal and liberals stressed so much, Hoffer wrote: "My kind of people do not feel that the world owes us anything, or that we owe anybody—white, black or yellow—a damn thing." Concerning

62. Lucius J. Barker and Jesse J. McCorry, Jr., *Black Americans and the Political System* (2d ed.; Cambridge, Mass., 1980), 60; *Newsweek,* October 21, 1963, pp. 47–57; Robert Blauner, "Whitewash Over Watts," in Robert M. Fogelson (ed.), *The Los Angeles Riots of 1965* (New York, 1969), 174.

63. *Newsweek,* October 21, 1963, pp. 47–57.

compensation to blacks for past oppression, the blue-collar philosopher proclaimed: "We believe that the Negro should have every right we have. But he can have no special claims on us, and no valid grievances against us. Our hands," Hoffer contended, "are more gnarled and work-broken than his, and our faces more lined and worn." [64]

In an earlier and less passionate article that year in the *Times*, Myrdal also rejected the idea of preferential treatment for blacks. He cautioned that such an effort would turn poor whites against blacks, and he constantly warned blacks against the coming ordeal of dog-eat-dog integration. At Howard University in 1962, he admonished black businessmen that they would have to give up the monopolies created by segregation. Myrdal also maintained that imminent integration meant the end of black institutions like Howard University. [65]

In truth, the evolving mood in the black community ensured that black colleges and universities would exist indefinitely. The civil rights movement peaked in 1965, and then it faltered and fragmented. Johnson's voting rights speech in March, 1965, marked one of the emotional high points of the crusade. Three months later the nation turned a deaf ear to the president's plea at Howard University for whites to extend more than just freedom to blacks. In August, just a few days after Johnson signed the strong Voting Rights Act, Watts, a suburb of Los Angeles, exploded in fury. The president, like the great majority of whites, could not comprehend the riot. According to one biographer, Johnson was struck dumb by Watts. "After all we've accomplished," the president repeated angrily to himself, "how could it be?" [66] Whites expressed dismay, anger, and fear over Watts and the long, hot Krakatoan summers that followed. But they felt little guilt. The majority believed that it had "given" blacks freedom and equal opportunity. Few whites felt that they owed Afro-Americans anything more.

Meanwhile, the fissures in the civil rights movement, perhaps best symbolized by the resegregation and radicalization of SNCC, became vast cleavages. The dilemma in the white mind shifted to the black mind as the minority frantically searched for new ways to change an increasingly hostile white America. Events also further tarnished the image of

64. *New York Times Magazine*, December 13, 1964, p. 28; Eric Hoffer, "The Negro Is Prejudiced Against Himself," *ibid.*, November 29, 1964, pp. 27, 100–114.

65. New York *Times*, January 24, 1964, p. 16; "The Negro Problem: A Prognosis," *New Republic*, July 9, 1962, pp. 11–12; Myrdal's Howard speech is reprinted in *Challenge to Affluence*, 163–72.

66. Kearns, *Lyndon Johnson*, 305.

the Myrdal study. As Charles Silberman put it in 1965: "Negro-white relations have entered a new and radically different stage—a stage so different from the recent past as to make the familiar approaches and solutions obsolete, irrelevant, and sometimes even harmful." [67] The racial dilemma, in the argot of the 1960s, it was "a-changing."

67. Charles Silberman, "Beware the Day They Change Their Minds," in Rainwater and Yancey (eds.), *Moynihan Report,* 428.

X

New Dilemmas, 1965–1969

In September, 1966, presidential adviser Harry McPherson relayed the following message to Lyndon Johnson: "The civil rights movement is obviously in a mess. . . . White resistance is great and still growing; the Negro community is fragmented." A few months earlier Charles Silberman, the ever-acute observer of the national scene, expressed fear that the pent-up frustrations and anger of the black rank and file might erupt at any moment and result in nihilistic and destructive, perhaps even suicidal, action.[1] His fears were not unfounded. In the remaining years of the decade, hundreds of riots broke out across the country, resulting in great loss of life and property.

The urban black riots contributed to a spiraling white backlash. White Americans showed no inclination to initiate the massive economic and social reconstruction of society demanded by black leaders and recommended by the 1968 report of the National Advisory Commission on Civil Disorders. The passage of strong civil rights bills in 1964 and 1965 basically eradicated from the white mind the dilemma that had been posed by *de jure* segregation and disfranchisement. But the race problem remained. And as the glue of the civil rights movement came unstuck in the late 1960s, the ever-present tension between white liberals and black activists deepened into sullen resentment and often open hostility.[2]

1. Harry McPherson, *A Political Education* (Boston, 1972), 355; Charles Silberman, "Beware the Day They Change Their Minds," in Rainwater and Yancey, (eds.), *Moynihan Report,* 428–31.
2. For others who designate 1965 as a turning point, see August Meier and Elliott Rudwick, *From Plantation to Ghetto* (rev. ed.; New York, 1970), 276–78, 280, 284; Sit-

Against the background of racial events from 1965 to 1969, Myrdal's influence declined rapidly. Occurrences in these years directly affected the study of race relations and altered attitudes toward the *Dilemma* by both blacks and whites. Scholars also discovered (or rediscovered) formidable barriers to Myrdal's vision of an integrated society, including new intellectual currents with conservative implications, disturbing new insights about the nature of racism, and by 1969 a presidential administration with a "southern strategy." These trends all reinforced the increasingly pessimistic view of black-white relations that had begun to take root in the early 1960s. This chapter discusses some of the events and trends that caused a growing number of academicians and racial reformers to discard Myrdal's upbeat model of race relations for the more problematic conflict model.

By 1965 most policy-oriented social scientists either pronounced Myrdal's ideas outdated or became somewhat indifferent to them. Far from indifferent, a great many black leaders and thinkers assigned Myrdal to the hottest part of Dante's inferno, usually with resounding invective. Although most of the black intelligentsia pragmatically endorsed Myrdal's study before the 1960s, they had always stressed economics, class solidarity, and power relations more than Myrdal had. But they had done so, for the most part, while still directing earnest appeals to the white conscience. After 1965 blacks increasingly appealed to white fears.

In the meantime, the cracks in the black movement became yawning chasms. The American dilemma for Afro-Americans was whether to make an all-out assault on the American system or to continue their painful efforts to enter it gradually. As one racial observer put it: "The division lay between those who still believed that the American dilemma might be resolved by the achievement of the American Dream and those who viewed the dream as a deception and the dilemma as unreconcilable." By the late 1960s younger and more militant blacks, many disillusioned integrationists, proclaimed the so-called American Dream to be an American Nightmare. In the summer of 1966 the slogan "black power" emerged from the March Against Fear launched by James Meredith. In the Mississippi march young Stokely Carmichael, the head of SNCC, used the slogan "black power" to steal the spotlight from Martin Luther King, who, like Carmichael, had rushed to Missis-

koff, *Struggle for Black Equality,* 199–200; John Herbers, *The Lost Priority: What Happened to the Civil Rights Movement?* (New York, 1970), xiv, 18, 46, 65, 176, 181.

sippi after Meredith had been wounded by a sniper. The cry of black power spread through the ghettos like wildfire. Some blacks acrimoniously debated the meaning of the new buzzword. Most black leaders, however, including King, appropriated and defined the slogan to suit their ideological likings. But Roy Wilkins of the NAACP denounced the concept of black power as "the father of hatred and the mother of violence." [3]

Whatever the slippery concept of black power meant, it fractured the ideological popular front of Martin Luther King, an admirer of Myrdal. Stokely Carmichael no longer talked about black and white together but about "offing pigs" and "killing honkies." H. Rap Brown, Carmichael's successor at SNCC, surmised that "America won't come around, so we're going to burn it down." The once idealistic "kids" of SNCC exchanged their Gandhi and Myrdal for Franz Fanon and Che Guevara. The former, a black physician from Algeria, excited young blacks with his book *The Wretched of the Earth* (1963). Fanon celebrated violence as a "cleansing force" that freed oppressed people from their inferiority complexes and transformed them into self-respecting individuals. [4]

To Myrdal's credit, he had acknowledged the potential for black violence. In the *Dilemma* he quoted his collaborator Ralph Bunche on that point: "There are Negroes too, who, fed up with frustration of their life here, see no hope and express an angry desire to 'shoot their way out of it.' I have on many occasions heard Negroes exclaim: 'Just give us machine guns and we'll blow the lid off the whole damn business.'" Myrdal indeed warned that America could "*never more regard its Negroes as a patient, submissive minority.*" But the Scandinavian devoted only slightly more than a page to "Negro aggression." Like most white liberals of the 1940s, he played down the possibility of black violence, stressing that black aggression was most often directed against blacks. Had Myrdal studied northern slums more and white consciences less, he might have been more prophetic about future black behavior in the urban centers. [5]

3. Thomas R. Brooks, *Walls Came Tumbling Down: A History of the Civil Rights Movement, 1940–1970* (Englewood Cliffs, N.J., 1974), 250, 259, 266–67, 274; Sitkoff, *Struggle for Black Equality,* 212–17; Roy Wilkins, "Whither Black Power?" in Meier, Rudwick, and Broderick (eds.), *Black Protest Thought in the Twentieth Century,* 596–98.

4. Sitkoff, *Struggle for Black Equality,* 215–17; Brooks, *Walls Came Tumbling Down,* 265; Franz Fanon, *The Wretched of the Earth* (New York, 1963), 94.

5. *AD,* 566–69, 763, 1004, 1014. For a study of black aggressive urges, see William Grier and Price M. Cobbs, *Black Rage* (New York, 1968), 212–13 and *passim.*

The assassination of Malcolm X in 1965 strengthened the appeal of revolutionary and, of course, defensive violence among young blacks. Published shortly after his death, Malcolm X's autobiography became required reading for budding black leaders. Malcolm X also preached the mystique of blackness, sometimes called "Soul" or "Negritude." Young intellectuals and activists such as Stokely Carmichael continued to disseminate these concepts. Like Ralph Ellison's "invisible man," some blacks feared that integration meant "ethnocide." Revealingly, Ellison's original and unpublished review of Myrdal's study in 1944 appeared in print in 1964 in a collection of his writings called *Shadow and Act*. Its publication proved as timely for black nationalists as the *Dilemma* had been for integrationists.[6]

In 1969, for instance, John H. Bracey, Jr., made extensive use of Ellison's review in a paper entitled *"An American Dilemma: A National-ist Critique."* Speaking at the annual meeting of the Southern Historical Association in a session that assessed the *Dilemma* on its twenty-fifth anniversary, Bracey skewered the Swedish economist for his failure to understand the wholesome uniqueness of Afro-American culture. He vehemently dissented from Myrdal's description of black culture as a pathological variant of white culture. Bracey labeled such a view "implicitly racist." Displaying a voguish Afro-American hairstyle, the black historian quoted Ellison's plaintive questions from the 1944 review of the *Dilemma:* "But can a people . . . live and develop for over three hundred years simply by *reacting?* Why cannot Negroes have made a life upon the horns of the white man's dilemma?" Far from wanting to imitate white culture, Bracey declared, blacks rejected much of it as malignant. Bracey denounced as arrogant a long excerpt from the *Dilemma* which argued that an all-black movement would be impractical. He further blasted Myrdal for taking a middle-class approach to the race question. The black scholar pointed out that Myrdal frankly had admitted in his book that the liberal-integrationist approach to race relations sacrificed the interest of lower-class blacks.[7] Like Ellison in 1944, Bracey assailed the Swede from both nationalist and leftist positions.

6. Malcolm Little, *The Autobiography of Malcolm X* (New York, 1965); Stokely Carmichael and Charles V. Hamilton, *Black Power: The Politics of Liberation in America* (New York, 1967), 44; Larry Neal, "New Space: The Growth of Black Consciousness in the Sixties," in Floyd B. Barbour (ed.) *The Black Seventies* (Boston, 1970), 23; Ralph Ellison, *"An American Dilemma,"* 303–17.

7. John H. Bracey, Jr., *"An American Dilemma:* A Nationalist Critique," paper delivered at the annual meeting of the Southern Historical Association, Washington, D.C., November 1, 1969, pp. 5, 8, copy in possession of the author.

In the late 1960s scores of scholars combed black neighborhoods to see whether Afro-Americans had created a new life on the horns of the white man's dilemma. Was black culture a variant of mainstream culture, a separate culture, or a culture in the making? Lee Rainwater's 1970 book *Soul* collected some of the best writings on these questions. No consensus existed, although Rainwater held that a black subculture had acquired a "limited functional autonomy." Actually, the old argument that had raged between Myrdal (or E. Franklin Frazier) and Melville Herskovits in the 1940s resumed in full force again in the 1960s. The difference was that black nationalist scholars tended to glamorize the ghetto culture for its adaptive and survivalist character, and white liberals tended to see lower-class blacks as hapless victims of white racism.[8]

Myrdal was not unaware of the nationalist streak in black thought. Even the nationalist Bracey conceded that Myrdal had glimpsed the truth when he wrote: "The Negro caste is, in a sense 'a nation within a nation.'" As the sociologist Michael Banton pointed out in 1968, Myrdal realized that Afro-Americans had to disparage everything considered "Negro" if they were to assimilate, and, paradoxically, this often drove blacks into voluntary isolation to preserve their self-respect. "The Negro," Myrdal had written, "is an alien in America."[9] Yet the European declined to follow up such insights. Myrdal's optimistic model required that blacks believe in the American creed and seek integration. Besides, Myrdal feared that any racially chauvinistic movement by blacks would frighten away white allies that the minority so desperately needed. The celebration of black culture in the late 1960s often did just that.

Black power advocates could find little hope in Myrdal's idealism about white America. Carmichael and Charles V. Hamilton declared that white culture was "anti-humanist." Malcolm X charged that the Caucasian conscience had been nourished in a "soulless womb." James

---

8. "Introduction," Lee Rainwater (ed.), *Soul* (Chicago, 1970), 3. Some important works not represented in *Soul* are Charles Keil, *Urban Blues* (Chicago, 1966); Elliott Liebow, *Tally's Corner: A Study of Streetcorner Men* (Boston, 1967); S. P. Fullinwider, *The Mind and Mood of Black America* (Homewood, Ill., 1969); Nathan Caplan, "The New Ghetto Man: A Review of Recent Empirical Studies," in David Boesil and Peter H. Rossi (eds.), *Cities Under Siege: An Anatomy of the Ghetto Riots, 1964–1968* (New York, 1971). On the "glamorization of the ghetto," see Donald Bogle, *Toms, Coons, Mulattoes, Mammies, and Bucks: An Interpretive History of Blacks in American Films* (New York, 1973), 234–35.

9. Bracey, *"An American Dilemma,"* 18; Michael Banton, *Race Relations* (New York, 1968), 358; *AD*, 657, 659, 799, 853.

Forman, who in 1969 demanded $500 million in reparations from white churches (or "15 dollars per nigger") stressed the unchanging attitudes of whites. "Racism," Forman declared, "is so pervasive . . . that only an armed, well-disciplined, black-controlled government can insure the stamping out of racism in this country." The nationalist Harold Cruse insisted that relations between groups never hinged on morality or compassion for the oppressed.[10]

Suspicion about virtually all white scholarship was rife among most black intellectuals. Their reaction to white offerings often paralleled Carter Woodson's bitter response to the *Dilemma* in 1944. One black social scientist complained that whites were always looking "through their little microscopes of manipulation." According to another scholar, blacks felt that social science findings had been "useless and false" for blacks and "useful and false" for whites. The Black Caucus of the American Sociological Society went so far as to demand predetermined results from social research. It called for sociologists to produce research "which validates social humanism, liberation, and the legitimacy of the struggle of oppressed people for self-determination." Many observers in the late 1960s noted the feelings of resentment and the great depths of disagreement and misunderstanding between black and white scholars at professional meetings of the various disciplines in the social sciences.[11]

A prime example of this resentment and misunderstanding could be seen in the black reaction to the famous Moynihan Report in the summer and fall of 1965—a reaction that typified black attitudes toward Myrdal as well. As the historian Bracey accused Myrdal of implicit racism, several blacks charged that Daniel Moynihan's sociological portrait of the black family constituted a "new form of subtle racism." The complicated controversy surrounding the report need not be fully explored here. For that purpose one should read the judicious book, *The*

10. Carmichael and Hamilton, *Black Power,* 41; John Henrik Clarke (ed.), *Malcolm X: The Man and His Times* (New York, 1969), 343; William R. Corson, *Promise or Peril: The Black College Student in America* (New York, 1970), 174; Peter Goldman, *Report from Black America* (New York, 1971), 93–94; Cruse, *Crisis of the Negro Intellectual,* 494.

11. Charles J. Levy, *Voluntary Servitude: Whites in the Negro Movement* (New York, 1968), vii; Barbara A. Sizemore, "Social Science and Education for a Black Identity," in James A. Banks and Jean Dresden Grambs (eds.), *Black Self-Concept: Implications for Education and Social Science* (New York, 1972), 151–56; James E. Blackwell, "Role Behavior in a Corporate Structure: Black Sociologists in the ASA," in Blackwell and Janowitz (eds.), *Black Sociologists,* 360; and "Introduction," *ibid.,* vii.

Moynihan Report and the Politics of Controversy, by Lee Rainwater and William L. Yancey. To be sure, Moynihan's brief government study contained many flaws, especially if viewed by normal academic standards. It did not, for instance, make it clear enough that the report concerned only the lower-class black family; and its omission of any recommendations for specific action obscured Moynihan's motivations. Many who read the report, or perused the distorted journalistic accounts "leaked" about the initially confidential report, did not know that the Harvard urbanologist considered jobs for black males to be the primary solution to the problem of black families. Many blacks instead believed that Moynihan had recommended white moral engineering of *all* black families instead of government programs for employment, job training, and education. The white sociologist was, in black parlance, "blaming the victim." [12]

In any event, Moynihan did not intend his report to be a balanced and scholarly study but a short, secret, and persuasive position paper to prod the government into a new and more profound stage of the civil rights movement. And, indeed, it did, for it provided the basis of President Johnson's eloquent speech at Howard University in June of 1965. This provocative speech called for government involvement that would go "beyond freedom" and move blacks toward equality of condition. Many of the same blacks who bitterly criticized the Moynihan Report had loudly cheered the Howard speech, not knowing, of course, that Moynihan was the principal architect of the courageous address. [13]

Conceptually, the Moynihan Report was little more than an update of Myrdal's analysis (borrowed mainly from E. Franklin Frazier). Moynihan, however, based some of his report on Kenneth Clark's valuable research on Harlem, which appeared in 1965 as *Dark Ghetto.* Clark, who had written frankly about the "pathology" in the ghetto, scolded Moynihan's critics for unfairness. "It's a kind of wolf pack operating in an undignified way," the black social psychologist wrote. "If Pat is a racist, I am. He highlights the total pattern of segregation and discrimi-

12. Rainwater and Yancey (eds.), *Moynihan Report,* 1–37, 159, 163, 216–45, 258, and *passim.* The Moynihan Report, published by the U.S. Department of Labor, *The Negro Family: The Case for National Action* (1965), is reprinted in Rainwater and Yancey, along with various reactions to the report and President Johnson's Howard University speech of June, 1965. See also James M. Jones, *Prejudice and Racism* (Reading, Mass., 1972), 47–52; and William Ryan, *Blaming the Victim* (New York, 1971).

13. Rainwater and Yancey (eds.), *Moynihan Report,* 25–32, 125–32, 188–89, 215, 298–300; Elkins, "Slavery Debate," 44.

nation. Is a doctor responsible for a disease simply because he diagnoses it?" Clark asked.[14] It would be a long time before the black intelligentsia would tolerate anything but celebratory history and sociology of Afro-Americans, especially by white scholars. Had Myrdal's book appeared in 1965, someone undoubtedly would have written a book called *The Myrdal Report and the Politics of Race.*

By the late 1960s moderate and integrationist blacks began to sound much like the more strident nationalists. Their pessimism about whites often differed only in degree from that of more radical blacks. In 1965 Clark announced in the New York *Times* that the "cancer of racism" might have advanced too far to be cured. In May of the same year the black psychologist joined some thirty noted scholars at a special conference on blacks sponsored by the Academy of Arts and Sciences. Clark coedited the nearly eight hundred pages of material presented at the conference. Published as *The Negro American,* this wide-ranging anthology included a foreword by President Johnson. In his editorial introduction to the book, Clark castigated the Myrdalian analysis of race relations. The message emanating from the conference, Clark summarized, was that "the American dilemma is one of power." This summary contrasted starkly with the introduction of Clark's coeditor, Talcott Parsons. The renowned white sociologist from Harvard claimed that the papers given at the conference clearly validated Myrdal's thesis.[15]

In his paper delivered at the conference, Clark argued that Martin Luther King's appeals to the white conscience were now "irrelevant to fundamental social change." In his book *Dark Ghetto*—appropriately subtitled *Dilemmas of Social Power*—Clark did not once refer to Myrdal's *Dilemma,* even though the Swede had written a foreword to his book. Instead he cited his old European friend's latest book, *Challenge to Affluence* (1963). Clark preferred the more recent Myrdal, who now based his optimism on economic necessity, to the one who had predicated progress on white guilt. In *Challenge to Affluence,* Myrdal claimed that a massive government jobs program was necessary to end economic stagnation. In a 1967 address to the Southern Regional Council, Clark directly disputed Myrdal's thesis and emphasized that the American dilemma had been transferred to the black mind. The dilemma in the black person's mind, Clark explained, hinged on "whether to persist in his insistence upon his unqualified rights without regard to

14. Rainwater and Yancey (eds.), *Moynihan Report,* 7, 263.
15. Clark quoted in "The Wonder Is There Have Been So Few Riots," in Milton L. Barron (ed.), *Minorities in a Changing World* (New York, 1967), 255; Clark, "The Dilemma of Power," in Clark and Parsons (eds.), *Negro American,* xviii–xix, xi, xxii.

the risks or consequences—or whether to accommodate the resistances by subtle or flagrant forms of withdrawal from the fray." His preference was clear. Clark condemned the black power separatists as latter-day Booker T. Washingtons.[16]

To be sure, black moderates stood far to the left of most white liberals in the post-Watts period. Like the radicals, they more frequently appealed to the fears of whites than to their consciences. Whitney Young, Jr., of the National Urban League, for example, urged blacks to instigate "creative confrontations" with whites to force them to allocate "*unequal* resources to enable all Americans to compete on an equal basis." If they did not, Young warned, the result would be general repression and the end of American democracy. Bayard Rustin and A. Philip Randolph astounded white liberals, including Lyndon Johnson, when they proposed a $185 billion "Freedom Budget" to prevent catastrophe in the urban centers. Rustin hinted that if Myrdal's "exaggerated Americans" were not appeased, they, like Samson, might bring the pillars of the American polity tumbling down.[17]

Even before Martin Luther King's death in 1968, the shaky coalition of black leaders had been shattered and ideological chaos reigned. Various factions denounced one another with a ferocity heretofore reserved for white racists. In *The Crisis of the Negro Intellectual*, Harold Cruse referred to the pleadings of black integrationists as "piddling intellectual civil writism [*sic*]." In a special issue of *Ebony* in August, 1969, editor Lerone Bennett, Jr., issued an earnest plea for "ideological clarity." Although a certain unity built around black pride and bitterness toward whites existed, no hint of ideological clarity could be found. On one page of *Ebony* a writer reveled in blackness and sounded the battle cry to "get whitey." On another page, advertisements featured hair straightener and skin bleach. A year later *Ebony* featured another special issue on the movement that carried the caption: "Which Way Black America: Separation, Integration or Liberation?"[18]

If polls reflected reality, the radicalism of black intellectuals and leaders was less evident among the populace. Analyzing the exhaustive

16. Clark and Parsons (eds.), *Negro American*, 613; Kenneth B. Clark, *Dark Ghetto: Dilemmas of Social Power* (New York, 1965), 141, 215, 238; Clark, "The Present Dilemma of the Negro," address given at the annual meeting of the Southern Regional Council, November 2, 1967, pp. 3–5, 8, copy in possession of the author.

17. Whitney Young, Jr., *Beyond Racism: Building an Open Society* (New York, 1969) 100–103, 153, 239, 254; Bayard Rustin, "From Protest to Politics," *Commentary*, XXXIX (February, 1965), 25–31; *Down the Line: The Collected Writings of Bayard Rustin* (Chicago, 1971), 115, 207.

18. Cruse, *Crisis of the Negro Intellectual*, 475; *Ebony*, XXIV (August, 1969), 36,

polls done for *Newsweek* in the 1960s, Peter Goldman revealed that most blacks professed to be moderate and optimistic. They preferred integrated neighborhoods and schools by wide margins. In 1969 more among the minority selected the term "Negro" than any other designation to describe their group. Yet it was clear that black militancy and distrust of whites grew significantly during the 1960s, especially among the young. In stark contrast to whites, about half the black population saw the urban riots as positive events. Even if most blacks remained integrationists, they viewed integration quite differently from whites. As Sterling Tucker phrased it, "Integration is not a passing gesture, a few thousand new jobs, more liberal welfare reparations. Integration is the full partnership of black and white. It is the redistribution of capital resources and power. Integration means white sacrifice."[19] If by 1969 Myrdal's insights about black feelings had not been proved entirely wrong, they most definitely had been transcended.

The racial events of the 1960s had an equally strong impact on the attitudes of whites toward Myrdal's book. American social scientists have generally been an optimistic group concerning social change, whether they believed in the benign determinism of Robert Park or the social engineering of Myrdal. But the decade that began with such high hopes ended in disillusionment for many. The 1960s unmercifully exposed many of the flaws in postindustrial America. The civil rights movement spun off angry revolts against society by youths, women, Indians, Hispanics, gays, and others. The American consensus reeled from the civic storm unleashed by the divisive Vietnam War. Amid the turmoil, academics took a less hopeful view of solving social problems. Exemplifying this mood were the essays in the lengthy 1967 book *The Use of Social Research in Federal Domestic Programs.* One sociologist advised his colleagues to "undersell" their product so as not to foster

---

70, 165, 172, 175; *ibid.,* XXV (August, 1970), cover. On inconsistencies, see also William H. Chafe, *Civilities and Civil Rights: Greensboro, North Carolina, and the Black Struggle for Freedom* (New York, 1980), 324.

19. Goldman, *Report from Black America,* 11–12, 63–66, 179, 207, 229–70; Caplan, "New Ghetto Man," 345; David O. Sears and T. M. Tomlinson, "Riot Ideology in Los Angeles: A Study of Negro Attitudes," *Social Science Quarterly,* XLIV (1968), 498, 502; Howard Schuman and Shirley Hatchett, *Black Power Attitudes: Trends and Complexities* (Ann Arbor, 1974), 6; Angus Campbell and Howard Schuman, "Black Views of Racial Issues," in Marcel L. Goldschmid (ed.), *Black Americans and White Racism: Theory and Research* (New York, 1970), 357–59; William Brink and Louis Harris, *Black and White* (New York, 1966), 135; Sterling Tucker, *Beyond the Burning: Life and Death of the Ghetto* (New York, 1968), 149.

undue expectations about the ability of the social sciences to deal with complex human problems.[20]

The lack of confidence and consensus could be detected at the special conference on the black minority held by the American Academy of Arts and Sciences in May of 1965, at which twenty-six racial experts delivered papers and discussed them for two days. First published in the journal *Daedalus,* the essays appeared later in *The Negro American,* edited by Kenneth Clark and Talcott Parsons. Clark maintained that the essays showed that the theme of power was at the heart of the American dilemma. The black social scientist stressed that the organization of power by blacks, aided by international economic and political forces, held the key to racial progress. Contrarily, Parsons judged that only a minority of the participants at the conference believed that power was the main determinant in race relations.[21] Actually, the conference participants were divided in their views. Many expressed uncertainty about the course of black-white relations. Whether they were optimistic or pessimistic sometimes seemed to depend on the last significant racial event.

Clearly, however, Parsons would not be budged from the Myrdalian camp. He praised the collection of essays in *The Negro American* as the best work on black-white relations since the *Dilemma.* The sociologist asserted that racial caste could not survive in America "for both moral and structural reasons." Parsons felt that the civil rights movement could never have gained momentum "without its strong *moral* resonance." Although the Harvard sociologist started from the radical premise that racism was endemic to Western culture and that color prejudice possessed a primordial quality, he still postulated that an "inclusion process" ensured the integration of blacks into American society; Parsons indicated that this process was based on the "moral values characterized by Myrdal as the American creed." In essence, the leader of the school of sociological functionalism combined a progressive determinism reminiscent of the Chicago School with the moral idealism of Myrdal.[22]

20. Research and Technical Programs Subcommittee of the House Committee on Government Operations, *The Use and Abuse of Social Research in Federal Domestic Programs* (1967), especially Pt. 3; Robert C. Angell, "The Ethical Problems of Applied Sociology," in Paul Lazarsfeld, William H. Sewell, and Harold Wilensky (eds.), *The Uses of Sociology* (New York, 1967), 728.

21. Talcott Parsons, "Why 'Freedom Now,' Not Yesterday?" in Clark and Parsons (eds.), *Negro American,* xix–xx.

22. *Ibid.,* xxiii; Parsons, "Full Citizenship for the Negro American?" *ibid.,* 740, 745; Parsons, "The Problem of Polarization on the Axis of Color," in John Hope Franklin

As an inveterate optimist, a defender of the American system, and one given to grand theories, Parsons took his lumps from both the right and left. The conservative Robert Nisbet linked him unflatteringly with the grand theorizers Hegel, Spencer, and Marx. Parsons' sociological theories, Nisbet complained, assumed that change was natural, continuous, and progressive. Optimists such as Parsons, he argued, ignored the concrete and the cataclysmic in history and mistook motion for change. In sum, Nisbet charged that Parsons' abstract construction lacked historicity.[23]

Alvin Gouldner, a leftist sociologist, assailed Parsons as a misleading metaphysician who wrote in "Germanically opaque prose." The Harvard professor, Gouldner averred, practiced a "sunshine sociology," which ignored evil in history and described events that deviated from his model as accidents. Additionally, Gouldner depicted Parsons as an addicted bourgeois booster who manipulated his work to glorify capitalism.[24]

In his paper presented at the Boston conference, Parsons characterized the race problem as a golden opportunity to "put the seal on the Marxist error in diagnosing American society." By extending equality to blacks, he promised, America would "present a true alternative to the Communist pattern on a world-wide basis, one which is not bound to the stereotype of 'capitalism.' "[25]

That several scholars in 1965 still considered the race problem an opportunity for America proved that Myrdalism had not perished in certain circles. The Harvard economist James Tobin, for example, began his essay with the statement: "I start from the presumption that the integration of Negroes into the American society and economy can be accomplished within existing political and economic institutions." Tobin asserted that the position of the Negro in American society had been an aberration that could not last. He concluded his address by saying: "The nation, its conscience aroused by the plight of the Negro, has the chance to make reforms which will benefit the whole society."[26]

(ed.), *Color and Race* (Boston, 1968), 367; Parsons, *Sociological Theory and Modern Society* (New York, 1967), 433–34.

23. Robert A. Nisbet, *Social Change and History: Aspects of Western Theory and Development* (New York, 1969), 76, 166–82, 228, 270–71, 281–82, 294, 304.

24. Gouldner, *Coming Crisis of Western Sociology*, 147, 199–200, 417–19, 501. On Parsons, see also Stanford M. Lyman, *The Black American in Sociological Thought: A Failure of Perspective* (New York, 1973), 145–69; and Mills, *Sociological Imagination*.

25. Parsons, "Full Citizenship for the Negro American?" 749.

26. James Tobin, "On Improving the Economic Status of the Negro," in Clark and Parsons (eds.), *Negro American*, 451, 469.

Several other participants put the race problem in a Myrdalian framework, perhaps fitting for a conference sponsored by the Carnegie Corporation. In a paper entitled "The American Dilemma in a Changing
World," Rupert Emerson and Martin Kilson recalled Myrdal's 1944
views on the relation of international affairs to the race issue. Among
the several quotations from the *Dilemma* in their essay was the frequently used one from the final chapter which predicted that the international prestige of the United States would hinge on the treatment of its
black minority. John H. Fichter, professor of Roman Catholic Studies at
Harvard Divinity School, lauded Myrdal for recognizing the moral dimension of the race problem. Paul A. Freund, a member of the Harvard
Law School faculty, concluded his presentation with these words: "On
balance, it is a hopeful sign that our problem is in truth an American
dilemma." Paul B. Sheatsley, an opinion analyst with the National
Opinion Research Center in Chicago, said of white attitudes toward
blacks: "Most of them know that racial discrimination is morally wrong
and recognize the legitimacy of the Negro protest." [27]

Still, many conferees saw no Myrdalian linings on the gathering racial clouds. Jean Mayer, a nutritionist from Harvard, blurted out during
the discussion: "I think we are too marked by the title of Gunnar Myrdal's book, *An American Dilemma.*" Several of the papers focused on
the dreary economic situation of blacks. St. Clair Drake, coauthor of
Black Metropolis, revealed that with the then current economic trends,
it would take the black man almost one hundred years to achieve oc-
cupational equality and more than two hundred years to achieve equality
of income. Raschi Fein's economic profile of the black American emphasized that the gap between blacks and whites was widening. [28]

Daniel Moynihan, soon to be the target of many black writers, also
pointed out that the economic position of the black ghetto dweller was
slipping. His scholarly essay at the conference avoided many of the pitfalls in the Moynihan Report that leaked from the Labor Department in
the summer of 1965. The future senator carefully explained that the
civil rights movement had reached a new and difficult stage wherein

27. Rupert Emerson and Martin Kilson, "The American Dilemma in a Changing
World: The Rise of Africa and the Negro American," *ibid.,* 651–52; John H. Fichter,
"American Religion and the Negro," *ibid.,* 416; Paul A. Freund, "The Civil Rights Move-
ment and the Frontiers of Law," *ibid.,* 369; Paul B. Sheatsley, "White Attitudes Toward
Negroes," *ibid.,* 323.

28. Jean Mayer quoted in Transcript of the Academy Discussion, May 14–15, 1965,
Daedalus, XCV (1966), 340; St. Clair Drake, "The Social and Economic Status of the
Negro in the United States," in Clark and Parsons (eds.), *Negro American,* 15, 18; Raschi
Fein, "An Economic and Social Profile of the Negro American," *ibid.,* 104.

blacks sought to go beyond freedom to equality of condition. Because of past oppression, Moynihan insisted, a condition of approximate equality would not be possible without a special and massive effort by the federal government to assist blacks educationally and economically. Paul Freund, who alluded to the wisdom of Myrdal in his essay, remarked that the old liberal fetish of color-blindness could no longer serve as a realistic guide for civil rights action. "I think that violation of the principle of color-blindness for the purpose of transition toward a greater equality," Freund submitted, "is perfectly consistent with the letter and spirit of the Constitution." [29]

The Harvard legalist grasped the changed nature of black-white relations. But Moynihan, like Myrdal, pointed out that Freund's confidence in the willingness of whites to support compensatory programs was unwarranted. No dilemma existed in the white mind on the idea of preferential treatment of blacks. Moynihan asserted that whites plainly considered affirmative action wrong and unacceptable. James Q. Wilson, a political scientist from Harvard, informed the conference that a liberal coalition of blacks and whites, not to mention a leftist one, was only a slight possibility. When a conferee asked Moynihan whether the problem of black poverty should be addressed apart from poverty in general, he replied: "We have to declare that we are doing it for everybody." Although he held that black poverty constituted a unique problem, Moynihan confessed that public officials had to advertise their programs as beneficial to everyone. Moynihan's idea of a camouflaged affirmative action program incited some of the liveliest discussion and disagreements of the session. [30]

At the conference Ralph Ellison, the longtime champion of cultural pluralism, posed as a watchdog against assimilators. He pointedly admonished the mostly white delegation that blacks would increasingly reject white culture, not just because whites spurned blacks but because white culture was not "good enough" for many Afro-Americans. [31] In sum, an atmosphere of uncertainty, tension, and crisis pervaded the scholarly conference. Many now felt that time no longer worked in favor of a resolution to the race problem. But, like Myrdal twenty years

29. Moynihan, "Employment, Income and the Negro Family," in Clark and Parsons (eds.), 134–59; Transcript, *Daedalus*, XCV (1966), 361–63, 379–80.

30. James Q. Wilson, "The Negro in Politics," in Clark and Parsons (eds.), *Negro American*, 440–44; Moynihan, "Employment, Income and the Negro Family," *ibid.*, 134–59; Transcript, *Daedalus*, XCV (1966), 288–90, 292, 294, 301, 304, 361–63, 379–88.

31. Transcript, *Daedalus*, XCV (1966), 435–41.

earlier, some scholars still perceived the racial crisis as an opportunity to usher in the final triumph of American ideals.

A different view was expressed at the International Conference on Race and Color convened in Copenhagen in September, 1965. Shortly before the conference, the Watts riot occurred, and simultaneously in Malaysia massive violence erupted between brown Malayans and yellow Chinese. These events and the repeated observations of enduring racial discrimination around the world served to underscore the tragic meaning of color consciousness in human affairs. As John Hope Franklin, the black American historian and editor of the Copenhagen papers, put it: "They had learned that the specter of color haunts every nook and corner of the world, consuming an inordinate amount of mankind's energies and attention that are so desperately needed to solve major problems of peace and survival." [32] Virtually no one at the Copenhagen conference saw a resolution of the international race problem on the horizon. Certainly none touted the world racial situation as a good opportunity to effect the high ideals of human brotherhood.

The seventeen articles derived from the conference, first published in *Daedalus* and then in a book called *Color and Race,* painted a somber picture. These essays graphically illustrated how skin color served as a source of human suffering and injustice. Leon Carl Brown of Princeton University felt constrained to explain in a footnote that perhaps his "muted" optimism about race relations in northern Africa had been overstated. In truth, Brown had not found color discrimination to be inconsequential, but compared to the essays about other parts of the world, his paper seemed encouraging. [33]

Unlike the scholars who attended the conference of the American Academy of Arts and Sciences, the scholars at Copenhagen hardly mentioned Myrdal. Philip Mason, the director of the London Institute of Race Relations, proved to be the exception. His interest in Myrdal probably stemmed from a massive study of Britain's race problem that his organization had begun and patterned after the Carnegie collaboration. Mason, however, discussed and quoted Myrdal primarily to refute his idea that blacks desired integration into white culture. Rather, the Britisher maintained that blacks everywhere in the world were in revolt against Western culture, making a bad racial situation worse. [34]

32. "Introduction: Color and Race in the Modern World," in Franklin (ed.), *Color and Race,* viii.
33. Leon Carl Brown, "Color in Northern Africa," *ibid.,* 186–204.
34. Philip Mason, "The Revolt Against Western Values," *ibid.,* 53–54, 60.

Several of the conferees at Copenhagen brushed aside the familiar complaints of such cultural anthropologists as Franz Boas and Ashley Montagu about the misuse of the concept "race." In most cases they simply substituted "color" for the problematic term "race," arguing that nobody could deny that pigmentation played a large role in human affairs. The participants alluded to authorities from Augustine to Freud to explain the prevalence of racism in the world. In the lead article in *Color and Race,* Edward Shils of the University of Chicago expressed a view of color consciousness that many at the conference endorsed. "Self-identification by color," Shils proclaimed, "has its origins in a sense of primordial connection with which human beings find it difficult to dispense." Kenneth J. Gergen, a social psychologist from Harvard, believed that many racial studies erred in using color to designate the "battle lines" without considering the obvious possibility that color was responsible for the battle itself. Harold R. Isaacs, a professor of political science at Massachusetts Institute of Technology, declared: "Of all the factors involved in the great rearrangement of human relationships taking place today, skin color is the most glandular." Whereas a generation of cultural anthropologists and Myrdalians had soft-pedaled the issue of race as a real problem, the specialists at Copenhagen maintained that color loomed as the most elemental and explosive ingredient generating hostility between people around the world.[35]

The renewed awareness of the universal nature of the race problem made Myrdal's 1939 decision to avoid comparative studies look highly questionable. True, several followers of Robert Park, who generally had taken a longer and broader view of the race question, accused Myrdal of ignoring the world outside America. But it was not until the 1960s that Myrdal's critics could be counted on to condemn the *Dilemma* for making the study of race relations in America provincial and ethnocentric. Comparative race studies, of course, became commonplace in the 1970s and 1980s. Consequently, Americans could no longer view their racial situation as exceptional. That revelation gave comfort to many Americans who accepted the racial *status quo,* but it further damaged the credibility of Myrdal's analysis.[36]

35. Edward Shils, "Color, the Universal Intellectual Community, and the Afro-Asian Intellectual," *ibid.,* 3–4, 14; Kenneth J. Gergen, "The Significance of Skin Color in Human Relations," *ibid.,* 112, 115, 121–25; Harold R. Isaacs, "Group Identity and Political Changes: The Role of Color and Physical Characteristics," *ibid.,* 75.

36. Stressing international racism were Everett C. Hughes and Helen M. Hughes, *Where People Meet* (Glencoe, Ill., 1952), 8–9; and Andrew Lind's Introduction to Lind (ed.), *Race Relations in World Perspective* (Honolulu, 1955). Several textbooks on race

After 1965 the world perspective on the race problem, coupled with a greater appreciation for the historical approach to the issue by social scientists, led to a decidedly less cheerful outlook about black-white relations in America. No scholar better illustrated this approach or criticized Myrdal more persuasively than Pierre L. van den Berghe. Although trained under the Myrdal-influenced Talcott Parsons and Gordon Allport at Harvard, van den Berghe tartly criticized the popular liberal outlook. In his 1967 book, *Race and Racism: A Comparative Approach*, he dismissed most liberal scholarship in America as ahistorical. Van den Berghe claimed that the *"Herrenvolk"* democracy in the United States had never included blacks. He argued that the *Dred Scott* decision of 1857, which denied that blacks had any rights that whites were bound to respect, spoke for the overwhelming majority of whites. Accordingly, van den Berghe found few traces of an "American dilemma" before 1940. Though not denying that some sort of dilemma arose after World War II, he stressed group power as the key to race relations. Gathering his data from around the globe, van den Berghe scoffed at the optimism of Myrdalian liberals. That racism was ancient, universal, and tenacious, he proclaimed, was an inescapable, if unpalatable, truth. "Whenever phenotypical differences have existed between groups of people," he counseled, "racial prejudice seems to have arisen." [37]

Van den Berghe also lambasted many of the major precepts of Myrdal and his liberal followers. Whereas Myrdal had assumed that "modernization" would eliminate the "cultural lag" that perpetuated the old-style racism, the Harvard-trained sociologist held that the new order only shifted race relations from a paternalistic to a competitive mode. He chided Myrdal for thinking that his explicit declaration of value premises exonerated him from the charge of ideological distortion. In fact, van den Berghe charged, Myrdal's approach constituted a shallow

---

relations reflected the trend toward an international perspective. In 1957 Milton L. Barron's textbook was entitled *American Minorities*. He changed the title to *Minorities in a Changing World* (New York, 1967), and added Part 2, "Minorities in Various Societies." For later studies, see Richard A. Schermerhorn, *Comparative Ethnic Relations: A Framework for Theory and Research* (New York, 1970); Melvin Tumin (ed.), *Comparative Perspectives on Race Relations* (Boston, 1969); Philip Mason, *Patterns of Dominance* (New York, 1970); George M. Fredrickson, *White Supremacy: A Comparative Study in American and South African History* (New York, 1981).

37. Van den Berghe, *Race and Racism*, 4–8, 77–78, 126. See also van den Berghe's article, "Paternalistic Versus Competitive Race Relations: An Ideal-Type Approach," in Norman K. Yetman and C. Hoy Steele (eds.), *Majority and Minority: The Dynamics of Racial and Ethnic Relations* (Boston, 1971), 77.

"kind of exorcism" or "intellectual purification ritual," which the reformist Swede shrewdly used to make his idealistic assumptions about
mankind appear plausible and scientific.[38]

Scholars such as van den Berghe sensed that blunt conclusions about
the race problem did not receive easy acceptance by many Americans.
The 1968 report of the National Advisory Commission on Civil Disorders, popularly known as the Kerner Report, illustrated this point. This
historic presidential commission put the blame for the black ghetto's
formation and its perpetuation squarely on racism of the white community. It warned that the nation was "moving toward two societies, one
black, one white—separate and unequal." (Hard-nosed observers said
this was already the case.) The report advised the public to tax itself for
"a greatly enlarged national action" that would allocate massive resources to bring blacks into the mainstream of American life.[39]

Although the Kerner Commission engaged in a significant amount of
Myrdalian exhortation as well as apocalyptic rhetoric, it utterly failed to
awaken the white conscience of the nation or succeed in getting crucial
support for costly government programs for blacks. Several social scientists praised the report for its candor, but President Johnson turned his
back on his own commission. The racial specialist Norval D. Glenn
judged that politically the Kerner Report proved "largely irrelevant."[40]

In the 1960s race relations experts began to subject Myrdal's dilemma thesis to more vigorous testing. Legions of scholars and activists
had confidently quoted and paraphrased Myrdal's thesis for two decades, but seldom had anyone empirically tested the Swede's impressionistic hypothesis. In 1965, however, Frank Westie published his extensive
testing of Myrdal's thesis. Studying the city of Indianapolis, Westie
found what he considered to be substantial evidence that a strong dilemma about blacks existed in the white mind. But he also conceded that
the most blatant inconsistencies in values went unrecognized by about
half of those polled. Even when whites recognized the contradiction between their democratic professions and their feelings about blacks, they
often introduced a third set of values to rationalize their racial prejudice. So strong were the racist norms in Indianapolis that those who

38. Van den Berghe, *Race and Racism*, 7, 145.
39. U.S. Commission on Civil Disorders, *Report of the National Advisory Commission on Civil Disorders* (New York [Bantam Book ed.], 1968), ix, 1, 10, 410.
40. Norval D. Glenn, "The Kerner Report, Social Scientists, and the American Public," in Norval D. Glenn and Charles M. Bonjeans (eds.), *Blacks in the United States* (San
Francisco, 1969), 516–18.

expressed a willingness to treat blacks according to the American creed went to great lengths to justify their consistency. In other words, those with liberal attitudes toward blacks displayed more guilt in defying racist norms than those who deviated from the democratic creed. A few scholars saw Westie's study as a vindication of Myrdal, but it had actually stood the dilemma thesis on its head and left it all the more tenuous.[41]

A later empirical study of Myrdal's thesis clearly demonstrated its increasing lack of validity. After extensive research on a Virginia city, Scott Cummings and Charles Pinnel concluded that the 1968 followers of the segregationist George Wallace strongly opposed black demands for legal equality *"without having to evoke specific myths and stereotypes about blacks."* The authors showed that whites relied on values of law and order, liberty, and free enterprise to defend white supremacy. Biological racism ceased to be a necessary weapon in the arsenal of white racists. The old clash of values dissipated, but the relationship of the races changed little.[42]

More general studies of white attitudes toward blacks had similar implications for Myrdal's analysis. Rose Helper's study of the real estate business, for instance, found that its practitioners clung to a professional value system that took precedence over the general American creed. There values condoned, indeed demanded, black exclusion on the grounds that integrated housing threatened the white family. In a study of 204 white liberals in California, Judith Caditz found little intellectual discomfort among those who opposed busing, affirmative action, and integrated housing. By various mechanisms of "dissonance reduction," white liberals easily solved value conflicts about blacks in favor of their individual liberty, their family, and pluralism. She pointed out that liberals increasingly allied themselves with "Wallacites, Birchites . . . 'hard hats,' and Governor Reagan and others defined as conservatives with respect to the Civil Rights Movement." Reminiscent of

41. Frank Westie, "The American Dilemma: An Empirical Test," *American Sociological Review,* XXX (1965), 527–38. For comments on the Westie article, see Glenn and Bonjeans (eds.), *Blacks in the United States,* 195; Arnold Rose, "On an Empirical Test of An American Dilemma," *American Sociological Review,* XXXI (1966), 103; Jerome Green, "When Moral Prophecy Fails," *Catalyst,* IV (Spring, 1969), 67.

42. Scott Cummings and Charles Wellford Pinnel III, "Racial Double Standard of Morality in a Small Southern Community: Another Look at Myrdal's An American Dilemma," *Journal of Black Studies,* IX (1978), 67–86. See also Alan W. Wicker, "Attitudes Versus Action: The Relationship of Verbal and Overt Behavioral Responses to Attitude Objectives," *Journal of Social Issues,* XXV (Fall, 1969), 41–78.

Bertram Wyatt-Brown's Old South whites, growing numbers of white liberals, it seemed, evaded troubling moral considerations in racial matters by reverting to a "primal honor" that compelled them to protect the racial integrity of their kin and their neighborhood. F. Scott Fitzgerald once remarked that "the test of a first-rate intelligence is the ability to hold two opposing ideas in the mind at the same time, and still retain the ability to function." [43] By this reasoning, white Americans had become infinitely more intelligent in dealing with their mental dilemmas concerning Afro-Americans.

No one could deny that white racism had diminished by the 1960s, at least in its more overt forms. But numerous studies revealed that racism was still deeply entrenched in American society. After polling extensively in fifteen cities, Angus Campbell surmised that "the white population . . . is far from a general acceptance of the principle and practice of racial equality." In 1970 one study showed that about 70 percent of whites believed that Afro-Americans received just treatment. [44]

Such lingering evidence led many race relations scholars to question the conventional understanding of racism set forth by liberals in Myrdal. New assumptions and new concepts arose to explain the tenacity and nature of racism. Studies in this period, for example, stressed children's early awareness of color. Although most social scientists still took pains to affirm that prejudice was learned, they revealed that children between the ages of three and five expressed definite color preferences. There seemed to be a compulsion for human beings to categorize people so as to simplify the world around them. Unfortunately, categories based on color and certain physical features came effortlessly to the very young. In the context of American society, they all too often blossomed into a racism that permeated the culture. [45]

43. Rose Helper, *Racial Policies and Practices of Real Estate Brokers* (Minneapolis, 1969), 21–22, 276, 301; Judith Caditz, *White Liberals in Transition: Current Dilemmas of Ethnic Integration* (New York, 1976), 135–72; Bertram Wyatt-Brown, *Southern Honor: Ethics and Behavior in the Old South* (New York, 1981), 34, 402–403, 436, and *passim;* F. Scott Fitzgerald, *The Crack Up* (New York, 1959), 69. In addition to Caditz, see David T. Wellman, *Portraits of White Racism* (New York, 1977), for a study that goes beyond statistics.

44. Angus Campbell, *White Attitudes Toward Black People* (Ann Arbor, 1971), 5, 162, and *passim.* Similar evidence can be found in Charles S. Bullock III and Harrel R. Rodgers, Jr., *Racial Equality in America: In Search of an Unfulfilled Goal* (Pacific Palisades, Calif., 1975), 154–61; and Gertrude J. Selznick and Stephen Steinberg, *The Tenacity of Prejudice: Anti-Semitism in Contemporary America* (New York, 1969).

45. Cheryl A. Renninger and John E. Williams, "Black-White Color Connotations

After 1965 Myrdal's critics claimed that the Swede had misled a hopeful generation by focusing too much on the overt bigot whose infidelity to the American creed was obvious and dramatic. Scholars began to deemphasize individual prejudice that sprang from the conventional sources of prejudgment, authoritarianism, and irrationality. Instead they concentrated on institutional racism, or on the structural arrangements that kept blacks subordinate. Scholars, too, sought to show that racism provided real economic, social, and psychological advantages for whites. In 1944 Myrdal stated that "the interest motivation seldom explicitly or consciously enters the ordinary white man's mind." In the 1960s, however, social scientists argued that whites consciously gained from black subordination in the labor market.[46] Psychologists further stressed the psychological sustenance that normal, nonauthoritarian personalities gained from black subordination. Peter Lowenberg maintained that prejudice acted as a form of therapy for whites. It helped them maintain their identity and function better in society. In short, racism was not necessarily (or even usually) aberrant, irrational behavior. As the psychologist Joel Kovel phrased it: "Racism served as a stabilizing function in American culture for many generations. Indeed it was a source of gratification to whites. It defined a social universe, absorbed aggression, and facilitated a sense of virtue in white America— a trait which contributed to America's material success. Racism was an integral part of a stable and productive cultural order."[47]

Viewed in this light, racism was a constant factor, or independent variable, that operated to maintain racial privilege in America. Closer scrutiny of white attitudes showed that the well-educated, middle-class

and Racial Awareness in Pre-School Children," in Goldschmid (ed.), *Black Americans and White Racism*, 311–20; Julius Trubowitz, *Changing the Racial Attitudes of Children: The Effects of an Activity Group Program in New York City Schools* (New York, 1969), vii, 131–32; Henri Taifel, "Cognitive Aspects of Prejudice," *Journal of Social Issues*, XXV (Fall, 1969), 79–97; Introduction to Martin Deutsch, Irwin Katz, and Arthur Jensen (eds.), *Social Class, Race, and Psychological Development* (New York, 1968), 3.

46. Herbert H. Blalock, Jr., *Toward a Theory of Minority Group Relations* (New York, 1970), 132–33; *AD*, 585; L. Paul Metzger, "American Sociology and Black Assimilation: Conflicting Perspectives," *American Journal of Sociology*, LXXVI (1971), 627–47; Norval D. Glenn, "Benefits to Whites from the Subordination of Negroes," *American Sociological Review*, XXVIII (1963), 443–48; Glenn, "White Gains from Negro Subordination," *Social Problems*, XIV (1966), 159–78.

47. Peter Lowenberg, "The Psychology of Racism," in Gary B. Nash and Richard Weiss (eds.), *The Great Fear: Race in the Mind of America* (New York, 1970), 197; Joel Kovel, *White Racism: A Psychohistory* (New York, 1970), 4.

whites who ranked high on tolerance scales opposed black demands just as surely as did lower-class whites. But better-educated whites were more able to verbalize their beliefs in the tenets of the American creed and cover up racism when it existed. As black demands hit closer to home—affirmative action in academia and in management positions, for example—educated whites skillfully repudiated them in the name of liberty, family, property rights, local control, and so on. Racism became so subtle and elusive that only in-depth interviewing of individuals, not simple polls, could expose it.[48]

While behavioral scientists examined the changing nature of racism in the present, historians carefully explored the phenomenon in the past. What they uncovered gave little hope that the solution to the race problem was imminent. In his book *White over Black* (1968), Winthrop D. Jordan traced the origins of American racism back to sixteenth-century England. In contrast to the economic determinists, Jordan argued strongly that a virile racism preceded the institution of slavery in the English colonies. He found scant evidence of a white dilemma in early American history and concluded that after the American Revolution, the leaders of the United States proclaimed the nation a white man's country. Extrapolating his historical findings into the future, Jordan sadly concluded that there was little in the American past to suggest that whites would succeed in solving their most enduring social malady.[49]

As indicated in the previous chapter of this book, Myrdal figured in the revision of American racial history. Jordan, however, charged that historians had relied too heavily on the works of Myrdal, Rose, and Montagu, all of whom had underestimated the extent of racism in the past. The Berkeley historian advised his colleagues to be wary of all social science writings on race done before 1960.[50]

The Pulitzer Prize–winning historian Carl Degler ultimately reached a similar verdict. In his 1959 history of America, Degler cited the *Dilemma* and the works of the Brazilian Gilberto Freyre as evidence that two races could live together in harmony and equality. But subsequent research on slavery and race relations in Brazil and the United States altered his views considerably. In a 1969 article in the New York *Times*,

48. Caditz, *White Liberals in Transition*, 27, 166–72; Wellman, *Portraits of White Racism*, 1–44.

49. Winthrop D. Jordan, *White over Black: American Attitudes Toward the Negro, 1550–1812* (Chapel Hill, 1968), xi–xiii, 581–82. See also Gilbert Osofsky, "The Enduring Ghetto," *Journal of American History*, LV (1968), 243–55.

50. Jordan, *White over Black*, 604, 607, 609.

the Stanford professor reviewed the *Dilemma* on its twenty-fifth anniversary. Citing a number of specifics, Degler branded Myrdal a false
prophet. His major mistake, the historian wrote, was his excessive optimism. Degler's research on Brazil convinced him that racism kept
blacks down there just as it did in America. Brazil's racism, greatly
complicated by class, was more complex and subtle than America's. But
that made it all the harder to combat; and the form of racism prevalent in
Brazil was beginning to predominate in America. Degler concluded that
racism was universal and did not have to be learned, although it could
be. What had to be learned, he advised, was toleration because "observable physical differences between people encourage, or at least provide the basis for, discrimination. When in addition there are also advantages of status or wealth to be derived from discrimination, then it
will occur unless actively countered."[51]

   As Jordan, Degler, and a host of discerning scholars made clear,
nothing fostered racism more than interracial sex. When polled, an increasingly large majority of whites rejected the idea that blacks were
innately inferior, but a large majority also held negative feelings toward
interracial dating, sex, and marriage. A national public opinion study
disclosed that more than 80 percent of whites agreed that "most adults
get upset when they see an interracial couple."[52]

   Myrdal, of course, was not unaware that interracial sex caused white
fear and hostility. The European marveled at the mystical significance
whites attached to "Negro blood," and he judged the fear of amalgamation to be "the most powerful rationalization" for the caste system. But
Myrdal's influential discussion of interracial sex was one-dimensional
and deceptive. He did not explore deeply the "dynamics of interracial
sex" as the historian Jordan did in his suggestive title, *White over
Black*. Nor did he boldly examine the relation of racism and sex as the
black writer Calvin C. Hernton did in 1965, or as the white sociologist
Charles H. Stember did over a decade later in his provocative book,
Sexual Racism. These scholars rightly singled out Myrdal as one of the
most important purveyors of half-truths about interracial sex. Stember
charged that the Swedish economist shied away from any discussion of

51. Carl N. Degler, *Out of Our Past: The Forces That Shaped Modern America*
(New York, 1959), 27–28, 39, 185–86; "The Negro in America—Where Myrdal Went
Wrong," *New York Times Magazine*, December 7, 1969, pp. 64ff.; and *Neither Black nor
White: Slavery and Race Relations in Brazil and the United States* (New York, 1971).
   52. Hazel Erskine, "The Polls: Interracial Socializing," *Public Opinion*, XXXVII
(1973), 283; Joan Down, "Black/White Dating," *Life*, May 28, 1971, pp. 66–67.

blacks that might put them in a bad light or serve the interests of white racists.[53]

Although Myrdal recognized the depths of feeling about interracial sex, he dismissed all white sexual fears of blacks as totally unfounded. He interpreted white attitudes as mere rationalizations to keep blacks down socially and economically. His optimistic rank order of discriminations taught that interracial marriage was of no practical importance to blacks. Even though Myrdal found that the prevention of interracial sex and marriage was paramount to whites, he asserted that, given the real attitudes of blacks, the issue would not be a significant barrier to civil rights progress. The sex issue was to him just a matter of educating whites away from sexual myths. He dutifully exposed the white complex about rape, pointing out that only 23 percent of the blacks lynched had been accused of rape.[54]

When Myrdal devised his hopeful rank order of discriminations, he included both interracial marriage and "sexual intercourse" on the white scale. But when he discussed the black rank order, he curiously referred only to intermarriage, which he assured whites was "of rather distant and doubtful interest" to blacks. Myrdal's avoidance of black attitudes (especially male attitudes) toward casual sex with whites now appears to have been a glaring omission. Recent studies suggest that interracial sex rather than interracial marriage is the key issue for whites. Indeed, white revulsion toward interracial sex on the part of the black man is greater than intermarriage because whites seem to feel that the former gives pleasure without responsibility. Also, when Myrdal wrote that black men preferred light-skinned Afro-American women with Caucasian features, he failed to pursue this revealing line of logic very far.[55] The environmentalist Swede did not consider the possibility that centuries of white racism might have saddled blacks with sexual "hang-ups" just as it had whites.

"Sexual racism" surely was one of the most formidable obstacles to an integrated society. This hardly constituted a new idea. In the early

53. *AD*, 58-59, 100, 108, 562, 591-92; Jordan, *White over Black*, 32-40, 136-78; Calvin C. Hernton, *Sex and Racism* (Garden City, N.Y., 1965), 3-4; Charles H. Stember, *Sexual Racism: The Emotional Barrier to an Integrated Society* (New York, 1978), 11-13.

54. *AD*, 60-64, 561, 563, 591.

55. *Ibid.*, 60-64, 697-99; Stember, *Sexual Racism*, 15; Winthrop D. Jordan, Introduction to Grace Halsell, *Black/White Sex* (New York, 1972), 10; Gary I. Schulman, "Race, Sex, and Violence: A Laboratory Test of the Sexual Threat of the Black Male Hypothesis," *American Journal of Sociology*, LXXIX (1974), 1260-77.

twentieth century, James Weldon Johnson, a black writer and activist, declared that "the heart of the race problem is the sex problem." And hard-core white racists had always considered it so. But Myrdalian liberals of the postwar years tended to avoid the full dimensions of the problem. This was no longer true in the 1960s. Several scholars at the Copenhagen Conference of 1965 maintained that the victims of Western imperialism often adopted the color preference of their oppressors. Conferee C. Eric Lincoln pursued Myrdal's insight that black males preferred the fair-skinned women of their race to say that black men preferred white women. Hiroshi Wagatsuma of Japan demonstrated that the people of his country, which had escaped Western colonization, favored pale skin over darker hues and regarded black people as ugly in appearance. Most scholars nevertheless still seemed reluctant to discuss frankly the sexual aspects of racism, other than to denounce the often condemned white rape complex. The only part of Myrdal's rank order of discriminations virtually to go unchallenged for two decades was the hypothesis that blacks had no desire to cross the color line in sexual matters.[56]

Whatever void Myrdal and liberal scholars left on the sexual question was amply filled by black writers in the 1960s. Unlike the Scandinavian, black militants had little concern for the reaction of the white racist or the white liberal. Post–civil rights blacks discussed feelings long avoided or denied by whites sympathetic to the civil rights movement. In a book entitled *Sex and Racism* in 1965, for instance, the black writer Calvin C. Hernton criticized Myrdal for claiming that black men had no interest in white women. According to Hernton, the truth was that "the Negro man is secretly tormented every second of his wakeful life by the presence of white women in his midst, whom he cannot or had not better touch. Despite the severe penalties for associating with white women—lynching, castration, electrocution—Negroes risk their lives for white flesh, and an occasional few actually commit rape."[57]

Hernton asserted that the Madison Avenue media had completely sexualized American life. Scantily clad white women had become the ubiquitous sex symbol. Consequently, the idealization of the white woman made it impossible for the black man to resist her. Not only did

---

56. Johnson quoted in Stember, *Sexual Racism,* ix; E. Eric Lincoln, "Color and Group Identity in the United States," in Franklin, (ed.), *Color and Race,* 254; Hiroshi Wagatsuma, "The Social Perception of Skin Color in Japan," *ibid.,* 129–65.

57. Hernton, *Sex and Racism,* 3–4.

black men prefer white women, Hernton argued, but the warped racist society caused white men to desire black women, black women to desire white men, and white women to desire black men. All the interracial fantasies and liaisons, he maintained, were greatly complicated by simultaneous feelings of love, hate, and guilt.[58]

Many of Hernton's ideas received support from the writings of noted black militants. Malcolm X, who had once roamed the underworld of crime, recalled how he flaunted his white lover as a status symbol. As a procurer, the black nationalist found that white men sought the blackest possible females as hired lovers. As for black men, "All you had to do," Malcolm X wrote in his autobiography, "was to put a white girl anywhere close to the average black man, and he would respond."[59]

Eldridge Cleaver, the Black Panther leader, revealed in *Soul on Ice* (1968) that he became politicized when a white guard tore down his white pin-up from the wall of his cell. Hatred and shame engulfed Cleaver when he realized that he preferred white women to those of his own race. Out of jail, he resorted to raping white women, "rape on principle" or rape as "insurrectionary act," he called it. Later he used more conventional, if radical, means to fight for black liberation.[60]

The interest of black militants in white women and the guilt (or voyeurism) of numerous liberal white women increased interracial unions. Julius Lester of SNCC described one such affair: "She gloried in my blackness, wearing me like a mink stole. . . . We were emotional cripples using each other as crutches." The phenomenon of "daytime nationalism" and "nighttime integration" became a topic of common discussion in the late 1960s. The nationalist Cecil M. Brown tried to justify "talking black and sleeping white" to angry black females. Brown explained that the black male activist had to "pierce the abstraction of the white women" before he could engage in effective liberation work. Black pride, he pleaded, depended in part on "the conquest of the White Bitch."[61]

Although Martin Luther King, the moderate saint of the movement, was not prone to engage in the fashionable confessional of the period, his biographers could not avoid the subject of sex. The Baptist preacher's hearty sexual appetite and J. Edgar Hoover's surveillance of him made the

58. *Ibid.*, 6, 21, 39, 62, 64–65, 84–85, 95, 151.
59. Little, *Autobiography of Malcolm X*, 67–70, 94–97.
60. Eldridge Cleaver, *Soul on Ice* (New York, 1968), 8, 10, 14.
61. Julius Lester, *All Is Well* (New York, 1976), 91; Brown quoted in Stember, *Sexual Racism*, 110.

topic unavoidable. King's biographers agree that the black leader had an eye for the ladies, especially the ones he classified as "light sisters." It is less known that King fell in love with a white woman while in seminary and was talked out of marriage by friends. The head of the FBI, of course, took great delight in revealing the black minister's extramarital affairs, some of which apparently were interracial.[62]

Although black militants did not condemn interracial love and marriage *per se*, they regretted that a racist society had caused them to succumb to the ideal of white beauty, and they refuted the myth of the hypersexual black man. Some blacks, however, seemed determined to strengthen the myth. In *The Fire Next Time*, James Baldwin depicted America as "an Anglo-Teutonic, anti-sexual country" and described its white inhabitants as having "sexless little voices." Both Baldwin and LeRoi Jones opined that blacks played better jazz than whites because of the Afro-American's superior sexuality. The intellectual historian Ronald Berman suggested that such writers as Baldwin and Jones had trivialized the civil rights movement by basing black culture on genitality.[63]

The point here is not to engage in sexual gossip (or fact). The idea is that the supersexualization of society in the 1960s added to the old racism created an explosive mixture that posed a major stumbling block to racial harmony and progress.[64] Myrdal, like most liberals, tried to skirt the problem. If whites feared blacks sexually as much as research suggests, the revelations by Hernton, Malcolm X, Cleaver, Brown, Baldwin, and others surely must have fortified their reservations about the thrust of the black revolution.

Another development that ran counter to the Myrdalian outlook in this period was the rejuvenation of "scientific racism." Although equalitarian social scientists had routed the biological racists in the 1930s and 1940s, a growing group of scholars challenged the consensus view about race in the 1960s. In a 1967 book on the neoracists, the historian Idus A. Newby warned that there had been "a renascence of scientific racism." The segregationists could present only pathetically weak responses to the equalitarians in the civil rights cases of the 1940s and 1950s, but by

62. Lewis, *King*, 32–33; Oates, *Let the Trumpet Sound*, 16, 29, 265–67, 283–85. See also David J. Garrow, *The FBI and Martin Luther King, Jr.* (New York, 1983).

63. Baldwin, *Fire Next Time*, 44, 56; LeRoi Jones, *Home: Social Essays* (New York, 1966), 221–33; Ronald Berman, *America in the Sixties: An Intellectual History* (New York, 1968), 105–106.

64. Schulman, "Race, Sex, and Violence," 1260–77; and Grier and Cobbs, *Black Rage*.

the 1960s the advocates of massive resistance could draw on a number
of behavioral scientists to support their cause. Those scholars most
often cited by the segregationists were Frank C. J. McGurk, Audrey
Shuey, A. James Gregor, and Wesley C. George. Even the nonracist anthropologist Carleton C. Coon supplied material for white supremacists
with his theory of polygenesis, or multiple creations. With the publication of *Race and Reason* in 1961, Carleton Putnam, a Yankee businessman, became the undisputed popularizer of pseudo-scientific racism in
America.[65]
   Arthur Jensen, however, provided the biggest boost for "scientific
racism" with his 1969 article in the *Harvard Educational Review*. In
this lengthy piece, Jensen, a professor of psychology at the University of
California at Berkeley, a nonsoutherner, and at least a nominal sup-
porter of the civil rights movement, indicted social scientists for conspicuously ignoring the "biological basis of educability." He argued that
the evidence clearly showed that genetics accounted for most of the
fifteen-point difference between the average white and black I.Q.'s.
Challenging the argument that I.Q. tests were culturally loaded against
blacks, he revealed that Afro-Americans scored even lower on nonver-
bal and noncultural tests. Thus he concluded that it was a liberal myth
that the education gap between whites and blacks could be closed by
compensatory programs like Head Start.[66]
   To be sure, most social scientists rejected Jensen's views. Joshua
Lederberg, a recipient of the Nobel Prize in genetics, almost immediately labeled Jensen's research as "premature and sloppy" and declared
that he had done a great disservice to society. But another Nobel Prize
winner, William Shockley, who switched his concentration from phys-
ics to genetics, supported Jensen. The inventor of the transistor claimed
that there was "a difference in the wiring patterns" of black and white
minds. Although the theories of Jensen or Shockley never achieved
great respectability among social scientists, their views were not with-

65. Newby, *Challenge to the Court*, ix; Frank C. J. McGurk, "Scientist's Report on
Race Differences," *U.S. News & World Report*, September 21, 1956, pp. 92–96; Audrey
Shuey, *The Testing of Negro Intelligence* (Lynchburg, Va., 1958); A. James Gregor, "The
Law, Social Science, and School Segregation: An Assessment," *Western Reserve Law
Review*, XIV (1963), 621–36; Wesley C. George, *The Biology of the Race Problem*
([Montgomery, Ala.?], 1962); Carleton C. Coon, *The Origins of the Races* (New York,
1962); Putnam, *Race and Reason*.
   66. Arthur Jensen, "How Much Can We Boost I.Q. and Scholastic Achievement?"
Harvard Educational Review, XXXIX (1969), 81–82.

out impact. In fact, by the 1970s fewer social scientists expressed total certainty on the nature-nurture question, and fewer still claimed that race meant nothing.[67]

The disillusionment about race relations in the late 1960s coincided with broader intellectual currents that had pessimistic implications for society. In 1969 a troubled Ashley Montagu responded to what he perceived as a powerful revival of the concept of original sin. The well-known anthropologist opined that the old idea of the innate depravity of man had been dressed up in modern scientific garb. Montagu, a former Myrdal collaborator, singled out for blame such works as William Golding's *Lord of the Flies*, Konrad Lorenz's *On Aggression*, Robert Ardrey's *African Genesis* and *The Territorial Imperative*, and Desmond Morris' *The Naked Ape*. He reported that these authors falsely traced man's aggressiveness to instincts inherited from lower animals; none, he added, held out much hope for taming man's animal nature. Montagu theorized that such books were popular because they absolved erring mankind from responsibility and guilt. By implication, racism could be explained away as a part of man's nature. Not surprisingly, in the January, 1969, issue of the *Journal of Social Issues*, two articles dealt with the "sociology of evil." [68]

Blacks and white liberals no doubt found it easier to contemplate evil with the inauguration of Richard M. Nixon as president in 1969. Nixon openly revived the old "southern strategy" of the Republican party, which aimed at luring southern segregationists away from the Democratic fold (and from the third-party candidate, George Wallace). In the North the Republican candidate exploited the white backlash with a "law and order" campaign, and he took broad swipes at the Kerner Report for blaming racial unrest and poverty on white racism. In 1969 Daniel Moynihan, one of the president's few liberal advisers (although greatly distrusted by blacks), acknowledged that "the winds of [Arthur] Jensen" were blowing through the White House. The Civil Rights Com-

67. Joshua Lederberg and other equalitarians answered Jensen in the *Harvard Educational Review*, XXXIX (Spring, 1969); Shockley quoted in John Neary, "A Scientist's Variation on a Disturbing Theme," *Life*, June 12, 1970, pp. 58–65; Newby, *Challenge to the Court*, 138; Jordan, *White over Black*, 609; Blalock, *Toward a Theory of Minority-Group Relations*, 111.

68. Ashley Montagu, "'Original Sin' Redivivus," *Journal of Historical Studies*, II (1969), 132–33, 145–46; Lewis A. Coser, "The Visibility of Evil," *Journal of Social Issues*, XXV (January, 1969), 101–109; Kurt H. Wolff, "For a Sociology of Evil," *ibid.*, 111–25.

mission's first report on the Nixon administration charged that black
rights risked nullification through lack of enforcement. According to
Whitney Young, the chief executive faced "a credibility gap of enormous proportions."[69]

And, after 1965, so did Myrdal's study. In the late 1960s publication
after publication cataloged the alleged errors of the *Dilemma*. A legion
of critics branded the Swede an all-too-powerful false prophet. For
many, Myrdal's book symbolized a quarter century of liberal nostrums,
which consisted of "pious ideology, pious sociology, pious government,
pious goodwill and intentions." One social scientist hailed black studies
as "a response to the bankruptcy of the 'American Dilemma' view of
black-white relations." John Horton brusquely assigned Myrdal to a
school of sociology he labeled "consensual liberalism." This school, he
wrote, laced its sociology with middle-class, liberal values, and it mistook highly impressionistic concepts like "moral dilemma" for objective facts. Horton asserted that the dilemma thesis was an untested fan-
tasy, which perhaps made good politics but poor sociology.[70]

In 1969 Jerome Green assaulted the Swede with a stridency hardly
matched since the philippics aimed at Myrdal by the Marxists Herbert
Aptheker and Oliver Cox in the 1940s. Contesting Myrdal's thesis at
every point, Green proclaimed that guilt feelings had never once in history induced the "haves" to share their loot with the "have-nots." Obviously irritated by the thought that the European economist still had
some stature, Green lamented that Myrdal still strutted about in various
American forums wearing the mantle of a prophet—apparently oblivious to Watts, Detroit, and the persistence of white racism. To him,
Myrdal had initiated a "climate of moral prophecy," which had emascu-
lated the sociological imagination since World War II.[71]

Unlike the prophecy of Myrdal, the forecasts of several scholars in
the late 1960s resembled jeremiads. In an age when many intellectuals

69. Meier and Rudwick, *From Plantation to Ghetto,* 295–97; "A Whig in the White
House: Daniel P. Moynihan," *Time,* March 16, 1970, pp. 26–27; Moynihan quoted in
Neary, "A Scientist's Variation on a Disturbing Theme," 58D; U.S. Commission on Civil
Rights, *Federal Civil Rights Enforcement* (1970), 209, 980–83, 1070, 1089, 1094; Young
quoted in "Northern-Southern Strategy," *Time,* August 3, 1970, p. 7.

70. Truman Nelson, *The Right to Revolution* (Boston, 1968), 107; Wilson Record,
"Response of Sociologists to Black Studies," in Blackwell and Janowitz (eds.), *Black Sociologists,* 372; John Horton, "Order and Conflict Theories of Social Problems as Competing Ideologies," *American Journal of Sociology,* LXXI (1966), 701–13.

71. Green, "When Moral Prophecy Fails," 63–78.

seemed to lust for the apocalypse, two authors posed especially chilling questions in their studies of black-white relations. In his book *The Impossible Revolution?* Lewis Killian approached a mood of almost total despair. He feared that if whites could not respond compassionately to Martin Luther King's moderate movement, the country could not cope with the increasingly radicalized black movement without resorting to a police state. Given the black mood, the sociologist believed it possible that Afro-Americans might opt for violent revolution; but if they did, he believed that outgunned blacks would suffer disaster.[72]

Similarly, Sidney M. Wilhelm suggested the possibility of genocide in *Who Needs the Negro?* Wilhelm reasoned that since whites no longer needed blacks economically, they could afford to vent their racism more fully. He drew an analogy between red-white relations in the past and black-white relations in the present. Whites, Wilhelm asserted, would try to confine superfluous blacks to the ghetto reservations. Or they might madden slum dwellers into armed resistance and slaughter them, just as they had decimated the economically useless Indians.[73]

Not all, it should be stressed, abandoned hope in the Myrdal model of race relations. The esteemed Harvard sociologists Talcott Parsons and Thomas F. Pettigrew, for example, held to the optimistic tradition. In the special session on Myrdal at the Southern Historical Association in 1969, Elliott Rudwick vigorously defended Myrdal against the historians Carl Degler and John Bracey, who also participated in the session. Rudwick, a sociologist, scolded the Swede's critics for tearing his ideas and statements out of a complex and comprehensive context. He pointed out that Martin Luther King's crusade, which ironically thrived on conflict, had based its successful strategy on the American dilemma thesis. Rudwick maintained that if white Americans did not take the American creed seriously, black militants would be in concentration camps. After the urban riots, however, the kindest words for Myrdal usually came not from liberals such as Rudwick but from exuberant American boosters of the "neoconservative" stripe.[74]

---

72. Lewis M. Killian, *The Impossible Revolution? Black Power and the American Dream* (New York, 1968). In *The Urban Guerrilla* (Chicago, 1969), Martin Oppenheimer, a white Marxist, pleads with blacks not to start the revolution prematurely.

73. Sidney M. Wilhelm, *Who Needs the Negro?* (Cambridge, Mass., 1970).

74. Thomas F. Pettigrew, *Racially Separate or Together?* (New York, 1971), 113, 118; "Race Relations in the United States: A Sociological Perspective," in Talcott Parsons (ed.), *American Sociology: Perspectives, Problems, Methods* (New York, 1968), 258–71; Elliott Rudwick, "American Values and Social Change: How Right Was Gunnar Myrdal?"

In sum, after Watts, racial analysts embraced the conflict model of race relations in droves.[75] Gone from the vocabulary of the race specialist were such concepts as "brothers under the skin," or "people want to be rational and good." In chorus, social scientists proclaimed that white racism reflected basic values in American culture. About the future of race relations, academicians displayed less certainty. It was evident to them that the civil rights movement had raised black expectations far beyond white America's willingness to fulfill them. Some therefore foresaw the continuation of large-scale violence or even revolution. Others, however, conjectured that most blacks would remain committed to the American system. But even those who predicted peaceful racial progress predicated their forecasts on massive compensatory programs and far-reaching institutional changes designed to lift blacks rapidly into the mainstream of American life. These prerequisites, however, failed to materialize because of the economic stagnation and the conservative resurgence in the 1970s and 1980s. By then, the American dilemma defined by Myrdal had all but vanished, but the race problem persisted.

---

paper presented at the annual meeting of the Southern Historical Association, Washington, D.C., November 1, 1969. For conservatives' use of Myrdal, see Edward C. Banfield, *The Unheavenly City: The Nature and Future of Our Urban Crisis* (Boston, 1970), 258–59; Nathan Glazer, "The Negro's Stake in the American Future," in Raymond Mack (ed.), *Prejudice and Race Relations* (Chicago, 1970), 241.

75. Horton, "Order and Conflict Theories," 712–13; Blalock, *Toward a Theory of Minority-Group Relations,* 48, 109–42, 204–21; Joseph S. Himes, "The Functions of Racial Conflict," *Social Forces,* XLV (1966), 1–10; Schermerhorn, *Comparative Ethnic Relations,* xi–xii; Roger Daniels and Harry H. L. Kitano, *American Racism: Exploration of the Nature of Prejudice* (Englewood Cliffs, N.J., 1970), 124.

XI

The *Dilemma* and Black-White Relations After Forty Years Plus: Some Reflections

In a century so taken by the deterministic theories of Darwin, Marx, and Freud, and a host of others more ancient and recent, one could easily slight the power of ideas and values to alter history. Myrdal's study serves as a reminder that ideas and values do play a part in the process of social change. They can and do shape external reality, especially in the matter of color.

The amazing success of the *Dilemma* depended on many factors. One can hardly overemphasize the exquisite timing of the book. Had it come a decade earlier, the country would not have been primed for its message. Had it been undertaken in the age of McCarthyism, the Carnegie Corporation probably would have bypassed the left-leaning Swedish economist. Had it appeared in the black power era, it would have proved as ineffectual in promoting racial change as the Moynihan and Kerner reports.

Much of *Dilemma*'s appeal came from Myrdal's ability to dress the American creed in "scientific garb." The Scandinavian wrapped his version of "science" in the American flag and Judaeo-Christian values. With Henry R. Luce, he proclaimed the "American Century" at a time when Americans were reveling in a wave of exultant nationalism.[1] Indeed, sometimes Myrdal's message seemed as much aimed at the Soviet challenge as at race relations. Equally important, he pointed out a "middle way" of racial reform that appealed to centrist American liber-

---

1. August Meier, "Review Essay/Whither the Black Perspective on Afro-American Historiography?" *Journal of American History*, LXX (1983), 104; Henry R. Luce, *The American Century* (New York, 1941).

als. Taking George Bernard Shaw's advice, the European economist tried to reach Americans through their religion. In straining the multi-tudinous racial facts through the American ethos, Myrdal created a classic synthesis and an environmental paradigm that, for good or ill, dominated liberal thinking on the race issue after World War II.

In his brilliant work on scientific revolutions, Thomas Kuhn pointed out that young thinkers were more inclined to ignore controlling paradigms or models and create new ones, especially if they were new to the field.[2] On both accounts, Myrdal came eminently equipped to forge a new vision of race relations. Not yet forty when the Carnegie project began, he knew next to nothing about blacks.

Frederick Keppel's choice of Myrdal was a stroke of genius. Even those who resented or disliked the foreigner agreed that no other scholar they knew could have produced such a utilitarian work under the circumstances. Keppel understood that Americans valued imported critics over native products. C. Vann Woodward vouched that southern intellectuals paid more attention to Myrdal because he was not a Yankee.[3] In short, in the late 1930s the right man and the right situation converged, and race relations in America entered a period of unprecedented change. As with most great works (and great people), the *Dilemma* was both cause and effect. The times shaped the book, and the book helped shape history. The study not only described a "dilemma" but helped create or strengthen one in the minds of many leading Americans. Myrdal's role in race relations might be likened to that of George F. Kennan in foreign policy. A major architect of America's Cold War strategy, Kennan intellectualized the containment doctrine in his famous long telegram from Moscow in 1946 (and publicly in his "X" article in *Foreign Affairs* a year later). In truth, Kennan only supplied a scholarly blueprint for what the Truman administration was already practicing by dead reckoning. Similarly, the long tome via Stockholm provided a compelling framework for civil rights advocates, policy makers, and opinion molders for nearly a quarter of a century in the battle for black rights that was already under way by World War II.[4] But Kennan, the foreign policy real-

2. Kuhn, *Structure of Scientific Revolutions*, 89.
3. Guion Johnson, COHP, 64–66; Charles Dollard, COHP, 87, 325; Guy Johnson, COHP, 27; Frederick Osborn, COHP, 1, 54–55; record of conversation, Frederick Keppel and E. L. Thorndike, May 29, 1939, Negro Study, roll 1; C. Vann Woodward to the author, August 12, 1984.
4. On George Kennan's impact, see John Lewis Gaddis, *Strategies of Containment: A Critical Appraisal of Postwar American National Security Policy* (New York, 1982),

ist, ventured only a prescription for containing a palpable evil, whereas Myrdal designed a plan to roll back the iron curtain of racism, and with all possible speed.

As events unfolded in the late 1940s and ensured Kennan's reputation, the changes in race relations between the war and 1965 caused social analysts to hail Myrdal as a prophet. In his 1964 paperback condensation of the *Dilemma*, Arnold Rose marveled at the accumulated changes in race relations since 1944—all of which, he boasted, were in line with the Swede's prognosis. Myrdal's chief collaborator and subsequent booster predicted even swifter changes in the future. The caste system and racism had been so debilitated, Rose proclaimed, that even informal segregation and discrimination would be a "mere shadow" in twenty years.[5] The march of events from 1965 to 1969, however, cast a pall over Rose's forecast and the Myrdalian outlook in general. By the end of the 1960s many wondered how the Swedish economist could have been so naïve.

Time would inevitably reveal a host of faulty assumptions and erroneous extrapolations in a book as vast and daring as the *Dilemma*. Many of these miscalculations could have been prevented or mitigated had Myrdal not succumbed to what his critics rightly considered his gravest fault: excessive optimism. The European scholar greatly underestimated the tenacity of American racism, and he missed the tragic aspect of the race problem that lay beyond legal equality. A better appreciation of history would have improved Myrdal's analysis. Unfortunately, the racial history available to Myrdal in the late 1930s was limited. Since the 1960s the works of historians such as Leon F. Litwack, Thomas F. Gossett, Rayford W. Logan, John Hope Franklin, Winthrop D. Jordan, George M. Fredrickson, Idus A. Newby, Ronald T. Takaki, and Joel Williamson—and many others too numerous to mention—have demonstrated the lurid depths of racism in the American past, in the North as well as the South.[6] Such works cautioned against the optimism expressed by Myrdal, for they recognized the old evil of racism in contemporary guises.

35–53; John H. Stanfield, "Race Relations Research and Black Americans Between the Two World Wars," *Journal of Ethnic Studies*, XI (Fall, 1983), 61, 80–81.

    5. Arnold Rose, *The Negro in America* (New York, 1964), xxxiii.

    6. Leon F. Litwack, *North of Slavery: The Negro in the Free States, 1790–1860* (Chicago, 1961); Thomas F. Gossett, *Race: The History of an Idea* (Dallas, 1963); Rayford W. Logan, *The Betrayal of the Negro: From Rutherford B. Hayes to Woodrow Wilson* (New York, 1965); John Hope Franklin, *Reconstruction After the Civil War* (Chicago, 1961); Jordan, *White over Black;* Fredrickson, *The Black Image in the White Mind;* Idus A.

Having dealt with a stupefying amount of material written on race relations since 1969—only a hint of which can be given in the bibliography—I am tempted to comment on it; but that would take another book. Besides, one quickly realizes how difficult it is to sustain an even-handed, historical demeanor in dealing with recent publications, many of them highly controversial and contentious. It is enough to say here that the writings of social scientists and others have rendered many of the hypotheses of the *Dilemma* tenuous.

In the past fifteen years many social scientists have talked more frequently in tones reminiscent of the pre-Myrdalian concept of "consciousness of kind." In his study *Slavery and Race Relations in the Americas* (1973), Harmannus Hoetink argued that "every multiracial society was racist in the sense that in its mechanism of social selection and mobility a general preference is shown for individuals who more than others correspond to the social definition of race that the dominant group applies to itself." Many social scientists have suggested that race has a life of its own, that it takes on a character that is seemingly primordial, metaphysical, or transhistorical. Joel Kovel's 1984 update of his thought-provoking *White Racism* maintained that "metaracism" has replaced the older "aversive racism." Metaracism originated in the "late-capitalistic society" and was subtle, complex, and systemic.[7]

Many social scientists doubted that conventional polls—which have shown an ever-decreasing belief in biological racism—could accurately gauge complex and changing racial feelings. By the late 1970s, however, the interpreters of polls were producing eminently more sophisticated and realistic analyses of prejudice than had the optimistic Myrdalians of the 1950s and 1960s. A recent study of attitudinal polls over the past forty years by Howard Schuman and associates reveals that despite steady progress toward the acceptance of equalitarian principles by whites, underlying racism thrives. They found that the belief in the abstract value of equality clearly is not matched by support for relevant forms of implementation. Ambivalent whites apparently prefer a society that practices "something in between" segregation and integration.

Newby, *Jim Crow's Defense: Anti-Negro Thought in America, 1900–1930* (Baton Rouge, 1965); Ronald T. Takaki, *Iron Cages: Race and Culture in Nineteenth-Century America* (New York, 1979); Joel Williamson, *The Crucible of Race: Black-White Relations in the American South Since Emancipation* (New York, 1984).

7. Harmannus Hoetink, *Slavery and Race Relations in the Americas: Comparative Notes on Their Nature and Nexus* (New York, 1973), 170 and *passim;* Kovel, *White Racism,* ix–xi.

"America," Schuman and his colleagues conclude, "is not much more color-blind today than it ever was." In-depth interviews of whites by such scholars as Judith Caditz and David T. Wellman tended to support the analysis of the poll watchers. And those who have focused on interracial sex have been particularly persuasive in demonstrating the continued importance of skin color in America. A 1985 Roper Poll, for example, showed that 75 percent of American women would accept an interreligious marriage by their daughter but only 23 percent would tolerate an interracial union. Indeed, on the question of race and intermarriage, arguably the acid test of egalitarian principles, white attitudes have remained virtually unchanged for a decade.[8]

Given racism's complex and gut-wrenching nature, it is not surprising that the phenomenon provokes disagreements about its meaning. To Myrdal in the 1940s, racism meant white belief in the genetic inferiority of blacks. In the 1960s several analysts, especially black nationalists, expanded the definition to include what they considered invidious comparisons between black and white culture, a tendency that prompted some commentators to brand as racist such environmentalists as Myrdal and Daniel Moynihan. More recently, David O. Sears and others have postulated that old-fashioned racism has been replaced by a more elusive kind of racism, one they call "symbolic racism." This racism manifests itself in fierce opposition to such policies as busing and affirmative action. These scholars maintain that whites respond negatively to such policies less from concrete self-interest than from gossamer predispositions acquired in early life. These early inclinations involve racial imagery that evokes moralistic resentment toward blacks, resulting in white perceptions that the minority violates such basic American values as "self-reliance, the work ethic, obedience, and discipline." If this is true, the American creed now serves essentially as a white device to rationalize the inferior position of the black minority in American society. More extreme analysts such as Wellman tend to classify as racist anyone, even the nonprejudiced, who supports a system of governance that does not propel blacks toward equality of condition.[9] Many racists, no doubt, are

8. Schuman, Steeh, and Bobo, *Racial Attitudes in America,* 5–6, 84, 176–79, 194–95, 201; Caditz, *White Liberals in Transition;* Wellman, *Portraits of White Racism;* the Roper poll is in "Women Ease Views on Sex," St. Louis *Post-Dispatch,* October 20, 1985. On interracial sex, see Stember, *Sexual Racism;* Grace Halsell, Introduction by Winthrop D. Jordan, *Black/White Sex* (New York, 1972); and Shulman, "Race, Sex, and Violence."

9. Bracey, *"An American Dilemma,"* 5; Rainwater and Yancey (eds.), *Moynihan Re-*

fairly indicted in this sweeping definition of racism, but such a view un-
fairly brands as bigots too many politically conservative but nonracist
people, black and white alike.

Nevertheless, just because racism cannot be defined or measured precisely (or because every person cannot be judged innocent or guilty of it
beyond a reasonable doubt) is no reason for denying its crucial bearing
on black-white relations. The sociologist Alvin W. Gouldner exclaimed
that whites do not just *"believe"* that blacks are lazy and bad, they *"feel"*
it, and feel it strongly. These feelings, he stated, "entail a hormone-
eliciting, muscle-tensing, tissue-embedded, fight-or-flight disposition
of the total organism." Myrdal had said as much in the *Dilemma: "The
'reality' of his* [the Negro's] *inferiority is the white man's own indubitable sensing of it, and that feeling applies to every single Negro."* [10] But
the Swede did not dwell on this social dynamic, and, unlike many current scholars, he believed that visceral antiblack feelings could be eradicated through social engineering.

Many, however, have challenged the idea that white racism is "primordial" or "transhistorical" and have even suggested that such views
help perpetuate racism. Marxists have always dismissed race as "false
consciousness," and many non-Marxists still stress class as the major
fault line in human affairs. In his 1978 book *The Declining Significance
of Race,* William J. Wilson argued this increasingly popular view. But
several scholars took strong exception to Wilson's thesis. The Association of Black Sociologists condemned it. In their comparative studies of
South Africa and the American South, John W. Cell and Stanley B.
Greenberg claimed that color had been and still remained the major
source of black oppression. According to Hoetink: "The conviction . . .
that prejudice and racism within a multiracial society are closely related to a specific socio-economic structure is not based on plausible
evidence." [11]

port, 216–45; David O. Sears, Carl P. Hensler, and Leslie K. Speer, "Whites' Opposition
to 'Busing': Self-Interest of Symbolic Politics?" *American Political Science Review,*
LXXIII (1979), 370–71, 379–82; Donald R. Kinder and David O. Sears, "Prejudice and
Politics: Symbolic Racism Versus Racial Threats to the Good Life," *Journal of Personality
and Social Psychology,* XL (1981), 416; Wellman, *Portraits of White Racism,* 31–37,
216–20, 234–36.

    10. Gouldner, *Coming Crisis in Western Sociology,* 37; *AD,* 100.

    11. Barbara J. Fields, "Ideology and Race in American History," in J. Morgan
Kousser and James M. McPherson (eds.), *Region, Race, and Reconstruction* (New York,
1982), 144, 151, 168; William J. Wilson, *The Declining Significance of Race: Blacks and*

Those on the left who hope for a class revolution or significant structural changes in American society seem more utopian than did Myrdal in the 1940s. Class cleavages in America may have widened in both the black and white communities, but no evidence of a reform coalition along class lines exists. In his insightful analysis of the conservative resurgence in America, *The New Politics of Inequality* (1984), Thomas Byrne Edsall documented growing class conflict, but he offered no solace for needy blacks. The shift in power, he revealed, was toward the wealthy. The left was nonexistent, he concluded, and the center was in disarray. Only the right was coherent.[12]

Black nationalism faded ingloriously in the 1970s. Nationalism had represented an understandable reaction to white insensitivity and intransigence and also gave many whites a rationalization to go slow on integration ("They really do want to stay with their kind"). When militant blacks began to emphasize what divided people rather than what united them, they lost what Myrdal saw as their best weapon: the moral edge. Black ethnicity, moreover, generated a white ethnic revival or "New Pluralism," which white groups used to protect their neighborhoods and their psyches from outsiders. Myrdal had warned about "romantic ethnicity" in the *Dilemma,* and he and others condemned it in the 1970s. They argued that ethnic politics equaled conservatism. Black ethnicity, a product of coping with an oppressive history and sometimes one of free choice, created what one author refers to as "black styles," behavior that fosters misunderstanding, resentment, fear, and hatred among the white majority.[13]

Changing American Institutions (Chicago, 1978); Cell, *Highest Stage of White Supremacy,* 14–20, 171–91; Stanley B. Greenberg, *Race and State in Capitalist Development: Comparative Perspectives* (New Haven, 1980), 242, 385, 394–95; Hoetink, *Slavery and Race,* 193. For a complex, eclectic analysis of racism, see Robert Blauner, *Racial Oppression in America* (New York, 1972).

12. Thomas Byrne Edsall, *The New Politics of Inequality* (New York, 1984).

13. For the rise of white ethnicity, see Andrew M. Greely, *Why Can't They Be Like Us? American White Ethnic Groups* (New York, 1971); William K. Newman, *American Pluralism: A Study of Minority Groups and Social Theory* (New York, 1973); Michael Novak, *The Rise of the Unmeltable Ethnics: Politics and Culture in the Seventies* (New York, 1971). For attacks on what some call "defensive pluralism," see Gunnar Myrdal, "The Case Against Romantic Ethnicity," *Center Magazine,* VII (July–August, 1974), 26–30; Howard F. Stein and Robert F. Hill, *The Ethnic Imperative: Examining the New White Ethnic Movement* (University Park, Pa., 1977); Orlando Patterson, *Ethnic Chauvinism: The Reactionary Impulse* (New York, 1977). On black and white "styles," see Thomas Kochman, *Black and White Styles in Conflict* (Chicago, 1981).

In the 1970s many erstwhile black nationalists drifted into the academic world of empiricism, often opting for a respectable neo-Marxism. Conversely, some abandoned Marxism for the black mystique. Most blacks, however, including former Black Panthers such as Huey Newton and Eldridge Cleaver, practiced conventional politics. Some blacks who had once been optimistic grew despondent. In 1973 E. Frederic Morrow, a black aide to President Dwight D. Eisenhower in the 1950s, wrote that he was glad his parents had died before they realized that their children would not overcome. He now believed that it was impossible for a black male to be accepted as a "complete man" in American society. These changes in black strategies, tactics, and moods played into the hands of the white opposition, who demanded that their victims be consistent. In 1944 Myrdal discussed the black propensity for ideological and tactical flip-flops as follows: "*Negroes seem to be held in a state of eternal preparedness for a great number of contradictory opinions—* ready to accept one type [of ideas] or another depending upon how they are driven by pressures or where they see an opportunity." [14]

To be sure, the situation in the 1970s and 1980s posed wrenching dilemmas for the black movement. Blacks almost unanimously supported the Democratic party, which suffered bruising national defeats in 1972, 1980, and 1984. Many of the policies that black leaders deemed necessary for progress elicited indifference or angry opposition from whites. Former white activists now divided on the issues of busing, affirmative action, and foreign policy. The conflict between blacks and Jews hastened the end of the civil rights coalition. [15]

In this period the divisions within the black community also became more pronounced, and individuals became more ambiguous about policy. Charles V. Hamilton, the philosopher of black power in the 1960s,

14. Meier, "Review Essay," 105; Thomas L. Blair, *Retreat to the Ghetto: The End of a Dream?* (New York, 1977), 152–62; E. Frederic Morrow, *Way Down South Up North* (Philadelphia, 1973), 120–22; *AD,* 782.

15. Nat Hentoff (ed.), *Black Anti-Semitism and Jewish Racism* (New York, 1969). On the busing and affirmative action controversies, see Raymond Wolters, *The Burden of Brown: Thirty Years of School Desegregation* (Knoxville, 1984); Jennifer L. Hochschild, *The New American Dilemma: Liberal Democracy and School Desegregation* (New Haven, 1984); Richard A. Pride and J. David Woodard, *The Burden of Busing: The Politics of Desegregation in Nashville, Tennessee* (Knoxville, 1985); Nathan Glazer, *Affirmative Discrimination* (New York, 1974); Charles Murray, "Affirmative Racism," *New Republic,* December 31, 1984, pp. 18–23; Douglas B. Huron, "But Government Can Help: Sometimes Racial Quotas Are Justified," Washington *Post,* August 12, 1984, Sec. B, p. 1.

would later say of affirmative action: "It's a dilemma. I don't know quite how to deal with it." With the change to a conservative administration in 1981, blacks on the right found more outlets for their views. Black scholars such as Thomas Sowell, a prolific writer and an intellectual soul brother of Milton Friedman, and Glenn C. Loury, a professor of public policy at the John F. Kennedy School of Government at Harvard, advocated self-help policies and denounced preferential treatment of blacks. Clarence Pendleton, Jr., President Ronald Reagan's appointee to head the Civil Rights Commission, branded established liberal black leaders as the "new racists."[16]

Still, most black leaders continue to call for busing to integrate schools and affirmative action in various forms. In 1983 thirty-two main-line black leaders met at Tarrytown, New York, for a policy session. The group emphasized the decline of the civil rights movement, white racism, black unemployment, and the state of the black family. These black leaders criticized the federal government for not doing enough to advance Afro-Americans into the mainstream of American life.[17]

The emphasis on the problem of the black family at Tarrytown was ironic. As the black columnist William Raspberry reported, for nearly twenty years the breakdown of the black family was an "unmentionable." In the 1980s, however, Raspberry pointed out that minority leaders seemed to talk of little else. In 1984 a joint meeting of the NAACP and the National Urban League concluded that the "tangle of pathology," which Moynihan had discovered two decades earlier, had worsened. When Moynihan issued his controversial report in 1965, the number of female-headed black families barely topped 20 percent. In 1984 the figure had soared to 47 percent. And the rate of illegitimacy had risen from 38 to 55 percent, with almost 40 percent of the babies being born to teenage mothers.[18]

16. "Redefining the American Dilemma," *Time*, November 11, 1985, pp. 33–36; Hamilton quoted in Ken Auletta, *The Underclass* (New York, 1982), 314; Thomas Sowell, *Race and Economics* (New York, 1975); Sowell, "Black Progress Can't Be Legislated," Washington *Post*, August 12, 1984, Sec. B, p. 1; Glenn C. Loury, "A New American Dilemma," *New Republic*, December 31, 1984, pp. 14–18; William Raspberry, "Pendleton Spoiler in Fight for Rights," St. Louis *Post-Dispatch*, March 3, 1985. For another conservative black view, see Walter E. Williams, *The State Against Blacks* (New York, 1982).

17. Joint Center for Political Studies, *A Policy Framework for Racial Justice* (Washington, 1983), 1–13.

18. William Raspberry, "Blacks Confront Family Breakdown," St. Louis *Post-Dispatch*, February 9, 1984; Ann Hulbert, "Children as Parents," *New Republic*, September 10, 1984, pp. 15–23; Loury, "New American Dilemma," 14.

In the 1960s militant black writers were so enthusiastic about black culture that they tended to celebrate the extended lower-class black family as adaptive, utilitarian, and loving. The mere recitation of negative data about the ghetto family by white scholars was enough to provoke a verbal storm in the black community. By the 1980s, however, John Jacob of the National Urban League advised blacks to abandon their knee-jerk defensiveness and begin a constructive dialogue on the catastrophe of the family. Glenn C. Loury, a more conservative black spokesman, held that the plight of the black underclass family could no longer be attributed mainly to white racism. Not surprisingly, in 1986 Loury appeared as a commentator on Bill Moyers' dramatic and well-received television production "The Vanishing Family—Crisis in Black America." [19]

When Senator Moynihan delivered the Godkin Lectures at Harvard University in 1985, he could relate family structure to poverty and other social pathologies without fear of retribution. The so-called "feminization of poverty" and the increasing postindustrial problems of the white family took much of the racial edge off Moynihan's updating of the statistical black family. But time had also blunted the New Yorker's Myrdalian faith in social engineering. "It is neither possible nor desirable," the senator warned, "to attempt to construct a family policy on the basis of presumed social science knowledge. Far too little is known, or perhaps knowable." [20]

Ironically, in the past two decades the conservatives and neoconservatives have often expressed the highest regard for Myrdal's optimism. In a 1973 article in *Commentary*, Ben J. Wattenberg and Richard M. Scammon stridently denounced the liberal prophets of gloom and doom, arguing that the 1960s had brought great gains for blacks. They claimed that 52 percent of Afro-Americans had entered the middle class. Hungering for good news after the Vietnam War and the Watergate scandals, Americans seized upon the article. *Time* used it as a basis for proclaiming the rise of the black middle class. [21]

19. Hulbert, "Children as Parents," 16, 23; Loury, "New American Dilemma," 14; "The Vanishing Family—Crisis in Black America," television documentary, Columbia Broadcasting System, January 25, 1986.

20. "Moynihan, I Told You So," *Newsweek*, April 22, 1985, p. 30; Daniel P. Moynihan, "Family and Nation," Godkin Lectures, April 8–9, 1985, pp. i, 8–10, 23–28, copy in possession of author.

21. Ben J. Wattenberg and Richard Scammon, "Black Progress and Liberal Rhetoric," *Commentary*, LV (April, 1973), 35–43; "Decade of Progress," *Time*, April 16, 1973, pp. 16–17; "America's Rising Black Middle Class," *Time*, June 17, 1974, pp. 19–28. Wattenberg continues to spread optimism in *The Good News Is That Bad News Is Wrong* (New York, 1984).

The Wattenberg-Scammon article also noted, but did not stress, the increase in broken black homes, the surge of blacks onto the welfare rolls, and the spiraling incidence of crime and illegitimacy. In the 1960s educated and skilled blacks did advance promisingly toward parity with whites. But a large minority of blacks did not achieve adequate education or skills, and several recessions and a generally stagnant economy after 1972 battered the Wattenberg-Scammon thesis, which scholars such as Alphonso Pinkney charge was exaggerated in the first place. Pinkney additionally claimed that neoconservatives such as Wattenberg and Scammon had a compulsion to prove the racial progressivity of America.[22]

In any event, numerous studies show that economic trends since 1970 have wiped out several of the black gains. Black unemployment soared above 10 percent, more than doubling that of whites. In *Twenty Years After Brown*, the United States Commission on Civil Rights reported that one-half of black Americans were falling further behind whites. In 1975 a massive study financed by the Ford Foundation concluded: "Blacks are worse off because the cards have been, and remain stacked against them." Arguing before the Supreme Court in the *Bakke* case, Archibald Cox pleaded that "no racially blind" admission policy would enroll "more than a trickle of minority students in the nation's . . . professions." All the while, social scientists gathered mountains of data on the burgeoning black underclass. The Reagan administration, however, tended to view blacks as lagging economic indicators. When in December, 1985, a White House spokesman rejoiced that the unemployment rate had fallen to 7 percent, the lowest in the Reagan presidency, he neglected to point out that joblessness for blacks had increased by 0.9 percent to 15.9 percent. For black teenagers the unemployment rate had risen 5 percent to 46.1 percent. Figures such as these prompted the *Crisis* to devote its March, 1986, issue to answering the question, "Black Males in Jeopardy?" A series of sobering articles answered affirmatively.[23]

22. Alphonso Pinkney, *The Myth of Black Progress* (New York, 1984), 11–17, 46–57.

23. U.S. Commission on Civil Rights, *Twenty Years After Brown: Equality of Economic Condition* (1975), 76; Sar A. Levitan, William B. Johnston, and Robert Teggart, *Still a Dream: The Changing Status of Blacks Since 1960* (Cambridge, Mass., 1975), 267; Archibald Cox quoted in New York *Times*, October 13, 1977, p. 30; Auletta, *Underclass;* Douglas G. Glasgow, *The Black Underclass: Poverty, Unemployment and Entrapment of Ghetto Youth* (New York, 1982); "Unemployment Rate Drops to 7 Pct.," St. Louis *Post-Dispatch*, December 7, 1985; "Black Males in Jeopardy?" *Crisis*, XCIII (March, 1986). Some other studies showing limited black progress are Blair, *Retreat to the Ghetto;* Lester

Undeniably, the gap between the American promise and racial reality remained wide in the 1980s. This discrepancy, however, no longer agitated the white superego. Myrdal's analysis of the race problem nevertheless continued to irritate scholars. In his penetrating critique of the *Dilemma*, Stanford M. Lyman argued that Myrdal's break with traditional sociology had not been sharp enough. Lyman judged that the Myrdal study presented only a slightly "softer" determinism than that of Sumner or Park. By stressing the dynamics of society, the American sociologist maintained, the Swede had failed to see the continuity of history. Lyman railed against Myrdal's liberal assumptions about social change: that it was natural, unidirectional, continuous (orderly), and necessary.[24]

Several southern liberals, who had once been hopeful about their region, ultimately became less sanguine. Lewis Killian, a trenchant Myrdal critic, adopted a tragic vision of his society that was reminiscent of older southern liberals such as David Cohn. In 1982 C. Vann Woodward, a once optimistic summoner of the "Silent South," testified before a congressional committee that if the Voting Rights Act of 1965 were not renewed, the white South would "abridge, diminish and dilute, if not emasculate, the power of the black vote." In his long and pessimistic work on his native South, *The Crucible of Race* (1984), Joel Williamson contrasted his findings with those of Myrdal by saying: "What was so clear from the aracial heights of Sweden was all but invisible in the biracial bogs of the South. Ideally, neatly logical, there should have been a dilemma. In the real and conscious mind of the South," he lamented, "there was none."[25]

Myrdal's critics have been better at tearing down his analysis than constructing a new model for race relations, at least one that offers reasonable hope for racial justice. As Howard Odum said of Myrdal in 1944, in the theories of neither Lyman, nor Killian, nor Williamson is there shown a way out. Lyman held that since the Afro-American past was so calamitous and discontinuous, predictions about future race rela-

---

C. Thurow, *The Zero Sum Society: Distribution and the Possibilities for Economic Change* (Baltimore, 1981), 185–89; and "Black Gains Halted, U.S. Study [of 1980 Census] Finds," St. Louis *Post-Dispatch*, August 22, 1983.

24. Lyman, *Black American in Sociological Thought*, 99–120, 176–82.

25. Killian, *The Impossible Revolution?*; Killian, "Optimism and Pessimism in Sociological Analysis," *American Sociologist*, VI (1971), 281–86; Woodward quoted in Thomas Ottenad, "Blacks' Fight Moves from Street to Court," St. Louis *Post-Dispatch*, May 16, 1982; Williamson, *Crucible of Race*, 248.

tions were fatuous. Despairingly, he announced that the black American's "present is problematic, his past unknown, and his future uncertain." In an existential funk, Lyman could only talk vaguely about a "sociology of the absurd." [26]

Though time has made many of Myrdal's shortcomings disturbingly obvious, many of his critics have been less than fair. They have frequently caricatured Myrdal's large and complex book, often viewing it with tunnel vision or through some distorting ideological lens. Detractors strongly denounced the Swedish economist for being an imperfect prophet. In 1973 an exasperated Myrdal exclaimed that his book had only ventured short-range prognostications based on the trends of the early 1940s. Although the Swede overplayed his thesis, it should be remembered that he, like Du Bois, preached that blacks had to move forward on all fronts at once. He consistently taught that there was no basic factor in social change. [27] To use the famous insight of Isaiah Berlin, Myrdal was a fox who knew many truths rather than a hedgehog, such as Freud or Marx, who clung to one overarching truth. Above all, Myrdal saw that federal intervention and desegregation were the *sine qua non* of significant racial change. Such can be said of few American social scientists before World War II.

Questions of policy relevancy aside, the *Dilemma* still provides a valuable historical landmark that depicts a vital phase in American race relations. Scholars continue to use the book as a starting or finishing point for studies of black-white relations, creating a kind of BM and AM dichotomy (before and after Myrdal). [28] Furthermore, Myrdal still often sets the terms of debate. A case in point is Jennifer L. Hochschild's 1984 book, *The New American Dilemma: Liberal Democracy and School Desegregation*. In this impassioned plea for integrated education—through elite-mandated metropolitan busing if necessary—a self-proclaimed child of the 1960s carries on a running debate with

26. Odum, "Problem and Methodology in *An American Dilemma*," 98; Lyman, *Black American in Sociological Thought*, 182; Lyman and Marvin B. Scott, *A Sociology of the Absurd* (New York, 1970), 1–27.

27. Gunnar Myrdal, "The Unity of the Social Sciences," *Human Organization*, XXXIV (1975), 328; *Against the Stream*, 295.

28. See, for example, Dorothy K. Newman *et al.*, *Protest, Politics and Prosperity: Black Americans and White Institutions, 1940–1975* (New York, 1978), v; Wacker, *Ethnicity, Pluralism and Race: Race Relations Theory in America Before Myrdal*; Benjamin B. Ringer, *"We the People" and Others: Duality and America's Treatment of Its Minorities* (New York, 1983); C. Eric Lincoln, *Race, Religion, and the Continuing American Dilemma* (New York, 1984).

Myrdal. In the 1940s the foreign scholar based his optimistic forecast on observable social trends. Hochschild, however, concedes that her scenario for change bucks all the trends. In her references to "Myrdal and his ilk" (there are eleven citations in the index), she makes some telling criticisms of the *Dilemma*. Hochschild links Myrdal with those scholars who have held that white racism is anomalous to American liberalism. She insists, however, that American liberalism and racism have been and remain symbiotic. Anyone who has studied American history must take this point seriously.[29]

The racial debate goes on, as does the race problem. The dilemma nonetheless sadly languishes. Is it possible, as Samuel P. Huntington contends, that a new wave of "creedal passion" will sweep over America again?[30] If such were to happen, perhaps Myrdalian optimism will have a rebirth. It should be remembered, though, that the price of freedom alone has been blood, sweat, tears, and a long, grinding vigilance. Surely no less will be required for racial justice.

29. Hochschild, *New American Dilemma*, xi–xii, xix, 1–5, 8, 35, 91, 149, 190–91, 209, and *passim*. See the highly negative review of Hochschild's book by Chester E. Finn, Jr., "Choice and Coercion," *New Republic*, March 11, 1985, pp. 35–39.

30. Samuel P. Huntington, "American Ideals Versus American Institutions," *Political Science Quarterly*, XCVII (1982), 10; see generally Huntington's *American Politics: The Promise of Disharmony* (Cambridge, Mass., 1981).

Epilogue: Myrdal to Reexamine
the American Dilemma

In 1962 Myrdal disclosed that he had often been asked to review his original findings on the American race problem. He explained that although he was tempted to do so, several projects had preempted his time far into the future. "As I did not want to express views on a subject on which I could no longer constantly follow the discussion," Myrdal announced, "I have refrained from further comments on the Negro issue and even from answering criticisms of my own study." Myrdal vowed that the *Dilemma* would be his final contribution to the issue.[1] For almost thirty years the Swedish scholar resisted answering his critics (or closely following the arguments), but he hardly refrained from commenting on America's race problem.

During Myrdal's ten-year stint as head of the United Nations Economic Commission for Europe starting in 1947, he turned his attention to world poverty. Over the next two decades he published many well-received articles and books on the subject. Because he was a noted synthesizer of the social sciences, the Swede's work on social theory and methodology gained wide circulation, and some of his pre-*Dilemma* books were translated into English. In 1968 his extensive research on Eastern poverty culminated in the publication of the three-volume work *Asian Drama*, another monumental and collaborative work which Myrdal called a methodological "replica of *An American Dilemma.*" Reviewing this herculean effort, John Fischer postulated that the European economist was the only person in recent memory who had written two books capable of changing history.[2]

1. *AD* (1962 ed.), xxiv.
2. The following works are by Gunnar Myrdal: *An International Economy: Problems and Prospects* (New York, 1956): *Rich Lands, Poor Lands: The Road to World Prosperity*

For thirty years after the publication of the *Dilemma,* Myrdal made frequent, almost annual, trips to the United States. Not surprisingly, Myrdal was in America serving as a visiting professor at the City University of New York when he learned that he had won the 1974 Nobel Prize for economics. A popular speaker, he lectured before civil rights groups, college audiences, professional gatherings, and television viewers. He collected a trunkload of honorary degrees from renowned American universities. Given his many influential friends, his ties with the academic establishment in America were strong, and they were no doubt strengthened by the marriage of his daughter to Derek C. Bok, the president of Harvard.[3]

When asked for his views on the race question, Myrdal incessantly repeated the ideas found in his 1944 book. In 1958, for example, he told Americans that he never had the slightest doubt that they would make great racial strides because of their belief in the ideals of democracy and fair play. "This is something that is found not only in the Constitution," he exclaimed, "but in the hearts of the people of America, even the white 'crackers' in the South." Even in the deepening gloom of the late 1960s, Myrdal retained his cheerful outlook. After the election of Richard Nixon in 1968, he expressed confidence that a new and wiser Nixon was sincere in his desire to unite the country. To do so, Myrdal judged, the president would "have to go back to the American Dream and the American Conscience."[4]

In fairness it should be pointed out that although Myrdal continued to stress the alleged moral dilemma as the primary factor in race rela-

---

(New York, 1958); *Beyond the Welfare State: Economic Planning and Its International Implications* (New Haven, 1960); *Asian Drama: An Inquiry into the Poverty of Nations* (New York, 1968); *The Challenge to World Poverty: A World Anti-Poverty Program in Outline* (New York, 1970). On theory and methodology, see "How Scientific Are the Sciences?" in Myrdal, *Against the Stream;* "The Unity of the Social Sciences," *Human Organization,* XXXIV (Winter, 1975), 328; *Objectivity in Social Science Research* (New York, 1969); Myrdal quoted in an unpublished report for the World Bank, February 21, 1983, in the author's possession; John Fischer, "Western Intellectuals vs. Myrdal's Brutal Facts," *Harper's,* June, 1968, p. 12. For some of Myrdal's pre-*Dilemma* writing, see *The Political Element* and *Value in Social Theory.*

3. Solveytchick, "Europe's Not So Quiet Corner," 287; Werner Wiskari, "Gunnar Myrdal: A Man of Two Roles," New York *Times,* March 11, 1968, p. 14; "Myrdal and von Hayek Share a Nobel," New York *Times,* October 10, 1974, p. 1; "Unretiring Economist Whose Energy Defies Age," New York *Times,* October 10, 1974, p. 79.

4. New York *Times,* December 4, 1958, p. 6; "The American Conscience," *Look,* December 24, 1968, pp. 32, 34.

tions, he tended to emphasize economics and class more. On numerous occasions, he depicted the race problem as actually a "poverty problem." He encouraged blacks to form alliances with poor whites to promote racial change. When pressed by critics that this view clashed with his thesis in the *Dilemma*, Myrdal admitted that solidarity among the poor was not natural, as Marxists taught, but he claimed that it could be achieved through education. There existed no comparable ambivalence about the questions of black separatism and affirmative action. He consistently opposed both in the 1960s and 1970s.[5]

By 1970 Myrdal had retired from his professorship at the University of Stockholm and had completed his exhaustive *Asian Drama*. Once again the Swedish social scientist turned his primary attention to black-white relations in America. In late 1971 he told members of the African-American Studies Department at Harvard that he intended to take another deep look at the race problem. Two years later in a collection of essays entitled *Against the Stream*, the economist devoted a full chapter labeled "Gunnar Myrdal's *An American Dilemma*—Has It Been Resolved?" For the first time he lashed out specifically at some of his critics. In this discussion he also announced that he would soon be issuing a book called *An American Dilemma Revisited: The Racial Crisis in the United States in Perspective*. In various articles between 1971 and 1975, Myrdal and the press promoted the anticipated sequel to the *Dilemma*.[6]

But Myrdal never got very far with his sequel in the 1970s. As a fellow at the Center for the Study of Democratic Institutions in California and as a visiting professor in New York in 1973 and 1974, he gave some serious thought to black-white relations. But the Swede's initial investigation educated him to the tremendous amount of work that had been done on the subject since 1944 and made him realize that he could hardly write another volume like the original. Additionally, in his late seventies, he now suffered from Parkinson's disease and deteriorating

5. Gunnar Myrdal, "Social Trends in America and Strategic Approaches to the Negro Problem," *Phylon*, IX (1948), 208; "Myrdal Says Negro Against Revolting," Atlanta *Constitution*, December 4, 1968; Myrdal, "American Conscience," *Look*, December 24, 1968, p. 35; "The American Dilemma: 1967—An Interview with Gunnar Myrdal," *Center Magazine*, I (October–November, 1967), 32–36; Degler, "Negro in America," 155–56.

6. Myrdal, *Against the Stream*, 293–367; "Myrdal Plans Book on Racism," St. Louis *Post-Dispatch*, November 7, 1971; Myrdal, "Mass Passivity in America," *Center Magazine*, VII (March–April, 1974), 72; "Myrdal and von Hayek," New York *Times*, p. 79; Victor S. Navasky, "In Cold Print: American Dilemma," *New York Times Book Review*, May 18, 1975.

eyesight. Furthermore, he was unable to find a new Arnold Rose to assist him. He gave up on the project.[7]

Despite the resurgence of conservatism in the 1970s and the election of Ronald Reagan in 1980, Myrdal still tended to look on the bright side. In 1982 he conceded that there might be temporary setbacks, but the long-run prospects for race relations were good because Americans never ceased "feeling the dilemmas between their ideals and their every-' day actions." By 1983, however, the octogenarian seemed less positive about the future. In a two-page public letter for the Fund for an Open Society, Myrdal spoke in uncharacteristically somber tones. He condemned President Reagan for allowing the racial situation to worsen, and he lamented that the once-pathbreaking Supreme Court had reversed its salutary course on black-white questions. Myrdal added that white racism still thrived, that many blacks still remained trapped in dire economic straits, and that the vicious circle still worked its evil in the America of the 1980s.[8]

Apparently, the racial situation prodded Myrdal to return his attention to his promised review. By early 1985 the eighty-six-year-old Scandinavian had drafted several chapters of *An American Dilemma Revisited*, which was scheduled for release sometime in late 1986.[9] Entering the twilight of his life, Myrdal seemed compulsively drawn back to the country and the subject that first brought him international acclaim.

7. Myrdal to the author, February 6, March 13, 1984.
8. Myrdal to the author, April 7, 1982; letter for the Fund for an Open Society, received December 6, 1983.
9. Carolyn Marsh (Pantheon Books) to the author, April 4, 1985.

Selected Bibliography

This bibliography barely touches on the large and amorphous body of sources that have shaped this book. Because virtually everything written on race relations since the 1930s, and much before, constituted a potential source for this book, a complete bibliography would not be feasible.

This bibliography selects some of the sources that effectively did one or more of the following: (1) commented at length or insightfully on *An American Dilemma;* (2) helped provide the historical and social context or a conceptual framework for analyzing Myrdal's book; (3) introduced me to the various disciplines in the behavioral sciences; or (4) expressed a view of the *Dilemma* that represented an important mode of thought in America.

Although much of my information derived from published sources, several archival collections yielded useful material, especially those in the Truman Library and the Library of Congress. *Facts on Film,* more than 150 rolls of microfilm gathered by the Southern Education Reporting Service, proved valuable in writing about the South in the 1950s and 1960s. The microfilm of the Negro Study—General Correspondence from the Carnegie Files was indispensable for writing the first two chapters, and they gave me a better feel for Myrdal's book. The files on the Myrdal study, for reasons unclear to me, disappeared sometime in the 1950s. In 1943 Myrdal asked that no files be destroyed without his approval. Most, but obviously not all, of the files were microfilmed and are now available to researchers. When I first began research on Myrdal in the late 1960s, persons connected with the Carnegie Corporation and the Myrdal project seemed reluctant to encourage the use of the founda-

311

tion's files to tell the story about the making of Myrdal's book. For example, Florence Anderson, who worked on the Myrdal manuscript in 1943 and was still with Carnegie in 1968, wrote me that Myrdal's preface and Keppel's foreword adequately told the story of the Carnegie project. Anderson advised me that such details would, in any case, have no bearing on the influence of Myrdal's book. Besides, she continued, the "files on the study have been pretty well cleaned out." She said nothing about the records having been microfilmed. Charles Dollard, who with Keppel was closest to the Myrdal project, likewise directed me to the *Dilemma*'s preface and foreword concerning the origins and making of the study. He said that anything that remained in the foundation's files would probably be of little use to me. Only in 1982 did I discover from a secretary at the Carnegie Corporation that the Myrdal files had been microfilmed in 1956.

The Carnegie Corporation Oral History Project, undertaken by Columbia University in the late 1960s, was not available when I first began writing on Myrdal. It added a revealing source. Unfortunately, some parts of the interviews, many of which are massive, are still closed to researchers. Others require permission for use.

Manuscript, Oral History, and Microfilm Collections

Carnegie Corporation Oral History Project. Columbia University, New York, 1969.

Carnegie Research Memoranda. Schomburg Collection, New York Public Library (available on microfilm).

Facts on Film. Southern Education Reporting Service, Nashville, 1958–67.

Gunnar Myrdal Name File. White House Central Files. John F. Kennedy Library, Boston.

Gunnar Myrdal Name File. White House Central Files. Lyndon Johnson Library, Austin, Texas.

La Farge, John. Papers. Georgetown University Library, Washington, D.C.

"Logan, *What the Negro Wants* File." University of North Carolina Press Records, Southern Historical Collection, University of North Carolina, Chapel Hill.

National Association for the Advancement of Colored People. Papers. Library of Congress, Washington, D.C.

Nash, Pilleo. Papers. Harry S. Truman Library, Independence, Mo.

Negro Study—General Correspondence. Carnegie Corporation, New York, 1956 (2 rolls of microfilm).

Odum, Howard W. Papers. Southern Historical Collection, University of North Carolina, Chapel Hill.

Records of the President's Committee on Civil Rights, 1946–47. Harry S. Truman Library, Independence, Mo.

Records of the President's Commission on Equality of Treatment and Opportunity in the Armed Forces. Harry S. Truman Library, Independence, Mo.

Rose, Arnold M. Papers. University of Minnesota, Minneapolis.

Scarlett, William. Papers. Archives of the Episcopal Church, Austin, Texas.

Spingarn, Stephen. Papers. Harry S. Truman Library, Independence, Mo.

Truman, Harry S. Papers. Harry S. Truman Library, Independence, Mo.

Vance, Rupert B. Papers. Southern Historical Collection, University of North Carolina, Chapel Hill.

U.S. Supreme Court. Records and Briefs. Law Library, Library of Congress, Washington, D.C.

Waring, J. Waties. Papers. Moorland Spingarn Research Center, Howard University Library, Washington, D.C.

Wofford, Harris. Oral History Collection. John F. Kennedy Library, Boston, 1965–68.

Government Publications

Congressional Record, 1944–69.

Hearings, Committee on the Judiciary. Senate. 84th Cong., 2nd Sess., April 24–July 13, 1956.

Hearings, Subcommittee No. 5 of the Committee on the Judiciary. House. 85th Cong., 1st Sess., February 4–26, 1957.

Hearings, Subcommittee on Constitutional Rights, Judiciary Committee. Senate. 85th Cong., 1st Sess., February 14–March 5, 1957.

Hearings, Committee on the Judiciary. Senate. 88th Cong., 1st Sess. "Civil Rights—The President's Program, 1963." July 16–September 11, 1963.

Hearings, Committee on the Judiciary. House. 88th Cong., 1st Sess. "Civil Rights." October 15–16, 1963.

Hearings, Subcommittee No. 5 of the Committee on the Judiciary. House. 88th Cong., 1st Sess., July 26, 1963.

President's Commission on Higher Education. *Higher Education for American Democracy.* 2 vols. 1947.

President's Committee on Civil Rights. *To Secure These Rights.* 1947.

President's Committee on Equality of Treatment and Opportunity in the Armed Forces. *Freedom to Serve.* 1950.

Select Committee to Investigate Tax-Exempt Foundations and Comparable Organizations. House. 82d Cong., 2d Sess. *Tax-Exempt Foundations.* November 18–December 30, 1952.

Special Committee to Investigate Tax-Exempt Foundations and Comparable Organizations. House. 83d Cong., 2d Sess. May 10–July 9, 1954.

U.S. Commission on Civil Disorders. *Report of the National Advisory Commission on Civil Disorders.* New York, 1968.

U.S. Commission on Civil Rights. *Affirmative Action in the 1980's: Dismantling the Process of Discrimination.* 1981.

———. *Federal Civil Rights Enforcement.* 1970.

———. *1961 United States Civil Rights Commission Report.* 5 vols. 1961.

———. *Report of the United States Commission on Civil Rights 1959.*

———. *Twenty Years After Brown: Equality of Economic Opportunity.* 1975.

Books, Articles, Dissertations, and Unpublished Papers

Adams, Barry D. "Inferiorization and 'Self-Esteem.'" *Social Psychology,* XLI (1978), 47–53.

Adorno, Theodore, *et al. The Authoritarian Personality.* New York, 1950.

Allport, Gordon. *The Nature of Prejudice.* Cambridge, Mass., 1954.

Apostle, Richard A., *et al. The Anatomy of Racial Attitudes.* Berkeley, Calif., 1983.

Aptheker, Herbert. *The Negro People in America: A Critique of Gunnar Myrdal's "An American Dilemma."* New York, 1946.

Auletta, Ken. *The Underclass.* New York, 1982.

Bahr, Howard M., Theodore Johnson, and M. Kay Seitz. "Influential Scholars and Works in Sociology of Race and Minority Relations, 1944–1968." *American Sociologist,* VI (1971), 296–98.

Baldwin, James. *The Fire Next Time.* New York, 1963.

Banks, James A., and Jean D. Grambs, eds. *Black Self-Concept: Implications for Education and Social Science.* New York, 1972.

Bartley, Numan V. *The Rise of Massive Resistance: Race and Politics in the South During the 1950's.* Baton Rouge, 1969.

Bartley, Numan V., and Hugh D. Graham. *Southern Politics and the Second Reconstruction.* Baltimore, 1975.

Bass, Jack. *Unlikely Heroes: The Dramatic Story of the Southern Judges of the Fifth Circuit Who Translated the Supreme Court's Brown Decision into a Revolution for Equality.* New York, 1981.

Berman, William C. *The Politics of Civil Rights in the Truman Administration.* Columbus, Ohio, 1970.

Bernard, Jesse. "Where Is the Modern Sociology of Conflict?" *American Journal of Sociology,* LVI (1950), 11–16.

Berry, Mary Frances, and John W. Blassingame. *Long Memory: The Black Experience in America.* New York, 1982.

Berstein, Barton J., ed. *The Politics of Civil Rights in the Truman Administration.* Chicago, 1970.

Blackwell, James E., and Morris Janowitz, eds. *Black Sociologists: Historical and Contemporary Perspectives.* Chicago, 1974.

Blair, Thomas L. *Retreat to the Ghetto: The End of a Dream?* New York, 1977.

Blauner, Robert. *Racial Oppression in America.* New York, 1972.

Blumer, Herbert. "Race Relations as a Sense of Group Position." *Pacific Sociological Review,* I (1958), 3–7.

Bobo, Lawrence. "Whites' Opposition to Busing: Symbolic Racism or Realistic Group Conflict?" *Journal of Personality and Social Psychology,* XLV (1983), 1196–1210.

Boesil, David, and Peter H. Rossi, eds. *Cities Under Siege: An Anatomy of the Ghetto Riots, 1964–1968.* New York, 1971.

Bogart, Leo, ed. *Social Research and the Desegregation of the U.S. Army.* Chicago, 1969.

Bonacich, Edna. "Advanced Capitalism and Black/White Relations in the United States: A Split Labor Market Interpretation." *American Sociological Review,* XLI (1976), 34–51.

Bottomore, Tom, and Robert Nisbet, eds. *A History of Sociological Analysis.* New York, 1978.

Bracey, John H., Jr. "*An American Dilemma:* A Nationalist Critique." Paper delivered at the annual meeting of the Southern Historical Association, Washington, D.C., November 1, 1969.

Bracey, John H., Jr., August Meier, and Elliott Rudwick, eds. *Conflict and Competition: Studies in the Recent Black Protest Movement.* Belmont, Calif., 1971.

Brauer, Carl M. *John F. Kennedy and the Second Reconstruction.* New York, 1977.

Brink, William, and Louis Harris. *Black and White.* New York, 1966.

———. *The Negro Revolution in America.* New York, 1964.

Bromley, David G., and Charles F. Longino, Jr., eds. *White Racism and Black Americans.* Cambridge, Mass., 1972.

Brooks, Thomas R. *Walls Came Tumbling Down: A History of the Civil Rights Movement, 1940–1970.* Englewood Cliffs, N.J., 1974.

Burk, Robert F. *The Eisenhower Administration and Black Civil Rights.* Knoxville, 1984.

Caditz, Judith. *White Liberals in Transition: Current Dilemmas of Ethnic Integration.* New York, 1976.

Campbell, Angus. *White Attitudes Toward Black People.* Ann Arbor, 1971.

Campbell, Ernest Q. "Moral Comfort and Racial Segregation: An Examination of the Myrdal Hypothesis." *Social Forces,* XXXIX (1961), 228–34.

———. *Racial Tensions and National Identity.* Nashville, 1972.

Carey, James T. *Sociology and Public Affairs: The Chicago School.* Beverly Hills, Calif., 1975.

Carlson, Allan C. "The Myrdals, Pro-Natalism, and Swedish Social Democracy." *Continuity,* VI (Spring, 1983), 71–94.

Carmichael, Stokely, and Charles V. Hamilton. *Black Power: The Politics of Liberation in America.* New York, 1967.

Carson, Clayborne. *In Struggle: SNCC and the Black Awakening of the 1960s.* Cambridge, Mass., 1981.

Carter, Hodding. *Southern Legacy.* Baton Rouge, 1950.

Cell, John W. *The Highest Stage of White Supremacy: The Origins of Segregation in South Africa and the American South.* New York, 1982.

Clark, Kenneth B. "The Present Dilemma of the Negro." Address before a meeting of the Southern Regional Council, November 2, 1967.

Clark, Kenneth B., and John Hope Franklin. *The Nineteen Eighties: Prologue and Prospect.* Washington, 1981.

Clark, Kenneth B., and Kate Clark Harris. "What Do Blacks Really Want?" *Ebony,* XL (January, 1985), 110–15.

Clark, Kenneth B., and Talcott Parsons, eds. *The Negro American.* Boston, 1966.

Cleaver, Eldridge. *Soul on Ice.* New York, 1968.

Collins, Charles Wallace. *Whither the Solid South?* New Orleans, 1947.

Cook, Samuel DuBois. Review of *The Negro in America,* by Arnold Rose. *Journal of Negro History,* XLIX (1964), 207–209.

Coser, Lewis. *The Functions of Social Conflict.* Glencoe, Ill., 1956.

Couch, W. T. "Publisher's Introduction." In *What the Negro Wants,* edited by Rayford W. Logan. Chapel Hill, 1944.

Cox, Oliver C. "An American Dilemma: A Mystical Approach to the Study of Race Relations." *Journal of Negro Education,* XIV (1945), 132–48.

Crespi, Leo. "Is Gunnar Myrdal on the Right Track?" *Public Opinion Quarterly,* IX (1945), 201–12.

Cross, Theodore. *The Black Power Imperative: Racial Inequality and the Politics of Nonviolence.* New York, 1984.

Cruse, Harold. *The Crisis of the Negro Intellectual.* New York, 1967.

Cummings, Scott, and Charles W. Pinnel III. "Racial Double Standard of Morality in a Small Southern Community: Another Look at Myrdal's An American Dilemma." *Journal of Black Studies,* IX (1978), 67–86.

Dabney, Virginius. "Nearer and Nearer the Precipice." *Atlantic,* CLXXI (January, 1943), 94–100.

Dalfiume, Richard M. *Desegregation of the U.S. Armed Forces: Fighting on Two Fronts, 1939–1953.* Columbia, Mo., 1969.

————. "The 'Forgotten Years' of the Negro Revolution." *Journal of American History,* LV (1968), 90–106.

Daniels, Roger, and Harry H. L. Kitano. *American Racism: Exploration of the Nature of Prejudice.* Englewood Cliffs, N.J., 1970.

Degler, Carl N. "The Negro in America—Where Myrdal Went Wrong." *New York Times Magazine,* December 7, 1969, pp. 64ff.

————. *Neither Black nor White: Slavery and Race Relations in Brazil and the United States.* New York, 1971.

Dollard, John. *Caste and Class in a Southern Town.* New Haven, 1937.

Donald, David. "Writing About Slavery." *Commentary,* LIX (January, 1975), 86–90.

Drake, St. Clair, and Horace Cayton. *Black Metropolis: A Study of Negro Life in a Northern City.* New York, 1945.

Draper, Theodore. *The Rediscovery of Black Nationalism.* New York, 1970.

"Dr. Gunnar Twistmaul." *National Review,* January 26, 1957, pp. 78–79.

Du Bois, W. E. B. Review of *An American Dilemma*, by Gunnar Myrdal. *Phylon* V (1944), 118–24.

Dulles, Foster Rhea. *The Civil Rights Commission, 1957–1965*. East Lansing, 1968.

Elkins, Stanley M. *Slavery: A Problem in American Institutional and Intellectual Life*. Chicago, 1959.

———. "The Slavery Debate." *Commentary*, LX (December, 1975), 40–54.

Ellison, Ralph. "*An American Dilemma*: A Review." In *Shadow and Act*. New York, 1964, pp. 303–17.

Essien-Udom, E. U. *Black Nationalism: A Search for an Identity in America*. Chicago, 1962.

Farley, Reynolds. *Blacks and Whites: Narrowing the Gap?* Cambridge, Mass., 1984.

Festinger, Leon. *A Theory of Cognitive Dissonance*. Evanston, Ill., 1957.

Franklin, John Hope, ed. *Color and Race*. Boston, 1968.

Frazier, E. Franklin. Review of *An American Dilemma*, by Gunnar Myrdal. *Crisis*, LI (1944), 104–105, 126.

———. Review of *An American Dilemma*, by Gunnar Myrdal. *American Journal of Sociology*, L (1945), 555–57.

Fredrickson, George M. *The Black Image in the White Mind: The Debate on Afro-American Character and Destiny, 1817–1914*. New York, 1971.

———. *White Supremacy: A Comparative Study in American and South African History*. New York, 1981.

Friedman, Lawrence M., and Stewart McCaulay, eds. *Law and the Behavioral Sciences*. Indianapolis, 1969.

Friedman, Leon, ed. *Argument: The Oral Argument Before the Supreme Court in Brown v. Board of Education of Topeka, 1952–55*. New York, 1969.

Gallagher, Buell. *Color and Conscience: The Irrepressible Conflict*. New York, 1946.

Gavins, Raymond. *The Perils and Prospects of Southern Black Leadership: Gordon Blaine Hancock, 1884–1970*. Durham, N.C., 1977.

Glasgow, Douglas G. *The Black Underclass: Poverty, Unemployment, and Entrapment of Ghetto Youth*. New York, 1980.

Glazer, Nathan, and Daniel P. Moynihan. *Beyond the Melting Pot*. Cambridge, Mass., 1963.

Goldman, Peter. *Report from Black America*. New York, 1971.

Goldschmid, Marcel L., ed. *Black Americans and White Racism: Theory and Research*. New York, 1970.

Golightly, Cornelius L. "Race, Values, and Guilt." *Social Forces,* XXVI (1947), 125–39.

Gossett, Thomas F. *Race: The History of an Idea in America*. Dallas, 1963.

———. *Uncle Tom's Cabin and American Culture*. Dallas, 1985.

Gould, Stephen Jay. *The Mismeasure of Man*. New York, 1981.

Gouldner, Alvin W. *The Coming Crisis of Western Sociology*. New York, 1970.

Green, Jerome. "When Moral Prophecy Fails." *Catalyst,* IV (Spring, 1969), 63–78.

Greenberg, Stanley B. *Race and State in Capitalist Development: Comparative Perspectives*. New Haven, 1980.

Grier, William H., and Price M. Cobbs. *Black Rage*. New York, 1968.

Grossack, Martin M., ed. *Mental Health and Segregation*. New York, 1963.

Guterman, Stanley S., ed. *Black Psyche: The Modal Personality Patterns of Black Americans*. Berkeley, 1972.

Gwaltney, John Langston. *Drylongso: A Self-Portrait of Black Americans*. New York, 1980.

Handlin, Oscar. Review of *An American Dilemma*, by Gunnar Myrdal. *New York Times Book Review,* April 21, 1963, pp. 1ff.

Harris, William H. *The Harder We Run: Black Workers Since the Civil War*. New York, 1982.

Haselden, Kyle. *The Racial Problem in Christian Perspective*. New York, 1959.

Haskell, Thomas L. *The Emergence of Professional Social Science: The American Social Science Association and the Nineteenth-Century Crisis of Authority*. Urbana, Ill., 1977.

Height, Dorothy I. "What Must Be Done About Children Having Children?" *Ebony,* XL (March, 1985), 76–84.

Helper, Rose. *Racial Policies and Practices of Real Estate Brokers*. Minneapolis, 1969.

Hentoff, Nat, ed. *Black Anti-Semitism and Jewish Racism*. New York, 1969.

Hernton, Calvin C. *Sex and Racism*. Garden City, N.Y., 1965.

Herskovits, Melville J. *The Myth of the Negro Past*. New York, 1941.

Higham, John. "Integration vs. Pluralism: Another American Dilemma." *Center Magazine,* VII (July–August, 1974), 67–73.

Himes, Joseph S. "The Functions of Racial Conflict." *Social Forces,* XLV (1966), 1–10.

Hirsch, Arnold R. *Making the Second Ghetto: Race and Housing in Chicago, 1940–1960* New York, 1983.

Hochschild, Jennifer L. *The New American Dilemma: Liberal Democracy and School Desegregation.* New Haven, 1984.

Hoetink, Harmannus. *Slavery and Race Relations in the Americas: Comparative Notes on Their Nature and Nexus.* New York, 1973.

Horton, John. "Order and Conflict Theories of Social Problems as Competing Ideologies." *American Journal of Sociology,* LXXI (1966), 701–13.

Hulbert, Ann. "Children as Parents." *New Republic,* September 10, 1984, pp. 15–23.

Isaacs, Harold R. *The New World of the Negro Americans.* New York, 1963.

Jensen, Arthur. "How Much Can We Boost I.Q. and Scholastic Achievement?" *Harvard Educational Review,* XXXIX (1969), 1–123.

Joint Center for Political Studies. *A Policy Framework for Racial Justice.* Washington, 1983.

Jones, LeRoi. *Home: Social Essays.* New York, 1966.

Jordan, Winthrop D. *White over Black: American Attitudes Toward the Negro, 1550–1812.* Chapel Hill, 1968.

Kaiser, Ernest. "Racial Dialectics: The Aptheker-Myrdal School Controversy." *Phylon,* IX (1948), 295–302.

Kecskemeti, Paul. "The Psychological Theory of Prejudice: Does It Underrate the Role of Social History?" *Commentary,* XVIII (1954), 359–66.

Keil, Charles. *Urban Blues.* Chicago, 1966.

Kellogg, Peter J. "Northern Liberals and Black America: A History of White Attitudes, 1936–1952." Ph.D. dissertation, Northwestern University, 1971.

Key, V. O. *Southern Politics in State and Nation.* New York, 1949.

Killian, Lewis M. "Optimism and Pessimism in Sociological Analysis." *American Sociologist,* VI (November, 1971), 281–86.

Killian, Lewis M., and Charles Grigg. *Racial Crisis in America.* Englewood Cliffs, N.J., 1964.

———. "Rank Orders of Discrimination of Negroes and Whites in a Southern City." *Social Forces,* XXXIX (1961), 235–39.

Kilpatrick, James J. *The Southern Case for School Segregation.* New York, 1962.

Kinder, Donald R., and David O. Sears. "Prejudice and Politics: Symbolic Racism Versus Racial Threats to the Good Life." *Journal of Personality and Social Psychology,* XL (1981), 414–31.

King, Martin Luther, Jr. *Stride Toward Freedom: The Montgomery Story.* New York, 1958.

———. *Where Do We Go From Here: Chaos or Community?* New York, 1967.

———. *Why We Can't Wait.* New York, 1964.

Kirby, John B. *Black Americans in the Roosevelt Era: Liberalism and Race.* Knoxville, 1980.

Kluger, Richard. *Simple Justice: The History of Brown v. Board of Education and Black America's Struggle for Equality.* New York, 1976.

Kneebone, John T. *Southern Liberal Journalists and the Issue of Race, 1920–1944.* Chapel Hill, 1985.

Knowles, Louis L., and Kenneth Prewitt, eds. *Institutional Racism in America.* Englewood Cliffs, N.J., 1969.

Kochman, Thomas. *Black and White Styles in Conflict.* Chicago, 1981.

Kolchin, Peter. "Reevaluating the Antebellum Slave Community: A Comparative Perspective." *Journal of American History,* LXX (1983), 579–601.

Kovel, Joel. *White Racism: A Psychohistory.* New York, 1970.

Krueger, Thomas A. *And Promises to Keep: The Southern Conference for Human Welfare, 1938–1948.* Nashville, 1967.

Kuhn, Thomas S. *The Structure of Scientific Revolutions.* Chicago, 1962.

Ladner, Joyce A., ed. *The Death of White Sociology.* New York, 1973.

Levine, Lawrence W. *Black Culture and Black Consciousness: Afro-American Folk Thought from Slavery to Freedom.* New York, 1977.

Levitan, Sar, William B. Johnston, and Robert Teggart. *Still a Dream: The Changing Status of Blacks Since 1960.* Cambridge, Mass., 1975.

Levy, Charles J. *Voluntary Servitude: Whites in the Negro Movement.* New York, 1968.

Lewis, Anthony. *Portrait of a Decade: The Second American Revolution.* New York, 1964.

Lewis, David L. *King: A Critical Biography.* New York, 1970.

Lieberman, Leonard. "The Debate over Race: A Study in the Sociology of Knowledge." *Phylon,* XXIX (1968), 127–41.

Liebow, Elliot. *Tally's Corner: A Study of Streetcorner Men.* Boston, 1967.

Lincoln, C. Eric. *Race, Religion, and the Continuing American Dilemma.* New York, 1984.

Little, Malcolm. *The Autobiography of Malcolm X.* New York, 1965.

Logan, Rayford W., ed. *What the Negro Wants.* Chapel Hill, 1944.

Lomax, Louis E. *The Negro Revolt.* New York, 1962.

Lyman, Stanford M. *The Black American in Sociological Thought: A Failure of Perspective.* New York, 1973.

McClosky, Herbert. "Consensus and Ideology in American Politics." *American Political Science Review,* LVIII (1964), 361–82.

McConahay, John B., Betty B. Hardee, and Valerie Batts. "Has Racism Declined in America? It Depends on Who Is Asking and What Is Asked." *Journal of Conflict Resolution,* XXV (1981), 563–79.

McCoy, Donald R., and Richard T. Ruetten. *Quest and Response: Minority Rights and the Truman Administration.* Lawrence, Kan., 1973.

McDowell, Sophia Fagen. "Teaching Note on the Use of the Myrdal Concept of 'An American Dilemma' with Regard to the Race Problem in the United States." *Social Forces,* XXX (1951), 87–91.

MacGregor, Morris J., Jr. *Integration of the Armed Forces, 1940–1965.* Washington, 1981.

McMillen, Neil R. *The Citizens' Council: Organized Resistance to the Second Reconstruction, 1954–64.* Urbana, Ill., 1971.

Mason, Philip. *Patterns of Dominance.* New York, 1970.

Masuoka, Jitsuichi, and Preston Valien, eds. *Race Relations: Problems and Theory.* Chapel Hill, 1961.

Matthews, Donald R., and James W. Prothro. *Negroes and the New Southern Politics.* New York, 1966.

Matthews, Fred H. *Quest for an American Sociology: Robert E. Park and the Chicago School.* Montreal, 1977.

Matusow, Allen J. "From Civil Rights to Black Power: The Case of SNCC, 1960–1966." In Barton J. Bernstein and Allen J. Matusow, eds., *Twentieth Century America: Recent Interpretations.* 2d ed. New York, 1972.

Medalia, Nahum. "Myrdal's Assumptions on Race Relations: A Conceptual Commentary." *Social Forces,* XL (1962), 223–27.

Meier, August, Elliott Rudwick, and Francis L. Broderick, eds. *Black Protest Thought in the Twentieth Century.* 2d ed. Indianapolis, 1971.

Merton, Robert K. "Discrimination and the American Creed." In

Robert M. MacIver, ed., *Discrimination and National Welfare*. New York, 1949.

Metzger, L. Paul. "American Sociology and Black Assimilation: Conflicting Perspectives." *American Journal of Sociology*, LXXVI (1971), 627–47.

Mills, C. Wright. *The Sociological Imagination*. New York, 1959.

Montagu, M. F. Ashley. *Man's Most Dangerous Myth*. 2d ed. New York, 1945.

————, ed. *Race and I.Q.* New York, 1975.

Murray, Charles. *Losing Ground: American Social Policy, 1950–1980*. New York, 1984.

Muse, Benjamin. *The American Negro Revolution: From Nonviolence to Black Power, 1963–1967*. Bloomington, Ind., 1968.

————. *Ten Years of Prelude: The Story of Integration Since the Supreme Court's 1954 Decision*. New York, 1964.

Myrdal, Gunnar. *Against the Stream: Critical Essays on Economics*. New York, 1973.

————, with the assistance of Richard Sterner and Arnold Rose. *An American Dilemma: The Negro Problem and Modern Democracy*. New York, 1944.

————. *Challenge to Affluence*. New York, 1963.

————. *The Political Element in the Development of Economic Theory*. Translated by Paul Streeten. *Cambridge, Mass., 1955*.

————. *Value in Social Theory: A Selection of Essays on Methodology by Gunnar Myrdal*. Translated and edited by Paul Streeten. New York, 1958.

Nagel, Ernest. "The Value-Oriented Bias of Social Inquiry." In May Brodbeck, ed., *Readings in the Philosophy of the Social Sciences*. New York, 1968.

Namorato, Michael V., ed. *Have We Overcome? Race Relations Since Brown*. Jackson, Miss., 1979.

Nash, Gary B., and Richard Weiss, eds. *The Great Fear: Race in the Mind of America*. New York, 1970.

Neary, John. "A Scientist's Variation on a Disturbing Theme." *Life*, June 12, 1970, pp. 58–65.

Newby, Idus A. *Challenge to the Court: Social Scientists and the Defense of Segregation, 1954–1966*. Baton Rouge, 1967.

Newman, Dorothy K., *et al. Protest, Politics, and Prosperity: Black Americans and White Institutions, 1940–1975*. New York, 1978.

Newman, William K. *American Pluralism: A Study of Minority Groups and Social Theory.* New York, 1973.

Nisbet, Robert A. *Social Change and History: Aspects of Western Theory and Development.* New York, 1969.

Novak, Michael. *The Rise of the Unmeltable Ethnics: Politics and Culture in the Seventies.* New York, 1971.

Oates, Stephen B. *Let the Trumpet Sound: The Life of Martin Luther King, Jr.* New York, 1982.

O'Brien, Michael. *The Idea of the American South, 1920–1941.* Baltimore, 1979.

Odum, Howard W. "Problem and Methodology in *An American Dilemma.*" *Social Forces,* XXIII (1944), 94–98.

――――. *Race and Rumors of Race.* Chapel Hill, 1943.

Pahl, Brother Denis. "An Empirical Study of Some Underlying Theories in Myrdal's *An American Dilemma.*" Ph.D. dissertation, University of Wisconsin, 1970.

Parrish, Noel F. "The Segregation of Negroes in the Army Air Forces." Air University Thesis, Maxwell Field, Ala., 1947.

Parsons, Talcott. *The Structure of Social Action.* New York, 1937.

Patterson, Orlando. "The Moral Crisis of the Black American." *Public Interest,* XXII (Summer, 1973), 43–69.

――――. *Slavery and Social Death: A Comparative Study.* Cambridge, Mass., 1982.

――――. "Toward a Future That Has No Past—Reflections on the Fate of Blacks in America." *Public Interest,* XXVII (Spring, 1972), 25–62.

Peltason, Jack W. *Fifty-Eight Lonely Men: Southern Federal Judges and School Desegregation.* New York, 1961.

Pinkney, Alphonso. *The Myth of Black Progress.* New York, 1984.

Porter, Judith D. R. *Black Child, White Child.* Cambridge, Mass., 1971.

Putnam, Carleton. *Race and Reason: A Yankee View.* Washington, 1961.

Rainwater, Lee, ed. *Soul.* Chicago, 1970.

Rainwater, Lee, and William L. Yancey, eds. *The Moynihan Report and the Politics of Controversy.* Cambridge, Mass., 1967.

Ravitch, Diane. *The Troubled Crusade: American Education, 1945–1980.* New York, 1983.

Reimers, David M. *White Protestantism and the Negro.* New York, 1965.

Riesman, Frank. *The Culturally Deprived Child.* New York, 1962.

Ringer, Benjamin B. *"We the People" and Others: Duality and America's Treatment of Its Racial Minorities.* New York, 1983.

Robinson, Armstead L., Craig C. Foster, and Donald C. Ogilvie, eds. *Black Studies in the University: A Symposium.* New Haven, 1969.

Roosevelt, Archibald, and Zymund Dobbs. *The Great Deceit: Social-Psuedo Sciences.* West Sayville, N.Y., 1964.

Rose, Arnold. *Libel and Academic Freedom: A Lawsuit Against Political Extremists.* Minneapolis, 1968.

Rose, Peter I. *The Subject Is Race: Traditional Ideologies and the Teaching of Race Relations.* New York, 1968.

Rosen, Paul L. *The Supreme Court and Social Science.* Urbana, Ill., 1972.

Rothschild, Mary A. *A Case of Black and White: Northern Volunteers and Southern Freedom Summers, 1964–1965.* Westport, Conn., 1982.

Roucek, Joseph. "Minority-Majority Relations in Their Power Aspects." *Phylon,* XVII (1956), 24–30.

Rudwick, Elliott, "American Values and Social Change: How Right Was Gunnar Myrdal?" Paper presented at the annual meeting of the Southern Historical Association, Washington, D.C., November 1, 1969.

Rustin, Bayard. "From Protest to Politics." *Commentary,* XXXIX (February, 1965), 25–31.

Ryan, William. *Blaming the Victim.* New York, 1971.

Schermerhorn, Richard A. *Comparative Ethnic Relations: A Framework for Theory and Research.* New York, 1970.

Schulman, Gary I. "Race, Sex, and Violence: A Laboratory Test of the Sexual Threat of the Black Male Hypothesis." *American Journal of Sociology,* LXXIX (1974), 1260–77.

Schumann, Howard, and Shirley Hatchett. *Black Racial Attitudes: Trends and Complexities.* Ann Arbor, 1974.

Schuman, Howard, Charlotte Steeh, and Lawrence Bobo. *Racial Attitudes in America: Trends and Interpretations.* Cambridge, Mass., 1985.

Schwartz, Barry, and Robert Disch, eds. *White Racism: Its History, Pathology, and Practice.* New York, 1970.

Sears, David O., Carl P. Hensler, and Leslie K. Speer. "Whites' Opposition to 'Busing': Self-Interest or Symbolic Politics?" *American Political Science Review,* LXXIII (1979), 369–84.

Selznick, Gertrude J., and Stephen Steinberg. *The Tenacity of Preju-*

dice: Anti-Semitism in Contemporary America. New York, 1969.

Semas, Philip W. "How Influential Is Sociology?" *Chronicle of Higher Education*, September 19, 1977, p. 4.

Shore, Laurence. "The Poverty of Tragedy in Historical Writing on Southern Slavery." *South Atlantic Quarterly*, LXXXV (1986), 147–64.

Silberman, Charles E. *Crisis in Black and White*. New York, 1964.

Silver, James W. *Mississippi: The Closed Society*. New York, 1963.

Singal, Daniel. *The War Within: From Victorian to Modernist Thought in the South, 1919–1945*. Chapel Hill, 1982.

Singer, Lester. "Ethnogenesis and Negro Americans Today." *Social Research*, XXIX (1962), 419–32.

Sitkoff, Harvard. *A New Deal for Blacks: The Emergence of Civil Rights as a National Issue*. New York, 1978.

————. "Racial Militancy and Interracial Violence in the Second World War." *Journal of American History*, LVIII (1971), 661–81.

————. *The Struggle for Black Equality, 1954–1980*. New York, 1981.

Smith, Lillian. *Killers of the Dream*. New York, 1949.

Soloveytchik, George. "Europe's Not So Quiet Corner." *Survey Graphic*, XXXV (August, 1946), 282–87.

Sosna, Morton. *In Search of the Silent South: Southern Liberals and the Race Issue*. New York, 1977.

Southern, David W. "*An American Dilemma* Revisited: Myrdalism and White Southern Liberals." *South Atlantic Quarterly*, LXXV (1976), 182–97.

————. "Beyond Jim Crow Liberalism: Judge Waring's Fight Against Segregation in South Carolina, 1942–52." *Journal of Negro History*, LXVI (1981), 209–27.

Sowell, Thomas. "Black Progress Can't Be Legislated." *Washington Post*, August 12, 1984, Sec. B, pp. 1ff.

————. *Race and Economics*. New York, 1975.

Stanfield, John H. "Race Relations and Black Americans Between the Two World Wars." *Journal of Ethnic Studies*, XI (Fall, 1983), 61–93.

Staples, Robert. *Introduction to Black Sociology*. New York, 1976.

Stein, Howard F., and Robert F. Hill. *The Ethnic Imperative: Examining the New White Ethnic Movement*. University Park, Pa., 1977.

Steinberg, Stephen. *The Ethnic Myth: Race, Ethnicity, and Class in America*. New York, 1982.

Steinfels, Peter. *The Neoconservatives: The Men Who Are Changing America.* New York, 1979.

Stember, Charles H. *Education and Attitude Change: The Effects of Schooling on Attitude Change.* New York, 1961.

————. *Sexual Racism: The Emotional Barrier to an Integrated Society.* New York, 1978.

Stocking, George W., Jr. *Race, Culture, and Evolution: Essays in the History of Anthropology.* New York, 1968.

Taeuber, Karl E., and Alma K. Taeuber. *Negroes in Cities: Residential Segregation and Neighborhood Change.* Chicago, 1965.

Takaki, Ronald T. *Iron Cages: Race and Culture in Nineteenth-Century America.* New York, 1979.

Thurow, Lester C. *Poverty and Discrimination.* Washington, 1969.

Trubowitz, Julius. *Changing the Racial Attitudes of Children: The Effect of an Activity Group Program in New York City Schools.* New York, 1969.

Vance, Rupert B. "Tragic Dilemma: The Negro and the American Dream." *Virginia Quarterly Review,* XX (1944), 440–44.

Van den Berghe, Pierre. *Race and Racism: A Comparative Approach.* New York, 1967.

Wacker, R. Fred. "An American Dilemma: The Racial Theories of Robert E. Park and Gunnar Myrdal." *Phylon,* XXXVII (1976), 117–25.

————. *Ethnicity, Pluralism and Race: Race Relations Theory in America Before Myrdal.* Westport, Conn., 1983.

Wasby, Steven, Anthony A. D'Amato, and Rosemary Metrailer. *Desegregation from Brown to Alexander: An Explanation of Supreme Court Strategies.* Carbondale, Ill., 1977.

Wattenberg, Ben J., and Richard M. Scammon. "Black Progress and Liberal Rhetoric." *Commentary,* LV (April, 1973), 35–44.

Watters, Pat. *Down to Now: Reflections on the Southern Civil Rights Movement.* New York, 1971.

Wellman, David T. *Portraits of White Racism.* New York, 1977.

Westie, Frank. "The American Dilemma: An Empirical Test." *American Sociological Review,* XXX (1965), 527–38.

Wicker, Alan W. "Attitudes Versus Action: The Relationship of Verbal and Overt Behavioral Responses to Attitude Objectives." *Journal of Social Issues,* XXV (Fall, 1969), 41–78.

Wilhelm, Sidney M. *Blacks in a White America.* Cambridge, Mass., 1984.

————. *Who Needs the Negro?* Cambridge, Mass., 1970.

Wilkinson, J. Harvie III. *From Brown to Bakke: The Supreme Court and School Integration, 1954–1978.* New York, 1979.

Williamson, Joel. *The Crucible of Race: Black-White Relations in the American South Since Emancipation.* New York, 1984.

Willie, Charles V., *et al. Racism and Mental Health.* Pittsburgh, 1973.

Wilson, James Q. *Negro Politics: The Search for Leadership.* Glencoe, Ill., 1960.

Wilson, William J. *The Declining Significance of Race: Blacks and Changing American Institutions.* Chicago, 1978.

Wofford, Harris. *Of Kennedys and Kings: Making Sense of the Sixties.* New York, 1980.

Wolters, Raymond. *The Burden of Brown: Thirty Years of School Desegregation.* Knoxville, 1984.

Woodward, C. Vann. "Equality: America's Deferred Commitment." *American Scholar,* XXVII (1958), 459–72.

————. *The Strange Career of Jim Crow.* New York, 1955. (Several subsequent editions published.)

————. "What Happened to the Civil Rights Movement?" *Harper's,* CCXXXIV (January, 1967), 29–37.

Wyzanski, Charles E., Jr. Review of *An American Dilemma,* by Gunnar Myrdal. *Harvard Law Review,* LVIII (1944), 285–91.

Yetman, Norman R., and C. Hoy Steele, eds. *Majority and Minority: The Dynamics of Racial and Ethnic Relations.* Boston, 1971.

Young, Donald R. *American Minority People: A Study in Racial and Cultural Conflict in the United States.* New York, 1932.

Zetterberg, Hans L., ed. *Sociology in the United States of America.* Paris, 1956.

Newspapers

Arkansas Gazette, 1944.
Atlanta *Constitution,* 1944.
Atlanta *Journal,* 1944.
Charleston *News and Courier,* 1944.
Charlotte *Observer,* 1944.
Chicago *Defender,* 1944.
Chicago *Tribune,* 1944.
Dallas *Morning News,* 1944.
Detroit *News,* 1944.

Jackson *Clarion Ledger*, 1944.
Louisville *Courier-Journal*, 1944.
Memphis *Commercial Appeal*, 1944.
Minneapolis *Tribune*, 1944.
Montgomery *Advertiser*, 1944.
New Orleans *Picayune*, 1944.
New York *Herald Tribune*, 1944.
New York *Times*, 1938–1984.
Philadelphia *Inquirer*, 1944.
Pittsburgh *Courier*, 1944.
Raleigh *News and Observer*, 1944.
Richmond *News Leader*, 1944.
Richmond *Times-Dispatch*, 1944.
San Francisco *Examiner*, 1944.
St. Louis *Post-Dispatch*, 1970–1986.
Washington *Post*, 1944.

Correspondence: Letters to the Author

Anderson, Florence, April 18, 1968.
Brauer, Carl M. June 19, 1981.
Couch, W. T., July 21, 1984.
Dollard, Charles, April 30, 1968.
Dutton, Frederick, July 7, 1981.
Fischer, John, June 18, 1968.
Hesburgh, Theodore, July 19, 1981.
Johnson, Guion, 1981–84.
Johnson, Guy, 1981–84.
Kazenbach, Nicholas deB., July 14, 1981.
Kirkendall, Richard, November 7, 1969.
Humphrey, Hubert H., November 13, 1969.
McDonald, D., October 28, 1969.
McPherson, Harry, July 8, 1981.
Marshall, Burke, July 14, 1981.
Moyers, Bill, July 13, 1981.
Myrdal, Gunnar, 1968, 1970, 1981–84.
Parrish, Noel, May 18, 1970.
Reedy, George, July 18, 1981.
Rose, Caroline B., July 16, 1969.
Rusk, Dean, July 20, 1981.

Schlesinger, Arthur, Jr., October 5, 1981.
Schriffrin, Andre, July 11, 1984.
Snelling, Paula, September 29, 1969.
Sorensen, Theodore, July 19, 1981.
Stampp, Kenneth, December 27, 1982.
Symington, Stuart, May 15, 1968.
White, Lee, July 23, 1981.
Wofford, Harris, July 28, 1981.
Woodward, C. Vann, August 12, 1984.

Index

Abbott, Robert S., 9
Abrams, Charles, 134
Adams, Barry D., 217
Adorno, Theodore, 210
Affirmative action, 274, 279, 292, 300–301
Africa, 67, 68, 232, 275, 298; "African-isms," 17, 43; African heritage, 30, 43; "African survivals," 218, 221
Afro-Americans. *See* Blacks
Alexander, Will, 39, 84, 158, 159, 161–62, 200
Allport, Gordon, 110, 182, 194, 203–204, 277
American Academy of Arts and Sciences, 218, 268, 271, 275
"American Century," 50, 74, 293
American consensus, 219–20, 223, 270
American Council on Race Relations, 109, 110, 134
American creed, 12, 34, 50, 59, 64, 69, 83, 96, 115, 142, 150, 166, 188, 194, 201, 203, 209–10, 212, 219, 230, 234, 238–39, 265, 271, 279, 282, 293, *passim;* defined by Myrdal, xiii, 55–57; as key to race problem, 32–33; as dynamic force, 58; and living standards, 63. *See also* Values; Moral dilemma
Amici curiae, 134–35, 137, 241
American Dilemma, An: as classic, xiii;

theme of, xiii; rank among influential books, xiv; sales, xv, 46; origins of, 1–8; making of, 8–9, 15–48; outline of, 29, 31–34; cost of, 35; collaborators on, 15–16, 19–21, 23–24, 37; and Sterner and Rose, 38–39, 44–47; critics of manuscript, 39–41; style of, 40–41; on the South, 42; on sexism and racism, 43; lack of history in, 43; on black culture, 43–45; title for, 48, 56; size of, 54; first reviews of, 71–99; and civil rights cases, 127–55; southern liberals react to, 157–71; southern conservatives react to, 171–78, 183–85; liberal scholars on, 187–88, 193–201; and academia, 188–89, 201–206, 208–10, 219–23, 277–86, 290–92, 304–307; and college students, 196; and historians, 211–18; and civil rights, 225–34; black militants react to, 234–40, 264–65; and Eisenhower, 241–42; and Congress, 243–44; and Civil Rights Commission, 244–48; and John F. Kennedy, 248–52; and Lyndon B. Johnson, 253–55; impact on history, 294–96; as landmark, 305. *See also* Gunnar Myrdal
American School of Ethnology, 147
American Sociological Society, 17
"American state religion," 32–33